Course Student Guid

Transitions Throughout the Life Span

for use with

RICHARD O. STRAUB

Coast
LEARNING SYSTEMS

The course ***Transitions Throughout the Life Span*** is produced by the Coast Community College District in cooperation with Worth Publishers and KOCE-TV, Channel 50.

Distributed by: **Coast Learning Systems**
Coastline Community College
11460 Warner Avenue
Fountain Valley, CA 92708
telephone: (800) 547-4748 ◆ fax: (714) 241-6286
e-mail: CoastLearning@coastline.edu ◆ web site: www.CoastLearning.org

Published by Worth Publishers

Printed in the United States of America

ISBN-10: 1-4292-5252-9
ISBN-13: 978-1-4292-5252-2

First printing 2009

Worth Publishers
41 Madison Avenue
New York, NY 10010
www.worthpublishers.com

Contents

Introduction		***v***
Lesson 1	Introduction: Theories of Development	**1**
Lesson 2	Developmental Study as a Science	**33**
Lesson 3	The Beginnings: Heredity and Environment	**51**
Lesson 4	The Beginnings: Prenatal Development and Birth	**75**
Lesson 5	The First Two Years: Biosocial Development	**97**
Lesson 6	The First Two Years: Cognitive Development	**115**
Lesson 7	The First Two Years: Psychosocial Development	**135**
Lesson 8	The Play Years: Biosocial Development	**157**
Lesson 9	The Play Years: Cognitive Development	**177**
Lesson 10	The Play Years: Psychosocial Development	**197**
Lesson 11	The School Years: Biosocial Development	**219**
Lesson 12	The School Years: Cognitive Development	**239**
Lesson 13	The School Years: Psychosocial Development	**257**
Lesson 14	Adolescence: Biosocial Development	**273**
Lesson 15	Adolescence: Cognitive Development	**291**
Lesson 16	Adolescence: Psychosocial Development	**309**
Lesson 17	Early Adulthood: Biosocial Development	**329**
Lesson 18	Early Adulthood: Cognitive Development	**347**
Lesson 19	Early Adulthood: Psychosocial Development	**363**
Lesson 20	Middle Adulthood: Biosocial Development	**381**
Lesson 21	Middle Adulthood: Cognitive Development	**397**
Lesson 22	Middle Adulthood: Psychosocial Development	**419**
Lesson 23	Late Adulthood: Biosocial Development	**441**
Lesson 24	Late Adulthood: Cognitive Development	**461**
Lesson 25	Late Adulthood: Psychosocial Development	**481**
Lesson 26	Epilogue: Death and Dying	**503**

Acknowledgments

Several of the individuals responsible for the creation of this course are listed on the copyright page of this book. In addition, appreciation is expressed for these contributions:

Members of the Telecourse Advisory Committee

The following gifted scholars, professionals, and teachers helped focus the approach and content of the video lessons, faculty manual, and course student guide to ensure accuracy, academic validity, accessibility, significance, and instructional integrity.

Pauline Abbott, Ed.D., California State University, Fullerton
Mary Belcher, M.A., Orange Coast College
Joyce Bishop, Ph.D., Golden West College
Fredda Blanchard-Fields, Ph.D., Georgia Institute of Technology
Michael Catchpole, Ph.D., R. Psych., North Island College, British Columbia, Canada
Chuansheng Chen, Ph.D., University of California, Irvine
Donald Cusumano, Ph.D., St. Louis Community College
Linda Flickinger, M.A., St. Clair County Community College
Andrea R. Fox, M.D., M.P.H., University of Pittsburgh and VA Pittsburgh Healthcare System
Ellen Greenberger, Ph D., University of California, Irvine
Jutta Heckhausen, Ph.D., University of California, Irvine
Sally Hill, M.A., Bakersfield College
Sandra J. McDonald, M.S., Sierra College
Mary K. Rothbart, Ph.D., University of Oregon
Susan Siaw, Ph.D., California State Polytechnic University, Pomona
Barbara W. K. Yee, Ph.D., University of South Florida
Judy Yip, Ph.D., University of Southern California
Elizabeth Zelinski, Ph.D., University of Southern California

Lead Academic Advisors

Roberta Beam, M.A., Tyler Junior College
Amy Himsel, M.A., University of California, Irvine
Doug Hughey, M.A., Mt. San Antonio College
Jeanne Ivy, M.S., L.P.A., Tyler Community College
Phyllis Lembke, M.A., Coastline Community College
Robert D. Nash, M.S.Ed., Coast Learning Systems

Video Production Team

Vanessa Chambers, Jason Daley, Sharon Dymmel, Liz Ervin, Jim Jackson, Becky Koppenhaver, Alejandro Lopez, Dorothy McCollom, Laurie R. Melby, Salma Montez, Evelyn Moore, Harry Ratner, Greg Rogers, Mike Rust, Wendy Moulton-Tate, Charlie Powell, and the many other talented people who helped make the programs.

Special thanks are extended to Maureen Zweig, M.A., who helped review this edition of the course student guide.

Introduction

To the Student

Welcome to ***Transitions Throughout the Life Span***. This course has been designed to cover the concepts, vocabulary, and subjects that are typical of an on-campus, college-level human development course. This course introduces the development process in three distinct categories or domains—biosocial, cognitive, and psychosocial.

While most people achieve developmental milestones, each person will take his or her own unique path. The twenty-six half-hour video lessons feature an assortment of real-life examples, historical footage, and an array of subject-matter experts. Throughout this course we will emphasize how the development principles you will be learning can be used to improve the quality of your everyday life, as well as those around you.

As with any college-level course, this course has a textbook, a student guide, assignments, and tests. In lieu of classroom lectures, however, you will be watching half-hour video programs. The designers, academic advisors, and producers of this course have produced an engaging and comprehensive course that will entertain you as you learn about the fascinating subject of human development.

Course Goals

From its inception, this course was designed to provide the concepts, vocabulary, and subjects that are needed for a college-level introductory course on human development. The designers, academic advisors, and producers of this course have specified the following learning outcomes for students taking ***Transitions Throughout the Life Span***. After successfully completing the course assignments, you should be able to:

1. Describe the developing person from conception through death in terms of biosocial, cognitive, and psychosocial development, and discuss how these three domains interact.
2. Consider how the interplay of nature (genetics) and nurture (environment) affects development across the life span.
3. Discuss how developmental concepts apply to "real-life" situations.
4. Identify the major theories of development, discuss their strengths and weaknesses, and summarize what they tell us about how, when, and why a human develops.
5. Describe how the scientific method is used in research on human development, and explain how theoretical perspectives and research findings influence one another.
6. Outline observational and analytical skills that can be used to examine and interpret human behavior objectively.
7. Consider how contextual issues—including age, gender, culture, socioeconomic status, and ethnicity—broaden our understanding of human development, and note how the multidisciplinary nature of human development contributes to this understanding.

Course Components

Student Guide

The course student guide is an integral part of this course. Think of this guide as your "road map." It gives you a starting point for each lesson, as well as directions and exercises that will help you successfully navigate your way through the course. Reading this guide will provide you with the information that you normally would receive in the classroom if you were taking this course on campus. Each lesson in this course student guide includes the following components:

- **Preview:** An overview of the lesson that informs you of the importance of the subject you are about to study and gives you a snapshot of the upcoming video lesson.
- **Prior Telecourse Knowledge:** A list of concepts, theories, terms, and other knowledge presented in previous lessons that you should recall in order to prepare for the current lesson.
- **Learning Objectives:** Your instructional goals for the lesson, which will guide your reading, viewing, thinking, and studying. Upon completing each lesson, you should be able to satisfy each of the learning objectives. (Hint: Instructors often develop test questions directly from learning objectives.)
- **Reading Assignment:** Description of page numbers and sections in the textbook that should be read for each lesson.
- **Viewing Assignment:** Instructions on which video lesson to view, as well as mention of each segment within the video lesson.
- **Summary:** A summary of the lesson—to be read after reading the textbook and viewing the video lesson—that clarifies key points.
- **Key Terms:** Much of education is learning the meaning of new terms and concepts. It is important to be able to define each of the key terms and concepts for each lesson.
- **Practice Questions:** These self-test questions (multiple-choice, matching, and true-false questions) help you review and master basic facts and definitions presented in each lesson.
- **Applying Your Knowledge:** These self-test questions (multiple-choice) help you evaluate your understanding of the lesson's broader and conceptual material and its application to real-world situations.
- **Answer Key:** Answers to the key terms and self-test items are conveniently located at the end of each lesson so that you can get immediate feedback. The answers reference pages in the textbook and segments in the video lesson where the information is presented, as well as the learning objective the question covers. After completing the Key Terms section and other self-tests, be sure to check the Answer Key to make sure you correctly understand the material.
- **Lesson Review:** This chart has been designed to act as a study tool to help you achieve each learning objective. It lists pages in the textbook, segments in the video lesson, and sections in the student guide where you can find more information on each objective. Use this tool to master concepts and skills that you feel are your weak points.

Textbook

The recommended textbook for this course is *Invitation to the Life Span*, by Kathleen Stassen Berger (Worth Publishers, 2010). In much the same way as the course lessons, the textbook is complete with real-life stories—some funny, some dramatic, others quite personal. This textbook allows you to learn about human development by observing and hearing about the lives of real, ordinary people. This condensed presentation of the topics found in Berger's best-selling textbooks helps address challenges that face instructors and students as they cover the entire life span within the limits of an accelerated academic calendar.

Video Programs

Each of the video lessons features a real-life situation—a story line that will help you recognize and appreciate how development affects the lives of ordinary people. The award-winning producers and directors at Coast Learning Systems have brought together top professionals from various fields of psychology and development to help explain different aspects of human development.

How to Take a Distance Learning Course

If this is your first experience with a college-level distance learning course, welcome. Distance learning courses are designed for busy people whose schedules do not permit them to take a traditional on-campus college course.

This guide is designed to help you study effectively and learn the material presented in both the textbook and the video lessons. To complete a distance learning course successfully, you will need to schedule sufficient time to watch each lesson, read the textbook, and study the materials outlined in this guide. This course guide is a complement to the textbook and the video lessons. It is not a substitute. By following the instructions in this guide, you should easily master the learning objectives for each lesson.

To complete this course successfully, you will need to:

- Find and read the syllabus or handbook for this course provided by your instructor. This course syllabus will list and explain what you will be required to do to complete the course successfully. The syllabus describes assignments, explains the course grading scale, and offers a schedule for quizzes, exams, and review sessions.
- Purchase a copy of the course textbook.
- Read and study this course student guide and the textbook.
- View each video lesson in its entirety. (The course syllabus or handbook should explain how you can view the lesson videos.)
- Focus your study time so you can achieve the Learning Objectives for each lesson.
- Complete the Review Exercises in this guide.
- Complete any additional assignments your instructor may require.
- If you have questions about what you are supposed to do in this course, look for the answer in your syllabus. If you are still unsure, contact your instructor.

Even though you do not have a scheduled class to attend each week, please keep in mind that this is a college-level course. It will require the same amount of work as a traditional, classroom version of this course and at the same level of difficulty. As a distance learner, however, it will be up to you alone to keep up with your deadlines. It is important that you schedule sufficient time to watch, read, study, and reflect.

Do your best to keep up with the work. In a distance learning course, it is very difficult to catch up if you allow yourself to get behind schedule. We strongly recommend that you set aside specific times each week for reading, viewing the videos, completing the assignments, and studying for quizzes and exams. You will be more likely to succeed if you make a formal study schedule and stick to it schedule.

When you watch each video lesson, try to do so without any interruptions. If you are interrupted, you may miss an important point. If possible, view the videos in a recorded mode so you can stop the program and take notes. Also, take some time immediately after watching the video program to reflect on what you have just seen. This is an excellent time to discuss the video lesson with a friend or family member. Your active thinking and involvement will promote your success.

Study Recommendations

Everyone has his or her own unique learning style. Some people learn best by reading alone the first thing each morning, others by discussing ideas with a group of friends, still others by listening to experts and taking notes. While there is no "best" way to learn, psychologists and educators have identified several things you can do that will help you study and learn more effectively.

One of the advantages of distance learning is that you have many choices in how you learn and study. You can tailor this course to fit your "best" way to learn. Below are several study tips. These are proven methods that will help you learn and retain what you are studying. Please take the time to read through this list. You will discover that by using one or more of these techniques you can significantly improve your ability to learn and remember new information.

Open your mind: One of the major obstacles to learning new information is that new information often differs from what we already "know." For example, if you believe that obesity is caused by depression, it will be difficult for you to learn about new information that reveals that there is no cause-and-effect relationship between obesity and depression. To learn, you need to have an open mind. We are not suggesting you simply believe everything you are told. We want you to think critically about what you are told. However, be cautious and guard against letting old beliefs or opinions stop you from learning anything new.

Reduce interference: One of the major reasons for forgetting information is that new information interferes with other information. When you are studying more than one subject at a time, you are increasing the likelihood of interference occurring. If possible, focus your study on one subject at a time. If you must take multiple subjects, try to take courses with very different subjects, such as art and psychology or math and history. For example, it would not be a good idea to take Human Development and Introduction to Psychology during the same semester. Also, do your best to avoid interruptions while you are studying.

Find a quiet room with a good desk, chair, and adequate lighting. Try to avoid distractions so your mind can focus and give yourself enough time to absorb new information.

Don't cram: You probably already know that staying up all night cramming for an exam the following morning is not a good way to study. The opposite of cramming is, in fact, one of the best ways to study. Spacing out your studying into smaller and more frequent study periods will improve retention. Instead of studying for six hours in one evening, you will learn more and retain more if you study one hour per night for six nights.

Reduce stress: In addition to being bad for your health, stress is bad for learning. Stress and anxiety interfere with learning. You will learn more and enjoy it more if you are relaxed when you study. One of the most effective ways of relaxing that does not interfere with learning is exercise. A good brisk walk or run before you settle in to study is a good prescription for success. Ideally, you would study some, take a break, then get some exercise while you think about what you have just learned. And later, when you are relaxed, return and study some more.

Be a Smart Student: Most top students have one thing in common. They all have excellent study habits. Students who excel have learned, or were fortunate enough to have someone teach them, how to study effectively. There is no magic formula for successful studying. However, there are a few universal guidelines.

Do make a commitment to yourself to learn.

Don't let other people interrupt you when you are studying.

Do make a study schedule and stick to it.

Don't study when you are doing something else, like watching television.

Do create a specific place to study.

Don't study if you are tired, upset, or overly stressed.

Do exercise and relax before you study.

Don't study for extended periods of time without taking a break.

Do give yourself ample time to study.

Don't complain that you have to go study.

Do take a positive approach to learning.

Make the most of your assignments: You will master this material more effectively if you make a commitment to completing all your assignments. The lessons will make more sense to you, and you will learn more, if you follow these instructions:

Think about what you have learned: You are much more likely to remember new information if you use it. Remember that learning is not a passive activity. Learning is active. As soon as you learn something, try to repeat it to someone or discuss it with a friend. If you will think about what you just learned, you will be much more likely to retain that information. The reason we remember certain information has to do mostly with (1) how important that information is to us, and (2) whether or not we actively use the information. For example, if you suffer from headaches and the textbook or video is discussing various headache remedies, this information will be valuable to you. Because of your personal interest in this subject, you will have little difficulty remembering this information. What do you do, however, when you need to learn some information that is not personally valuable or interesting to you? The best way to remember this type of information is to reinforce it—and the best reinforcer is actively using the information.

Get feedback on what you are studying: Study alone, learn with others. You need feedback to help reinforce learning. Also, feedback helps make sure you correctly understand the information. The study activities and self-tests in this guide are specifically designed to give you feedback and reinforce what you are learning. The more time and practice you devote to learning, the better you will be at remembering that information. When you take a self-test, make sure you immediately check your answers with the answer key. Don't wait and check your answers later. If you miss a question, review that section of the textbook to reinforce the correct understanding of the material.

A good gauge of how well you understand some information is your ability to explain that information to another person. If you are unable to explain some term or concept to a friend, you probably will need to review and study that term or concept further.

Contact your instructor: If you are having an especially difficult time with learning some information, contact your instructor. Your instructor is there to help you. Often a personal explanation will do wonders in helping you clear up a misunderstanding. Your instructor wants to hear from you and wants you to succeed. Don't hesitate to call, write, e-mail, or visit your instructor.

Collaborate with study groups or partners: Some students do better with study groups; others do better studying alone. If study groups are helpful to you, let your instructor know of your preference. However, be aware that study groups are not a substitute for studying alone. Because study groups can sometimes turn into friendly chats, without much learning going on, you should use your group time wisely. Remember that study groups are not a substitute for individual effort.

Learn it well: Retention is the key to long-term knowledge. One of the best methods to increase your retention is to overlearn material. It is a common mistake to think that just because you can answer a question or give a brief definition of a term or concept, you really know and will remember that term or concept. Think back about how many things you have already "learned." How much do you really remember? Much of what we learn is quickly forgotten. If you want to really learn some information, learn it in a way that you will not forget it—overlearn it.

Enjoy learning: You do not need to suffer to learn. In fact, the opposite is true. You will learn more if you enjoy learning. If you have the attitude that "I hate to study" or "schoolwork is boring," you are doing yourself a real disservice.

You will progress better and learn more if you adopt a positive attitude about learning and studying. Since you are choosing to learn, you will be well served by also choosing to enjoy the adventure!

Lesson 1

Introduction:
Theories of Development

Preview

The first lesson of this telecourse introduces the **scientific study of human development**, beginning with a description of the domains into which development is often divided, a description of the scope of the field, and an overview of the major **developmental theories** that have guided research over the past century. A philosopher once said that "nothing is more practical than a good theory," and such has proven to be the case in developmental psychology. Theories help psychologists organize large amounts of information, and focus their research on specific, testable ideas about development.

In an effort to organize this course, human development has been divided into three major domains: biosocial, cognitive, and psychosocial. The **biosocial domain** includes all the growth and change that occur in a person's body, and the genetic, nutritional, and health factors that affect that growth and change. The **cognitive domain** includes all the mental processes that are used to obtain knowledge or to become aware of the environment. It includes all the processes people use to think, decide, and learn. The **psychosocial domain** includes development of emotions, temperament, and social skills. The influence of family, friends, the community, the culture, and the larger society are particularly central to this domain. Very few factors, however, belong exclusively to one domain or another. Each aspect of development is related to all three domains.

Several major themes are introduced in this lesson that will be woven into lessons throughout the telecourse, including the idea that development is influenced as much by external factors as by internal factors. This theme, framed initially by philosophers many years ago, continues to drive the field today as researchers weigh the relative contributions of biological factors (such as heredity) and environmental factors (such as learning) in development.

The impact of external factors on development is revealed in the many contexts in which development occurs (such as the family), as well as the many contexts that have an influence on society at large (such as culture). Each of us as individuals is affected by, and affects, other individuals (such as family members and friends) and groups of individuals (such as the neighborhood and community). Furthermore, our development is also affected by the influence of larger systems in the environment (such as ethnicity and culture.)

A third theme of the lesson and telecourse is that development is a lifelong process. Although some early theorists believed that our personalities and fates are fully shaped by the end of childhood, developmental psychologists today recognize that people continue to grow and change from the day they are born until the day they die.

Learning Objectives

Use this information to guide your reading, viewing, thinking, and studying. After successfully completing this lesson, you should be able to:

1. Define the life-span perspective of development, and identify five characteristics or principles of development.
2. Identify and describe the three domains into which human development is often separated.
3. Describe the ecological-systems approach to human development, and explain how this approach leads to an understanding of the overlapping contexts in which people develop.
4. Discuss the nested levels (microsystems, exosystems and macrosystems) of Urie Bronfenbrenner's ecological systems approach to human development and demonstrate an understanding of how these levels fit into the three broader overlapping contexts of culture, ethnicity, and socioeconomic status (SES).
5. Define developmental theory, and describe how developmental theories help explain human behavior and development.
6. Discuss the major focus of psychoanalytic theories, and describe the conflicts that occur during Freud's stages of psychosexual development.
7. Describe the crises of Erikson's theory of psychosocial development, and contrast them with Freud's stages.
8. Discuss the major focus of behaviorism, and explain the basic principles of classical and operant conditioning.
9. Discuss social learning theory as an extension of learning theory.
10. Identify the primary focus of cognitive theory, and briefly describe Piaget's stages of cognitive development.
11. Discuss the process that, according to Piaget, guides cognitive development.
12. Discuss the basic ideas of Vygotsky and define the concept of guided participation.

13. Define the term "epigenetic," and discuss how an epigenetic understanding relates to the nature/nurture controversy.
14. Summarize the contributions and criticisms of the major developmental theories, and explain the eclectic perspective of contemporary developmentalists.
15. Define developmental science and discuss the three crucial elements in the definition as specifically noted in your textbook.

Read Chapter 1, "The Science of Development," pages 3–25.

View the video for Lesson 1, "The Developing Person."

Segment 1: *Contexts and Systems*

Segment 2: *Theories of Development*

Segment 3: *The Life-Span Perspective*

Summary

The scientific study of human development is the science that seeks to understand how and why people change with increasing age, and how and why they remain the same.

The **life-span perspective** underscores the fact that development is lifelong, multidirectional, multicontextual, multicultural, multidisciplinary, and plastic. Human development is also multidimensional in that it includes many dimensions of many domains. The three major domains of development include the **biosocial domain** (brain and body as well as changes in them and the social influences that guide them), the **cognitive domain** (thought processes, perceptual abilities, and language mastery, as well as the educational institutions that encourage them), and the **psychosocial domain** (emotions, personality, and interpersonal relationships with family, friends, and the wider community).

According to Urie Bronfenbrenner's **ecological-systems approach**, human development is supported by systems at three nested levels: the microsystem (immediate social setting), the exosystem (the community structures and local educational, medical, employment, and communications systems that directly affect the various microsystems and indirectly affect everyone in those microsystems), and the macrosystem (cultural values, political philosophies, economic patterns, and social conditions). The larger perspective fostered by the ecological approach makes it imperative that development be understood in its social context—which includes its historical, cultural, ethnic, and socioeconomic contexts.

Psychoanalytic theory interprets human development in terms of intrinsic drives and motives, many of which are irrational and unconscious. According to Sigmund Freud, development progresses through five psychosexual stages; at each stage, sexual interest and pleasure is focused on a particular part of the body—the mouth during infancy (the oral stage), the anus during early childhood (the anal stage), and the genitalia later in the preschool years (the phallic stage). Following a 5- or

6-year stage of sexual latency, the individual enters the fifth stage, the genital stage, which lasts throughout adulthood.

In his psychosocial theory of human development, Erik Erikson proposed eight developmental stages, each of which is characterized by a particular challenge, or developmental crisis (for example, young adults are faced with the challenge of establishing intimate relationships). Erikson emphasized each person's interactions in the social environment and the importance of family and cultural influences in determining how well-prepared individuals are to meet and resolve these crises.

Proponents of **behaviorism (learning theory**) formulated laws of behavior that are presumed to operate at every age. As demonstrated by Ivan Pavlov, classical conditioning involves learning by association: the subject comes to associate a neutral stimulus with a meaningful response. In operant conditioning, proposed by B. F. Skinner, the individual learns that a particular behavior produces a particular consequence. **Social learning theory** emphasizes the ways in which people learn new behaviors by observing and imitating, or **modeling**, the behavior of other people they consider admirable, powerful, or similar.

Cognitive theory focuses on the structure and development of the individual's thought processes and their effect on his or her understanding of the world—focusing on how children's thinking differs from adults' thinking. Jean Piaget viewed cognitive development as a process that follows a universal sequence of age-related periods: sensorimotor, preoperational, concrete operational, and formal operational. According to Piaget, each individual strives for **cognitive equilibrium**—that is, a state of mental balance achieved through the development of mental concepts that explain his or her experiences.

Lev Vygotsky believed that the development of cognitive competencies results from social interaction between children and more mature members of the society in what has been called an "apprenticeship in thinking." The basis of this apprenticeship is *guided participation*, in which a skilled tutor engages the learner in joint activities.

The Berger textbook emphasizes that genes alone do not determine development. **Epigenetic** is a term that refers to the effects of environmental forces on the expression of our genes. Some of these forces include nourishing food and freedom to play, as well as potentially disruptive factors such as injury, temperature, or crowding. "Genetic" refers both to the genes that make each person unique and to the genes humans share with all other humans. This theory also points out that changes in one part of the individual's system may cause corresponding adjustments and changes in every other part.

The five theories complement one another, as each emphasizes a somewhat different aspect of development and, as such, is too restricted to account for the diversity of human behavior. **Psychoanalytic theory** calls attention to the importance of early childhood experiences and "hidden dramas" that influence daily life. **Behaviorism** highlights the effect of the immediate environment on behavior. **Cognitive theory** promotes a greater understanding of how intellectual processes and thinking affect our behavior.

Developmentalists agree that the interaction between nature and nurture is the crucial influence on any particular aspect of development at any point in time during the life span. Today, most developmentalists take an eclectic perspective: instead of limiting themselves to only one school of thought, they apply insights drawn from various theoretical views.

Review all reading assignments for this lesson.

As assigned by your instructor, complete the optional online component for this lesson.

Key Terms

Using your own words, write a brief definition or explanation of each of the following terms on a separate piece of paper.

1. science of human development
2. nature
3. nurture
4. biosocial domain
5. cognitive domain
6. psychosocial domain
7. critical period
8. sensitive period
9. difference-equals-deficit error
10. life-span perspective
11. cohort
12. socioeconomic status (SES)
13. guided participation
14. ethnic group
15. social construction
16. epigenetic
17. mirror neurons
18. developmental theory
19. psychoanalytic theory
20. behaviorism (learning theory)
21. conditioning
22. classical conditioning
23. operant conditioning
24. reinforcement
25. social learning theory
26. modeling
27. cognitive theory
28. cognitive equilibrium
29. ecological-systems approach
30. socioemotional selectivity theory
31. dynamic-systems theory
32. eclectic perspective

Practice Questions I

Multiple-Choice Questions

1. The science of human development is defined as the study of
   a. how and why people change or remain the same over time.
   b. psychosocial influences on aging.
   c. individual differences in learning over the life span.
   d. all of the above.

2. The cognitive domain of development includes
   a. perception.
   b. thinking.
   c. language.
   d. all of the above.

3. Changes in height, weight, and bone thickness are part of the _________________ domain.
   a. cognitive
   b. biosocial
   c. psychosocial
   d. physical

4. Psychosocial development focuses primarily on personality, emotions, and
   a. intellectual development.
   b. sexual maturation.
   c. relationships with others.
   d. perception.

5. The ecological-systems approach to developmental psychology focuses on the
   a. biochemistry of the body systems.
   b. cognitive domain only.
   c. internal thinking processes.
   d. overall environment of development.

6. Researchers who take a life-span perspective on development focus on
   a. the sources of continuity from the beginning of life to the end.
   b. the sources of discontinuity throughout life.
   c. the "nonlinear" character of human development.
   d. all of the above.

7. During the 1960s, American society tilted toward a youth culture. This is a vivid example of the effect of ________________ on society.

    a. the "baby boom" cohort
    b. the biosocial domain
    c. the cognitive domain
    d. the microsystem

8. A developmentalist who is interested in studying the influences of a person's immediate environment on his or her behavior is focusing on which system?

    a. mesosystem
    b. macrosystem
    c. microsystem
    d. exosystem

9. Socioeconomic status (SES) is determined by a combination of variables, including

    a. age, education, and income.
    b. income, ethnicity, and occupation.
    c. income, education, and occupation.
    d. age, ethnicity, and occupation.

10. The purpose of a developmental theory is to

    a. provide a broad and coherent view of the complex influences on human development.
    b. offer guidance for practical issues encountered by parents, teachers, and therapists.
    c. generate testable hypotheses about development.
    d. do all of the above.

11. Which developmental theory emphasizes the influence of unconscious drives and motives on behavior?

    a. psychoanalytic
    b. learning
    c. cognitive
    d. sociocultural

12. Which of the following is the correct order of the psychosexual stages proposed by Freud?
    a. oral stage; anal stage; phallic stage; latency; genital stage
    b. anal stage; oral stage; phallic stage; latency; genital stage
    c. oral stage; anal stage; genital stage; latency; phallic stage
    d. anal stage; oral stage; genital stage; latency; phallic stage

13. Erikson's psychosocial theory of human development describes
    a. eight crises all people are thought to face.
    b. four psychosocial stages and a latency period.
    c. the same number of stages as Freud's, but with different names.
    d. a stage theory that is not psychoanalytic.

14. Which of the following theories does **NOT** belong with the others?
    a. psychoanalytic
    b. sociocultural
    c. learning
    d. cognitive

15. An American psychologist who explained complex human behaviors in terms of operant conditioning was
    a. Lev Vygotsky.
    b. Ivan Pavlov.
    c. B. F. Skinner.
    d. Jean Piaget.

16. Pavlov's dogs learned to salivate at the sound of a bell because they associated the bell with food. Pavlov's experiment with dogs was an early demonstration of
    a. classical conditioning.
    b. operant conditioning.
    c. positive reinforcement.
    d. social learning.

17. The nature–nurture controversy considers the degree to which traits, characteristics, and behaviors are the result of

    a. early or lifelong learning.
    b. genes or heredity.
    c. heredity or experience.
    d. different historical concepts of childhood.

18. Modeling, an integral part of social learning theory, is so called because it

    a. follows the scientific model of learning.
    b. molds character.
    c. follows the immediate reinforcement model developed by Albert Bandura.
    d. involves people's patterning their behavior after that of others.

19. Which term suggests that each person is born with genetic possibilities that must be nurtured in order to grow?

    a. sociocultural
    b. cognitive
    c. learning
    d. epigenetic

20. Which of the following are reflected by a family's socioeconomic status (also known as SES)?

    a. income
    b. education
    c. occupation
    d. all of the above

21. Which is the correct sequence of stages in Piaget's theory of cognitive development?

    a. sensorimotor, preoperational, concrete operational, formal operational
    b. sensorimotor, preoperational, formal operational, concrete operational
    c. preoperational, sensorimotor, concrete operational, formal operational
    d. preoperational, sensorimotor, formal operational, concrete operational

22. When an individual's existing understanding no longer fits his or her present experiences, the result is called
    a. a psychosocial crisis.
    b. equilibrium.
    c. disequilibrium.
    d. negative reinforcement.

23. According to your textbook, developmental study is
    a. a science.
    b. a new area of study that does not require the use of the scientific method.
    c. an area of study that is only applied to children from birth to 18 years of age.
    d. an area of study reserved for evaluating disabled children.

24. Which of Vygotsky's ideas can occur via direct instruction in school, but usually occurs informally?
    a. cognitive dissonance
    b. guided participation
    c. classical conditioning
    d. heredity

25. Nature is to nurture as
    a. *tabula rasa* is to blank slate.
    b. Jean Rousseau is to John Locke.
    c. B. F. Skinner is to Ivan Pavlov.
    d. Urie Bronfenbrenner is to Kurt Lewin.

Matching Items

Match each definition or description with its corresponding term.

Terms

26. __________ psychoanalytic theory
27. __________ nature
28. __________ learning theory
29. __________ social learning theory
30. __________ cognitive theory
31. __________ nurture
32. __________ conditioning
33. __________ modeling
34. __________ epigenetic theory
35. __________ difference-equals-deficit error
36. __________ critical period

Descriptions or Definitions

a. emphasizes the impact of the immediate environment on behavior
b. time when a particular type of growth must happen
c. emphasizes that people learn by observing others
d. environmental influences that affect development
e. a process of learning, as described by Pavlov or Skinner
f. emphasizes the "hidden dramas" that influence behavior
g. mistaken belief that deviation from the norm is somehow inferior
h. emphasizes how our thoughts shape our actions
i. the process whereby a person learns by imitating someone else's behavior
j. emphasizes the interaction of genes and environmental forces
k. traits that are inherited

Practice Questions II

Multiple-Choice Questions

1. When developmentalists discuss the "context" of individual development, they are referring to
   a. microsystem and mesosystem.
   b. exosystem.
   c. macrosystem.
   d. microsystem, mesosystem, exosystem, and macrosystem.

2. People often mistakenly believe that most developmental changes
   a. originate within each individual as a result of genetic factors.
   b. take place in a larger social context.
   c. are temporary.
   d. occur in the same way in all people.

3. According to the ecological-systems approach, the macrosystem would include
   a. the peer group.
   b. the community.
   c. cultural values.
   d. the family.

4. A cohort is defined as a group of people
   a. of similar national origin.
   b. who share a common language.
   c. born within a few years of each other.
   d. who share the same religion.
5. Which developmental theorist has been criticized for suggesting that every child, in every culture, in every nation, passes through certain fixed stages?
   a. Sigmund Freud
   b. Erik Erikson
   c. Jean Piaget
   d. all of the above.
6. Of the following terms, the one that does **NOT** describe a stage of Freud's theory of childhood sexuality is
   a. phallic.
   b. oral.
   c. anal.
   d. sensorimotor.
7. We are more likely to imitate the behavior of others if we particularly admire and identify with them. This belief finds expression in
   a. stage theory.
   b. sociocultural theory.
   c. social learning theory.
   d. Pavlov's experiments.
8. According to Erikson, an adult who has difficulty establishing a secure, mutual relationship with a life partner might never have resolved the crisis of
   a. initiative versus guilt
   b. autonomy versus shame
   c. intimacy versus despair
   d. trust versus mistrust

9. Who would be most likely to agree with the statement, "Anything can be learned"?

   a. Jean Piaget
   b. Lev Vygotsky
   c. John Watson
   d. Erik Erikson

10. Classical conditioning is to ________________ as operant conditioning is to ____________________.

   a. Skinner; Pavlov
   b. Watson; Vygotsky
   c. Pavlov; Skinner
   d. Vygotsky; Watson

11. Learning theorists have found that they can often solve a person's seemingly complex psychological problem by

   a. analyzing the patient.
   b. admitting the existence of the unconscious.
   c. altering the environment.
   d. administering well-designed punishments.

12. According to Piaget, an infant first comes to know the world through

   a. sucking and grasping.
   b. naming and counting.
   c. preoperational thought.
   d. instruction from parents.

13. According to Piaget, the stage of cognitive development that generally characterizes preschool children (2 to 6 years old) is the

   a. preoperational stage.
   b. sensorimotor stage.
   c. oral stage.
   d. psychosocial stage.

14. In Piaget's theory, cognitive equilibrium refers to

   a. a state of mental balance.
   b. a kind of imbalance that leads to cognitive growth.
   c. the ultimate stage of cognitive development.
   d. the first stage in the processing of information.

15. You teach your dog to "speak" by giving her a treat each time she does so. This is an example of
    a. classical conditioning.
    b. respondent conditioning.
    c. reinforcement.
    d. modeling.

16. A child who must modify an old idea in order to incorporate a new experience is using the process of
    a. assimilation.
    b. accommodation.
    c. cognitive equilibrium.
    d. guided participation.

17. All of the following are stage theories **EXCEPT**
    a. Freud's psychosexual theory.
    b. Piaget's cognitive theory.
    c. Erikson's psychosocial theory.
    d. Skinner's learning theory.

18. According to Jean-Jacques Rousseau, human development is
    a. influenced more by nature than by nurture.
    b. influenced more by nurture than by nature.
    c. equally affected by both nature and nurture
    d. too complex to understand in terms of nature and nurture.

19. Stimulus is to response as
    a. action is to reaction.
    b. reaction is to action.
    c. nature is to nurture.
    d. nurture is to nature.

20. The concept of how effective people think they are at changing themselves or altering their social context is
    a. self-efficacy.
    b. self-understanding.
    c. self-determination.
    d. none of the above.

21. Many fields, including education, neuroscience, psychology, and anthropology, contribute to the science of development. This is
    a. multidirectional.
    b. multicontextual.
    c. multicultural.
    d. multidisciplinary.

22. Body strength increases during early life and then begins to decline with age. This is an example of
    a. multidirectionality.
    b. multicontextuality.
    c. multicultural influence.
    d. multidisciplinarity.

23. Change is ongoing and can occur at any point throughout the life span. This is representative of
    a. multidirectionality.
    b. continuity.
    c. plasticity.
    d. the life-span perspective.

True or False Items

Write T (for true) or F (for false) on the line in front of each statement.

24. _____ Behaviorists study what people actually do, not what they might be thinking.

25. _____ Erikson's eight developmental stages are centered not on a body part but on each person's relationship to the social environment.

26. _____ Most developmentalists agree that the nature–nurture controversy has been laid to rest.

27. _____ Few developmental theorists today believe that humans have instincts or abilities that arise from our species' biological heritage.

28. _____ Of the major developmental theories, cognitive theory gives the most emphasis to the interaction of genes and experience in shaping development.

29. _____ A critical period is a time when things must occur for normal development.

30. _____ According to Piaget, a state of cognitive equilibrium must be attained before cognitive growth can occur.

31. _____ In part, cognitive theory examines how an individual's understandings and expectations affect his or her behavior.

32. _____ According to Piaget, children begin to think only when they reach preschool age.

33. _____ Most contemporary researchers have adopted an eclectic perspective on development.

Applying Your Knowledge

1. Dr. Ramirez conducts research on the psychosocial domain of development. She is most likely to be interested in a child's
   a. perceptual abilities.
   b. brain-wave patterns.
   c. emotions.
   d. use of language.

2. Jahmal is writing a paper on the role of the social context in development. He would do well to consult the writings of
   a. Jean Piaget.
   b. Sigmund Freud.
   c. Urie Bronfenbrenner.
   d. B. F. Skinner.

3. Dr. Wong looks at human development in terms of the individual's supporting ecosystems. Evidently, Dr. Wong subscribes to the _______________ approach.
   a. psychosocial
   b. ecological-systems
   c. biosocial
   d. cognitive

4. When we say that the idea of old age as we know it is a "social construction," we are saying that
   a. the idea is built on the shared perceptions of members of society.
   b. old age has only recently been regarded as a distinct period of life.
   c. old age cannot be defined.
   d. the idea is based on a well-tested hypothesis.

5. When a pigeon is rewarded for producing a particular response, and so learns to produce that response to obtain rewards, psychologists describe this chain of events as

   a. operant conditioning.
   b. classical conditioning.
   c. modeling.
   d. reflexive actions.

6. Dr. Cleaver's research focuses on the biological forces that shape each child's characteristic way of reacting to environmental experiences. Evidently, Dr. Cleaver is working from a(n) ________________ perspective.

   a. psychoanalytic
   b. cognitive
   c. sociocultural
   d. epigenetic

7. Which of the following is the best example of guided participation?

   a. After watching her mother change her baby sister's diaper, four-year-old Brandy changes her doll's diaper.
   b. To help her son learn to pour liquids, Linda engages him in a bathtub game involving pouring water from cups of different sizes.
   c. Seeing his father shaving, three-year-old Jack pretends to shave by rubbing whipped cream on his face.
   d. After reading a recipe in a magazine, Kyle gathers ingredients from the cupboard.

8. A child who calls all furry animals "doggie" will experience cognitive ________________ when she encounters a hairless breed for the first time. This may cause her to revamp her concept of "dog" in order to ________________ the new experience.

   a. disequilibrium; accommodate
   b. disequilibrium; assimilate
   c. equilibrium; accommodate
   d. equilibrium; assimilate

9. A confirmed neo-Freudian, Dr. Thomas strongly endorses the views of Erik Erikson. She would be most likely to disagree with Freud regarding the importance of

   a. unconscious forces in development.

   b. irrational forces in personality formation.

   c. early childhood experiences.

   d. sexual urges in development.

10. After watching several older children climbing around a new jungle gym, five-year-old Jennie decides to try it herself. Which of the following best accounts for her behavior?

   a. classical conditioning

   b. modeling

   c. guided participation

   d. reinforcement

11. I am 8 years old, and although I understand some logical principles, I have trouble thinking about hypothetical concepts. According to Piaget, I am in the ____________________ stage of development.

   a. sensorimotor

   b. preoperational

   c. concrete operational

   d. formal operational

12. Two-year-old Bjorn has a simple understanding for "dad," and so each time he encounters a man with a child, he calls him "dad." When he learns that these other men are not "dad," Bjorn experiences

   a. conservation.

   b. cognition.

   c. equilibrium.

   d. disequilibrium.

13. Most adults become physiologically aroused by the sound of an infant's laughter. These interactive reactions, in which caregivers and babies elicit responses in each other,

   a. help ensure the survival of the next generation.

   b. do not occur in all human cultures.

   c. are the result of conditioning very early in life.

   d. are more often found in females than in males.

14. The school psychologist believes that each child's developmental needs can be understood only by taking into consideration the child's broader social and cultural background. Evidently, the school psychologist is working within the ____________________ perspective.

   a. psychoanalytic
   b. epigenetic systems
   c. social learning
   d. sociocultural

15. Four-year-old Rashad takes great pride in successfully undertaking new activities. Erikson would probably say that Rashad is capably meeting the psychosocial challenge of

   a. trust vs. mistrust.
   b. initiative vs. guilt.
   c. industry vs. inferiority.
   d. identity vs. role confusion.

16. Dr. Bazzi's developmental research draws upon insights from several theoretical perspectives. Evidently, Dr. Bazzi is working from a(n) ____________________ perspective.

   a. cognitive
   b. learning
   c. eclectic
   d. sociocultural

17. Dr. Ivey believes that development is a lifelong process of gradual and continuous growth. Based on this information, with which of the following theories would Dr. Ivey most likely agree?

   a. Piaget's cognitive theory
   b. Erikson's psychosocial theory
   c. Freud's psychoanalytic theory
   d. learning theory

18. Professor Villa believes that a person's social convoy is a powerful determinant of the motivational changes that occur in his or her life. Professor Villa is evidently an advocate of

   a. behaviorism.
   b. socioemotional selectivity theory.
   c. epigenetic systems theory.
   d. cognitive theory.

19. According to socioemotional selectivity theory, ____________ goals become paramount when people perceive their futures as being ____________.
    a. emotional; limited
    b. emotional; open-ended
    c. knowledge; limited
    d. knowledge; unpredictable

Answer Key

Key Terms

1. The science of human development is the science that seeks to understand how and why people change, and how and why they remain the same, as they grow older. (p. 4; video lesson, introduction & segment 3; objective 1)
2. Nature refers to all the traits, capacities, and limitations that a person inherits at the moment of conception. (pp. 5, 12–14; video lesson, introduction; objective 13)
3. Nurture refers to all the environmental influences that affect a person's development following the moment of conception. (pp. 5, 12–14; video lesson, introduction; objective 13)
4. The biosocial domain is concerned with brain and body changes and the social influences that guide them. (entire video; objective 2; telecourse student guide, pp. 1, 3)
5. The cognitive domain is concerned with thought processes, perceptual abilities, and language mastery, and the educational institutions that encourage these aspects of development. (entire video; objective 2; telecourse student guide, pp. 1, 3)
6. The psychosocial domain is concerned with emotions, personality, and interpersonal relationships with family, friends, and the wider community. (entire video; objective 2; telecourse student guide, pp. 1, 3)
7. A critical period in human development refers to a time when a particular type of developmental growth (in body or behavior) must happen if it is ever going to happen. (p. 5; objective 15)
8. A sensitive period in human development is a time when a certain type of development is most likely to happen, although it may still happen later with more difficulty. For example, early childhood is considered a sensitive period for language learning. (pp. 5–6; objective 15)
9. The Berger textbook refers to the difference-equals-deficit error as the mistaken belief that a deviation from some norm is necessarily inferior to behavior or characteristics that meet the standard. (p. 6; objective 15)
10. The life-span perspective on human development recognizes that human growth is lifelong and characterized by both continuity (as in personality)

and discontinuity (as in the number of brain cells). (p. 7; video lesson, segment 3; objective 1)

11. A cohort is a group of people who, because they were born within a few years of each other, experience many of the same historical and social emotions. (p. 9; objective 4)
12. An individual's socioeconomic status (SES) is determined by his or her income, education, place of residence, and occupation. (p. 10; objective 4)
13. Guided participation is a learning process in which the learner is tutored, or mentored, through social interaction with a skilled teacher. (p. 11; objective 12)
14. An ethnic group is a collection of people who share certain attributes, such as national origin, religion, ancestry, and/or language and who, as a result, tend to identify with each other and have similar daily encounters with the social world. (p. 11; objectives 3 & 4)
15. A social construction is an idea about the way things are, or should be, that is built more on the shared perceptions of members of a society than on objective reality. (p. 12; objective 4)
16. The term epigenetic emphasizes the genetic origins of behavior but also stresses that genes, over time, are directly and systematically affected by environmental forces. (p. 12; objective 13)
17. Mirror neurons are brain cells that respond to actions performed by someone else, as if the observer had done that action. Mirror neuron research provides an example of how developmental psychology benefits from an interdisciplinary approach (p. 15; objective 1)
18. A developmental theory is a systematic statement of principles and generalizations that explains behavior and development and provides a framework for future research. (p. 17; video lesson, segment 2; objective 5)
19. Psychoanalytic theory, a grand theory, interprets human development in terms of intrinsic drives and motives, many of which are irrational and unconscious. (p. 17; video lesson, segment 2; objective 6)
20. Behaviorism emphasizes the sequences and processes of conditioning that underlie most of human and animal behavior. (p. 19; video lesson, segment 2; objective 8)
21. Conditioning is the learning process that occurs either through the association of two stimuli (classical conditioning) or through the use of positive or negative reinforcement or punishment (operant conditioning). (p. 20; video lesson, segment 2; objective 8)
22. Put forth by Pavlov, classical conditioning is a learning process in which a meaningful stimulus, such as the smell of food to a hungry animal, gradually comes to be connected with a neutral stimulus, such as a particular sound, that had no special meaning before the learning process began. Also referred to as *respondent conditioning*. (p. 20; video lesson, segment 2; objective 8)

23. Put forth by B. F. Skinner, operant conditioning is the learning process in which a particular action is followed either by something desired (which makes the animal or person repeat the action) or something unwanted (which makes the action less likely to be repeated). Also referred to as *instrumental conditioning*. (p. 21; video lesson, segment 2; objective 8)
24. Reinforcement is the process by which the consequences of a particular behavior strengthen the behavior, making it more likely that the behavior will be repeated. (p. 21; video lesson, segment 2; objective 8)
25. An extension of behaviorism, social learning theory emphasizes that people often learn new behaviors through observation and imitation of other people. (p. 22; video lesson, segment 2; objectives 8 & 9)
26. Modeling refers to the process by which we observe other people's behavior and then pattern our own after it. (p. 22; video lesson, segment 2; objectives 8 & 9)
27. Cognitive theory emphasizes that the way people think and understand the world shapes their perceptions, attitudes, and actions. (p. 22; video lesson, segment 2; objective 10)
28. In Piaget's theory, cognitive equilibrium is a state of mental balance, in which a person's thoughts about the world seem not to clash with each other or with his or her experiences. (p. 23; video lesson, segment 2; objective 11)
29. According to Urie Bronfenbrenner's ecological-systems approach or model, human development is supported by systems at three nested levels: the microsystem, the exosystem, and the macrosystem. (p. 24; video lesson, segment 1; objectives 3 & 4)
30. According to socioemotional selectivity theory, the goals people set during their lifetimes reflect their sense of time: When time is limited, emotionally meaningful goals become paramount; when the future seems unending, knowledge-related goals are given higher status. (video lesson, segment 3; objective 5)
31. Dynamic-systems theory describes a process in which changes within a person or group are systematically connected to each other. That means that each aspect of a person's development can potentially affect all other aspects. (p. 24; objectives 1 & 3)
32. Developmentalists who work from an eclectic perspective accept elements from several theories, instead of adhering to only a single perspective. (video lesson, segment 3; objective 14)

Practice Questions I

Multiple-Choice Questions

1. a. is the correct answer. (p. 4; video lesson, segment 3; objective 15)

   b. & c. are incorrect. The study of development is concerned with a broader range of phenomena, including biosocial aspects of development, than these answers specify.

2. d. is the correct answer. (p. 7; objective 2; telecourse student guide, pp. 1, 3)
3. b. is the correct answer. (p. 7; objective 2; telecourse student guide, pp. 1, 3)

   a. is incorrect. This domain is concerned with thought processes.

   c. is incorrect. This domain is concerned with emotions, personality, and interpersonal relationships.

   d. is incorrect. This is not a domain of development.
4. c. is the correct answer. (p. 7; objective 2; telecourse student guide, pp. 1, 3)

   a. is incorrect. This falls within the cognitive and biosocial domains.

   b. is incorrect. This falls within the biosocial domain.

   d. is incorrect. This falls within the cognitive domain.
5. d. is the correct answer. This approach sees development as occurring within four interacting levels, or environments. (p. 24; video lesson, segment 1; objectives 3 & 4)
6. d. is the correct answer. (pp. 7–16; video lesson, segment 3; objective 1)
7. a. is the correct answer. (pp. 9–11, 24; objectives 3 & 4)

   b. is incorrect. The biosocial domain is concerned with brain and body changes.

   c. is incorrect. The cognitive domain is concerned with thought processes in individuals and the factors that influence them.
8. c. is the correct answer. (p. 24; objective 4)

   a. is incorrect. This refers to systems that link one microsystem to another.

   b. is incorrect. This refers to cultural values, political philosophies, economic patterns, and social conditions.

   d. is incorrect. This includes the community structures that affect the functioning of smaller systems.
9. c. is the correct answer. (p. 10; objectives 3 & 4)
10. d. is the correct answer. (p. 17; video lesson, segment 2; objective 5)
11. a. is the correct answer. (pp. 17–18; video lesson, segment 2; objective 6)

   b. is incorrect. Learning theory emphasizes the influence of the immediate environment on behavior.

   c. is incorrect. Cognitive theory emphasizes the impact of conscious thought processes on behavior.

   d. is incorrect. Sociocultural theory emphasizes the influence on development of social interaction in a specific cultural context.
12. a. is the correct answer. (pp. 17–19; video lesson, segment 2; objective 6)
13. a. is the correct answer. (pp. 18–19; video lesson, segment 2; objective 7)

b. & c. are incorrect. Whereas Freud identified five stages of psychosexual development, Erikson proposed eight psychosocial stages.

d. is incorrect. Although his theory places greater emphasis on social and cultural forces than Freud's did, Erikson's theory is nevertheless classified as a psychoanalytic theory.

14. b. is the correct answer. Sociocultural theory is an emergent theory. (video lesson, segment 2; objective 5)

    a., c., & d. are incorrect. Each of these is an example of a grand theory.

15. c. is the correct answer. (pp. 20–21; video lesson, segment 2; objective 8)

16. a. is the correct answer. In classical conditioning, a neutral stimulus—in this case, the bell—is associated with a meaningful stimulus—in this case, food. (p. 21; video lesson, segment 2; objective 8)

    b. is incorrect. In operant conditioning, the consequences of a voluntary response determine the likelihood of its being repeated. Salivation is an involuntary response.

    c. & d. are incorrect. Positive reinforcement and social learning pertain to voluntary, or operant, responses.

17. c. is the correct answer. (pp. 5, 12–14; objective 13)

    a. is incorrect. These are both examples of nurture.

    b. is incorrect. Both of these refer to nature.

    d. is incorrect. The impact of changing historical concepts of childhood on development is an example of how environmental forces (nurture) shape development.

18. d. is the correct answer. (p. 22; video lesson, segment 2; objective 9)

    a. & c. are incorrect. These can be true in all types of learning.

    b. is incorrect. This was not discussed as an aspect of developmental theory.

19. d. is the correct answer. (p. 12; objective 13)

    a. & c. are incorrect. Sociocultural and learning theories focus almost entirely on environmental factors (nurture) in development.

    b. is incorrect. Cognitive theory emphasizes the developing person's own mental activity but ignores genetic differences in individuals.

20. d. is the correct answer. (p. 10; objectives 3 & 4)

21. a. is the correct answer. (pp. 22–23; video lesson, segment 2; objective 10)

22. c. is the correct answer. (p. 23; objective 11)

    a. is incorrect. This refers to the core of Erikson's psychosocial stages, which deals with people's interactions with the environment.

    b. is incorrect. Equilibrium occurs when existing schemes do fit a person's current experiences.

    d. is incorrect. Negative reinforcement is the removal of a stimulus as a consequence of a desired behavior.

23. a. is the correct answer. (p. 4; video lesson; introduction; objective 15)
24. b. is the correct answer. (p. 11; objective 12)
25. b. is the correct answer. Locke believed that the mind at birth is a *tabula rasa,* or "blank slate," onto which learning (nurture) leaves its mark. Rousseau emphasized the natural (biological) goodness of human beings. (video lesson, introduction; objective 13)

Matching Items

26. f (pp. 17–19; video lesson, segment 2; objective 6)
27. k (p. 5; video lesson, introduction; objectives 13 & 15)
28. a (pp. 19–20; video lesson, segment 2; objective 8)
29. c (p. 22; video lesson, segment 2; objective 9)
30. h (p. 22; objective 10)
31. d (p. 5; video lesson, introduction; objectives 13 & 15)
32. e (p. 20; objective 8)
33. i (p. 22; video lesson, segment 2; objective 9)
34. j (pp. 12–13; objective 13)
35. g (p. 6; objective 15)
36. b (p. 5; objective 15)

Practice Questions II

Multiple-Choice Questions

1. d. is the correct answer. (pp. 9–11, 24; objectives 3 & 4)
2. a. is the correct answer. (pp. 7–16; video lesson; segment 1; objective 1)

   b. is incorrect. This is the emphasis of the newer, ecological-systems approach.

   c. & d. are incorrect. The textbook does not suggest that people commonly make these assumptions.
3. c. is the correct answer. (p. 24; video lesson, segment 1; objectives 3 & 4)

   a. & d. are incorrect. These are part of the microsystem.

   b. is incorrect. This is part of the exosystem.
4. c. is the correct answer. (p. 9; objective 4)

   a., b., & d. are incorrect. These are attributes of an ethnic group.
5. d. is the correct answer. (pp. 17–25; video lesson, segment 2; objective 14)
6. d. is the correct answer. This is one of Piaget's stages of cognitive development. (p. 19; video lesson, segment 2; objective 6)
7. c. is the correct answer. (p. 22; video lesson, segment 2; objective 9)
8. d. is the correct answer. (pp. 18–19; video lesson, segment 2; objective 7)
9. c. is the correct answer. (pp. 19–20; objective 8)

   a. is incorrect. Piaget formulated a cognitive theory of development.

b. is incorrect. Vygotsky formulated a sociocultural theory of development.

d. is incorrect. Erikson formulated a psychoanalytic theory of development.

10. c. is the correct answer. (pp. 19–21; video lesson, segment 2; objective 8)

11. c. is the correct answer. (pp. 20–21; video lesson, segment 2; objective 8)

    a. & b. are incorrect. These are psychoanalytic approaches to treating psychological problems.

    d. is incorrect. Learning theorists generally do not recommend the use of punishment.

12. a. is the correct answer. These behaviors are typical of infants in the sensorimotor stage. (pp. 22–23; video lesson, segment 2; objective 10)

    b., c., & d. are incorrect. These are typical of older children.

13. a. is the correct answer. (p. 23; video lesson, segment 2; objective 10)

    b. is incorrect. The sensorimotor stage describes development from birth until age 2.

    c. is incorrect. This is a psychoanalytic stage described by Freud.

    d. is incorrect. This is not the name of a stage; "psychosocial" refers to Erikson's stage theory.

14. a. is the correct answer. (p. 23; video lesson, segment 2; objective 11)

    b. is incorrect. This describes disequilibrium.

    c. is incorrect. This is formal operational thinking.

    d. is incorrect. Piaget's theory does not propose stages of information processing.

15. c. is the correct answer. (p. 21; video lesson, segment 2; objective 8)

    a. & b. are incorrect. Teaching your dog in this way is an example of operant, rather than classical (respondent), conditioning.

    d. is incorrect. Modeling involves learning by imitating others.

16. b. is the correct answer. (p. 23; objectives 10 & 11)

    a. is incorrect. Assimilation occurs when new experiences do not clash with existing ideas.

    c. is incorrect. Cognitive equilibrium is mental balance, which occurs when ideas and experiences do not clash.

    d. is incorrect. This is Vygotsky's term for the process by which a mentor engages a child in shared learning activities.

17. d. is the correct answer. (pp. 12–23; video lesson, segment 2; objective 14)

18. a. is the correct answer. (pp. 5, 12–14; video lesson, introduction; objective 13)

19. a. is the correct answer. (pp. 19–21; video lesson, segment 2; objective 8)

    b. is incorrect. This answer would have been correct had the question read "Response is to stimulus as…"

c. & d. are incorrect. Nature and nurture refer to internal and external influences on development, respectively.

20. a. is the correct answer (p. 22; objective 9)
21. d. is the correct answer (pp. 7–16; video lesson, segment 3; objective 1)
22. a. is the correct answer (p. 8; video lesson, segment 3; objective 1)
23. c. is the correct answer (pp. 15–16; objective 1)

True or False Items

24. T (pp. 19– 21; video lesson, segment 2; objective 8)
25. T (pp. 18–19; video lesson, segment 2; objective 7)
26. F Although most developmentalists believe that nature and nurture interact in shaping development, the practical implications of whether nature or nurture plays a greater role in certain abilities keep the controversy alive. (pp. 5, 12–14; video lesson, introduction; objective 13)
27. F This assumption lies at the heart of epigenetic systems theory. (pp. 5, 12–14; objective 13)
28. F Epigenetic theory emphasizes the interaction of genes and experience. (pp. 12– 14; objective 13)
29. T (p. 5; objective 15)
30. F On the contrary, disequilibrium often fosters greater growth. (p. 23; objective 11)
31. T (pp. 22–23; video lesson, segment 2; objective 10)
32. F The hallmark of Piaget's theory is that, at every age, individuals think about the world in unique ways. (pp. 22–23; video lesson, segment 2; objective 10)
33. T (video lesson, segment 3; objective 14)

Applying Your Knowledge

1. c. is the correct answer. (p. 7; objectives 2 & 15)

   a. & d. are incorrect. These pertain to the cognitive domain.

   b. is incorrect. This pertains to the biosocial domain.

2. c. is the correct answer. (p. 24; video lesson, segment 1; objectives 3 & 4)

   a. is incorrect. Piaget is notable in the area of cognitive development.

   b. is incorrect. Freud was a pioneer of psychoanalysis.

   d. is incorrect. Skinner is notable in the history of learning theory.

3. b. is the correct answer. (p. 24; video lesson, segment 1; objectives 3 & 4)

   a., c., & d. are incorrect. These are the three domains of development.

4. a. is the correct answer. (p. 17; objective 5)

5. a. is the correct answer. This is an example of operant conditioning because a response recurs due to its consequences. (p. 21; video lesson, segment 2; objective 8)

   b. & d. are incorrect. In classical conditioning, the individual learns to associate a neutral stimulus with a meaningful stimulus.

   c. is incorrect. In modeling, learning occurs through the observation of others, rather than through direct exposure to reinforcing consequences, as in this example.

6. d. is the correct answer. (p. 12; objective 13)

   a. is incorrect. Psychoanalytic theorists focus on the role of unconscious forces in development.

   b. is incorrect. Cognitive theorists emphasize how the developing person actively seeks to understand experiences.

   c. is incorrect. Sociocultural theorists focus on the social context, as expressed through people, language, and customs.

7. b. is the correct answer. (p. 11; objective 12)

   a. & c. are incorrect. These are both examples of modeling.

   d. is incorrect. Guided participation involves the coaching of a mentor. In this example, Kyle is simply following written directions.

8. a. is the correct answer. (p. 23; objective 11)

   b. is incorrect. Because the dog is not furry, the child's concept of dog cannot incorporate (assimilate) the discrepant experience without being revamped.

   c. & d. are incorrect. Equilibrium exists when ideas (such as what a dog is) and experiences (such as seeing a hairless dog) do not clash.

9. d. is the correct answer. (pp. 18–19; video lesson, segment 2; objective 7)

10. b. is the correct answer. Evidently, Jennie has learned by observing the other children at play. (p. 22; video lesson, segment 2; objective 9)

    a. is incorrect. Classical conditioning is concerned with the association of stimuli, not with complex responses, as in this example.

    c. is incorrect. Guided participation involves the interaction of a mentor and a child.

    d. is incorrect. Reinforcement is a process for getting a response to recur.

11. c. is the correct answer. (p. 23; video lesson, segment 2; objective 10)

12. d. is the correct answer. When Bjorn experiences something that conflicts with his existing understanding, he experiences disequilibrium. (p. 23; objective 11)

    a. is incorrect. Conservation is the ability to recognize that objects do not change when their appearances change.

b. is incorrect. Cognition refers to all mental activities associated with thinking.

c. is incorrect. If Bjorn's thinking were in equilibrium, all men would be "dad"!

13. a. is the correct answer. (pp. 12–14; objective 13)

    b. & c. are incorrect. Infant social reflexes and adult caregiving impulses occur in all cultures (b), which indicates that they are the product of nature rather than nurture (c).

    d. is incorrect. The textbook does not address the issue of gender differences in infant reflexes or caregiving impulses.

14. d. is the correct answer. (video lesson, segment 2; objective 12)
15. b. is the correct answer. (pp. 18–19; video lesson, segment 2; objective 7)

    a. is incorrect. According to Erikson, this crisis concerns younger children.

    c. & d. are incorrect. In Erikson's theory, these crises concern older children.

16. c. is the correct answer. (video lesson, segment 3; objective 14)

    a., b., & d. are incorrect. These are three of the many theoretical perspectives upon which someone working from an eclectic perspective might draw.

17. d. is the correct answer. (pp. 17, 19–21; video lesson, segment 2; objectives 5 & 8)

    a., b., & c. are incorrect. Each of these theories emphasizes that development is a discontinuous process that occurs in stages.

18. b. is the correct answer. (video lesson, segment 2; objective 5)
19. a. is the correct answer. (video lesson, segment 2; objective 5)

Lesson Review

Lesson 1

Introduction
Theories of Development

Please Note: Use this matrix to guide your study and achieve the learning objectives of this lesson. It will also help you to view the video, which defines and demonstrates important concepts and skills as they relate to everyday life.

Learning Objective	Textbook	Telecourse Student Guide	Video Lesson
1. Define the life-span perspective of development, and identify five characteristics or principles of development.	pp. 7–16	Key Terms: 1, 10, 17, 31; Practice Questions I: 6; Practice Questions II: 2, 21, 22, 23.	Segment 1: *Contexts and Systems* Segment 3: *The Life-Span Perspective*
2. Identify and describe the three domains into which human development is often separated.	p. 7, (Figure 1.1)	Key Terms: 4, 5, 6; Practice Questions I: 2, 3, 4; Applying Your Knowledge: 1.	Introduction
3. Describe the ecological-systems approach to human development, and explain how this approach leads to an understanding of the overlapping contexts in which people develop.	pp. 9–11 & 24	Key Terms: 14, 29, 31; Practice Questions I: 5, 7, 9, 20; Practice Questions II: 1, 3; Applying Your Knowledge: 2, 3.	Segment 1: *Contexts and Systems*
4. Discuss the nested levels (microsystems, exosystems and macrosystems) of Urie Bronfenbrenner's ecological systems approach to human development and demonstrate an understanding of how these levels fit into the three broader overlapping contexts of culture, ethnicity, and socioeconomic status (SES).	pp. 9–11 & 24	Key Terms: 11, 12, 14, 15, 29; Practice Questions I: 5, 7, 8, 9, 20; Practice Questions II: 1, 3, 4; Applying Your Knowledge: 2, 3.	Segment 1: *Contexts and Systems*
5. Define developmental theory, and describe how developmental theories help explain human behavior and development.	p. 17	Key Terms: 18, 30; Practice Questions I: 10, 14; Applying Your Knowledge: 4, 17, 18, 19.	Segment 2: *Theories in Development;* Segment 3: *The Life-Span Perspective*

Learning Objective	**Textbook**	**Telecourse Student Guide**	**Video Lesson**
6. Discuss the major focus of psychoanalytic theories, and describe the conflicts that occur during Freud's stages of psychosexual development.	pp. 17–19, Table 1.3	Key Terms: 19; Practice Questions I: 11, 12, 26; Practice Questions II: 6.	Segment 2: *Theories in Development*
7. Describe the crises of Erikson's theory of psychosocial development, and contrast them with Freud's stages.	pp. 18–19	Practice Questions I: 13; Practice Questions II: 8, 25; Applying Your Knowledge: 9, 15.	Segment 2: *Theories in Development*
8. Discuss the major focus of behaviorism, and explain the basic principles of classical and operant conditioning.	pp. 19–21	Key Terms: 20, 21, 22, 23, 24, 25, 26; Practice Questions I: 15, 16, 28, 32; Practice Questions II: 9, 10, 11, 15, 19, 24; Applying Your Knowledge: 5, 17.	Segment 2: *Theories in Development*
9. Discuss social learning theory as an extension of learning theory.	p. 22	Key Terms: 25, 26; Practice Questions I: 18, 29, 33; Practice Questions II: 7, 20; Applying Your Knowledge: 10.	Segment 2: *Theories in Development*
10. Identify the primary focus of cognitive theory, and briefly describe Piaget's stages of cognitive development.	pp. 22–23	Key Terms: 27; Practice Questions I: 21, 30; Practice Questions II: 12, 13, 16, 31, 32; Applying Your Knowledge: 11.	Segment 2: *Theories in Development*
11. Discuss the process that, according to Piaget, guides cognitive development.	p. 23	Key Terms: 28; Practice Questions I: 22; Practice Questions II: 14, 16, 30; Applying Your Knowledge: 8, 12.	Segment 2: *Theories in Development*
12. Discuss the basic ideas of Vygotsky and define the concept of guided participation.	p. 11	Key Terms: 13; Practice Questions I: 24; Applying Your Knowledge: 7, 14.	Segment 2: *Theories in Development*
13. Define the term "epigenetic," and discuss how an epigenetic understanding relates to the nature/nurture controversy.	pp. 5 & 12–14	Key Terms: 2, 3, 16; Practice Questions I: 17, 19, 25, 27, 31, 34; Practice Questions II: 18, 26, 27, 28; Applying Your Knowledge: 6, 13.	Introduction

Learning Objective	Textbook	Telecourse Student Guide	Video Lesson
14. Summarize the contributions and criticisms of the major developmental theories, and explain the eclectic perspective of contemporary developmentalists.	pp. 17–23	Key Terms: 32; Practice Questions II: 5, 17, 33; Applying Your Knowledge: 16.	Segments 2: *Theories in Development;* Segment *3: The Life-Span Perspective*
15. Define developmental science and discuss the three crucial elements in the definition as specifically noted in your textbook.	pp. 4–7	Key Terms: 7, 8, 9; Practice Questions I: 1, 23, 27, 31, 35, 36; Practice Questions I: 29; Applying Your Knowledge: 1.	Introduction

Lesson 2

Developmental Study as a Science

Preview

The scientific study of human development is the science that seeks to understand how and why people change with increasing age, and how and why they remain the same. Central to this science is the set of principles and procedures scientists use to produce the most objective results possible. Lesson 2 discusses these principles and procedures, beginning with the **scientific method** and including **scientific observation**, correlational research, **experiments**, **surveys**, and case studies. To study people over time, developmentalists have created several research designs: cross-sectional, longitudinal, and cross-sequential. As these methods are described, several classic developmental psychology studies are summarized.

The final section of the lesson discusses the ethics of research with humans. In addition to ensuring confidentiality and safety, developmentalists who study children are especially concerned that the benefits of research outweigh the risks.

Prior Telecourse Knowledge that Will Be Used in this Lesson

This lesson focuses primarily on research methods, drawing on material from each of the three domains of development. Recall from Chapter 1 that the three domains of development include the biosocial domain (brain and body as well as changes in them and the social influences that guide them), the cognitive domain (thought processes, perceptual abilities, and language mastery, as well as the educational institutions that encourage them), and the psychosocial domain (emotions, personality, and interpersonal relationships with family, friends, and the wider community). All three domains are important at every age, and each of the domains is affected by the other two.

Learning Objectives

Use this information to guide your reading, viewing, thinking, and studying. After successfully completing this lesson, you should be able to:

1. List and describe the basic steps of the scientific method as it applies to the study of human development.
2. Describe scientific observation and correlation as research strategies.
3. Discuss why scientists carry out experiments, and describe the components of an experiment.
4. Describe surveys and case studies, noting at least one advantage (or strength) and one disadvantage (or weakness) of each.
5. Describe three basic research designs used by developmental psychologists.
6. Discuss the code of ethics that should be followed by researchers in the field of developmental psychology.

Read Chapter 1, "The Science of Development," pages 4, 9, and 26–39.

View the video for Lesson 2, "A Scientific Approach."

Segment 1: *The Scientific Method*

Segment 2: *Research Methods*

Segment 3: *Studying Changes over Time*

Summary

The **scientific method** consists of five basic steps: (1) formulate a research question, (2) develop a **hypothesis**, (3) test the hypothesis, (4) draw conclusions, and (5) make the findings available. **Replication** of research findings verifies the findings and leads researchers to more definitive and extensive conclusions.

Because the variables in research are numerous, it is difficult to determine whether all the relevant ones have been identified in a particular investigation. Developmentalists deal with both intrapersonal variation, which occurs from day to day in each person, and interpersonal variation, which occurs between people or groups.

In designing research, scientists are concerned with four issues: validity, accuracy, generalizability, and usefulness. There are many ways to test hypotheses. One method is **scientific observation** of people in their natural environment or in a laboratory setting. Naturalistic observation is limited in that it tells us only if two variables are correlated.

Correlation is a statistical term indicating that two variables are related. It does not prove causality. **Experiments** can reveal cause-and-effect relationships by allowing experimenters to observe whether a change in an **independent variable**

affects some specific behavior, or **dependent variable**. Experiments are not, however, without their limitations. Even if subjects behave normally in an experiment, their performance may not be applicable to the real world.

To determine whether a difference between two groups occurred purely by coincidence, or chance, researchers apply a mathematical test of statistical significance. Generally, coincidence is ruled out if there is less than 1 possibility in 20 that the difference could have occurred by chance.

The scientific **survey** is especially vulnerable to bias: the phrasing of the questions may affect the responses obtained; people may give answers they think the researcher wants to hear.

In **cross-sectional research**, groups of people who are different in age but similar in all other important ways are compared on the characteristic that is of interest to the researcher(s). One limitation of cross-sectional research is that it is always possible that some variable other than age differentiates the groups. In **longitudinal research**, the same people are studied over a period of time. Longitudinal research is particularly useful in studying developmental trends that occur over a long age span.

Both longitudinal and cross-sectional researchers must bear in mind that research on a single **cohort** may not be valid for people developing in an earlier or later cohort. In **cross-sequential research**, several groups of people at different ages (cross-sectional component) are followed over time (longitudinal component).

When studying people, scientists take special care to ensure that participation is voluntary and harmless and that the study's benefits outweigh its costs. Sometimes scientists conduct a meta-analysis, or a compilation of data from many other sources, so that no participants are directly involved.

Review all reading assignments for this lesson.

As assigned by your instructor, complete the optional online component for this lesson.

Key Terms

Using your own words, write a brief definition or explanation of each of the following terms on a separate piece of paper.

1. scientific method
2. hypothesis
3. replication
4. variable
5. scientific observation
6. correlation
7. experiment
8. independent variable
9. dependent variable
10. experimental group
11. comparison group
12. survey
13. cross-sectional research
14. longitudinal research
15. cross-sequential research
16. quantitative research
17. qualitative research
18. code of ethics
19. attachment
20. the Strange Situation
21. random assignment
22. cohort

Practice Questions I

Multiple-Choice Questions

1. The scientific study of human development is defined as the study of
   a. how and why people change or remain the same over time.
   b. psychosocial influences on aging.
   c. individual differences in learning over the life span.
   d. all of the above.

2. A hypothesis is a
   a. conclusion.
   b. prediction to be tested.
   c. statistical test.
   d. correlation.

3. A disadvantage of experiments is that
   a. people may behave differently in the artificial environment of the laboratory.
   b. control groups are too large to be accommodated in most laboratories.
   c. they are the method most vulnerable to bias on the part of the researcher.
   d. proponents of the ecological approach overuse them.

4. In an experiment testing the effects of group size on individual effort in a tug-of-war task, the number of people in each group is the

   a. hypothesis.

   b. independent variable

   c. dependent variable.

   d. level of significance.

5. Which research method would be most appropriate for investigating the relationship between parents' religious beliefs and their attitudes toward middle school sex education?

   a. experimentation

   b. longitudinal research

   c. naturalistic observation

   d. the survey

6. Developmentalists who carefully observe the behavior of schoolchildren during recess are using a research method known as

   a. the case study.

   b. cross-sectional research.

   c. scientific observation.

   d. cross-sequential research.

7. In an experiment to determine the effects of attention on memory, memory is the

   a. control condition.

   b. intervening variable.

   c. independent variable.

   d. dependent variable.

8. The emotional tie that develops between an infant and his or her primary caregiver is called

   a. self-awareness.

   b. synchrony.

   c. affiliation.

   d. attachment.

9. Harry Harlow found that when monkeys were reared in social isolation, they would seek
   a. contact comfort as much as nourishment.
   b. nourishment over contact comfort.
   c. the company of other monkeys that had been socially isolated.
   d. no food, water, or nourishment of any kind.

10. If shoe size and IQ are negatively correlated, which of the following is true?
    a. People with large feet tend to have high IQs.
    b. People with small feet tend to have high IQs.
    c. People with small feet tend to have low IQs.
    d. IQ is unpredictable based on a person's shoe size.

11. To protect participants, scientists who study human development are bound by
    a. a code of ethics.
    b. a code of honor.
    c. a chain of bonds.
    d. none of the above.

Matching Items

Match each definition or description with its corresponding term.

Terms

12. __________ cross-sequential
13. __________ correlation
14. __________ scientific observation
15. __________ hypothesis
16. __________ scientific method
17. __________ cross-sectional
18. __________ longitudinal research

Definitions or Descriptions

a. a general procedural model that helps researchers remain objective
b. a testable prediction regarding development
c. a statistical measure of relationship between two variables
d research study retesting one group of people at several different times
e. research study comparing people of different ages at the same time
f. research study that follows groups of people of different ages over time
g. unobtrusively watching and recording of the behavior of a group of research subjects

Practice Questions II

Multiple-Choice Questions

1. Professor Cohen predicts that because "baby boomers" grew up in an era that promoted independence and assertiveness, people in their 40s and 50s will respond differently to a political survey than will people in their 20s and 30s. The professor's prediction regarding political attitudes is an example of a(n)

   a. meta-analysis.

   b. hypothesis.

   c. independent variable.

   d. dependent variable.

2. A cohort is defined as a group of people

   a. of similar national origin.

   b. who share a common language.

   c. born within a few years of each other.

   d. who share the same religion.

3. In a test of the effects of noise, groups of students performed a proofreading task in a noisy or a quiet room. To what group were students in the noisy room assigned?

   a. experimental

   b. control

   c. randomly assigned

   d. dependent

4. If developmentalists discovered that poor people are happier than wealthy people are, this would indicate that wealth and happiness are

   a. unrelated.

   b. positively correlated.

   c. negatively correlated.

   d. causally related.

5. In an experiment testing the effects of noise level on mood, mood is the

   a. hypothesis.

   b. independent variable.

   c. dependent variable.

   d. scientific observation.

6. Which of the following research strategies would be best for determining whether alcohol causes impairments to memory?

   a. case study

   b. naturalistic observation

   c. survey

   d. experiment

7. Well-conducted surveys measure attitudes using ______________________ phrasing.

   a. random

   b. experimental

   c. highly controlled

   d. unbiased

8. Which of the following research methods does **NOT** belong with the others?

   a. case study

   b. survey

   c. experiment

   d. observation

9. Repeating a study, using the same procedures on another group of participants, to verify or refute the original study's conclusions is called

   a. variable controlling.

   b. replication.

   c. representative sampling.

   d. stratification.

10. In a test of the effects of noise, groups of students performed a proofreading task in a noisy or a quiet room. To what condition were students in the quiet room exposed?

    a. experimental

    b. comparison

    c. randomly assigned

    d. dependent

Matching Items

Match each definition or description with its corresponding term.

Terms

11. __________ independent variable
12. __________ dependent variable
13. __________ experiment
14. __________ replicate
15. __________ experimental group
16. __________ comparison group
17. __________ survey

Definitions or Descriptions

a. the "treatment-absent" condition in an experiment
b. the "treatment-present" condition in an experiment
c. the research strategy in which a representative sample of individuals is questioned
d. to repeat an experiment to check the reliability of its results
e. the variable manipulated in an experiment
f. to test a hypothesis in a controlled situation
g. the variable measured in an experiment

Applying Your Knowledge

1. When researchers find that the results of a study are statistically significant, this means
   a. they may have been caused purely by chance.
   b. it is unlikely they could be replicated.
   c. it is unlikely they could have occurred by chance.
   d. that the sample population was representative of the general population.

2. If height and weight are correlated, which of the following is true?
   a. There is a cause-and-effect relationship between height and weight.
   b. A person's height is related to his or her weight.
   c. Height and weight are completely unrelated.
   d. None of the above statements are true.

3. To study the effects of temperature on mood, Dr. Sanchez had students fill out questionnaires in very warm or very cool rooms. What was the independent variable?
   a. the number of subjects assigned to each group
   b. the students' responses to the questionnaire
   c. the room temperature
   d. the subject matter of the questions

4. Esteban believes that high doses of caffeine slow a person's reaction time. To test his belief, he has five friends each drink three 8-ounce cups of coffee and then measures their reaction time on a learning task. What is wrong with Esteban's research strategy?
   a. No independent variable is specified.
   b. No dependent variable is specified.
   c. There is no control condition.
   d. There is no provision for replication of the findings.

5. Which of the following is an example of longitudinal research?
   a. A researcher compares how many different age groups perform on a memory test.
   b. A researcher compares how the same group of people, at different ages, performs on a test of memory.
   c. An investigator compares the performance of an experimental group and a control group of subjects on a memory test.
   d. A researcher compares the performance of several different age groups on a test of memory as each group is tested repeatedly over a period of years.

6. For her developmental psychology research project, Lakia decides she wants to focus on just one person. You advise her to conduct
   a. a survey.
   b. an experiment.
   c. a cross-sectional study.
   d. a case study.

7. Dr. Weston is comparing research findings for a group of 30-year-olds with findings for the same individuals at age 20, as well as with findings for groups who were 30 in 1990. Which research method is she using?
   a. longitudinal research
   b. cross-sectional research
   c. case study
   d. cross-sequential research

8. A psychologist studies the play behavior of third-grade children by watching groups during recess at school. Which research technique is being used?
   a. correlation
   b. case study
   c. experimentation
   d. naturalistic observation

Answer Key

Key Terms

1. The scientific method is a general procedural model that helps researchers remain objective as they study behavior. The five basic steps of the scientific method are (1) formulate a research question; (2) develop a hypothesis; (3) test the hypothesis; (4) draw conclusions; and (5) make the findings available. (p. 4; video lesson, segment 1; objective 1)
2. In the scientific method, a hypothesis is a specific, testable prediction regarding development. (p. 4; video lesson, segment 1; objective 1)
3. To replicate a test of a research hypothesis is to repeat it and obtain the same results using a different but related set of subjects or procedures in order to test its validity. (p. 4; objective 1)
4. A variable is any quantity, characteristic, or action that can take on different values within a group of individuals or a single individual. (p. 28; video lesson, segment 2; objective 3)
5. Scientific observation is the unobtrusive watching and recording of subjects' behavior in a situation that is being studied, either in the laboratory or in a natural setting. (p. 26; video lesson, segment 2; objective 2)
6. Correlation is a statistical term that merely indicates whether two variables are related to each other such that one is likely (or unlikely) to occur when the other occurs or one is likely to increase (or decrease) when the other increases (or decreases). (p. 34; video lesson, segment 2; objective 2)
7. The experiment is the research method in which an investigator tests a hypothesis in a controlled situation in which the relevant variables are limited and can be manipulated by the experimenter. (p. 28; video lesson, segment 2; objective 3)
8. The independent variable is the variable that is manipulated in an experiment. (p. 28; video lesson, segment 2; objective 3)
9. The dependent variable is the variable that is being studied in an experiment. (p. 28; video lesson, segment 2; objective 3)

   Example: In the study of the effects of a new drug on memory, the subjects' memory is the dependent variable.
10. The experimental group of an experiment is one in which subjects are exposed to the independent variable being studied. (p. 28; video lesson, segment 2; objective 3)

11. The comparison group (also known as a control group) of an experiment is one in which the treatment of interest, or independent variable, is withheld so that comparison to the experimental group can be made. (p. 28; video lesson, segment 2; objective 3)
12. The scientific survey is the research method in which information is collected from a large number of people, either through written questionnaires or through interviews. (p. 29; video lesson, segment 2; objective 4)
13. In cross-sectional research, groups of people who differ in age but share other important characteristics are compared with regard to the variable under investigation. (p. 30; video lesson, segment 3; objective 5)
14. In longitudinal research, the same group of individuals is studied over a period of time to measure both change and stability as they age. (pp. 30, 32; video lesson, segment 3; objective 5)
15. Cross-sequential research follows a group of people of different ages over time, thus combining the strengths of the cross-sectional and longitudinal methods. (pp. 30, 33; objective 5)
16. Quantitative research produces data that can be expressed with numbers. Since it can be categorized, ranked, or numbered, it can be translated across cultures to draw comparisons between diverse populations. (p. 36; objective 5)
17. Qualitative research produces data that can describe particular conditions and participants' expressed ideas in narrative, rather than numerical, form. Such research reflects cultural and contextual diversity, but it is also more vulnerable to bias and difficult to replicate. (p. 36; objective 5)
18. Developmental psychologists and other scientists work from a code of ethics, which is a set of moral principles that guides their research. (p. 36; video lesson, segment 3; objective 6)
19. Attachment refers to the relationship between an infant and his or her caregiver. (video lesson, segment 1; objective 5)
20. The Strange Situation is a laboratory research procedure used to measure an infant's attachment to his or her caregiver. (video lesson, segment 2; objective 5)
21. Random assignment is the procedure of assigning participants to the experimental and control conditions of an experiment by chance in order to minimize preexisting differences between the groups. (video lesson, segment 2; objective 3)
22. A cohort is a group of people who, because they were born within a few years of each other, experience many of the same historical and social conditions. (p. 9; video lesson, segment 3; objective 5)

Practice Questions I

Multiple-Choice Questions

1. a. is the correct answer. (p. 4; video lesson, introduction; objective 1)

   b. & c. are incorrect. The study of development is concerned with a broader range of phenomena, including biosocial aspects of development, than these answers specify.

2. b. is the correct answer. (p. 4; video lesson, segment 1; objective 1)

3. a. is the correct answer. (pp. 28–29; objective 3)

4. b. is the correct answer. (p. 28; video lesson, segment 2; objective 3)

   a. is incorrect. A possible hypothesis for this experiment would be that the larger the group, the less hard a given individual will pull.

   c. is incorrect. The dependent variable is the measure of individual effort.

   d. is incorrect. Significance level refers to the numerical value specifying the possibility that the results of an experiment could have occurred by chance.

5. d. is the correct answer. (p. 29; video lesson, segment 2; objective 4)

   a. is incorrect. Experimentation is appropriate when one is seeking to uncover cause-and-effect relationships; in this example, the researcher is only interested in determining whether the parents' beliefs predict their attitudes. Experimenters cannot manipulate religious beliefs.

   b. is incorrect. Longitudinal research would be appropriate if the researcher sought to examine the development of these attitudes over a long period of time.

   c. is incorrect. Mere observation would not allow the researcher to determine the attitudes of the subjects.

6. c. is the correct answer. (pp. 26–27; video lesson, segment 2; objective 2)

   a. is incorrect. In this method, one subject is studied over a period of time.

   b. & d. are incorrect. In these research methods, two or more groups of subjects are studied and compared.

7. d. is the correct answer. (p. 28; video lesson, segment 2; objective 3)

   a. is incorrect. The control condition is the comparison group, in which the experimental treatment is absent.

   b. is incorrect. Memory is the dependent variable in this experiment.

   c. is incorrect. Attention is the independent variable, which is being manipulated.

8. d. is the correct answer. (video lesson, segment 1; objective 5)

   a. is incorrect. Self-awareness refers to the infant's developing sense of "me and mine."

   b. is incorrect. Synchrony, which will be discussed in a later lesson, describes the coordinated inaction between infant and caregiver.

c. is incorrect. Affiliation describes the tendency of people at any age to seek the companionship of others.

9. a. is the correct answer. (video lesson, segment 1; objective 5)
10. b. is the correct answer. (video lesson, segment 2; objective 2)

    a. & c. are incorrect. These answers would have been correct had the question stated that there is a *positive* correlation between shoe size and IQ. Actually, there is probably no correlation at all!

11. a. is the correct answer (p. 36; video lesson, segment 3; objective 6)

Matching Items

12. f (pp. 30, 33; objective 5)
13. c (pp. 34–35; video lesson, segment 2; objective 2)
14. g (pp. 26–27; video lesson, segment 2; objective 2)
15. b (p. 4; video lesson, segment 1; objective 1)
16. a (p. 4; video lesson, segment 1; objective 1)
17. e (pp. 30–31; video lesson, segment 3; objective 5)
18. d (pp. 30, 32–33; video lesson, segment 3; objective 5)

Practice Questions II

Multiple-Choice Questions

1. b. is the correct answer. (p. 4; video lesson, segment 1; objective 1)

    a. is incorrect. In a meta-analysis, the results of a number of separate research studies are combined.

    c. & d. are incorrect. Variables are treatments (independent) or behaviors (dependent) in experiments, which this situation clearly is not.

2. c. is the correct answer. (p. 9; video lesson, segment 3; objective 5)

    a., b., & d. are incorrect. These are attributes of an ethnic group.

3. a. is the correct answer. The experimental group is the one in which the variable or treatment—in this case, noise—is present. (p. 28; video lesson, segment 3; objective 3)

    b. is incorrect. Students in the quiet room would be in the control condition.

    c. is incorrect. Presumably, all students in both groups were randomly assigned to their groups.

    d. is incorrect. The word *dependent* refers to a kind of variable in experiments; groups are either experimental or control.

4. c. is the correct answer. (video lesson, segment 2; objective 2)

    a. is incorrect. Wealth and happiness clearly are related.

    b. is incorrect. This answer would be correct if wealthy people were found to be happier than poor people.

    d. is incorrect. Correlation does not imply causation.

5. c. is the correct answer. (p. 28; video lesson, segment 2; objective 3)

    a. is incorrect. Hypotheses make specific, testable predictions.

b. is incorrect. Noise level is the independent variable.

d. is incorrect. Scientific observation is a research method in which subjects are watched, while their behavior is recorded unobtrusively.

6. d. is the correct answer. In an experiment, it would be possible to manipulate alcohol consumption and observe the effects, if any, on memory. (pp. 28–29; video lesson, segment 2; objective 3)

   a., b., & c. are incorrect because only by directly controlling the variables of interest can a researcher uncover cause-and-effect relationships.

7. d. is the correct answer (p. 29; objective 4)

8. c. is the correct answer. Only experiments can reveal cause-and-effect relationships; the other methods can only describe relationships. (pp. 26–28, 34–35; video lesson, segment 2; objectives 2 & 3)

9. b. is the correct answer. (p. 4; video lesson, segment 2; objectives 1 & 3)

   a., c., & d. are incorrect. None of these terms describes precautions taken in setting up groups for experiments.

10. b. is the correct answer. The comparison condition is the one in which the treatment—in this case, noise—is absent. (pp. 28–29; video lesson, segment 2; objective 3)

    a. is incorrect. Students in the noisy room would be in the experimental condition.

    c. is incorrect. Presumably, all students in both groups were randomly assigned. Random assignment is a method for establishing groups, rather than a condition.

    d. is incorrect. The word "dependent" refers to a kind of variable in experiments; conditions are either experimental or comparison.

Matching Items

11. f (pp. 28–29; video lesson, segment 2; objective 3)
12. h (pp. 28–29; video lesson, segment 2; objective 3)
13. g (pp. 28–29; video lesson, segment 2; objective 3)
14. e (p. 4; objective 1)
15. c (p. 28; video lesson, segment 2; objective 3)
16. b (p. 28; video lesson, segment 2; objective 3)
17. d (p. 29; video lesson, segment 2; objective 4)

Applying Your Knowledge

1. c. is the correct answer. (pp. 28–29; objective 1)
2. b. is the correct answer (pp. 34–35; video lesson, segment 2; objective 2)
3. c. is the correct answer. (p. 28; video lesson, segment 2; objective 3)
4. c. is the correct answer. In order to determine the effects of caffeine on reaction time, Esteban needs to measure reaction time in a control, or comparison, group that does not receive caffeine. (pp. 28–29; video lesson, segment 2; objective 3)

a. is incorrect. Caffeine is the independent variable.

b. is incorrect. Reaction time is the dependent variable.

d. is incorrect. Whether or not Esteban's experiment can be replicated is determined by the precision with which he reports his procedures, which is not an aspect of research strategy.

5. b. is the correct answer. (pp. 30, 32; video lesson, segment 3; objective 5)

   a. is incorrect. This is an example of cross-sectional research.

   c. is incorrect. This is an example of an experiment.

   d. is incorrect. This type of study is not described in the textbook.

6. d. is the correct answer. (p. 29; objective 4)

   a., b., & c. are incorrect. These research methods generally yield quantitative, rather than qualitative, data.

7. d. is the correct answer. (pp. 30, 33; objective 5)

   a., & c. are incorrect. In these research methods, only one group of subjects is studied.

   b. is incorrect. Dr. Weston's design includes comparison of groups of people of different ages over time.

8. d. is the correct answer. (pp. 26–28; video lesson, segment 2; objective 2)

Lesson Review

Lesson 2

Developmental Study as a Science

Please Note: Use this matrix to guide your study and achieve the learning objectives of this lesson. It will also help you to view the video, which defines and demonstrates important concepts and skills as they relate to everyday life.

Learning Objective	**Textbook**	**Telecourse Student Guide**	**Video Lesson**
1. List and describe the basic steps of the scientific method as it applies to the study of human development.	p. 4	Key Terms: 1, 2, 3; Practice Questions I: 1, 2, 15, 16; Practice Questions II: 1, 9, 14; Applying Your Knowledge: 1.	Introduction; Segment 1: *The Scientific Method* Segment 2: *Research Methods* Segment 3: *Studying Changes over Time*
2. Describe scientific observation and correlation as research strategies.	pp. 26–28, 34–35	Key Terms: 5, 6; Practice Questions I: 6, 10, 13, 14; Practice Questions II: 4, 8; Applying Your Knowledge: 2, 8.	Segment 2: *Research Methods*
3. Discuss why scientists carry out experiments, and describe the components of an experiment.	pp. 28–29	Key Terms: 4, 7, 8, 9, 10, 11, 21; Practice Questions I: 3, 4, 7; Practice Questions II: 2, 3, 5, 6, 8, 9, 10, 11, 12, 13, 15, 16; Applying Your Knowledge: 3, 4.	Segment 2: *Research Methods* Segment 3: *Studying Changes over Time*
4. Describe surveys and case studies, noting at least one advantage (or strength) and one disadvantage (or weakness) of each.	p. 29	Key Terms: 12; Practice Questions I: 5; Practice Questions II: 7, 17, 18; Applying Your Knowledge: 6.	Segment 2: *Research Methods*

Learning Objective	Textbook	Telecourse Student Guide	Video Lesson
5. Describe three basic research designs used by developmental psychologists.	pp. 9, 30–33	Key Terms: 13, 14, 15, 16, 17, 19, 20, 22; Practice Questions I: 8, 9, 12, 17, 18; Practice Questions II: 2; Applying Your Knowledge: 5, 7.	Segment 1: *The Scientific Method* Segment 2: *Research Methods* Segment 3: *Studying Changes over Time*
6. Discuss the code of ethics that should be followed by researchers in the field of developmental psychology.	pp. 36–37	Key Terms: 18; Practice Questions I: 11.	Segment 3: *Studying Changes over Time*

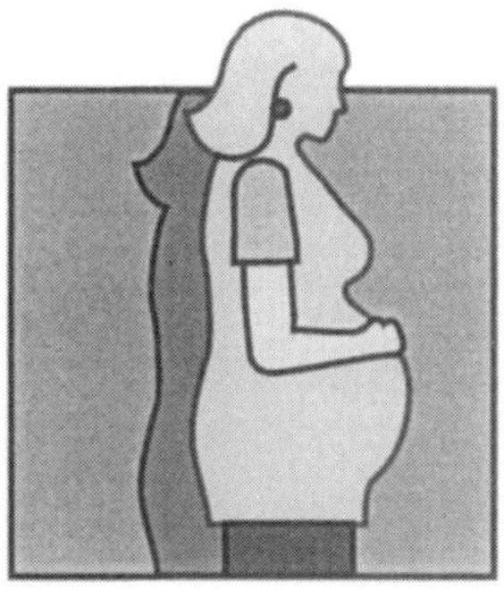

Lesson 3

The Beginnings: Heredity and Environment

Preview

Much is determined at the moment of conception, when a sperm and ovum unite to initiate the developmental processes that will culminate in the birth of a new human being. The genetic legacies of the mother and father influence virtually everything about the developing person—including physical attributes, such as gender and appearance, as well as intellectual and personality characteristics.

Lesson 3 describes the fusion of the ovum and the sperm and the biological mechanisms by which normal, and sometimes abnormal, **chromosomes** and **genes** are transmitted to the developing person. The reading assignment and program emphasize that although the direction a person's life takes is strongly influenced by **heredity**, its ultimate course depends on the interaction of many biological and environmental factors—that is, on both nature and nurture.

Lesson 3 also discusses the benefits of **genetic counseling** for prospective parents who are at risk of giving birth to children with genetic disorders. Prenatal diagnosis of genetic disorders has been greatly facilitated by recent advances in genetic testing techniques, allowing prospective parents to make more informed decisions about the risks of childbearing.

Prior Telecourse Knowledge that Will Be Used in this Lesson

This lesson focuses primarily on the biosocial domain of development. Recall from Chapter 1 that the biosocial domain is the part of human development that includes all the growth and changes that occur in a person's body, and the genetic, nutritional, and health factors that affect that growth and change. Remember, too, that although the division of human development into three domains makes it easier to study, development is holistic rather than piecemeal: Every aspect of human behavior reflects all three domains.

Learning Objectives

Use this information to guide your reading, viewing, thinking, and studying. After successfully completing this lesson, you should be able to:

1. Identify the mechanisms of heredity, and explain how sex is determined.
2. Discuss genetic continuity and diversity, and distinguish between monozygotic and dizygotic twins.
3. Differentiate genotype from phenotype, and explain the polygenic and multifactorial nature of human traits.
4. Explain the function of regulator genes, describe the additive and nonadditive patterns of genetic interaction, and give examples of the traits that result from each type of interaction.
5. Discuss dominant–recessive patterns in regard to blood types and other common phenotypic traits.
6. Explain how scientists distinguish the effects of genes and environment on development.
7. Identify some environmental variables that affect genetic inheritance, and describe how a particular trait, such as susceptibility to shyness (inhibition) or alcoholism, might be affected.
8. Describe the most common of the chromosomal abnormalities, focusing on abnormalities involving the sex chromosomes.
9. Discuss X-linked genes in terms of genotype and phenotype and describe four genetic disorders for which couples should seek genetic testing and counseling.
10. Explain the major methods of prenatal diagnosis, noting the advantages of each.

Read Chapter 2, "Genes and Prenatal Development," pages 42–57 and 71–79.

View the video for Lesson 3, "Nature and Nurture: The Dance of Life."

Segment 1: *The Beginning of Development*
Segment 2: *The Twin Perspective*
Segment 3: *From Genotype to Phenotype*
Segment 4: *Genetic and Chromosomal Abnormalities*

Summary

Conception occurs when the male **gamete** (or sperm) penetrates the membrane of the female gamete (the ovum); the gametes then fuse, and their genetic material combines to form the one-celled **zygote**. Within hours, the zygote initiates human development through the processes of duplication and division. Soon after, differentiation begins. Each body cell created from these processes carries an exact copy of the zygote's genetic instructions.

Genes, the basic units of **heredity**, are discrete segments of a **chromosome**, which is a DNA (deoxyribonucleic acid) molecule. Every human body cell, except the sperm and ovum, has 23 pairs of chromosomes (one chromosome in each pair from each parent). The sperm and ovum receive only one member of each chromosome pair when cells divide to produce gametes, and thus have only 23 single chromosomes each. The **twenty-third pair** of chromosomes, which determines sex, is designated **XY** in the male and **XX** in the female. The critical factor in the determination of the zygote's sex is which sperm reaches the ovum first, a Y sperm, creating a boy, or an X sperm, creating a girl.

Approximately once in every 270 pregnancies a single zygote splits into two separate identical cells that develop into genetically identical individuals, or **monozygotic twins**, who have the potential for developing the same physical appearance and psychological characteristics, and the same vulnerability to specific diseases. Dizygotic, or fraternal, twins occur about once in every sixty births. **Dizygotic twins** begin life as two separate zygotes and share no more genes than any other siblings (about 50 percent). The number of multiple births has doubled in many nations because of the increased use of fertility drugs and other methods of helping infertile couples.

Most traits are polygenic—that is, affected by many genes—and multifactorial—that is, influenced by many factors, including environmental factors. **Genotype** refers to the sum total of all the genes a person inherits. **Phenotype** refers to the sum total of all the genes that are actually expressed. In genetic terms, people are **carriers** of their unexpressed genes.

The various genes underlying height and skin color, for example, interact in an additive pattern: The phenotype in question reflects the sum of all the genes involved. Less commonly, genes interact in a nonadditive fashion. Genes that have a controlling influence over weaker, recessive genes are called dominant genes. Hundreds of physical characteristics follow this **dominant–recessive pattern** (a nonadditive pattern). Note that recessive genes are not always completely suppressed by their dominant gene counterparts, an outcome called incomplete dominance.

Behavioral genetics is the study of the genetic origins of psychological characteristics. Research in this field has revealed that most behavioral traits are affected by the interaction of large numbers of genes with environmental factors. When social scientists discuss the effects of the environment on the individual, they are referring to everything that can interact with the person's genetic inheritance at every point of life, from the first prenatal days to the last breath. Environment, as broadly defined, affects every human characteristic.

Scientists use twin research to identify genetic influences because for any given characteristic, if monozygotic twins are much more alike than dizygotic twins, it seems likely that genes play a significant role in the appearance of that trait. Another approach is to compare adopted children with both their biological and adoptive parents. Adopted children, however, are often placed in families that are similar to their birth families; thus, shared culture rather than shared genes may account for similarities. The best way to separate the effects of genes and environment is to study identical twins who have been separated at birth and raised in different families (to control for the fact that identical twins in a given family tend to be treated much more alike than dizygotic twins are).

An estimated half of all zygotes have too few or too many chromosomes. Most are spontaneously aborted. Once in every 200 births, however, a baby is born with a chromosomal abnormality that leads to a recognizable syndrome.

Although most known genetic disorders are dominant, recessive and multifactorial disorders claim many more victims. Among the more common recessive genetic disorders are cystic fibrosis, thalassemia, and sickle-cell anemia. For most of human history, couples at risk for having a child with a genetic problem did not know it. **Genetic counseling** is a means by which couples can learn more about their genes and make informed decisions about childbearing.

Genetic counseling is strongly recommended for individuals who have a parent, sibling, or child with a genetic condition; couples who have a history of spontaneous abortion, stillbirth, or infertility; couples who are from the same ethnic group or subgroup; and women over age 34. Couples who have a high probability of producing a baby with a serious genetic condition have several alternatives—from avoiding pregnancy to adoption to considering abortion. In cases where the consequences of a disease are variable, the decision making is often more difficult.

Review all reading assignments for this lesson.

As assigned by your instructor, complete the optional online component for this lesson.

Key Terms

Using your own words, write a brief definition or explanation of each of the following terms on a separate piece of paper.

1. DNA (deoxyribonucleic acid)
2. chromosome
3. gamete
4. zygote
5. genes
6. genotype
7. phenotype
8. allele
9. genome
10. monozygotic twins
11. dizygotic twins
12. XX
13. XY
14. polygenic
15. multifactorial
16. regulator gene
17. additive gene
18. dominant–recessive pattern
19. dominant gene
20. recessive gene
21. carrier
22. heritability
23. Down syndrome (trisomy-21)
24. fragile X syndrome
25. genetic counseling
26. phenylketonuria (PKU)
27. heredity
28. amniocentesis
29. gene therapy
30. environment

Practice Questions I

Multiple-Choice Questions

1. When a sperm and an ovum merge, a one-celled __________________ is formed.
   a. zygote
   b. reproductive cell
   c. gamete
   d. monozygote

2. Genes are discrete segments that provide the biochemical instructions that each cell needs to become
   a. a zygote.
   b. a chromosome.
   c. a specific part of a functioning human body.
   d. deoxyribonucleic acid.

3. In the male, the twenty-third pair of chromosomes is designated _______________; in the female, this pair is designated _______________.

   a. XX; XY
   b. XY; XX
   c. XO; XXY
   d. XXY; XO

4. Since the twenty-third pair of chromosomes in females is XX, each ovum carries an

   a. XX zygote.
   b. X zygote.
   c. XY zygote.
   d. X chromosome.

5. When a zygote splits, the two identical, independent clusters that develop become

   a. dizygotic twins.
   b. monozygotic twins.
   c. fraternal twins.
   d. trizygotic twins.

6. In scientific research, the best way to separate the effects of genes and the environment is to study

   a. dizygotic twins.
   b. adopted children and their biological parents.
   c. adopted children and their adoptive parents.
   d. monozygotic twins raised in different environments.

7. Most of the known genetic disorders are

   a. dominant.
   b. recessive.
   c. seriously disabling.
   d. sex-linked.

8. When we say that a characteristic is multifactorial, we mean that

   a. many genes are involved.
   b. many environmental factors are involved.
   c. many genetic and environmental factors are involved.
   d. the characteristic is polygenic.

9. Genes are segments of molecules of
   a. genotype.
   b. deoxyribonucleic acid (DNA).
   c. karyotype.
   d. phenotype.

10. Genetic diversity provides invaluable health benefits to human beings. Which of the statements below is true of genetic diversity?
    a. According to the Berger textbook, there are approximately 8 million possible combinations of chromosomes, which ensures genetic diversity from one generation to the next.
    b. Genetic diversity enables humans to adapt to many climates.
    c. In some instances, diversity protects humans against devastating diseases.
    d. All of the above are true.

11. A chromosomal abnormality that affects males only involves a(n)
    a. XO chromosomal pattern.
    b. XXX chromosomal pattern.
    c. YY chromosomal pattern.
    d. XXY chromosomal pattern.

12. Polygenic complexity is most apparent in ______________ characteristics.
    a. physical
    b. psychological
    c. recessive gene
    d. dominant gene

13. Most babies born with trisomy-21 (Down syndrome) often
    a. have specific facial characteristics.
    b. are unusually aggressive.
    c. are abnormally tall by adolescence.
    d. are blind.

14. To say that a trait is polygenic means that
    a. many genes make it more likely that the individual will inherit the trait.
    b. it is influenced by many genes.
    c. the trait is multifactorial.
    d. most people carry genes for the trait.

15. Some genetic diseases are recessive, so the child cannot inherit the condition unless both parents

   a. have Kleinfelter syndrome.
   b. carry the same recessive gene.
   c. have XO chromosomes.
   d. have the disease.

Matching Items

Match each definition or description with its corresponding term.

Terms

16. __________ gametes
17. __________ chromosome
18. __________ genotype
19. __________ phenotype
20. __________ dizygotic
21. __________ additive
22. __________ fragile X syndrome
23. __________ carrier
24. __________ zygote

Definitions or Descriptions

a. a person's entire genetic inheritance
b. sperm and ovum
c. the first cell of the developing person
d. a person who has a recessive gene in his or her genotype that is not expressed in the phenotype
e. fraternal twins
f. a pattern in which each gene in question makes an active contribution to the final outcome
g. a DNA molecule
h. the behavioral or physical expression of genetic potential
i. a chromosomal abnormality

Practice Questions II

Multiple-Choice Questions

1. Which of the following provides the best broad description of the relationship between heredity and environment in determining height?
   a. Heredity is the primary influence, with environment affecting development only in severe situations.
   b. Heredity and environment contribute equally to development.
   c. Environment is the major influence on physical characteristics.
   d. Heredity directs the individual's potential and environment determines whether and to what degree the individual reaches that potential.

2. Research studies of monozygotic twins who were raised apart suggest that
   a. virtually every human trait is affected by both genes and environment.
   b. only a few psychological traits, such as emotional reactivity, are affected by genes.
   c. most traits are determined by environmental influences.
   d. most traits are determined by genes.

3. Males with fragile X syndrome are
   a. feminine in appearance.
   b. less severely affected than females.
   c. frequently retarded intellectually.
   d. unusually tall and aggressive.

4. Disorders that are ______________________ are most likely to pass undetected from generation to generation.
   a. dominant
   b. dominant and polygenic
   c. recessive
   d. recessive and multifactorial

5. Dizygotic twins result when
   a. a single egg is fertilized by a sperm and then splits.
   b. a single egg is fertilized by two different sperm.
   c. two eggs are fertilized by two different sperm.
   d. either a single egg is fertilized by one sperm or two eggs are fertilized by two different sperm.

6. In humans, the molecules of DNA that are arranged by twenty-three complementary pairs are called
   a. zygotes.
   b. genes.
   c. chromosomes.
   d. ova.

7. Shortly after the zygote is formed, it begins the processes of duplication and division. Each resulting new cell has
   a. the same number of chromosomes as was contained in the zygote.
   b. half the number of chromosomes as was contained in the zygote.
   c. twice, then four times, then eight times the number of chromosomes as was contained in the zygote.
   d. all the chromosomes except those that determine sex.

8. If an ovum is fertilized by a sperm bearing a Y chromosome
   a. a female will develop.
   b. cell division will cease.
   c. a male will develop.
   d. spontaneous abortion will occur.

9. When the male cells in the testes and the female cells in the ovaries divide to produce gametes, the process differs from that in the production of all other cells. As a result of the different process, the gametes have
   a. one rather than both members of each chromosome pair.
   b. twenty-three chromosome pairs.
   c. X but not Y chromosomes.
   d. chromosomes from both parents.

10. Genotype is to phenotype as ____________________ is to ____________________.
   a. genetic potential; physical expression
   b. physical expression; genetic potential
   c. sperm; ovum
   d. gamete; zygote

11. The genes that influence height and skin color interact according to the ______________________ pattern.

a. dominant-recessive

b. X-linked

c. additive

d. nonadditive

12. X-linked recessive genes explain why some traits seem to be passed from

a. father to son.

b. father to daughter.

c. mother to daughter.

d. mother to son.

13. According to the textbook, the effects of the environment on genetic inheritance include

a. direct effects, such as nutrition, climate, and medical care.

b. indirect effects, such as the individual's broad economic, political, and cultural context.

c. irreversible effects, such as those resulting from brain injury.

d. everything that can interact with the person's genetic inheritance at every point of life.

True or False Items

Write T (for true) or F (for false) on the line in front of each statement.

14. _____ Most human characteristics are multifactorial, caused by the interaction of genetic and environmental factors.

15. _____ Less than 10 percent of all zygotes have harmful genes or an abnormal chromosomal makeup.

16. _____ Research suggests that susceptibility to alcoholism is at least partly the result of genetic inheritance.

17. _____ The human reproductive cells (ova and sperm) are called gametes.

18. _____ Only a very few human traits are polygenic.

19. _____ A couple should probably seek genetic counseling if several earlier pregnancies ended in spontaneous abortion.

20. _____ Many genetic conditions are recessive; thus, a child will have the condition even if only the mother carries the gene.

21. _____ Two people who have the same phenotype may have a different genotype for a trait such as eye color.

22. _____ When cells divide to produce reproductive cells (gametes), each sperm or ovum receives only twenty-three chromosomes, half as many as the original cell.

Applying Your Knowledge

1. Some men are color-blind because they inherit a particular recessive gene from their mother. That recessive gene is carried on the

   a. X chromosome.

   b. XX chromosome pair.

   c. Y chromosome.

   d. X or Y chromosome.

2. If your parents are much taller than your grandparents, the explanation probably lies in

   a. genetics.

   b. environmental factors.

   c. better family planning.

   d. good genetic counseling.

3. If a dizygotic twin develops schizophrenia, the likelihood of the other twin experiencing serious mental illness is much lower than is the case with monozygotic twins. This suggests that

   a. schizophrenia is caused by genes.

   b. schizophrenia is influenced by genes.

   c. environment is unimportant in the development of schizophrenia.

   d. monozygotic twins are especially vulnerable to schizophrenia.

4. A person's skin turns yellow-orange as a result of a carrot-juice diet regimen. This is an example of

   a. an environmental influence.

   b. an alteration in genotype.

   c. polygenic inheritance.

   d. incomplete dominance.

5. The personality trait of inhibition (shyness) seems to be partly genetic. A child who inherits the genes for shyness will be shy
   a. under most circumstances.
   b. only if shyness is the dominant gene.
   c. if the environment does not encourage greater sociability.
   d. if he or she is raised by biological rather than adoptive parents.

6. One of the best ways to distinguish the relative influence of genetic and environmental factors on behavior is to compare children who have
   a. the same genes and environments.
   b. different genes and environments.
   c. similar genes and environments.
   d. the same genes but different environments.

7. When identical twins have been reared apart, researchers have generally found
   a. strong behavioral and psychological similarities.
   b. strong behavioral, but not necessarily psychological, similarities.
   c. striking behavioral and psychological differences.
   d. that it is impossible to predict how such twins will develop.

8. Emily and Jim, who both have a history of alcoholism in their families, are concerned that the child they hope to have will inherit a genetic predisposition to alcoholism. Based on information presented in the text, what advice should you offer them?
   a. "Stop worrying, alcoholism is only weakly genetic."
   b. "It is almost certain that your child will become alcoholic."
   c. "Social influences, such as the family and peer environment, play a critical role in determining whether alcoholism is expressed."
   d. "Wait to have children until you are both middle aged, in order to see if the two of you become alcoholic."

9. A chromosomal abnormality in which an abnormal sex chromosome is present and at puberty a boy experiences breast development and a lack of penis growth is
   a. mental retardation.
   b. Alzheimer's disease.
   c. Kleinfelter syndrome.
   d. Huntington's disease.

10. Genetically, Evan's potential height is 6' 0". Because he did not receive a balanced diet, however, he grew to only 5' 9". Evan's actual height is an example of a

    a. recessive gene.
    b. dominant gene.
    c. genotype.
    d. phenotype.

11. Shannon inherited a gene from her mother that, regardless of her father's contribution to her genotype, will be expressed in her phenotype. Evidently, the gene Shannon received from her mother is a(n) _______________ gene.

    a. polygenic
    b. recessive
    c. dominant
    d. X-linked

Answer Key

Key Terms

1. DNA (deoxyribonucleic acid) is a nucleic acid molecule that determines our inherited characteristics by encoding the information needed to synthesize proteins and regulate all aspects of cellular metabolism. (p. 43; video lesson, segment 1; objective 1)
2. Chromosomes are molecules of DNA that contain the genes organized in precise sequences. (p. 43; video lesson, segment 1; objective 1)
3. Gametes are the human reproductive cells. (p. 43; objective 1)
4. The zygote (a term derived from the Greek word for "joint") is the fertilized egg, that is, the one-celled organism formed during conception by the fusion of sperm and ovum. (p. 44; video lesson, segment 2; objective 1)
5. Genes are discrete segments of a chromosome, which is a DNA molecule, that are the basic units of heredity. (p. 44; video lesson, segment 1; objective 1)
6. The sum total of all the genes a person inherits—his or her genetic potential—is called the genotype. (p. 44; video lesson, segment 3; objective 3)
7. The actual physical or behavioral expression of a genotype, the result of the interaction of the genes with each other and with the environment, is called the phenotype. (p. 44; video lesson, segment 3; objective 3)
8. A normal alteration is called an allele, one of several possible letter sequences that some genes have. Note that everyone has one allele or another of those variable genes. (p. 45; objective 1)

9. A genome is the full set of chromosomes, with all the genes they contain, that make up the genetic material of an organism. (p. 45; objective 1)
10. Monozygotic, or identical, twins develop from one zygote that splits in two, producing two genetically identical zygotes. (p. 46; video lesson, segment 2; objective 2)

    Memory aid: Mono means "one"; monozygotic twins develop from one fertilized ovum.
11. Dizygotic, or fraternal, twins develop from two separate ova fertilized by different sperm at roughly the same time, and therefore are no more genetically similar than ordinary siblings. (p. 47; video lesson, segment 2; objective 2)

    Memory aid: A fraternity is a group of two (di) or more nonidentical individuals.
12. XX is a twenty-third pair that consists of two X-shaped chromosomes, one from the mother and one from the father. (p. 47; objective 1)
13. XY is a twenty-third pair that consists of one X-shaped chromosome from the mother and one Y-shaped chromosome from the father. (p. 47; objective 1)
14. Most human traits, especially psychological traits, are polygenic traits; that is, they are affected by many genes. (p. 48; objective 3)
15. Most human traits are also multifactorial traits—that is, influenced by many factors, including genetic and environmental factors. (p. 48; objective 3)

    Memory aid: The roots of the words polygenic and multifactorial give their meaning: poly means "many" and genic means "of the genes"; multi means "several" and factorial obviously refers to factors.
16. Regulator genes direct the interactions of other genes, controlling their expression, duplication, and transcriptions. (p. 48; objectives 4 & 5)
17. An additive gene is one that, through interaction with other genes, affects a specific trait. The genes affecting height, for example, interact in this fashion. (p. 48; objective 4)
18. A dominant–recessive pattern involves the interaction of a pair of alleles in such a way that the phenotype reveals the influence of one allele (the dominant gene) more than that of the other (the recessive gene). (pp. 48–49; video lesson, segment 3; objective 5)
19. The dominant gene is the stronger of an interacting pair of alleles whose influence is more evident in the phenotype. (video lesson, segment 3; objective 5)
20. The recessive gene is the weaker of an interacting pair of alleles whose influence is less evident in the phenotype. (video lesson, segment 3; objective 5)

21. A person who has a recessive gene in his or her genotype that is not expressed in his or her phenotype is called a carrier of that gene. (p. 49; objective 7)
22. Heritability is a statistic that indicates what percentage of the variation in a particular trait within a particular population, in a particular context and era can be traced to genes. (p. 49; objective 7)
23. Down syndrome (trisomy-21) is a chromosomal disorder in which there is an extra chromosome at site 21. Most people with Down syndrome have distinctive physical and psychological characteristics, including a rounded face, short stature, and mental slowness. (p. 50; objective 8)
24. The fragile X syndrome is a single-gene disorder in which part of the X chromosome is attached by such a thin string of molecules that it seems about to break off. Although the characteristics associated with this syndrome are quite varied, some mental deficiency is relatively common. (p. 51; objective 9)
25. Genetic counseling involves a variety of tests through which couples can learn more about their genes, and can thus make informed decisions about their childbearing and child-rearing future. (p. 53; video lesson, segment 4; objective 9)
26. Phenylketonuria (PKU) is a genetic disorder in which a child's body is unable to metabolize an amino acit called phenylalanine. The resulting buildup of phenylalanine in body bluids causes brain damage, progressive mental retardation, and other symptoms. (pp. 55–56; video lesson, segment 3; objective 9)
27. Heredity refers to the transmission of traits and predispositions from parent to child through the genes. (video lesson, introduction; objective 6)
28. Amniocentesis is a prenatal diagnostic procedure in which a sample of amniotic fluid is withdrawn by syringe and tested to determine if the developing fetus is healthy. (video lesson, segment 4; objective 10)
29. Gene therapy (also called genetic engineering) involves the altering of an organism's genetic instructions through the insertion and addition of normal genes by way of a blood transfusion, bone marrow transplant, or direct insertion into a cluster of cells. (video lesson, segment 4; objective 10)
30. When social scientists discuss the effects of the environment on genes, they are referring to everything—from the impact of the immediate cell environment on the genes to the multitude of elements in the outside world, such as nutrition, climate, family interactions, and the cultural context—that can interact with the person's genetic inheritance at every point of life. (video lesson, segment 2; objective 6)

Practice Questions I

Multiple-Choice Questions

1. a. is the correct answer. (p. 44; video lesson, segment 2; objective 1)

   b. & c. are incorrect. The reproductive cells (sperm and ova), which are also called gametes, are individual entities.

   d. is incorrect. Monozygote refers to one member of a pair of identical twins.

2. c. is the correct answer. (p. 44; video lesson, segment 1; objective 1)

   a. is incorrect. The zygote is the first cell of the developing person.

   b. is incorrect. Chromosomes are molecules of DNA that carry genes.

   d. is incorrect. DNA molecules contain genetic information.

3. b. is the correct answer. (p. 47; objective 1)

4. d. is the correct answer. When the gametes are formed, one member of each chromosome pair splits off; because in females both are X chromosomes, each ovum must carry an X chromosome. (pp. 47–48; objective 1)

   a., b., & c. are incorrect. The zygote refers to the merged sperm and ovum that is the first new cell of the developing individual.

5. b. is the correct answer. Mono means "one." Thus, monozygotic twins develop from one zygote. (p. 46; video lesson, segment 2; objective 2)

   a. & c. are incorrect. Dizygotic, or fraternal, twins develop from two (di) zygotes.

   d. is incorrect. A trizygotic birth would result in triplets (tri), rather than twins.

6. d. is the correct answer. In this situation, one factor (genetic similarity) is held constant while the other factor (environment) is varied. Therefore, any similarity in traits is strong evidence of genetic inheritance. (video lesson, segment 2; objective 6)

7. a. is the correct answer. (p. 51; video lesson, segment 4; objective 9)

   c. & d. are incorrect. Most dominant disorders are neither seriously disabling, nor sex-linked.

8. c. is the correct answer. (p. 48; objective 3)

   a., b., & d. are incorrect. Polygenic means "many genes"; multifactorial means "many factors," which are not limited to either genetic or environmental ones.

9. b. is the correct answer. (pp. 43–44; video lesson, segment 1; objective 1)

   a. is incorrect. Genotype is a person's genetic potential.

   c. is incorrect. A karyotype is a picture of a person's chromosomes.

   d. is incorrect. Phenotype is the actual expression of a genotype.

10. d. is the correct answer. (pp. 45–47; video lesson, segment 1; objective 2)

11. d. is the correct answer. (pp. 50–51; objective 8)

    a. & b. is incorrect. These chromosomal abnormalities affect females.

    c. is incorrect. There is no such abnormality.

12. a. is the correct answer. (p. 48; objective 3)

    c. & d. are incorrect. The textbook does not equate polygenic complexity with either recessive or dominant genes.

13. a. is the correct answer. (p. 50; objective 8)

14. b. is the correct answer. (p. 48; objective 3)

15. b. is the correct answer. (p. 48; video lesson, segment 3; objective 9)

    a. & c. are incorrect. These abnormalities involve the sex chromosomes, not genes.

    d. is incorrect. In order for an offspring to inherit a recessive condition, the parents need only be carriers of the recessive gene in their genotypes; they need not actually have the disease.

Matching Items

16. b (p. 43; objective 1)
17. g (p. 43; video lesson, segment 1; objective 1)
18. a (p. 44; video lesson, segment 3; objective 3)
19. h (p. 44; video lesson, segment 3; objective 3)
20. e (p. 47; video lesson, segment 2; objective 2)
21. f (p. 48; objective 4)
22. i (pp. 51–52; objective 9)
23. d (p. 49; objective 7)
24. c (p. 44; video lesson, segment 2; objective 1)

Practice Questions II

Multiple-Choice Questions

1. d. is the correct answer. (p. 71; objective 6)

2. a. is the correct answer. (video lesson, segment 2; objective 2)

3. c. is the correct answer. (pp. 51–52; objective 8)

   a. is incorrect. Physical appearance is usually normal in this syndrome.

   b. is incorrect. Males are more frequently and more severely affected.

   d. is incorrect. This is true of the XYY chromosomal abnormality, but not the fragile X syndrome.

4. d. is the correct answer. (pp. 48–51; objective 8)

5. c. is the correct answer. (p. 47; video lesson, segment 2; objective 2)

   a. is incorrect. This would result in monozygotic twins.

   b. is incorrect. Only one sperm can fertilize an ovum.

d. is incorrect. A single egg fertilized by one sperm would produce a single offspring or monozygotic twins.

6. c. is the correct answer. (p. 43; video lesson, segment 2; objective 1)

   a. is incorrect. Zygotes are fertilized ova.

   b. is incorrect. Genes are the smaller units of heredity that are organized into sequences on chromosomes.

   d. is incorrect. Ova are female reproductive cells.

7. a. is the correct answer. (p. 44; video lesson, segment 1; objective 1)

8. c. is the correct answer. The ovum will contain an X chromosome, and with the sperm's Y chromosome, will produce the male XY pattern. (pp. 47–48; video lesson, segment 1; objective 1)

   a. is incorrect. Only if the ovum is fertilized by an X chromosome from the sperm will a female develop.

   b. is incorrect. Cell division will occur regardless of whether the sperm contributes an X or a Y chromosome.

   d. is incorrect. Spontaneous abortions are likely to occur when there are chromosomal or genetic abnormalities; the situation described is perfectly normal.

9. a. is the correct answer. (p. 43; objective 1)

   b. & d. are incorrect. These are true of all body cells except the gametes.

   c. is incorrect. Gametes have either X or Y chromosomes.

10. a. is the correct answer. Genotype refers to the sum total of all the genes a person inherits; phenotype refers to the actual expression of the individual's characteristics. (p. 44; video lesson, segment 3; objective 3)

11. c. is the correct answer. (p. 48; objective 4)

12. d. is the correct answer. X-linked genes are located only on the X chromosome. Because males inherit only one X chromosome, they are more likely than females to have these characteristics in their phenotype. (pp. 51–53; objective 9)

13. d. is the correct answer. (pp. 49, 71–74; objective 7)

True or False Items

14. T (pp. 44, 48; video lesson, segment 3; objective 3)

15. F An estimated half of all zygotes have an odd number of chromosomes. (pp. 70–71; video lesson, segment 4; objective 8)

16. T (pp. 71–75; objective 7)

17. T (p. 43; objective 1)

18. F (p. 48; objective 3)

19. T (video lesson, segment 4; objective 9)

20. F A trait from a recessive gene will be part of the phenotype only when the person has two recessive genes for that trait. (p. 48; video lesson, segment 4; objectives 4 & 5)
21. T (pp. 44, 48; video lesson, segment 3; objective 3)
22. T (pp. 43–44; objective 1)

Applying Your Knowledge

1. a. is the correct answer. (pp. 50–53; objective 9)

   b. is incorrect. The male genotype is XY, not XX.

   c. & d. are incorrect. The mother contributes only an X chromosome.

2. b. is the correct answer. This trend in increased height has been attributed to improved nutrition and medical care. (pp. 49, 71–75; objective 7)

   a., c., & d. are incorrect. It is unlikely that these factors account for height differences from one generation to the next.

3. b. is the correct answer. Since monozygotic twins are genetically identical, while dizygotic twins share only 50 percent of their genes, greater similarity of traits between monozygotic twins suggests that genes are an important influence. (pp. 71–75; video lesson, segment 2; objective 7)

   a. & c. are incorrect. Even though schizophrenia has a strong genetic component, it is not the case that if one twin has schizophrenia the other also automatically does. Therefore, the environment, too, is an important influence.

   d. is incorrect. This does not necessarily follow.

4. a. is the correct answer. (video lesson, segment 3; objective 3)

   b. is incorrect. Genotype is a person's genetic potential, established at conception.

   c. is incorrect. Polygenic inheritance refers to the influence of many genes on a particular trait.

   d. is incorrect. Incomplete dominance refers to the phenotype being influenced primarily, but not exclusively, by the dominant gene.

5. c. is the correct answer. (p. 49; objective 7)

   a. & b. are incorrect. Research on adopted children shows that shyness is affected by both genetic inheritance and the social environment. Therefore, if a child's environment promotes socializing outside the immediate family, a genetically shy child might grow up much less timid socially than he or she would have been with less outgoing parents.

   d. is incorrect. Either biological or adoptive parents are capable of nurturing, or not nurturing, shyness in their children.

6. d. is the correct answer. To separate the influences of genes and environment, one of the two must be held constant. (video lesson, segment 2; objective 6)

a., b., & c. are incorrect. These situations would not allow a researcher to separate the contributions of heredity and environment.

7. d. is the correct answer. (video lesson, segment 2; objective 6)

8. c. is the correct answer. (pp. 71–75; objective 7)

   a. is incorrect. Some people's inherited biochemistry makes them highly susceptible to alcoholism.

   b. is incorrect. Despite a strong genetic influence, the environment plays a critical role in the expression of alcoholism.

   d. is incorrect. Not only is this advice unreasonable, but it might increase the likelihood of chromosomal abnormalities in the parents' sperm and ova.

9. c. is the correct answer. (pp. 50–51; objective 8)

10. d. is the correct answer. (pp. 44, 48–49; video lesson, segment 4; objectives 3 & 4)

    a. & b. are incorrect. Genes are discrete segments of a chromosome.

    c. is incorrect. Genotype refers to genetic potential.

11. c. is the correct answer. (pp. 48–49; video lesson, segment 3; objective 5)

    a. is incorrect. There is no such thing as a "polygenic gene." Polygenic means "many genes."

    b. is incorrect. A recessive gene paired with a dominant gene will not be expressed in the phenotype.

    d. is incorrect. X-linked genes may be dominant or recessive.

Lesson Review

Lesson 3

The Beginnings
Heredity and Environment

Please Note: Use this matrix to guide your study and achieve the learning objectives of this lesson. It will also help you to view the video, which defines and demonstrates important concepts and skills as they relate to everyday life.

Learning Objective	Textbook	Telecourse Student Guide	Video Lesson
1. Identify the mechanisms of heredity, and explain how sex is determined.	pp. 43–48	Key Terms: 1, 2, 3, 4, 5, 8, 9, 12, 13; Practice Questions I: 1, 2, 3, 4, 9, 16, 17, 24; Practice Questions II: 6, 7, 8, 9, 17, 22.	Segment 1: *The Beginning of Development*
2. Discuss genetic continuity and diversity, and distinguish between monozygotic and dizygotic twins.	pp. 45–47	Key Terms: 10, 11; Practice Questions I: 5, 10, 20; Practice Questions II: 2, 5.	Segment 2: *The Twin Perspective*
3. Differentiate genotype from phenotype, and explain the polygenic and multifactorial nature of human traits.	pp. 44, 48	Key Terms: 6, 7, 14, 15; Practice Questions I: 8, 12, 14, 18, 19; Practice Questions II: 10, 14, 18, 21; Applying Your Knowledge: 4, 10.	Segment 3: *From Genotype to Phenotype*
4. Explain the function of regulator genes, describe the additive and nonadditive patterns of genetic interaction, and give examples of the traits that result from each type of interaction.	pp. 48–49	Key Terms: 16, 17; Practice Questions I: 21; Practice Questions II: 11, 20; Applying Your Knowledge: 10.	Segment 4: *Genetic and Chromosomal Abnormalities*
5. Discuss dominant–recessive patterns in regard to blood types and other common phenotypic traits.	pp. 48–49	Key Terms: 16, 18, 19, 20; Practice Questions II: 20; Applying Your Knowledge: 11.	
6. Explain how scientists distinguish the effects of genes and environment on development.	p. 71	Key Terms: 27, 30; Practice Questions I: 6; Practice Questions II: 1; Applying Your Knowledge: 6, 7.	Segment 2: *The Twin Perspective*

Learning Objective	Textbook	Telecourse Student Guide	Video Lesson
7. Identify some environmental variables that affect genetic inheritance, and describe how a particular trait, such as susceptibility to shyness (inhibition) or alcoholism, might be affected.	pp. 49, 71–75	Key Terms: 21, 22; Practice Questions I: 23; Practice Questions II: 13, 16; Applying Your Knowledge: 2, 3, 5, 8.	Segment 2: *The Twin Perspective*
8. Describe the most common of the chromosomal abnormalities, focusing on abnormalities involving the sex chromosomes.	pp. 50-51	Key Terms: 23; Practice Questions I: 11, 13; Practice Questions II: 3, 4, 15; Applying Your Knowledge: 9.	
9. Discuss X-linked genes in terms of genotype and phenotype and describe four genetic disorders for which couples should seek genetic testing and counseling.	pp. 51–53, 55–56	Key Terms: 24, 25, 26; Practice Questions I: 7, 15, 22; Practice Questions II: 12, 19; Applying Your Knowledge: 1.	Segment 4: *Genetic and Chromosomal Abnormalities*
10. Explain the major methods of prenatal diagnosis, noting the advantages of each.	pp. 54–55	Key Terms: 28, 29.	Segment 4: *Genetic and Chromosomal Abnormalities*

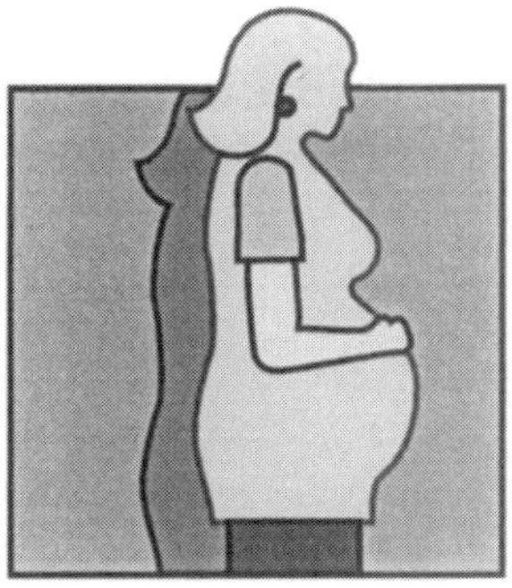

Lesson 4

The Beginnings:
Prenatal Development and Birth

Preview

Anticipating the birth of a child is one of life's most enriching experiences. As the video for this lesson begins, we meet Sandra and Darrin in the anxious moments just before Sandra gives birth. The personal experiences of this young family throughout Sandra's pregnancy and delivery form the backdrop for the lesson's exploration of prenatal development and birth.

The period of prenatal development is a time of incredibly rapid growth during which the emerging person develops from a single cell into a fully functioning individual. This lesson describes that development, along with some of the problems that can occur—including prenatal exposure to disease, drugs, and other hazards—and the factors that moderate the risks of that exposure.

A person's birth marks the most radical transition of the entire life span. No longer sheltered from the outside world, the newborn becomes a separate human being who begins life almost completely dependent upon its caregivers. This lesson also examines the process of birth, its possible variations and problems, and the parent–newborn bonding process.

As you complete this video, recall your experiences with pregnancy or those of someone you know. (You may want to interview that person during your study of this lesson.) What did the mother look and feel like during the early, middle, and final stages of this pregnancy? What sort of prenatal care did she receive? What did she do to stay healthy? For example, what did she eat and how did she exercise? Did she smoke, drink alcohol, or take any medications during the pregnancy? Was the baby born close to the "due date"? What was the birthing experience like? Where did the mother have the baby, in what type of facility? Did she have any surgical procedures performed? If so, which ones? Were there any complications during birth? If so, what were they, and how were the mother and baby treated? Did the mother and father both get to hold and bond with the baby in the first few hours after birth? Did the mother experience any depression in the days and weeks after birth? If so, how was she treated?

Prior Telecourse Knowledge that Will Be Used in this Lesson

- This lesson focuses primarily on the biosocial domain of development. Recall from Lesson 1 that biosocial development includes all the growth and changes that occur in a person's body, as well as the genetic, nutritional, and health factors that can affect that growth and change.
- This lesson begins with the development of the zygote after conception. Remember from Lesson 3 that conception occurs when the male's sperm and female's ovum unite. The resulting cell, called a zygote, then develops through a process of duplication and division.
- This lesson will also return to the epigenetic systems theory introduced in Lesson 1. Recall that the basic tenet of this theory is that our development is shaped not only by our genetics or by the environment in which we live, but rather by the interaction between the two. Nature *and* nurture make us who we are. This is just as true for prenatal development (before birth) as it is for postnatal development (after birth).

Learning Objectives

Use this information to guide your reading, viewing, thinking, and studying. After successfully completing this lesson, you should be able to:

1. Describe the significant developments of the germinal period.
2. Describe the significant developments of the embryonic period.
3. Describe the significant developments of the fetal period, noting the importance of the age of viability, and the fetus's various responses to its immediate environment (the womb).
4. Define teratogen, and identify at least five teratogens.
5. Outline the effects of teratogens on the developing embryo or fetus, and describe protective steps that can be taken to moderate the risk of exposure.
6. Distinguish among low-birthweight, preterm, and small-for-gestational-age (SGA) infants, and identify the causes of and treatments for low birthweight.
7. Describe the normal process of birth, specifying the events of each stage.
8. Describe the test used to assess the newborn's condition at birth.
9. Describe the options available for medical attention during the birthing process, and discuss the pros and cons of medical intervention and traditional birthing practices.
10. Explain the concept of parent–infant bonding and the current view of most developmentalists regarding early bonding in humans.

Read Chapter 2, "Genes and Prenatal Development," pages 57–79.

View the video for Lesson 4, "The Wondrous Journey."

Segment 1: *The First Trimester*

Segment 2: *Risk Reduction*

Segment 3: *The Second Trimester*

Segment 4: *The Third Trimester*

Summary

The first two weeks of prenatal development are called the **germinal period**. Within hours after conception, the one-celled zygote begins the process of cell division and growth as it travels down the fallopian tube. The **embryonic period** begins as the organism begins differentiating into three layers of tissue that will become the various body systems. At the end of the first month, the cardiovascular system is functioning; the eyes, ears, nose, mouth, and arm and leg buds start to form; and the embryo is about one-fifth of an inch (just 6 millimeters) long. By the end of the second month, the developing organism weighs about 1 gram, is 1 inch long, and has all the basic organs (except the sex organs) and features of a human being. During the third month, the **fetal period** begins, and the sex organs begin to take shape.

The crucial factor in the fetus's attaining the **age of viability**, beginning at about 22 to 24 weeks, is neurological maturation, which is essential to the regulation of the basic body functions of breathing, sucking, and sleeping. By 28 weeks, the typical fetus weighs about 1,300 grams (3 pounds) and has a greater than 50 percent chance of survival outside the womb.

Teratology is a science of risk analysis, which attempts to evaluate what factors can make prenatal harm more (or less) likely to occur. Three crucial factors that determine whether a specific teratogen will cause harm, and of what nature, are the timing of exposure, the amount of exposure, and the developing organism's genetic vulnerability to damage from the substance. Although each body structure has its own **critical period** during which it is most susceptible to teratogenic damage, for behavioral teratogens that affect the brain and nervous system the entire prenatal period is critical. Teratogens can also include conditions, such as maternal malnutrition and extreme levels of stress. Some **teratogens** have a cumulative effect on the developing individual. For other teratogens, there is a **threshold effect**; that is, the substance is virtually harmless until exposure reaches a certain frequency or dosage. However, the **interaction effect** of teratogens taken together may make them more harmful at lower dosage levels than they would be individually.

A major, preventable health hazard for the fetus is **low birthweight**, defined as birthweight that is less than 2,500 grams (5.5 pounds). Babies that weigh less than 3 pounds (1,500 grams) are classified as **very low birthweight**, while those that weigh less than 2 pounds (1,000 grams) are classified as **extremely low birthweight**. Infants who are born more than three weeks early are called **preterm**. Others, born close to the due date but weighing less than most full-term neonates, are called **small for gestational age (SGA)**.

The normal birth begins at about the 266th day after conception, when the fetus's brain signals the release of hormones that trigger uterine contractions in the mother. Labor usually lasts eight to twelve hours in first births and four to seven hours in subsequent births, but this can vary greatly. The **Apgar scale** is used to assign a score between 0 and 2 to the neonate's heart rate, breathing, muscle tone, color, and reflexes at one minute after birth and again at five minutes. A score of 7 or better indicates the newborn is not in danger; below 7, that the infant needs help in establishing normal breathing; and below 4, that the baby is in critical condition and needs immediate medical attention. Very few newborns score an immediate perfect 10, but most readily adjust to life outside the womb.

The quality of the birth experience depends on many factors, including the mother's preparation for birth, the support provided by others, and the nature and degree of medical intervention. Birth complications are much more likely if a fetus is at risk because of low weight, **preterm birth**, genetic abnormality, or teratogenic exposure, or because the mother is unusually young, old, or small, or in poor health. Cerebral palsy, for example, which was once thought to be solely caused by birth procedures (such as excessive analgesia or misapplied forceps) is now known to result from a combination of factors, including genetic vulnerability, exposure to teratogens, and **anoxia** (lack of oxygen) during birth.

The popular term **parent–infant bond** is used to emphasize the tangible as well as intangible attachment between parent and child in the early moments after birth. In many animals, early contact between mother and infant can be crucial to bonding. Most developmentalists now believe that the importance of early contact between a human mother and child has been overly popularized and that the events right after birth are just one episode in a long-term process of bonding and development.

Review all reading assignments for this lesson.

As assigned by your instructor, complete the optional online component for this lesson.

Key Terms

Using your own words, write a brief definition or explanation of each of the following terms on a separate piece of paper.

1. germinal period
2. embryonic period
3. fetal period
4. placenta
5. implantation
6. embryo
7. fetus
8. sonogram
9. age of viability
10. Apgar scale
11. doula
12. cesarean section (c-section)
13. low-birthweight (LBW)
14. very low-birthweight (VLBW)
15. extremely low-birthweight (ELBW)
16. preterm birth
17. small for gestational age (SGA)
18. kangaroo care
19. postpartum depression
20. parent–infant bond
21. fetal alcohol syndrome (FAS)
22. teratogens
23. threshold effect
24. anoxia
25. critical period
26. amniotic fluid
27. spina bifida
28. interaction effect

Practice Questions I

Multiple-Choice Questions

1. The first two weeks after conception are called the
   a. embryonic period.
   b. placental period.
   c. fetal period.
   d. germinal period.

2. Implantation occurs during the
   a. embryonic period.
   b. germinal period.
   c. uterine period.
   d. fetal period.

3. By the eighth week after conception, the embryo has almost all the basic organs **EXCEPT** the
   a. skeleton.
   b. elbows and knees.
   c. sex organs.
   d. fingers and toes.

4. The most critical factor in attaining the age of viability is development of the
   a. placenta.
   b. eyes.
   c. brain.
   d. skeleton.

5. Neural tube defects, such as spina bifida, have been linked to a deficiency of ____________________ in an expectant mother's diet.
   a. vitamin A
   b. zinc
   c. guanine
   d. folic acid

6. An embryo begins to develop male sex organs if ________________________, and female sex organs if ________________________.
   a. genes on the Y chromosome (the SRY gene) send a biochemical signal; no signal is sent from an X chromosome
   b. genes on the Y chromosome send a biochemical signal; genes on the X chromosome send a signal
   c. genes on the X chromosome send a biochemical signal; no signal is sent from an X chromosome
   d. genes on the X chromosome send a biochemical signal; genes on the Y chromosome send a signal

7. A teratogen
   a. cannot cross the placenta during the period of the embryo.
   b. is usually inherited from the mother.
   c. can be counteracted by good nutrition most of the time.
   d. may be a virus, drug, chemical, radiation, or environmental pollutants.

8. Among the characteristics of babies born with fetal alcohol syndrome are
   a. slowed physical growth and behavior problems.
   b. addiction to alcohol and methadone.
   c. deformed arms and legs.
   d. blindness.

9. The birth process begins
   a. when the fetus moves into the right position.
   b. when the uterus begins to contract at regular intervals to push the fetus out.
   c. about eight hours (in the case of firstborns) after the uterus begins to contract at regular intervals.
   d. when the baby's head appears at the opening of the vagina.

10. The Apgar scale is administered
    a. only if the newborn is in obvious distress.
    b. once, just after birth.
    c. usually twice, 1 minute and 5 minutes after birth.
    d. every two minutes for several hours.

11. Normal weight for most newborns is
    a. 5 pounds.
    b. 6 pounds.
    c. more than 5.5 pounds.
    d. none of the above.

12. Low-birthweight babies born near the due date but weighing substantially less than they should
    a. are classified as preterm.
    b. are called small for gestational age.
    c. usually have no sex organs.
    d. have undeveloped hands and feet.

13. A leading factor in the instances of low-birthweight births in the United States is maternal use of
    a. alcohol.
    b. tobacco.
    c. crack cocaine.
    d. household chemicals.

14. The idea of a parent–infant bond in humans arose from
    a. observations in the delivery room.
    b. data on adopted infants.
    c. animal studies.
    d. studies of disturbed mother–newborn pairs.

Matching Items

Match each definition or description with its corresponding term.

Terms

15. __________ embryonic period
16. __________ fetal period
17. __________ placenta
18. __________ preterm
19. __________ teratogen
20. __________ sonogram
21. __________ age of viability
22. __________ critical period
23. __________ low birthweight (LBW)
24. __________ fetal alcohol syndrome
25. __________ germinal period

Definitions or Descriptions

a. term for the period during which a developing baby's body parts are most susceptible to damage
b. external agents and conditions that can cause damage to the developing organism
c. the age when viability is attained
d. when a newborn weighs less than 2500 grams at birth
e. also called ultrasound
f. characterized by abnormal facial characteristics, slowed growth, behavior problems, and mental retardation
g. age at which the fetus can survive outside the mother's body
h. the life-giving organ that nourishes the embryo and fetus
i. when implantation occurs
j. the prenatal period when all major body structures begin to form
k. refers to a baby born three or more weeks early

Practice Questions II

Multiple-Choice Questions

1. The name for the developing human from about the third to the eighth week of gestation is
   a. an embryo.
   b. a fetus.
   c. a blastocyst.
   d. a placenta.

2. In order, the correct sequence of prenatal stages of development is
   a. embryo; germinal; fetal
   b. germinal; fetal; embryo
   c. germinal; embryo; fetal
   d. ovum; fetal; embryo

3. Tetracycline, retinoic acid, and most hormones
   a. can be harmful to the human fetus.
   b. have been proven safe for pregnant women after the embryonic period.
   c. will prevent spontaneous abortions.
   d. are safe when used before the fetal period.

4. A temporary lack of fetal oxygen during the birthing process that can cause brain damage is
   a. rubella (German measles).
   b. anoxia.
   c. acquired immune deficiency syndrome (AIDS).
   d. neural-tube defect.

5. Among the characteristics rated on the Apgar scale are
   a. shape of the newborn's head and nose.
   b. presence of body hair.
   c. interactive behaviors.
   d. muscle tone and color.

6. A newborn is classified as low birthweight if he or she weighs less than
   a. 7 pounds.
   b. 6 pounds.
   c. 5.5 pounds.
   d. 4 pounds.

7. A newborn weighing 2 pounds at birth would be classified as
   a. low birthweight.
   b. very low birthweight.
   c. extremely low birthweight.
   d. none of the above

8. Mothers who _______________ during pregnancy are most likely to give birth to infants who are small for gestational age (SGA).
   a. smoke
   b. are malnourished
   c. drink alcohol
   d. are HIV positive

9. Which Apgar score indicates that a newborn is in normal health?
   a. 4
   b. 5
   c. 6
   d. 7

10. Many low-birthweight babies are born to teenage mothers. This is primarily because teen mothers
    a. are less well nourished.
    b. have less education.
    c. have bodies that are too young to support a healthy pregnancy.
    d. are all of the above.

11. The critical period for preventing physical defects appears to be
    a. the period of the zygote.
    b. the embryonic period.
    c. only the third trimester.
    d. the entire pregnancy.

True or False Items

Write T (for true) or F (for false) on the line in front of each statement.

12. _____ Newborns can recognize some of what they heard while in the womb.

13. _____ Eight weeks after conception, the embryo has formed almost all the basic organs.

14. _____ In general, behavioral teratogens have the greatest effect during the period of the embryo.

15. _____ The effects of cigarette smoking during pregnancy remain highly controversial.

16. _____ The Apgar scale is used to measure vital signs such as heart rate, breathing, and reflexes.

17. _____ Newborns usually cry on their own, moments after birth.

18. _____ Research shows that immediate mother–newborn contact at birth is necessary for the normal emotional development of the child.

19. _____ Low-birthweight babies are more likely than other children to experience developmental difficulties in early childhood.

20. _____ Cesarean sections are rarely performed in the United States today because of the resulting danger to the fetus.

21. ____ Beginning at the 28th week, a fetus can hear and react to sounds outside the womb.

Applying Your Knowledge

1. Babies born to mothers who are powerfully addicted to a psychoactive drug are most likely to suffer from
   a. structural problems.
   b. behavioral problems.
   c. both a and b.
   d. neither a nor b.

2. I am about 1 inch long and 1 gram in weight. I have all of the basic organs (except sex organs) and features of a human being. What am I?
   a. a zygote
   b. an embryo
   c. a fetus
   d. an indifferent gonad

3. Elizabeth and Ethan report to their neighbors that, 5 weeks after conception, a sonogram of their child-to-be revealed female sex organs. The neighbors are skeptical of their statement because
   a. sonograms are never administered before the ninth week.
   b. sonograms only reveal the presence or absence of male sex organs.
   c. the fetus does not begin to develop female sex organs until about the ninth week.
   d. it is impossible to determine that a woman is pregnant until six weeks after conception.

4. Five-year-old Christopher can't sit quietly and concentrate on a task for more than a minute. Dr. Smith, who is a teratologist, suspects that Christopher may have been exposed to ______________ during prenatal development.
   a. human immunodeficiency virus
   b. a behavioral teratogen
   c. rubella
   d. lead

5. Megan and John, who are of British descent, are hoping to have a child. Doctor Snook asks for a complete nutritional history and is particularly concerned when she discovers that Megan may have a deficiency of folic acid in her diet. Doctor Snook is probably worried about the risk of ______________ in the couple's offspring.
   a. FAS
   b. brain damage
   c. neural-tube defects
   d. FAE

6. Three-year-old Taylor was born underweight and premature. Today, he is small for his age. His doctor suspects that
   a. Taylor is a victim of fetal alcohol syndrome.
   b. Taylor suffers from fetal alcohol effects.
   c. Taylor's mother smoked heavily during her pregnancy.
   d. Taylor's mother has a chromosomal abnormality.

7. Which of these fetuses is most likely to experience serious prenatal damage?
   a. a male whose 15-year-old mother has an unusually stressful home life
   b. a female whose mother did not begin to receive prenatal care until the second month of her pregnancy
   c. a female whose 30-year-old mother is on welfare
   d. a male whose mother was somewhat undernourished early in the pregnancy

8. Fetal alcohol syndrome is common in newborns whose mothers were heavy drinkers during pregnancy, whereas newborns whose mothers were moderate drinkers may suffer fetal alcohol effects. This finding shows that to assess and understand risk we must know
   a. the kind of alcoholic beverage (for example, beer, wine, or whiskey).
   b. the level of exposure to the teratogen.
   c. whether the substance really is teratogenic.
   d. the timing of exposure to the teratogen.

9. Your sister and brother-in-law, who are about to adopt a one-year-old, are worried that the child will never bond with them. What advice should you offer?
   a. Tell them that, unfortunately, this is true; they would be better off waiting for a younger child who has not yet bonded.
   b. Tell them that, although the first year is a biologically determined critical period for attachment, there is a fifty-fifty chance that the child will bond with them.
   c. Tell them that bonding is a long-term process between parent and child that is determined by the nature of interaction throughout infancy, childhood, and beyond.
   d. Tell them that if the child is female, there is a good chance that she will bond with them, even at this late stage.

10. Which of the following newborns would be most likely to have problems in body structure and functioning?
    a. Josh, whose Apgar score is 6.
    b. Christina, whose Apgar score is 7.
    c. Kingsley, whose Apgar score is 3.
    d. Corey, whose Apgar score is 5.

11. At birth, Pierre was classified as small for gestational age. It is likely that Pierre
    a. was born in a rural hospital.
    b. suffered several months of prenatal malnutrition.
    c. was born in a large city hospital.
    d. comes from a family with a history of such births.

12. Of the following, who is most likely to give birth to a low-birthweight child?
    a. twenty-one-year-old Lynn, who lives in the North
    b. twenty-five-year-old Thien, who lives in Vietnam
    c. sixteen-year-old Lori, who lives in a remote, rural part of the United States
    d. thirty-year-old Wendy, who lives in southern California

13. An infant born 266 days after conception, weighing 4 pounds, would be designated as which of the following?
    a. a preterm infant
    b. a low-birthweight infant
    c. a small-for-gestational-age infant
    d. b and c

14. The five characteristics evaluated by the Apgar scale are
    a. heart rate, length, weight, muscle tone, and color.
    b. orientation, muscle tone, reflexes, interaction, and responses to stress.
    c. reflexes, breathing, muscle tone, heart rate, and color.
    d. pupillary response, heart rate, reflex irritability, alertness, and breathing.

Answer Key

Key Terms

1. The first two weeks of development, characterized by rapid cell division and the beginning of cell differentiation, are called the germinal period. (pp. 57–59; video lesson, segment 1; objective 1)

   Memory aid: A germ cell is one from which a new organism can develop. The germinal period is the first stage in the development of the new organism.
2. The embryonic period is the third through the eighth week of prenatal development, when the rudimentary forms of all anatomical structures develop. (pp. 57, 60; video lesson, segment 1; objective 2)
3. From the ninth week until birth is the fetal period, when the organs grow in size and complexity. (pp. 60–62; video lesson, segment 1; objective 3)
4. The placenta is the organ that connects the mother's circulatory system with that of her growing embryo, providing nourishment to the developing organism and removing wastes. (p. 59; video lesson, segment 1; objective 1)
5. Implantation is the process by which the outer cells of the organism burrow into the uterine lining and rupture its blood vessels to obtain nourishment and trigger the bodily changes that signify the beginning of pregnancy. (p. 59; video lesson, segment 1; objective 1)
6. Embryo is the name for the developing organism from approximately three through eight weeks past conception. (p. 60; objective 2)
7. Fetus is the name for the developing organism from eight weeks after conception through birth. (p. 60; objective 3)

8. A sonogram is an image of an unborn fetus (or an internal organ) produced by scanning it with high-frequency sound waves. It is also called an ultrasound. (p. 61; objective 3)
9. About twenty-two weeks after conception, the fetus attains the age of viability, at which point it has at least some slight chance of survival outside the uterus if specialized medical care is available. (pp. 61–62; video lesson, segment 3; objective 3)
10. Newborns are rated at one and then at five minutes after birth according to the Apgar scale. This scale assigns a score of 0, 1, or 2 to each of five characteristics: heart rate, breathing, muscle tone, color, and reflexes. A score of 7 or better indicates that all is well. (p. 63; video lesson, segment 4; objective 8)
11. A doula helps a woman with the birthing process. In modern society, a doula often works with the hospital staff to assist the mother through labor and delivery. (p. 65; objective 9)
12. In a cesarean section (c-section), the fetus is removed from the mother surgically. (p. 65; objective 9)
13. Newborns who weigh less than 2,500 grams (5.5 pounds) are called low-birthweight (LBW) infants. Such infants are at risk for many immediate and long-term problems. (p. 67; video lesson, segment 3; objective 6)
14. A very low-birthweight (VLBW) infant is born weighing less than 3 lbs., 5 oz. (p. 67; objective 6)
15. An extremely low-birthweight (ELBW) infant is born weighing less than 2 lbs., 3 oz. (p. 67; objective 6)
16. Infants who are born three or more weeks before the due date are called preterm. (p. 68; objective 6)
17. Infants who weigh substantially less than they should, given how much time has passed since conception, are called small for gestational age (SGA), or small-for-dates. (p. 68; objective 6)
18. Kangaroo care is a type of care provided to low-birthweight infants where the mother holds the infant on her chest, often between her breasts, for at least an hour a day. (pp. 69–70; objective 6)
19. Postpartum depression is a profound feeling of sadness and inadequacy sometimes experienced by new mothers. (p. 70; objective 10)
20. The term parent–infant bond (or parent–newborn bond) describes the strong feelings of attachment between parent and child in the early moments of their relationship together. (p. 70; video lesson, segment 4; objective 10)
21. Prenatal alcohol exposure may cause fetal alcohol syndrome (FAS), which includes abnormal facial characteristics, slowed physical growth, behavior problems, and mental retardation. Likely victims are those who are genetically vulnerable and whose mothers drink three or more drinks daily during pregnancy. (p. 73; objective 5)

22. Teratogens are external agents and conditions, such as viruses, bacteria, drugs, chemicals, stressors, and malnutrition, that can cause damage to the developing organism. (p. 73; video lesson, segment 2; objective 4)
23. A threshold effect is the harmful effect of a substance that occurs when exposure to it reaches a certain level. (p. 76; video lesson, segment 2; objective 5)
24. Anoxia is a temporary lack of fetal oxygen during the birth process that, if prolonged, can cause brain damage or even death. (video lesson, segment 4; objective 8)
25. The first eight weeks, as well as thc last months, of pregnancy are often called the critical period, because teratogenic exposure during these time periods can produce malformations of basic body organs and structure. (p. 75; video lesson, segment 2; objective 5)
26. Amniotic fluid is a clear, slightly yellowish liquid that surrounds the unborn child (fetus) during pregnancy, protecting and cushioning its development. (video lesson, segment 1; objective 7)
27. Spina bifida (or cleft spine) is a birth defect that results from the failure of the spine to close properly during the first month of pregnancy. Research has shown that folic acid (a common B vitamin) is one factor that can reduce the risk of having a baby with neural tube defects such as spina bifida. (video lesson, segment 2; objective 5)
28. An interaction effect occurs when one teratogen intensifies the harmful effects of another. (video lesson, segment 2; objective 5)

Practice Questions I

Multiple-Choice Questions

1. d. is the correct answer. (pp. 57–59; video lesson, segment 1; objective 1)

   a. is incorrect. The period of the embryo is from the third through the eighth week after conception.

   b. is incorrect. This term, which refers to the germinal period, is not used in the lesson.

   c. is incorrect. The period of the fetus is from the ninth week until birth.
2. b. is the correct answer. (pp. 57–59; video lesson, segment 1; objective 1)
3. c. is the correct answer. The sex organs do not begin to take shape until the period of the fetus. (p. 60; video lesson, segment 1; objective 2)
4. c. is the correct answer. (pp. 61–62; video lesson, segment 3; objective 3)
5. d. is the correct answer. (pp. 75–77; video lesson, segment 2; objective 3)
6. a. is the correct answer. (pp. 60–63; objective 3)
7. d. is the correct answer. (pp. 73–77; video lesson, segment 2; objective 4)

   a. is incorrect. In general, teratogens can cross the placenta at any time.

b. is incorrect. Teratogens are agents in the environment, not heritable genes (although susceptibility to individual teratogens has a genetic component).

c. is incorrect. Although nutrition is an important factor in healthy prenatal development, the textbook does not suggest that nutrition alone can usually counteract the harmful effects of teratogens.

8. a. is the correct answer. (pp. 72–73; objective 5)
9. b. is the correct answer. (p. 63, video lesson, segment 4; objective 7)
10. c. is the correct answer. (p. 63; video lesson, segment 4; objective 8)
11. c. is the correct answer. (p. 63; objective 7)
12. b. is the correct answer. (p. 68; objective 6)
13. b. is the correct answer. (pp. 67–69; video lesson, segment 3; objective 6)
14. c. is the correct answer. (p. 70; video lesson, segment 4; objective 10)

Matching Items

15. j (p. 60; video lesson, segment 1; objective 2)
16. c (pp. 57, 60–63; video lesson, segment 1; objective 3)
17. h (p. 59; video lesson, segment 1; objective 1)
18. k (p. 68; objective 6)
19. b (p. 73; video lesson, segment 2; objective 4)
20. e (p. 61; objective 3)
21. g (pp. 61–62; video lesson, segment 3; objective 3)
22. a (p. 75; video lesson, segment 2; objective 3)
23. d (p. 67; video lesson, segment 3; objective 6)
24. f (p. 73; objective 5)
25. i (pp. 57–59; video lesson, segment 1; objective 1)

Practice Questions II

Multiple-Choice Questions

1. a. is the correct answer. (p. 60; video lesson, segment 1; objective 2)
2. c. is the correct answer. (pp. 58–62; video lesson, segment 1; objectives 1, 2, & 3)
3. a. is the correct answer. (video lesson, segment 2; objective 4)
4. b. is the correct answer. (p. 63; video lesson, segment 4; objective 9)
5. d. is the correct answer. (p. 63; video lesson, segment 4; objective 8)
6. c. is the correct answer. (p. 67; video lesson, segment 4; objective 6)
7. c. is the correct answer. (p. 67; video lesson, segment 3; objective 6)
8. a. is the correct answer. (pp. 68–69; objective 6)
9. d. is the correct answer. (p. 63; video lesson, segment 4; objective 8)

10. a. is the correct answer. (pp. 67–70; video lesson, segment 3; objective 6)
11. b. is the correct answer. (p. 60; video lesson, segment 2; objective 5)

True or False Items

12. T (pp. 60–62; video lesson, segment 1; objective 3)
13. T (p. 60; video lesson, segment 1; objective 2)
14. F Behavioral teratogens can affect the fetus at any time during the prenatal period. (p. 73; video lesson, segment 2; objective 4)
15. F There is no controversy about the damaging effects of smoking during pregnancy; tobacco is a dangerous teratogen. (pp. 73–77; objective 5)
16. T (p. 63; video lesson, segment 4; objective 8)
17. T (pp. 63–64; objective 8)
18. F Though highly desirable, mother–newborn contact at birth is not necessary for the child's normal development or for a good parent–child relationship. Many opportunities for bonding occur throughout childhood. (p. 70; video lesson, segment 4; objective 10)
19. T (pp. 67–69; video lesson, segment 3; objective 6)
20. F Approximately one in three births in the United States is now cesarean. (pp. 65–66; objective 9)
21. T (pp. 60–62; objective 3)

Applying Your Knowledge

1. b. is the correct answer. (pp. 73–77; video lesson, segment 2; objective 5)
2. b. is the correct answer. (p. 60; video lesson, segment 1; objectives 1, 2, & 3)

   a. is incorrect. The zygote is the fertilized ovum.

   c. is incorrect. The developing organism is designated a fetus starting at the ninth week.

   d. is incorrect. The indifferent gonad is the mass of cells that will eventually develop into female or male sex organs.
3. c. is the correct answer. (pp. 60–63; video lesson, segment 1; objective 3)
4. b. is the correct answer. (p. 73; objectives 4 & 5)

   a. is incorrect. This is the virus that causes AIDS.

   c. is incorrect. Rubella may cause blindness, deafness, and brain damage.

   d. is incorrect. The textbook does not discuss the effects of exposure to lead.
5. c. is the correct answer. (video lesson, segment 2; objective 5)

   a. is incorrect. FAS is caused in infants by the mother-to-be drinking three or more drinks daily during pregnancy.

   b. is incorrect. Brain damage is caused by the use of social drugs during pregnancy.

d. is incorrect. FAE is caused in infants by the mother-to-be drinking 1 ounce of alcohol per day.

6. c. is the correct answer. (pp. 67–69; video lesson, segment 2; objective 6)
7. a. is the correct answer. (p. 68; video lesson, segment 3; objective 6)
8. b. is the correct answer. (pp. 73–77; video lesson, segment 2; objectives 4 & 5)
9. c. is the correct answer. (p. 70; video lesson, segment 4; objective 10)

   a. & b. are incorrect. Bonding in humans is not a biologically determined event limited to a critical period, as it is in many other animal species.

   d. is incorrect. There is no evidence of any gender differences in the formation of the parent-infant bond.
10. c. is the correct answer. If a neonate's Apgar score is below 4, the infant is in critical condition and needs immediate medical attention. (p. 63; video lesson, segment 4; objective 8)
11. b. is the correct answer. (p. 68; objective 6)

   a., c., & d. are incorrect. Prenatal malnutrition and maternal tobacco use are the most common causes of a small-for-dates neonate.
12. c. is the correct answer. (pp. 67–69; objective 6)

   a., b., & d. are incorrect. The incidence of low birthweight is higher among teenaged mothers.
13. d. is the correct answer. (p. 68; objective 6)

   a. is incorrect. At 266 days, this infant is full term.
14. c. is the correct answer. (p. 63; video lesson, segment 4; objective 8)

Lesson Review

Lesson 4

The Beginnings
Prenatal Development and Birth

Please Note: Use this matrix to guide your study and achieve the learning objectives of this lesson. It will also help you to view the video, which defines and demonstrates important concepts and skills as they relate to everyday life.

Learning Objective	Textbook	Telecourse Student Guide	Video Lesson
1. Describe the significant developments of the germinal period.	pp. 57–59	Key Terms: 1, 4, 5; Practice Questions I: 1, 2, 17, 25; Practice Questions II: 2; Applying Your Knowledge: 2.	Segment 1: *The First Trimester*
2. Describe the significant developments of the embryonic period.	p. 60	Key Terms: 2, 6; Practice Questions I: 3, 15; Practice Questions II: 1, 2, 13; Applying Your Knowledge: 2.	Segment 1: *The First Trimester*
3. Describe the significant developments of the fetal period, noting the importance of the age of viability, and the fetus's various responses to its immediate environment (the womb).	pp. 60–63	Key Terms: 3, 7, 8, 9; Practice Questions I: 4, 5, 6, 16, 20, 21, 22; Practice Questions II: 2, 12, 21; Applying Your Knowledge: 2, 3.	Segment 1: *The First Trimester*; Segment 3: *The Third Trimester*
4. Define teratogen, and identify at least five teratogens.	pp. 73–75	Key Terms: 22; Practice Questions I: 7, 19; Practice Questions II: 3, 14; Applying Your Knowledge: 4, 8.	Segment 2: *Risk Reduction*
5. Outline the effects of teratogens on the developing embryo or fetus, and describe protective steps that can be taken to moderate the risk of exposure.	pp. 73–77	Key Terms: 21, 23, 25, 27, 28; Practice Questions I: 8, 24; Practice Questions II: 11, 15; Applying Your Knowledge: 1, 4, 5, 8.	Segment 2: *Risk Reduction*

Learning Objective	Textbook	Telecourse Student Guide	Video Lesson
6. Distinguish among low-birthweight, preterm, and small-for-gestational-age (SGA) infants, and identify the causes of and treatments for low birthweight.	pp. 67–69	Key Terms: 13, 14, 15, 16, 17, 18; Practice Questions I: 12, 13, 18, 23; Practice Questions II: 6, 7, 8, 10, 19; Applying Your Knowledge: 6, 7, 11, 12, 13.	Segment 3: *The Second Trimester*
7. Describe the normal process of birth, specifying the events of each stage.	pp. 63–65	Key Terms: 26; Practice Questions I: 9, 11.	Segment 1: *The First Trimester*; Segment 3: *The Third Trimester* Segment 4: *The Third Trimester*
8. Describe the test used to assess the newborn's condition at birth.	p. 63	Key Terms: 10, 24; Practice Questions I: 10; Practice Questions II: 5, 9, 16, 17; Applying Your Knowledge: 10, 14.	Segment 4: *The Third Trimester*
9. Describe the options available for medical attention during the birthing process, and discuss the pros and cons of medical intervention and traditional birthing practices.	pp. 65–67	Key Terms: 11, 12; Practice Questions II: 4, 20.	
10. Explain the concept of parent–infant bonding and the current view of most developmentalists regarding early bonding in humans.	p. 70	Key Terms: 19, 20; Practice Questions I: 14; Practice Questions II: 18; Applying Your Knowledge: 9.	Segment 4: *The Third Trimester*

Grow, Baby, Grow!

Lesson 5

The First Two Years: Biosocial Development

Preview

This is the first of a three-lesson unit that describes the developing person from birth to age 2 in terms of biosocial, cognitive, and psychosocial development. The biosocial domain is the part of human development that includes all the growth and changes that occur in a person's body and the genetic, nutritional, and health factors that affect that growth and change. It also includes the social, cultural, and environmental factors that affect biological development.

The lesson begins with observations on the overall growth and health of infants, including their size and shape and the importance of immunizations during the first two years. A discussion of brain growth and development follows, including how a child's experiences can affect his or her brain development. At birth, the brain contains more than 100 billion nerve cells, or **neurons**, but the networks of nerve fibers that interconnect them are incomplete. During the first few years of a child's life, extensive growth occurs in these neural pathways, enabling the emergence of new capabilities in each domain of development.

The lesson then turns to a discussion of how babies move and control their bodies and the ages at which the average infant advances in ability. Vision and hearing are discussed next, along with research on infant **perception**. The final section discusses the importance of nutrition during the first two years and describes the benefits of breastfeeding. During the video lesson, pediatricians and developmental psychologists provide expert commentary.

Prior Telecourse Knowledge that Will Be Used in this Lesson

This is the first lesson to focus on the biosocial domain of development. Remember, although the division of human development into three domains makes it easier to study, development is holistic rather than piecemeal: Every aspect of human behavior reflects all three domains. You may also wish to review epigenetic theory from Lesson 2.

Learning Objectives

Use this information to guide your reading, viewing, thinking, and studying. After successfully completing this lesson, you should be able to:

1. Describe the size and proportions of an infant's body, and discuss how babies change during the first two years and how their bodies compare with those of adults.
2. Describe public health concerns, such as immunization and risk factors for sudden infant death syndrome (SIDS), and list the methods that experts recommend for protecting infant health.
3. Describe the ways in which the brain changes or matures during infancy.
4. Discuss the role of experience and stimulation in brain development, and demonstrate an understanding of shaken baby syndrome and social deprivation.
5. Describe the basic reflexes of the newborn and distinguish between gross motor skills and fine motor skills.
6. Describe the basic pattern of motor-skill development, and discuss variations in the timing of motor-skill acquisition.
7. Distinguish between sensation and perception, and describe the extent and development of an infant's perceptual abilities using the sense of vision as an example.
8. Discuss the nutritional needs of infants and toddlers and list some benefits of breast-feeding.
9. Discuss undernutrition, failure to thrive, and malnutrition as they are explained in the video, identify the potential effects of these conditions on babies, and discuss methods of prevention.

Read Chapter 3, "The First Two Years: Body and Brain," pages 84–105.

View the video for Lesson 5, "Grow, Baby, Grow!"

Segment 1: *Physical Growth and Health*

Segment 2: *Brain Growth and Development*

Segment 3: *Basic Reflexes and Motor Skills*

Segment 4: *Infant Nutrition*

Summary

Biosocial development during the first two years is so rapid that infants often seem to change before their parents' very eyes. The newborn seems top-heavy in body proportions, with its head being one-fourth of total body length (in comparison to one-eighth of body length in an adult). By age two, the average toddler's body weight is about one-fifth adult weight and body length has increased to about one-half adult height.

Brain development is also rapid during infancy. By age two, the brain has attained about 75 percent of its adult weight, and there has been a fivefold increase in the density of **dendrite** networks in the **cortex**. As the brain develops, brain waves and physiological states become more cyclical and distinct.

The newborn's motor ability is limited to **reflexes**, including those that maintain adequate oxygen, body temperature, and nourishment. By 6 months, most babies can reach, grab, and hold onto dangling objects. The average child can walk with assistance at 9 months, stand momentarily at 10 months, and take steps unassisted at 12 months. Although all healthy infants develop the same **motor skills** in the same sequence, the age at which these skills are acquired varies greatly from infant to infant. Variations in the acquisition of motor skills can be attributed in part to inherited factors, such as activity level, rate of physical maturation, and body type. Environmental factors, such as medical care, nutrition, and patterns of infant care, are also influential. Note that the video for Lesson 5 draws a distinction between reflexes, which are involuntary responses to stimuli, and motor skills, which require voluntary participation. The textbook includes **reflexes**, along with **gross motor skills** and **fine motor skills**, as three types of motor skills.

At birth, both **sensation** and **perception** are apparent. Vision is the least well developed of the senses. Newborns can focus better on objects that are between 4 and 30 inches away. By 6 months, visual acuity approaches 20/20, and infants can use both eyes to track moving objects well. In contrast, hearing is comparatively acute in the newborn. Newborns can differentiate their mother's voice from those of other women; by 1 month, they can perceive differences between very similar sounds.

For its nutritional benefits, breast milk is the ideal food for most babies. It is always sterile and at body temperature, contains more essential vitamins and iron than cow's milk, is more digestible, and provides the infant with the mother's immunity to disease. In developed countries, severe infant **malnutrition** is unusual; more prevalent is **undernutrition**. Social and/or family problems are often responsible for undernutrition in developed countries.

Review all reading assignments for this lesson.

As assigned by your instructor, complete the optional online component for this lesson.

Key Terms

Using your own words, write a brief definition or explanation of each of the following terms on a separate piece of paper.

1. norms
2. head-sparing
3. neuron
4. cortex
5. axon
6. dendrites
7. synapses
8. neurotransmitter
9. prefrontal cortex
10. shaken baby syndrome
11. REM (rapid eye movement) sleep
12. reflexes
13. gross motor skills
14. fine motor skills
15. sensation
16. perception
17. binocular vision
18. immunization
19. sudden infant death syndrome (SIDS)
20. co-sleeping
21. transient exuberance
22. breathing reflex
23. sucking reflex
24. rooting reflex
25. motor skills
26. pincer grasp
27. malnutrition
28. undernutrition
29. failure-to-thrive
30. metabolism
31. enriched environment

Practice Questions I

Multiple-Choice Questions

1. The average North American newborn
   a. weighs approximately 6 pounds.
   b. weighs approximately 7 pounds.
   c. is "overweight" because of the diet of the mother.
   d. weighs 10 percent less than what is desirable.

2. Compared to the first year, growth during the second year

   a. proceeds at a slower rate.

   b. continues at about the same rate.

   c. includes proportionately more insulating fat.

   d. usually demonstrates drop-offs in percentile ranking.

3. The average newborn doubles her weight by __________ months, and triples it by __________________.

   a. 2 months; 8 months

   b. 4 months; 12 months

   c. 6 months; 18 months

   d. 12 months; 24 months

4. The interaction between inherited and environmental factors is responsible for

   a. variation in the age at which infants master specific motor skills.

   b. physical growth, but not the development of motor skills.

   c. the fact that babies in the United States walk earlier than do Ugandan babies.

   d. the fact that infants master motor skills more slowly today than they did fifty years ago.

5. The development of binocular vision at about 14 weeks results in

   a. a sudden improvement in the ability to focus the two eyes in a coordinated manner to see one image.

   b. the rapid development of distance vision.

   c. the refinement of the ability to discriminate colors.

   d. both a and b.

6. Proportionally, the head of the infant is about __________________ of total body length; the head of an adult is about __________________ of total body length.

   a. one-fourth; one-third

   b. one-eighth; one-fourth

   c. one-fourth; one-eighth

   d. one-third; one-fourth

7. Compared with formula-fed infants, breast-fed infants tend to have
   a. greater weight gain.
   b. fewer allergies and digestive upsets.
   c. less frequent feedings during the first few months.
   d. more social approval.

8. According to the video, when a child is not growing according to set parameters, she is
   a. malnourished.
   b. undernourished.
   c. demonstrating "failure to thrive."
   d. presenting a disease called marasmus.

9. The infant's first motor skills are not skills at all. They are
   a. fine motor skills.
   b. gross motor skills.
   c. reflexes.
   d. unpredictable.

10. Which of the following allows toddlers to begin walking?
    a. brain maturation
    b. practice
    c. muscle strength
    d. all of the above

11. Which of the following is true of motor-skill development in healthy infants?
    a. It follows the same basic sequence the world over.
    b. It occurs at different rates from individual to individual.
    c. It follows norms that vary from one ethnic group to another.
    d. All of the above are true.

12. Most of the nerve cells that a human brain will ever possess are present
    a. at conception.
    b. about 1 month following conception.
    c. at birth.
    d. at age 5 or 6.

Matching Items

Match each definition or description with its corresponding term.

Terms

13. __________	neuron	18. __________	fine motor skill
14. __________	dendrites	19. __________	reflex
15. __________	malnutrition	20. __________	sucking reflex
16. __________	enriched environment	21. __________	binocular vision
17. __________	gross motor skill	22. __________	transient exuberance

Definitions or Descriptions

a. a condition that occurs to babies who do not acquire the nutrients needed for proper development
b. picking up an object
c. ability to focus both eyes to see one image
d. provides highly nurturing and stimulating atmosphere in which to learn and grow
e. newborns suck anything that touches their lips
f. nerve fibers that allow communication among neurons
g. running or jumping
h. an involuntary response
i. the phenomenal increase in neural connections over the first 2 years
j. nerve cells

Practice Questions II

Multiple-Choice Questions

1. Dendrite is to axon as neural __________ is to neural __________.
   a. input; output
   b. output; input
   c. myelin; synapse
   d. synapse; myelin

2. A reflex is best defined as
   a. a fine motor skill.
   b. a motor ability mastered at a specific age.
   c. a responsive movement that seems automatic.
   d. none of the above.

3. Most babies can reach for, grasp, and hold onto an object by about the ____________ month.

    a. second

    b. sixth

    c. ninth

    d. fourteenth

4. Activity level, rate of physical maturation, and how fat the infant is affect the age at which an infant walks and acquires other motor skills. They are examples of

    a. norms.

    b. environmental factors.

    c. inherited factors.

    d. the interaction of environment and heredity.

5. During the first weeks of life, babies seem to focus reasonably well on

    a. little in their environment.

    b. objects at a distance of 4 to 30 inches.

    c. objects at a distance of 1 to 3 inches.

    d. objects several feet away.

6. An advantage of breast milk over formula is that it

    a. is always sterile and at body temperature.

    b. contains traces of medications ingested by the mother.

    c. can be given without involving the father.

    d. contains more protein and vitamin D than does formula.

7. Studies comparing breast-feeding to bottle-feeding show that

    a. breast-fed infants are less likely to get sick.

    b. breast-feeding is a necessity for all mothers.

    c. scientific improvements make bottle-feeding better than breast-feeding.

    d. none of the above statements are true.

8. The cause of sudden infant death syndrome (SIDS) is

    a. an inborn heart defect.

    b. a neurological disorder.

    c. inadequate infant care.

    d. a combination of factors.

9. Climbing is to using a crayon as __________ is to __________.
   a. fine motor skill; gross motor skill
   b. gross motor skill; fine motor skill
   c. reflex; fine motor skill
   d. reflex; gross motor skill

10. Some infant reflexes
   a. are essential to life.
   b. disappear in the months after birth.
   c. provide the foundation for later motor skills.
   d. do all of the above.

11. A common cause of undernutrition in young children is
   a. ignorance of the infant's nutritional needs.
   b. the absence of socioeconomic policies that reflect the importance of infant nutrition.
   c. problems in the family, such as maternal depression.
   d. all of the above.

12. Neurotransmitters are chemical messengers that diffuse across the
   a. axon.
   b. myelin sheath.
   c. dendrite.
   d. synaptic gap.

13. Reflexes are ________________ responses, whereas gross motor skills and fine motor skills ________________.
   a. involuntary; require active participation
   b. voluntary; are involuntary
   c. slow-to-develop; require extensive practice
   d. permanent; are temporary

True or False Items

Write T (for true) or F (for false) on the line in front of each statement.

14. _____ Reflexive hiccups, sneezes, and thrashing are signs that the infant's reflexes are not functioning properly.

15. _____ Infants of all ethnic backgrounds develop the same motor skills at approximately the same age.

16. _____ The typical two-year-old has achieved three-quarters their adult brain size and half their adult height.

17. _____ Vision is better developed than hearing in most newborns.

18. _____ Co-sleeping is a risk factor for sudden infant death syndrome (SIDS).

19. ____ Newborns have a high proportion of REM sleep.

20. ____ Over the first two years, the infant's metabolic activity decreases steadily.

Applying Your Knowledge

1. Newborns cry, shiver, and tuck their legs close to their bodies. This set of reflexes helps them
   a. ensure proper muscle tone.
   b. learn how to signal distress.
   c. maintain constant body temperature.
   d. communicate serious hunger pangs.

2. The last part of the brain to mature is the
   a. cortex.
   b. medulla oblongata.
   c. cerebellum.
   d. prefrontal cortex.

3. Dan has 20/400 vision and is able to discriminate subtle sound differences. Dan most likely
   a. is a preterm infant.
   b. has brain damage in the visual processing areas of the cortex.
   c. is a newborn.
   d. is slow-to-mature.

4. A baby turns her head and starts to suck when her receiving blanket is brushed against her cheek. The baby is displaying the
   a. sucking reflex.
   b. rooting reflex.
   c. Babinski reflex.
   d. Moro reflex.

5. Sensation is to perception as __________ is to __________.
   a. hearing; seeing
   b. detecting a stimulus; making sense of a stimulus
   c. making sense of a stimulus; detecting a stimulus
   d. tasting; smelling

6. Three-week-old Nathan should have the least difficulty focusing on the sight of
   a. stuffed animals on a bookshelf across the room from his crib.
   b. his mother's face as she holds him in her arms.
   c. the checkerboard pattern in the wallpaper covering the ceiling of his room.
   d. the family dog as it dashes into the nursery.

7. Geneva has been undernourished throughout childhood. It is likely that she will be
   a. smaller and shorter than her genetic potential would dictate.
   b. slow in intellectual development.
   c. less resistant to disease.
   d. all of the above.

Answer Key

Key Terms

1. Norms are age averages for the acquisition of a particular behavior, developed for a specific group population. (p. 86; objectives 1 & 6)
2. Head-sparing is a phenomenon in which the brain is biologically protected when malnutrition temporarily affects body growth. (p. 87; objectives 1 & 9)
3. A neuron, or nerve cell, is the main component of the central nervous system. (p. 88; video lesson, segment 2; objective 3)
4. The cortex is the thin outer layer of the brain that is involved in the voluntary, cognitive aspects of the mind. (p. 88; objective 3)

   Memory aid: Cortex in Latin means "bark." As bark covers a tree, the cortex is the "bark of the brain."
5. An axon is the nerve fiber extension that sends impulses from one neuron to the dendrites of other neurons. (p. 88; video lesson, segment 2; objective 3)
6. Dendrites are nerve fiber extensions that receive the impulses transmitted from other neurons via their axons. (p. 88; video lesson, segment 2; objective 3)
7. A synapse is the point at which the axon of a sending neuron meets the dendrites of a receiving neuron. At that point, brain chemicals called

neurotransmitters carry the impulse from axon to dendrites. (p. 88; objective 3)

8. A neurotransmitter is a brain chemical that carries information from the axon of a sending deuron to the dentrites of a receiving neuron. (p. 88; objective 3)
9. The prefrontal cortex is the last region of the brain to reach maturity. It is involved with planning, decision making, and emotion regulation, and it is largely inactive in infants. (p. 90; objectives 3 & 4)
10. Shaken baby syndrome is a condition brought about by the forceful shaking of an infant, often in an attempt by adults to stop the child from crying. This shaking breaks connections between neurons and ruptures blood vessels in the brain, usually resulting in long-term damage. (p. 91; objective 4)
11. REM (rapid eye movement) sleep is characterized by rapid brain activity, dreams, and movements of the eyes. The amount of time we spend in REM sleep is greatest in infancy, and declines across development. (p. 93; objective 3)
12. Reflexes are involuntary physical responses to specific stimuli. (p. 94; video lesson, segment 3; objective 5)
13. Gross motor skills are physical abilities that demand large body movements, such as climbing, jumping, or running. (p. 95; video lesson, segment 3; objective 5)
14. Fine motor skills are physical abilities that require precise, small movements, such as picking up a coin. (p. 96; video lesson, segment 3; objective 5)
15. Sensation is the process by which a sensory system detects a particular stimulus. (p. 97; objective 7)
16. Perception is the mental processing of sensory information, when the brain interprets a sensation (p. 97; objective 7)
17. Binocular vision is the ability to use both eyes together to focus on a single object. (pp. 98–99; objective 7)

    Memory aid: Bi- indicates "two"; ocular means something pertaining to the eye. Binocular vision is vision for "two eyes."
18. Immunization is a medical process that strengthens infants' resistance to potentially deadly diseases, such as smallpox, polio, and measles, by stimulating their immune systems to fight them off. (p. 100; objective 2)
19. The third leading cause of infant death in the United States, sudden infant death syndrome (SIDS) is diagnosed when autopsy suggests that the infant simply stopped breathing during sleep, with other possible causes ruled out. (p. 103; objective 2)
20. Also referred to as *bed-sharing*, co-sleeping occurs when parents and their children (usually infants) sleep in the same bed. (p. 103; objective 2)

21. Transient exuberance is the dramatic increase in neural connections that occurs in an infant's brain over the first two years of life. (video lesson, segment 2; objective 3)

22. The breathing reflex is an involuntary physical response that ensures that the infant has an adequate supply of oxygen and discharges carbon dioxide. (p. 94; video lesson, segment 3; objective 5)

23. The sucking reflex is the involuntary tendency of newborns to suck anything that touches their lips. This reflex fosters feeding. (p. 94; video lesson, segment 3; objective 5)

24. The rooting reflex, which helps babies find a nipple, causes them to turn their heads and start to suck when something brushes against their cheek. (p. 94; video lesson, segment 3; objective 5)

25. Motor skills are physical skills that involve large body movements, such as waving the arms, walking, and jumping (gross motor skills), and small body movements, such as picking up a coin or drawing (fine motor skills). (p. 94; video lesson, segment 3; objective 6)

26. The pincer grasp is when the thumb and forefinger are used together to hold an object. (video lesson, segment 3; objective 6)

27. Malnutrition (referred to as protein-calorie malnutrition in the textbook) occurs when a child does not consume the appropriate nutrients (of any kind) that it needs to grow and develop. (video lesson, segment 4; objective 9)

28. Undernutrition is a nutritional problem in which a child is noticeably underweight or short in stature compared to the norms. (video lesson, segment 4; objective 9)

29. Failure-to-thrive is undernutrition that involves a child who lives in an adequately nourished community but is not exhibiting normal childhood weight gain. (video lesson, segment 4; objective 9)

30. Metabolism refers to the physical and chemical processes in the body that promote growth and sustain life. For babies, major increases in the growth of the brain's communication system are fueled by a sharp increase in metabolism during the first two years. (video lesson, segment 2; objective 3)

31. An enriched environment is one that provides the developing child with a highly nurturing and stimulating atmosphere in which to grow and learn. (video lesson, segment 2; objective 4)

Practice Questions I

Multiple-Choice Questions

1. b. is the correct answer. (p. 86; objective 1)
2. a. (pp. 86–87; objective 1)
3. b. is the correct answer. (p. 86; video lesson, segment 1; objective 1)

4. a. is the correct answer. (pp. 94–96; objective 6)

   b. is incorrect. Inherited and environmental factors are important for both physical growth and the development of motor skills.

   c. is incorrect. On average, Ugandan babies walk earlier than do babies in the United States.

   d. is incorrect. In fact, just the opposite is true.
5. a. is the correct answer. (pp. 98–99; objective 7)
6. c. is the correct answer. (video lesson, segment 1; objective 1)
7. b. is the correct answer, because breast milk is more digestible than cow's milk or formula. (pp. 103–105; video lesson, segment 4; objective 8)

   a., c., & d. are incorrect. Breast- and bottle-fed babies do not differ in these attributes.
8. c. is the correct answer. (video lesson, segment 4; objective 9)
9. c. is the correct answer. (p. 94; video lesson, segment 3; objective 6)

   a. & b. are incorrect. These motor skills do not emerge until somewhat later; reflexes are present at birth.

   d. is incorrect. On the contrary, reflexes are quite predictable.
10. d. is the correct answer. (p. 95; video lesson, segment 3; objective 6)
11. d. is the correct answer. (pp. 94–97; video lesson, segment 3; objective 6)
12. c. is the correct answer. (pp. 88–90; video lesson, segment 2; objective 3)

Matching Items

13. j (p. 88; video lesson, segment 2; objective 3)
14. f (p. 88; video lesson, segment 2; objective 3)
15. a (video lesson, segment 4; objective 9)
16. d (video lesson, segment 2; objective 4)
17. g (p. 95; video lesson, segment 3; objective 5)
18. b (p. 96; video lesson, segment 3; objective 5)
19 h (pp. 94–95; video lesson, segment 3; objective 5)
20. e (p. 94; video lesson, segment 3; objective 5)
21. c (p. 98; objective 7)
22. i (video lesson, segment 2; objective 3)

Practice Questions II

Multiple-Choice Questions

1. a. is the correct answer. (p. 88; video lesson, segment 2; objective 3)
2. c. is the correct answer. (p. 94; video lesson, segment 3; objective 5)

   a., b., & d. are incorrect.
3. b. is the correct answer. (p. 96; video lesson, segment 3; objective 6)

4. d. is the correct answer. (pp. 94–97; objective 6)
5. b. is the correct answer. (pp. 98–99; objective 7)
6. a. is the correct answer. (pp. 103–105; video lesson, segment 4; objective 8)

   b. is incorrect. If anything, this is a potential disadvantage of breast milk over formula.

   c. is incorrect. So can formula.

   d. is incorrect. Breast milk contains more iron, vitamin C, and vitamin A than cow's milk; it does not contain more protein and vitamin D, however.
7. a. is the correct answer. (pp. 103–105; video lesson, segment 4; objective 8)
8. d. is the correct answer. (p. 103; objective 2)
9. b. is the correct answer. (pp. 95–97; video lesson, segment 3; objective 5)

   c. & d. are incorrect. Reflexes are involuntary responses; climbing and using a crayon are both voluntary responses.
10. d. is the correct answer. (pp. 93–97; video lesson, segment 3; objective 5)
11. d. is the correct answer. (video lesson, segment 4; objective 9)
12. d. is the correct answer. (p. 88; objective 3)
13. a. is the correct answer. (pp. 93–97; video lesson, segment 3; objective 5)

    b. & c. are incorrect. Reflexes are involuntary responses (therefore not b) that are present at birth (therefore not c).

    d. is incorrect. Some reflexes disappear with age.

True or False Items

14. F Hiccups, sneezes, and thrashing are common during the first few days, and they are entirely normal reflexes. (pp. 94–95; video lesson, segment 3; objective 5)
15. F Although all healthy infants develop the same motor skills in the same sequence, the age at which these skills are acquired can vary greatly from infant to infant. (pp. 96–97; objective 6)
16. T (p. 87; video lesson, segment 1; objective 1)
17. F Vision is relatively poorly developed at birth, whereas hearing is well developed. (pp. 98–99; objective 7)
18. T (p. 102; objective 2)
19. T (p. 93; objective 3)
20. F Metabolic activity increases, partly as a result of the dramatic growth occurring in the brain. (video lesson, segment 2; objective 3)

Applying Your Knowledge

1. c. is the correct answer. (p. 94; objective 5)
2. d. is the correct answer. (p. 90; objectives 3 & 4)
3. c. is the correct answer. (pp. 97–99; objective 7)

4. b. is the correct answer. (p. 94; video lesson, segment 3; objective 5)

   a. is incorrect. This is the reflexive sucking of newborns in response to anything that touches their lips.

   c. is incorrect. This is the response that infants make when their feet are stroked.

   d. is incorrect. In this response to startling noises, newborns fling their arms outward and then bring them together on their chests as if to hold on to something.

5. b. is the correct answer. (p. 97; objective 7)

   a. & d. are incorrect. Sensation and perception operate in all of these sensory modalities.

6. b. is the correct answer. This is true because, at birth, focusing is best for objects between 4 and 30 inches away. (pp. 97–99; objective 7)

   a., c., & d. are incorrect. Newborns have very poor distance vision; each of these situations involves a distance greater than the optimal focus range.

7. d. is the correct answer. (video lesson, segment 4; objective 9)

Lesson Review

Lesson 5

The First Two Years
Biosocial Development

Please Note: Use this matrix to guide your study and achieve the learning objectives of this lesson. It will also help you to view the video, which defines and demonstrates important concepts and skills as they relate to everyday life.

Learning Objective	Textbook	Telecourse Student Guide	Video Lesson
1. Describe the size and proportions of an infant's body, and discuss how babies change during the first two years and how their bodies compare with those of adults.	pp. 86–87	Key Terms: 1, 2; Practice Questions I: 1, 2, 3, 6; Practice Questions II: 16, 19.	Segment 1: *Physical Growth and Health*; Segment 2: *Brain Growth and Development*
2. Describe public health concerns, such as immunization and risk factors for sudden infant death syndrome (SIDS), and list the methods that experts recommend for protecting infant health.	pp. 100–103	Key Terms: 18, 19, 20; Practice Questions II: 8, 18.	
3. Describe the ways in which the brain changes or matures during infancy.	pp. 88–90	Key Terms: 3, 4, 5, 6, 7, 8, 9, 11, 21, 30; Practice Questions I: 12, 13, 14, 22; Practice Questions II: 1, 12, 19, 20; Applying Your Knowledge: 2.	Segment 2: *Brain Growth and Development*
4. Discuss the role of experience and stimulation in brain development, and demonstrate an understanding of shaken baby syndrome and social deprivation.	pp. 90–92	Key Terms: 9, 10, 31; Practice Questions I: 16; Applying Your Knowledge: 2.	Segment 2: *Brain Growth and Development*
5. Describe the basic reflexes of the newborn and distinguish between gross motor skills and fine motor skills.	pp. 93–97	Key Terms: 12, 13, 14, 22, 23, 24; Practice Questions I: 17, 18, 19, 20; Practice Questions II: 2, 9, 10, 13, 14; Applying Your Knowledge: 1, 4.	Segment 3: *Basic Reflexes and Motor Skills*

Learning Objective	Textbook	Telecourse Student Guide	Video Lesson
6. Describe the basic pattern of motor-skill development, and discuss variations in the timing of motor-skill acquisition.	pp. 94–97	Key Terms: 1, 25, 26; Practice Questions I: 4, 9, 10, 11; Practice Questions II: 3, 4, 15.	Segment 3: *Basic Reflexes and Motor Skills*
7. Distinguish between sensation and perception, and describe the extent and development of an infant's perceptual abilities using the sense of vision as an example.	pp. 97–99	Key Terms: 15, 16, 17; Practice Questions I: 5, 21; Practice Questions II: 5, 17; Applying Your Knowledge: 3, 5, 6.	
8. Discuss the nutritional needs of infants and toddlers and list some benefits of breast-feeding.	pp. 103–105	Practice Questions I: 7; Practice Questions II: 6, 7.	Segment 4: *Infant Nutrition*
9. Discuss undernutrition, failure to thrive, and malnutrition as they are explained in the video, and identify the potential effects of these conditions on babies, and discuss methods of prevention.		Key Terms: 2, 27, 28, 29; Practice Questions I: 8, 15, 21; Practice Questions II: 11; Applying Your Knowledge: 7.	Segment 4: *Infant Nutrition*

The Little Scientist

Lesson 6

The First Two Years: Cognitive Development

Preview

Lesson 6 is the first of the telecourse lessons to focus on the domain of *cognition,* by which we mean the mental processes involved in thinking. The lesson focuses on the various ways in which infant cognitive development is revealed: through perception (which, as you'll recall from Lesson 5, refers to the mental processing of sensory information), memory, intelligence, and language development. The lesson begins with a description of infant perception and the influential theory of affordances. Central to this theory is the idea that infants gain cognitive understanding of their world through affordances, that is, opportunities to perceive and interact with the objects and environments around them.

The lesson also discusses the key cognitive elements needed by infants to structure their environment. Using the habituation procedure, researchers have found that the speed with which infants recognize familiarity and seek something novel is related to later cognitive skill. It points out the importance of memory to cognitive development.

This video lesson, "The Little Scientist," outlines Jean Piaget's theory of **sensorimotor intelligence**, which maintains that infants think exclusively with their senses and motor skills. Piaget's six stages of sensorimotor intelligence are examined.

Finally, the lesson turns to the most remarkable cognitive achievement of the first two years, the acquisition of language. Beginning with a description of the infant's first attempts at language, the video and chapter follow the sequence of events that leads to the child's ability to utter two-word sentences. The lesson concludes with an examination of language learning as teamwork involving babies and adults, who, in a sense, teach each other the unique human process of verbal communication.

As you complete this lesson, think about a baby you know (and/or interview the child's parents, if time allows). Would you describe this child as a smart baby? How does this infant express his or her intelligence? Observe how this child reacts to new stimuli and assimilates new information. Study the child's usual environment. What objects, people, and situations does the child typically encounter that could afford him or her the opportunity to learn? What kinds of things can this baby remember, and under what circumstances? How far has this child's language advanced relative to other babies of the same age? What were his or her first vocalizations and/or first words? Speculate on how one could encourage language development in this child.

Prior Telecourse Knowledge that Will Be Used in this Lesson

- This lesson will return to Piaget's theory of cognitive development (Lesson 1) with a discussion of sensorimotor intelligence. (Recall that Piaget's theory specifies four major periods):
    1. **Sensorimotor (birth to 2 years) ← The First Two Years**
    2. Preoperational (2 to 6 years)
    3. Concrete Operational (7 to 11 years)
    4. Formal Operational (12 years through adulthood)
- You may wish to review the theories of B. F. Skinner and Lev Vygotsky (Lesson 1). They will come up again as the textbook and video lesson discuss how babies acquire language and what caregivers can do to help.
- In the section on perception, the textbook will refer to the importance of brain growth and development (Lesson 5). You may wish to review terms such as cortex, axons, and dendrites.

Learning Objectives

Use this information to guide your reading, viewing, thinking, and studying. After successfully completing this lesson, you should be able to:

1. Define information-processing theory and discuss the studies on depth perception as they relate to this theory.
2. Explain what object permanence is, how it is tested in infancy, and what these tests reveal.
3. Discuss research findings on infant memory and infants' understanding of cause-and-effect relationships.
4. Identify and describe Piaget's stages of sensorimotor intelligence, and give examples of the behavior associated with each stage.
5. Describe language development during the first two years, and identify its major hallmarks.
6. Contrast the theories of Skinner and Chomsky regarding early language development, and explain current views on language learning.
7. Explain the importance of child-directed speech, and identify its main features.

Read Chapter 3, "The First Two Years: Body and Brain," pages 105–121.

View the video for Lesson 6, "The Little Scientist."

Segment 1: *Sensorimotor Intelligence*

Segment 2: *Language Development*

Summary

During the first two years of life, cognitive development proceeds at a phenomenal pace as the infant is transformed from a baby who can know its world only through a limited set of basic reflexes into a toddler capable of imitating others, anticipating and remembering events, and pretending. According to Jean Piaget—often called the "father of cognitive development"—infants learn about their environment by using their senses and motor skills (**sensorimotor intelligence**). They begin by using and then adapting their reflexes (Stages 1 and 2); soon thereafter they become aware of their own and others' actions and reactions, and this awareness guides their thinking (Stage 3). By the end of the first year, they are able to set and achieve simple goals (Stage 4). During the second year, toddlers discover new ways to achieve their goals, first by actively experimenting with objects and actions (Stage 5) and then by manipulating mental images of objects and behaviors (Stage 6). Most significant among the advances of infancy is the development of language. By age 2, the average toddler has a relatively large vocabulary and is able to converse effectively with others.

By 3 months, infants have begun to organize their perceptual experience by identifying the boundaries of separate three-dimensional objects. One way young infants learn to deduce the boundaries of objects is by observing how the parts of the object move together through space. During the first 6 months, infants also establish a rudimentary understanding of perceptual constancy, the awareness that the size or shape of an object remains the same despite changes in its appearance due to a change in its location.

Infants' ability to coordinate sensory systems indicates extensive cognitive processing of perceptual information. Both intermodal perception (associating information from one sensory modality with information from another) and cross-modal perception (using information from one sensory modality to imagine something in another) are evident in the first months of life.

The remarkable speed and ease of infants' perceptual accomplishments have led some researchers to conclude that many of these basic perceptual skills are innate, or that infants are biologically endowed with the capacities to quickly acquire these abilities. Infants conceptualize their world in increasingly more meaningful ways that are relevant to their day-to-day encounters with objects and people.

Although standard Piagetian tasks suggest that infants do not search for hidden objects until about 8 months of age, studies using the habituation technique demonstrate that infants as young as 3.5–4.5 months have a basic understanding of **object permanence** long before they can demonstrate this on a hidden-object task. Infants as young as 3 months are capable of anticipating what will occur next in a sequence of events they have observed repeatedly. By 9 months, infants can show **deferred imitation** of a model whose actions they had observed a day earlier.

Infants are well equipped to learn language from birth, partly because of innate readiness and partly because of their auditory experiences during the final prenatal months. All children follow the same sequence of accomplishments in early language development, although their timing may vary considerably. They become competent first in language function (to understand and be understood) and later in language structure. At every stage of development—including the preverbal stage when infants use cries, cooing, **babbling**, and gestures to communicate—children understand much more than they are capable of expressing.

Toddlers differ in their vocabulary growth: some learn mainly naming words (referential), while others learn a higher proportion of words that facilitate social interaction (expressive). Toddlers initially show underextension of word meanings: words are applied more narrowly than they should be. Overextension, or overgeneralization, of a small set of words to inappropriate objects indicates that language development is proceeding normally, with the child forming and testing linguistic hypotheses. The first words, used as one-word sentences, occur by about 1 year, and the first two-word sentence at about 21 months.

Review all reading assignments for this lesson.

As assigned by your instructor, complete the optional online component for this lesson.

Key Terms

Using your own words, write a brief definition or explanation of each of the following terms on a separate piece of paper.

1. sensorimotor intelligence
2. assimilation
3. accommodation
4. object permanence
5. little scientist
6. information-processing theory
7. visual cliff
8. reminder session
9. child-directed speech
10. babbling
11. naming explosion
12. holophrase
13. language acquisition device (LAD)
14. adaptation
15. goal-directed behavior
16. mental combinations
17. deferred imitation
18. reduplicative babbling
19. semantics
20. intonation

Practice Questions I

Multiple-Choice Questions

1. According to the textbook, information-processing theory contrasts with
   a. Piaget's stage-based theories.
   b. Chomsky's ideas on the innate nature of language learning.
   c. B.F. Skinner's learning theories.
   d. none of the above.

2. According to Piaget, when a baby repeats an action that has just triggered a pleasing response from his or her caregiver, a stage __________ behavior has occurred.
   a. one
   b. two
   c. three
   d. six

3. Sensorimotor intelligence begins with a baby's first
   a. attempt to crawl.
   b. reflex actions.
   c. primary circular reaction.
   d. adaptation of a reflex.

4. Piaget would most likely agree that
   a. perception is largely automatic.
   b. language development is biologically predisposed in children.
   c. learning and perception are active cognitive processes.
   d. it is unwise to "push" children too hard academically.

5. By the end of the first year, infants usually learn how to
   a. accomplish simple goals.
   b. manipulate various symbols.
   c. construct mental combinations.
   d. pretend.

6. When an infant begins to understand that objects exist even when they are out of sight, she or he has begun to understand the concept of object
   a. displacement.
   b. importance.
   c. permanence.
   d. location.

7. It is thought that language learning is
   a. primarily the result of imitation of adult speech.
   b. a behavior that is determined primarily by biological maturation.
   c. a behavior determined entirely by learning.
   d. determined by both biological maturation and learning.

8. Children around the world
   a. attain language skills according to ethnically specific timetables.
   b. follow virtually the same sequence of early language development.
   c. routinely develop the same depth of linguistic ability despite cultural differences.
   d. attain language skills in a very different sequence because of cultural differences.

9. The average baby speaks a few words at about
   a. 6 months.
   b. 9 months.
   c. 12 months.
   d. 24 months.

10. A single word used by toddlers to express a complete thought is
    a. a holophrase.
    b. child-directed speech.
    c. reduplicative babbling.
    d. intonation.

11. A distinctive form of language, with a particular pitch, structure, and other elements, that adults use in talking to infants is called
    a. a holophrase.
    b. the LAD.
    c. child-directed speech.
    d. conversation.

12. A toddler who taps on the computer's keyboard after having observed her mother sending e-mail earlier in the day is demonstrating
   a. assimilation.
   b. accommodation.
   c. deferred imitation.
   d. dynamic perception.

Matching Items

Match each definition or description with its corresponding term.

Terms

13. __________	mental combinations	17. __________	babbling
14. __________	accommodation	18. __________	holophrase
15. __________	object permanence	19. __________	naming explosion
16. __________	sensorimotor intelligence	20. __________	reduplicative babbling

Definitions or Descriptions

a. repetitive utterance of certain syllables
b. a sudden increase in an infant's vocabulary
c. the realization that something that is out of sight continues to exist
d. trying out actions mentally
e. old ideas are restructured to include new experiences
f. a single word used to express a complete thought
g. thinking using the senses and motor skills
h. a type of babbling in which a baby puts two syllables together and repeats them over and over

Practice Questions II

Multiple-Choice Questions

1. Stage five (12 to 18 months) of sensorimotor intelligence is best described as
   a. first acquired adaptations.
   b. the period of the "little scientist."
   c. procedures for making interesting sights last.
   d. new means through symbolization.

2. Which of the following is evidence of object permanence during infancy?
   a. Babies are aware that an object or person continue to exist when they are no longer in sight.
   b. Babies form simple expectations of the path that a moving object will follow.
   c. Babies use movement cues to discern the boundaries of objects.
   d. Babies quickly grasp that even though objects look different when seen from different viewpoints, they are the same objects.

3. Recent research suggests that the concept of object permanence
   a. fades after a few months.
   b. is a skill some children never acquire.
   c. may occur earlier and more gradually than Piaget recognized.
   d. involves pretending as well as mental combinations.

4. Assimilation usually begins
   a. at birth.
   b. between 6 and 12 months.
   c. between 12 and 18 months.
   d. not until 24 months of age.

5. For Noam Chomsky, the "language acquisition device" refers to
   a. the human predisposition to acquire language.
   b. the portion of the human brain that processes speech.
   c. the vocabulary of the language the child is exposed to.
   d. all of the above.

6. The first stage of sensorimotor intelligence lasts until
   a. infants can anticipate events that will fulfill their needs.
   b. infants begin to adapt their reflexes to the environment.
   c. object permanence has been achieved.
   d. infants are capable of thinking about past and future events.

7. Piaget was incorrect in his belief that infants under 8 months do not have
   a. object permanence.
   b. intelligence.
   c. goal-directed behavior.
   d. all of the above.

8. The purposeful actions that begin to develop in sensorimotor stage four are called
   a. reflexes.
   b. affordances.
   c. goal-directed behaviors.
   d. mental combinations.

9. What is the correct sequence of language development in babies?
   a. crying, babbling, cooing, first word
   b. crying, cooing, babbling, first word
   c. crying, babbling, first word, cooing
   d. crying, cooing, first word, babbling

10. Compared with hearing babies, deaf babies
    a. are less likely to babble.
    b. are more likely to babble.
    c. begin to babble vocally at about the same age.
    d. begin to babble manually at about the same age as hearing babies begin to babble vocally.

11. According to Skinner, children acquire language
    a. as a result of an inborn ability to use the basic structure of language.
    b. through reinforcement and conditioning.
    c. mostly because of biological maturation.
    d. in a fixed sequence of predictable stages.

Matching Items

Match each definition or description with its corresponding term.

Terms

12. __________	goal-directed behavior	18. __________	little scientist
13. __________	information-processing theory	19. __________	accommodation
14. __________	intonation	20. __________	LAD
15. __________	assimilation	21. __________	semantics
16. __________	basic grammar	22. __________	child-directed speech
17. __________	naming explosion		

Definitions or Descriptions

a. incorporating new information into existing mental categories
b. according to Chomsky, all young children master this at about the same age

c. theory of human cognition that compares thinking to the ways in which a computer analyzes data
d. stage five toddler who "experiments" in order to see
e. dramatic increase in vocabulary that begins at about 18 months
f. a hypothetical device that facilitates language development
g. also called "motherese" or "baby talk"
h. Piaget's term for the stage-five toddler
i. purposeful actions
j. modifying an existing mental category to reflect new information
k. the cadence, tone, or emphasis of speech
l. the underlying meaning of words

Applying Your Knowledge

1. According to Skinner's theory, an infant who learns to delight his father by saying "da-da" is probably benefiting from
   a. social reinforcers, such as smiles and hugs.
   b. tertiary circular reaction.
   c. habituation.
   d. an innate ability to use language.

2. On the basis of experiments, developmentalists agree that very young infants can remember things if which of the following conditions are met?
   a. Experimental conditions are similar to real life.
   b. Motivation is high.
   c. Special measures aid memory retrieval.
   d. All of the above are true.

3. About nine months after speaking his or her first words, the typical child will
   a. have a vocabulary of around 50 words.
   b. begin to speak in holophrases.
   c. put words together to form rudimentary sentences.
   d. do all of the above.

4. A twenty-month-old girl who is able to try out various actions mentally without having to actually perform them is learning to solve simple problems by using
   a. dynamic perception.
   b. object permanence.
   c. intermodal perception.
   d. mental combinations.

5. A baby who repeats an action that has triggered a reaction in a parent is demonstrating an ability that typically occurs in which stage of sensorimotor development?
   a. Stage 1
   b. Stage 2
   c. Stage 3
   d. Stage 4

6. A baby who realizes that a rubber duck that has fallen out of the tub must be somewhere on the floor has certainly achieved
   a. object permanence.
   b. intermodal perception.
   c. mental combinations.
   d. cross-modal perception.

7. As soon as her babysitter arrives, twenty-one-month-old Christine holds on to her mother's legs and, in a questioning manner, says "bye-bye." Because Christine clearly is "asking" her mother if she is leaving, her utterance can be classified as
   a. babbling.
   b. an overextension.
   c. a holophrase.
   d. subject-predicate order.

8. The six-month-old infant's continual repetition of sound combinations such as "ba-ba-ba" is called
   a. cooing.
   b. reduplicative babbling.
   c. a holophrase.
   d. an overextension.

9. Like most Korean toddlers, Chul has acquired a greater number of words for __________ than his North American counterparts, who tend to acquire more words for __________.

a. objects; social interactions

b. social interactions; objects

c. people; actions

d. actions; people

Answer Key

Key Terms

1. Piaget's stages of sensorimotor intelligence (from birth to about 2 years old) are based on his theory that infants think exclusively with their senses and motor skills. (pp. 105–108; video lesson, segment 1; objective 4)
2. Assimilation is Piaget's term for a type of adaptation in which new experiences are interpreted to fit into, or assimilate with, old ideas. (p. 106; objective 4)
3. Accommodation is Piaget's term for a type of adaptation in which old ideas are restructured to include, or accommodate, new experiences. (p. 106; objective 4)
4. Object permanence is the understanding that objects continue to exist even when they cannot be seen, touched, or heard. (p. 107; video lesson, segment 1; objective 2)
5. "Little scientist" is Piaget's term for the stage-five toddler who learns about the properties of objects in his or her world through active experimentation. (p. 108; video lesson, segment 1; objective 4)
6. Information-processing theory is a theory of human cognition that compares thinking to the ways in which a computer analyzes data, through the processes of input, programming, and output. (pp. 108–109; objective 1)
7. A visual cliff is an apparent (but not actual) drop between one surface and another. (p. 109; objective 1)
8. A reminder session involves the experiencing of some aspect of an event that may trigger the entire memory of the event. (pp. 110–111; objective 3)
9. Child-directed speech is a form of speech used by adults when talking to infants. Its hallmark is exaggerated expressiveness; it employs more questions, commands, and repetitions and fewer past tenses, pronouns, and complex sentences; it uses simpler vocabulary and grammar; it has a higher pitch and more low-to-high fluctuations. It is also known as "baby talk" or "motherese." (p. 112; video lesson, segment 2; objective 7)

10. Babbling, which begins at 6 or 7 months, is characterized by the extended repetition of certain syllables (such as "ma-ma"). (p. 113; video lesson, segment 2; objective 5)
11. The naming explosion refers to the dramatic increase in the infant's vocabulary that begins at about 18 months of age. (p. 113; objective 5)
12. Another characteristic of infant speech is the use of the holophrase, in which a single word is used to convey a complete thought. (p. 114; objective 5)
13. According to Chomsky, children possess an innate language acquisition device (LAD) that enables them to acquire language, including the basic aspects of grammar. (p. 117; video lesson, segment 2; objective 6)
14. A key element of Piaget's theory, adaptation is the cognitive process by which information is taken in and responded to. (video lesson, segment 1; objective 4)
15. Goal-directed behavior refers to purposeful actions initiated by infants in anticipation of events that will fulfill their needs and wishes. (p. 107; video lesson, segment 1; objective 4)
16. In Piaget's theory, mental combinations are sequences of actions that are carried out mentally. Mental combinations enable stage-six toddlers to begin to anticipate and solve problems without resorting to trial-and-error experiments. (video lesson, segment 1; objective 4)
17. Deferred imitation is the ability to witness, remember, and later copy a behavior that has been witnessed. (video lesson, segment 1; objectives 3 & 4)
18. Reduplicative babbling is a form of speech in which babies, at about seven to nine months, string together two syllables and repeat them over and over. (video lesson, segment 2; objective 5)
19. Semantics refers to the set of rules by which we derive meaning from the spoken sounds in a given language; also, the study of the meaning of words. (video lesson, segment 2; objective 5)
20. Intonation refers to the cadence, tone, or emphasis of a given utterance. Babies learn a great deal about intonation, including how to adjust the intonation of their sounds to change the meaning of an utterance. (video lesson, segment 2; objective 5)

Practice Questions I

Multiple-Choice Questions

1. a. is the correct answer. (p. 108; objective 1)
2. c. is the correct answer. (p. 107; video lesson, segment 1; objective 4)
3. b. is the correct answer. This was Piaget's most basic contribution to the study of infant cognition—that intelligence is revealed in behavior at every age. (pp. 105–108; video lesson, segment 1; objective 4)

4. c. is the correct answer. (p. 106; objectives 1 & 4)

   b. is incorrect. This is Chomsky's position.

   d. is incorrect. This issue was not discussed in the textbook.

5. a. is the correct answer. (p. 108; video lesson, segment 1; objective 4)

   b. & c. are incorrect. These abilities are not acquired until children are much older.

   d. is incorrect. Pretending is associated with stage six (18 to 24 months).

6. c. is the correct answer. (p. 107; video lesson, segment 1; objective 2)

7. d. is the correct answer. This is a synthesis of the theories of Skinner and Chomsky. (pp. 115–119; video lesson, segment 2; objective 6)

8. b. is the correct answer. (pp. 114–115; video lesson, segment 2; objective 5)

   a., c., & d. are incorrect. Children the world over, and in every Piagetian stage, follow the same sequence and approximately the same timetable for early language development.

9. c. is the correct answer. (pp. 113–114; video lesson, segment 2; objective 5)

10. a. is the correct answer. (p. 114; objective 5)

    b. is incorrect. Child-directed speech is the speech adults use with infants.

    c. is incorrect. An overextension is a grammatical error in which a word is generalized to an inappropriate context.

    d. is incorrect. An underextension is the use of a word to refer to a narrower category of objects or events than the term signifies.

11. c. is the correct answer. (p. 112; video lesson, segment 2; objective 7)

    a. is incorrect. A holophrase is a single word uttered by a toddler to express a complete thought.

    b. is incorrect. According to Noam Chomsky, the LAD, or language acquisition device, is an innate ability in humans to acquire language.

    d. is incorrect. These characteristic differences in pitch and structure are precisely what distinguish child-directed speech from regular conversation.

12. c. is the answer (video lesson, segment 1; objective 3)

    a. & b. are incorrect. In Piaget's theory, these refer to processes by which mental concepts incorporate new experiences (assimilation) or are modified in response to new experiences (accommodation).

    d. is incorrect. Dynamic perception is perception that is primed to focus on movement and change.

Matching Items

13. d (video lesson, segment 1; objective 4)
14. e (p. 106; objective 4)
15. c (p. 107; video lesson, segment 1; objective 2)
16. g (p. 105; video lesson, segment 1; objective 4)
17. a (p. 113; video lesson, segment 2; objective 5)
18. f (p. 114; objective 5)
19. b (p. 113; objective 5)
20. h (video lesson, segment 2; objective 5)

Practice Questions II

Multiple-Choice Questions

1. b. is the correct answer. (p. 108; video lesson, segment 1; objective 4)

   a. & c. are incorrect. These are stages two and three.

   d. is incorrect. This is not one of Piaget's stages of sensorimotor intelligence.
2. a. is the correct answer. (p. 107; video lesson, segment 1; objective 2)
3. c. is the correct answer. (pp. 107–108; video lesson, segment 1; objective 2)
4. a. is the correct answer (p. 106; objective 4)
5. a. is the correct answer. Chomsky believed this device is innate. (p. 117; video lesson, segment 2; objective 6)
6. b. is the correct answer. (p. 106; video lesson, segment 1; objective 4)

   a. & c. Both of these occur later than stage one.

   d. is incorrect. This is a hallmark of stage six.
7. a. is the correct answer. (pp. 107–108; video lesson, segment 1; objective 2)
8. c. is the correct answer. (video lesson, segment 1; objective 4)

   a. is incorrect. Reflexes are involuntary (and therefore unintentional) responses.

   b. is incorrect. Affordances are perceived opportunities for interaction with objects.

   d. is incorrect. Mental combinations are actions that are carried out mentally, rather than behaviorally. Moreover, mental combinations do not develop until a later age, during sensorimotor stage six.
9. b. is the correct answer. (pp. 112–114; video lesson, segment 2; objective 5)

10. d. is the correct answer. (p. 113; objective 5)

    a. & b. are incorrect. Hearing and deaf babies do not differ in the overall likelihood that they will babble.

    c. is incorrect. Deaf babies begin to babble vocally several months later than hearing babies do.

11. b. is the correct answer. (pp. 116–117; video lesson, segment 2; objective 6)

    a., c., & d. are incorrect. These views on language acquisition describe the theory offered by Noam Chomsky.

Matching Items

12. i (p. 107; video lesson, segment 1; objective 4)
13. c (pp. 108–109; objective 1)
14. k (video lesson, segment 2; objective 5)
15. a (p. 106; objective 4)
16. b (p. 117; objective 6)
17. e (pp. 113–114; objective 6)
18. d (p. 108; video lesson, segment 1; objective 4)
19. j (pp. 106–107; objective 4)
20. f (p. 117; video lesson, segment 2; objective 6)
21. l (video lesson, segment 2; objective 5)
22. g (p. 112; video lesson, segment 2; objective 7)

Applying Your Knowledge

1. a. is the correct answer. The father's expression of delight is clearly a reinforcer in that it has increased the likelihood of the infant's vocalization. (pp. 115–116; video lesson, segment 2; objective 6)

   b. & c. are incorrect.

   d. is incorrect. This is Chomsky's viewpoint; Skinner maintained that language is acquired through learning.

2. d. is the correct answer (p. 110; objective 3)
3. c. is the correct answer. (pp. 112, 115; video lesson, segment 2; objective 5)

   a. is incorrect. At 18 months of age, most children have much smaller vocabularies.

   b. is incorrect. Speaking in holophrases is typical of younger infants.

4. d. is the correct answer. (p. 108; video lesson, segment 1; objective 4)

   a. is incorrect. Dynamic perception is perception primed to focus on movement and change.

   b. is incorrect. Object permanence is the awareness that objects do not cease to exist when they are out of sight.

c. is incorrect. Intermodal perception is the ability to associate information from one sensory modality with information from another.

5. c. is the correct answer. (p. 108; video lesson, segment 1; objective 4)
6. a. is the correct answer. Before object permanence is attained, an object that disappears from sight ceases to exist for the infant. (p. 107; video lesson, segment 1; objective 2)
7. c. is the correct answer. (p. 114; objective 5)

   a. is incorrect. Because Christine is expressing a complete thought, her speech is much more than babbling.

   b. is incorrect. An overextension is the application of a word the child knows to an inappropriate context, such as "doggie" to all animals the child sees.

   d. is incorrect. The ability to understand subject-predicate order emerges later, when children begin forming two-word sentences.
8. b. is the correct answer. (video lesson, segment 2; objective 5)

   a. is incorrect. Cooing is the pleasant-sounding utterances of the infant at about 2 months.

   c. is incorrect. The holophrase occurs later and refers to the toddler's use of a single word to express a complete thought.

   d. is incorrect. An overextension, or overgeneralization, is the application of a word to an inappropriate context, such as "doed" for the past tense of "do."
9. b. is the correct answer. (pp. 114–115; objective 6)

   c. & d. are incorrect.

Lesson Review

Lesson 6

The First Two Years
Cognitive Development

Please Note: Use this matrix to guide your study and achieve the learning objectives of this lesson. It will also help you to view the video, which defines and demonstrates important concepts and skills as they relate to everyday life.

Learning Objective	**Textbook**	**Telecourse Student Guide**	**Video Lesson**
1. Define information-processing theory and discuss the studies on depth perception as they relate to this theory.	pp. 108–109	Key Terms: 6, 7; Practice Questions I: 1, 4; Practice Questions II: 13.	
2. Explain what object permanence is, how it is tested in infancy, and what these tests reveal.	pp. 107–108	Key Terms: 4; Practice Questions I: 6, 15; Practice Questions II: 2, 3, 7; Applying Your Knowledge: 6.	Segment 1: *Sensorimotor Intelligence*
3. Discuss research findings on infant memory and infants' understanding of cause-and-effect relationships.	pp. 109–111	Key Terms: 8, 17; Practice Questions I: 12; Applying Your Knowledge: 2.	Segment 1: *Sensorimotor Intelligence*
4. Identify and describe Piaget's stages of sensorimotor intelligence, and give examples of the behavior associated with each stage.	pp. 105–108	Key Terms: 1, 2, 3, 5, 14, 15, 16, 17; Practice Questions I: 2, 3, 4, 5, 13, 14, 16; Practice Questions II: 1, 4, 6, 8, 12, 15, 18, 19; Applying Your Knowledge: 4, 5.	Segment 1: *Sensorimotor Intelligence*
5. Describe language development during the first two years, and identify its major hallmarks.	pp. 111–115	Key Terms: 10, 11, 12, 18, 19, 20; Practice Questions I: 8, 9, 10, 17, 18, 19, 20; Practice Questions II: 9, 10, 14, 21; Applying Your Knowledge: 3, 7, 8.	Segment 2: *Language Development*

Learning Objective	Textbook	Telecourse Student Guide	Video Lesson
6. Contrast the theories of Skinner and Chomsky regarding early language development, and explain current views on language learning.	pp. 115–119	Key Terms: 13; Practice Questions I: 7; Practice Questions II: 5, 11, 16, 17, 20; Applying Your Knowledge: 1, 9.	Segment 2: *Language Development*
7. Explain the importance of child-directed speech, and identify its main features.	pp. 112–113	Key Terms: 9; Practice Questions I: 11; Practice Questions II: 22.	Segment 2: *Language Development*

Lesson 7

The First Two Years: Psychosocial Development

Preview

Lesson 7 explores the emotional and social life of the developing person during the first two years. It begins with a description of the infant's emerging emotions and how they reflect increasing cognitive abilities. Newborns are innately predisposed to sociability, and are capable of expressing distress, sadness, contentment, and many other emotions, as well as responding to the emotions of other people.

This lesson also explores the social context in which a baby's emotions develop. By referencing their caregivers' signals, infants learn when and how to express their emotions. As **self-awareness** develops, many new emotions emerge, including embarrassment, shame, guilt, and pride. Parents who communicate effectively with their children are more responsive and tend to have children who are more skilled in communicating with others.

This lesson also presents the theories of Sigmund Freud and Erik Erikson that help us understand how the infant's emotional and behavioral responses begin to take on the various patterns that form personality. Important research on the nature and origins of **temperament**, which affects virtually every characteristic of the individual's developing personality, is also considered. Babies are not born with fully developed personalities. Instead, they come equipped with a basic set of temperamental tendencies in emotional expressiveness, activity level, and attention that, through their interactions with caregivers and others, are molded to form personality.

The final section of the lesson examines emotions and relationships from the perspective of parent–infant interaction. Videotaped studies of parents and infants, combined with laboratory studies, have greatly expanded our understanding of psychosocial development. In the video lesson, experts explain how the intricate patterns of parent–child interaction help infants learn to express and read emotions and promotes **attachment** to caregivers. Developmental psychologist Mary Ainsworth describes an experimental procedure she developed to measure the quality of attachment. The lesson concludes with a discussion of the impact of early day care on psychosocial development.

Prior Telecourse Knowledge that Will Be Used in this Lesson

- The developmental theories of Sigmund Freud and Erik Erikson (from Lesson 1) will be used to help explain psychosocial development during the school years.
- Recall (from Lesson 1) that Freud's theory specifies five major stages of **psychosexual development**, during which the sensual satisfaction associated with the mouth, anus, or genitals is linked to the major developmental needs and challenges that are associated with that stage. This lesson focuses on the first two stages:
    1. **Oral Stage (birth to 1 year)**
    2. **Anal Stage (1 to 3 years)**
    3. Phallic Stage (3 to 6 years)
    4. Latency Stage (7 to 11 years)
    5. Genital Stage (adolescence through adulthood)
- Recall (from Lesson 1) that Erik Erikson's theory specifies eight stages of **psychosocial development**, each of which is characterized by a particular challenge, or **developmental crisis**, that is central to that stage of life and must be resolved. This lesson focuses on the first two stages:
    1. **Trust versus Mistrust (birth to 1 year)**
    2. **Autonomy versus Shame and Doubt (1 to 3 years)**
    3. Initiative versus Guilt (3 to 6 years)
    4. Industry versus Inferiority (7 to 11 years)
    5. Identify versus Role Confusion (adolescence)
    6. Intimacy versus Isolation (adulthood)
    7. Generativity versus Stagnation (adulthood)
    8. Integrity versus Despair (adulthood)

Learning Objectives

Use this information to guide your reading, viewing, thinking, and studying. After successfully completing this lesson, you should be able to:

1. Describe the basic emotions expressed by infants during the first days and months.
2. Describe the main developments in the emotional life of the child between 6 months and 2 years.
3. Discuss the concept of social referencing, including its development and role in shaping later emotions.

4. Discuss the links between an infant's emerging self-awareness and his or her continuing emotional development, and explain the connection between the maturing brain, social impulses, and stress.
5. Describe how Freud's psychosexual stages can be used to explain the origins and development of personality.
6. Discuss how Erikson's psychosocial stages can be used to explain the origins and development of personality, and discuss how the concept of social learning fits into the behaviorist model of development.
7. Define and describe the concept of temperament, discuss its development as an interaction of nature and nurture, and explain the significance of research on temperament for parents and caregivers.
8. Describe the synchrony of parent–infant interaction during the first year, and discuss its significance for the developing person.
9. Define attachment, explain how it is measured and how it is influenced by context, and discuss the long-term consequences of secure and insecure attachment.
10. Discuss the potential effects of day care on a baby's development, and identify the factors that define high-quality day care.
11. Define ethnotheories and the child's "working model" and discuss how cognitive theory is linked to these two concepts.

Read Chapter 4, "The First Two Years: Psychosocial Development," pages 122–153.

View the video for Lesson 7, "Getting to Know You."

Segment 1: *Development through Crises*

Segment 2: *Attachment*

Segment 3: *Attachment and Day Care*

Summary

Contemporary developmentalists have revised a number of the traditional views of psychosocial development. It was once believed, for example, that infants did not have any real emotions. Researchers now know, however, that in the very first days and weeks of life, infants express and sense many emotions, including fear, anger, happiness, and surprise. Over the first two years, emotions change from a basic set of reactions to complex, self-conscious responses as infants become increasingly independent.

In the traditional view of personality development, the infant was seen as a passive recipient of the personality created almost entirely by the actions of his or her primary caregivers. Yet it is now apparent that many aspects of **temperament** are present in infants at birth and that active caregiver-infant interaction within a secure and nurturing environment is a central factor in the child's psychosocial development. During infancy, increasing independence, which Sigmund Freud explains in terms of the oral and anal stages, marks this development. Erik Erikson explains it in terms of "**trust versus mistrust**" and "**autonomy versus shame and doubt**."

A key factor in this psychosocial development is **attachment**—the affectional tie between infants and their primary caregivers. In infants the world over, attachment develops at about 7 months, when babies first become aware that other people stay in existence even when they're out of sight. **Secure attachment** helps ensure that the relatively helpless infant receives the adult care he or she needs in order to survive, and it sets the stage for the child's increasingly independent exploration of the world. By age 2, the toddler has a distinct personality that is the product of the social context and the innate temperament of the young infant.

Review all reading assignments for this lesson.

As assigned by your instructor, complete the optional online component for this lesson.

Key Terms

Using your own words, write a brief definition or explanation of each of the following terms on a separate piece of paper.

1. social smile
2. stranger wariness
3. separation anxiety
4. self-awareness
5. trust versus mistrust
6. autonomy versus shame and doubt
7. social learning
8. working model
9. ethnotheory
10. temperament
11. Big Five
12. proximal parenting
13. distal parenting
14. goodness of fit
15. synchrony
16. still-face technique
17. attachment
18. secure attachment
19. insecure-avoidant attachment
20. insecure-resistant/ambivalent attachment
21. disorganized attachment
22. Strange Situation
23. social referencing
24. family day care
25. center day care
26. contact-maintaining behaviors
27. insecure attachment
28. proximity-seeking behaviors

Practice Questions I

Multiple-Choice Questions

1. One of the first emotions that can be discerned in infancy is
   a. shame.
   b. distress.
   c. guilt.
   d. pride.

2. The social smile begins to appear
   a. at about 6 weeks.
   b. at about 8 months.
   c. after stranger wariness has been overcome.
   d. after the infant has achieved a sense of self.

3. An infant's fear of being left by the mother or other caregiver, called __________________, usually subsides after age __________________.
   a. separation anxiety; 24 months
   b. stranger wariness; 8 months
   c. separation anxiety; 8 months
   d. stranger wariness; 14 months

4. Social referencing refers to
   a. parenting skills that change over time.
   b. changes in community values regarding, for example, the acceptability of using physical punishment with small children.
   c. the support network for new parents provided by extended family members.
   d. the infant response of looking to trusted adults for emotional cues in uncertain situations.

5. Psychologists who favored the ____________________ perspective believed that the personality of the child was virtually "created" through reinforcement and punishment.
   a. psychoanalytic
   b. behaviorism
   c. psychosocial
   d. epigenetic

6. Freud's oral stage corresponds to Erikson's crisis of

   a. orality versus anality.

   b. trust versus mistrust.

   c. autonomy versus shame and doubt.

   d. secure versus insecure attachment.

7. Erikson feels that the development of a sense of trust in early infancy depends on the quality of the

   a. infant's food.

   b. child's genetic inheritance.

   c. relationship with caregiver.

   d. introduction to toilet training.

8. The increased tendency of toddlers to express frustration and anger is most closely linked to new developments in their cognitive abilities, especially those related to

   a. goal-directed actions.

   b. social referencing.

   c. self-awareness.

   d. stranger wariness.

9. "Easy," "slow to warm up," and "difficult" are descriptions of different

   a. forms of attachment.

   b. types of temperament.

   c. types of parenting.

   d. toddler responses to the Strange Situation.

10. Research studies of infant caregiving have found all of the following statements to be true **EXCEPT**:

    a. When both parents work outside the home, child care tends to be shared equally by mothers and fathers.

    b. Fathers can provide the emotional and cognitive nurturing that children need.

    c. Divorced fathers spend less time caring for infants than married fathers do.

    d. Contemporary fathers spend more time with their children than fathers did in 1970.

11. Synchrony is a term that describes

    a. the carefully coordinated interaction between parent and infant.

    b. a mismatch of the temperaments of parent and infant.

    c. a research technique involving videotapes.

    d. the concurrent evolution of different species.

12. The emotional tie that develops between an infant and his or her primary caregiver is called
    a. self-awareness.
    b. synchrony.
    c. affiliation.
    d. attachment.

13. An important effect of secure attachment is the promotion of
    a. self-awareness.
    b. curiosity and self-directed behavior.
    c. dependency.
    d. all of the above.

14. The sight of a friendly human face is most likely to produce a smile in a __________-month-old.
    a. three
    b. six
    c. nine
    d. twelve

15. Which of the following statements is true regarding cognitive theory?
    a. Thoughts and values determine a person's perspective.
    b. Thinking is affected by age and cultural values.
    c. Thoughts affect emotions.
    d. All of the above are true.

True or False Items

Write T (for true) or F (for false) on the line in front of each statement.

16. _____ Most developmentalists think that infants must learn to be sociable.

17. _____ The major difference between a six-month-old and a twelve-month-old is that emotions become less intense.

18. _____ A baby at 11 months is likely to display both stranger wariness and separation anxiety.

19. _____ Emotional development is affected by cognitive development.

20. _____ A securely attached toddler is most likely to stay close to his or her mother even in a familiar environment.

21. _____ Current research shows that the majority of infants in day care are insecurely attached.

22. _____ Temperament is genetically determined and is unaffected by environmental factors.

23. _____ Self-awareness enables toddlers to be self-critical and to feel guilt.

24. _____ Insecurely attached children display at least three different patterns of attachment behavior.

25. _____ Developmental psychologists express the greatest concerns about the early mental health of children who display insecure-resistant attachment.

26. _____ Studies show that the influence of center child care can be both positive and negative.

27. _____ In cognitive theory, a "working model" is a set of assumptions that an individual uses to organize perceptions and experience.

Practice Questions II

Multiple-Choice Questions

1. Infants give their first real smiles, called ___________, when they are about ___________ of age.
   a. play smiles; 3 months
   b. play smiles; 6 weeks
   c. social smiles; 3 months
   d. social smiles; 6 weeks

2. Freud's anal stage corresponds to Erikson's crisis of
   a. autonomy versus shame and doubt.
   b. trust versus mistrust.
   c. orality versus anality.
   d. identity versus role confusion.

3. Not until the sense of self begins to emerge do babies realize that they are seeing their own faces in the mirror. This realization usually occurs
   a. shortly before 3 months.
   b. at about 6 months.
   c. between 15 and 24 months.
   d. after 24 months.

4. Infants who are placed in day care are most likely to become insecurely attached if they are in day care more than 20 hours a week, if the day care quality is poor, and if
   a. their mothers are insensitive.
   b. they come from broken homes.
   c. they have a difficult temperament.
   d. their own parents were insecurely attached.

5. Emotions such as shame, guilt, embarrassment, and pride emerge at the same time that
   a. the social smile appears.
   b. aspects of the infant's temperament can first be discerned.
   c. self-awareness begins to emerge.
   d. parents initiate toilet training.

6. In the second six months, stranger wariness is a
   a. result of insecure attachment.
   b. result of social isolation.
   c. normal emotional response.
   d. setback in emotional development.

7. The caregiving environment can affect a child's temperament through
   a. the child's temperamental pattern and the demands of the home environment.
   b. parental expectations.
   c. both a and b.
   d. neither a nor b.

8. Compared to children who are insecurely attached, those who are securely attached are
   a. more independent.
   b. more curious.
   c. more sociable.
   d. characterized by all of the above.

9. The later consequences of secure and insecure attachment for children are
   a. subject to change due to the child's current rearing circumstances.
   b. irreversible, regardless of the child's current rearing circumstances.
   c. more significant in girls than in boys.
   d. more significant in boys than in girls.

10. Beginning at __________ of age, infants begin to associate emotional meaning with different facial expressions of emotion.

   a. 3 months
   b. 4 months
   c. 5 months
   d. 6 months

11. Compared with mothers, fathers are more likely to

   a. engage in noisier, more boisterous play.
   b. encourage intellectual development in their children.
   c. encourage social development in their children.
   d. read to their toddlers.

12. Unlike Freud, Erikson believed that

   a. problems arising in early infancy can last a lifetime.
   b. experiences later in life can alter the effects of early experiences.
   c. the first two years of life are fraught with potential conflict.
   d. all of the above are true.

Matching Items

Match each theorist, term, or concept with its corresponding description or definition.

Theorists, Terms, or Concepts

13. _______ temperament
14. _______ Erik Erikson
15. _______ the Strange Situation
16. _______ synchrony
17. _______ trust versus mistrust
18. _______ Sigmund Freud
19. _______ social referencing
20. _______ autonomy versus shame and doubt
21. _______ self-awareness
22. _______ Mary Ainsworth
23. _______ proximity-seeking behaviors
24. _______ contact-maintaining behaviors
25. _______ ethnotheories

Descriptions or Definitions

a. looking to caregivers for emotional cues
b. the crisis of infancy
c. the crisis of toddlerhood
d. approaching, following, and climbing
e. theorist who described psychosexual stages of development
f. researcher who devised a laboratory procedure for studying attachment
g. laboratory procedure for studying attachment

h. the relatively consistent, basic dispositions inherent in a person
i. clinging and resisting being put down
j. coordinated interaction between parent and infant
k. theorist who described psychosocial stages of development
l. a person's sense of being distinct from others
m. a set of ideas in which the values and practices of a culture are embedded

Applying Your Knowledge

1. In laboratory tests of attachment, when the mother returns to the playroom after a short absence, a securely attached infant is most likely to
   a. cry and protest the mother's return.
   b. climb into the mother's lap, then leave to resume play.
   c. climb into the mother's lap and stay there.
   d. continue playing without acknowledging the mother.

2. After a scary fall, eighteen-month-old Joey looks to his mother to see if he should cry or laugh. Joey's behavior is an example of
   a. proximity-seeking behavior.
   b. social referencing.
   c. insecure attachment.
   d. the crisis of trust versus mistrust.

3. Which of the following is a clear sign of an infant's attachment to a particular person?
   a. The infant turns to that person when distressed.
   b. The infant protests when that person leaves a room.
   c. The infant may cry when strangers appear.
   d. All of the above are signs of infant attachment.

4. If you had to predict a newborn baby's temperament "type" solely on the basis of probability, which classification would be the most likely?
   a. easy
   b. slow to warm up
   c. difficult
   d. There is not enough information to make a prediction.

5. One way in which infant psychosocial development has changed is that today
   a. many infants have their first encounters with other infants at a younger age.
   b. parental influence is less important than it was in the past.
   c. social norms are nearly the same for the sexes.
   d. infants tend to have fewer social encounters than in the past.

6. Ethan's mother left him alone in the room for a few minutes. When she returned, Ethan seemed indifferent to her presence. According to Mary Ainsworth's research with children in the Strange Situation, Ethan is probably
   a. a normal, independent infant.
   b. an abused child.
   c. insecurely attached.
   d. securely attached.

7. Mary and Chris, who are first-time parents, are concerned because their one-month-old baby has a high activity level. They are worried that they are doing something wrong. You inform them that their child is probably that way because
   a. they are reinforcing the child's tantrum behaviors.
   b. they are not meeting some biological need of the child.
   c. of his or her inherited temperament.
   d. at one month of age all children are difficult to care for and hard to soothe.

8. Two-year-old Anna and her mother visit a day-care center. Seeing an interesting toy, Anna runs a few steps toward it, then stops and looks back to see if her mother is coming. Anna's behavior illustrates
   a. the crisis of autonomy versus shame and doubt.
   b. synchrony.
   c. dyssynchrony.
   d. social referencing.

9. Frankie eats, chews, and talks excessively in quest of pleasures that were denied in infancy. Freud would probably say that Frankie is
   a. anally expulsive.
   b. anally retentive.
   c. fixated in the oral stage.
   d. experiencing the crisis of trust versus mistrust.

10. A researcher at the child development center places a dot on an infant's nose and watches to see if the infant reacts to her image in a mirror by touching her nose. Evidently, the researcher is testing the child's
    a. attachment.
    b. temperament.
    c. self-awareness.
    d. social referencing.

11. Four-month-old Carl and his thirteen-month-old sister Paula are left in the care of a babysitter. As their parents are leaving, it is to be expected that
    a. Carl will become extremely upset, while Paula will calmly accept her parents' departure.
    b. Paula will become more upset over her parents' departure than will Carl.
    c. Carl and Paula will both become quite upset as their parents leave.
    d. Neither Carl nor Paula will become very upset as their parents leave.

12. You have been asked to give a presentation on "Mother–Infant Attachment" to a group of expectant mothers. Basing your presentation on the research of Mary Ainsworth, you conclude your talk by stating that mother–infant attachment depends mostly on
    a. an infant's innate temperament.
    b. the amount of time mothers spend with their infants.
    c. sensitive and responsive caregiving in the early months.
    d. whether the mother herself was securely attached as an infant.

Answer Key

Key Terms

1. The social smile—a smile of pleasure in response to a human face or voice—appears at about 6 weeks. (p. 124; objective 1)
2. A common early fear, stranger wariness (also called fear of strangers) is first noticeable at about 6 months. (p. 125; objective 2)
3. Separation anxiety, which is the infant fear of being left by the mother or other caregiver, emerges at about 8 or 9 months, peaks at about 14 months, and then gradually subsides. (p. 125; objective 2)
4. Self-awareness refers to a person's sense of himself or herself as being distinct from other people that makes possible many new self-conscious emotions, including shame, guilt, embarrassment, and pride. (p. 126; objective 4)

5. In Erikson's theory, the crisis of infancy is one of trust versus mistrust, in which the infant learns whether the world is a secure place in which basic needs will be met. (p. 131; video lesson, segment 1; objective 6)
6. In Erikson's theory, the crisis of toddlerhood is one of autonomy versus shame and doubt, in which toddlers strive to rule their own actions and bodies. (p. 131; video lesson, segment 1; objective 6)
7. Social learning is the acquisition of behavior patterns by observing the behavior of others. (p. 132; objective 6)
8. According to cognitive theory, infants use social relationships to develop a set of assumptions called a working model that organizes their perceptions and experiences. (p. 133; objective 11)
9. Ethnotheory is a theory that underlies the values and practices of a culture but is not usually apparent to the people within the culture. (p. 133; objective 11)
10. Temperament refers to the set of innate tendencies, or dispositions, that underlie and affect each person's interactions with people, situations, and events. (p. 134; video lesson, segment 1; objective 7)
11. The Big Five are the five basic clusters of personality traits that remain quite stable throughout life: openness, conscientiousness, extroversion, agreeableness, and neuroticism. (p. 135; objective 7)
12. Parents who focus on close, physical contact with their infants (e.g., often holding or cuddling them) are engaged in proximal parenting. (p. 136; objective 9)
13. Distal parenting is defined as a focus on intellect and conversation more than on physical contact. (p. 136; objective 9)
14. Goodness of fit is the match between the child's temperamental pattern and the demands of the environment. (p. 139; objective 7)
15. Synchrony refers to the coordinated interaction between caregiver and infant that helps infants learn to express and read emotions. (p. 140; video lesson, segment 2; objective 8)
16. The still-face technique occurs when a parent maintains an expressionless face while maintaining eye contact with their child, an experience that is very stressful for the infant. (p. 141; objective 8)
17. Attachment is the enduring emotional tie that a person or animal forms with another. (p. 141; video lesson, segment 2; objective 9)
18. A secure attachment is one in which the infant derives comfort and confidence from the "secure base" provided by a caregiver. (p. 142; video lesson, segment 2; objective 9)
19. Insecure-avoidant attachment is a form of insecure attachment in which the child is likely to disregard or avoid a caregiver. (p. 143; video lesson, segment 2; objective 9)

20. Insecure-resistant/ambivalent attachment is a form of attachment in which children become very upset when they are separated from a caregiver, yet also fail to find comfort when the primary caregiver returns. (p. 143; video lesson, segment 2; objective 9)

21. Disorganized attachment is a form of attachment in which infants display inconsistent attachment behaviors, acting both avoidantly and resistantly to their primary caregivers. (p. 143; video lesson, segment 2; objective 9)

22. The Strange Situation is a laboratory procedure developed by Mary Ainsworth for assessing attachment. Infants are observed in a playroom, in several successive episodes, while the caregiver (usually the mother) and a stranger move in and out of the room. (p. 143; video lesson, segment 2; objective 9)

23. When infants engage in social referencing, they are looking to trusted adults for emotional cues on how to interpret uncertain situations. (p. 145; video lesson, segment 2; objective 3)

24. When an adult establishes a child care center in his/her own home, it is referred to as family day care. Typically, such caregivers are paid a lower rate and care for several children of different ages at once. (p. 147; objective 10)

25. Center day care (or infant day care) refers to caregiving provided by day-care workers and other adults who are not the child's biological parents and/or have no legal relationship to the child. (p. 147; video lesson, segment 3; objective 10)

26. Clinging, resisting being put down, and other contact-maintaining behaviors are intended to keep a person near another person to whom he or she is attached. (video lesson, segment 2; objective 9)

27. Insecure attachment is characterized by the infant's fear, anger, or seeming indifference toward the caregiver. (p. 143; video lesson, segment 2; objective 9)

28. Following, approaching, and other proximity-seeking behaviors are intended to place an individual close to another person to whom he or she is attached. (video lesson, segment 2; objective 9)

Practice Questions I

Multiple-Choice Questions

1. b. is the correct answer. (p. 124; objective 1)

   a., c., & d. are incorrect. These emotions emerge later in infancy, at about the same time as self-awareness emerges.

2. a. is the correct answer. (p. 124; objective 1)
3. a. is the correct answer. (p. 125; objective 2)

   b. & d. are incorrect. This fear, which is also called fear of strangers, peaks by 10 to 14 months.

4. d. is the correct answer. (p. 145; video lesson, segment 2; objective 3)

5. b. is the correct answer. (pp. 132–133; objective 7)

   a. is incorrect. Reinforcement and punishment have no place in the psychoanalytic perspective.

   c. is incorrect. This is Erikson's theory, which sees development as occurring through a series of basic crises.

   d. is incorrect. This perspective analyzes how genes and environment contribute to development.

6. b. is the correct answer. (p. 131; objectives 5 & 6)

   a. is incorrect. Orality and anality refer to personality traits that result from fixation in the oral and anal stages, respectively.

   c. is incorrect. According to Erikson, this is the crisis of toddlerhood, which corresponds to Freud's anal stage.

   d. is incorrect. This is not a developmental crisis in Erikson's theory.

7. c. is the correct answer. (p. 131; video lesson, segment 1; objective 6)

8. a. is the correct answer. Anger increases with age because toddlers are able to anticipate events and realize that other people's actions sometimes block their own efforts. (pp. 125–126; objective 2)

9. b. is the correct answer. (pp. 134–135; video lesson, segment 1; objective 7)

   a. is incorrect. "Secure" and "insecure" are different forms of attachment.

   c. is incorrect. The lesson does not describe different types of parenting.

   d. is incorrect. The Strange Situation is a test of attachment, rather than of temperament.

10. a. is the correct answer. (video lesson, segment 2; objective 9)

11. a. is the correct answer. (p. 140; video lesson, segment 2; objective 8)

12. d. is the correct answer. (pp. 141–143; video lesson, segment 2; objective 9)

    a. is incorrect. Self-awareness refers to the infant's developing sense of "me and mine."

    b. is incorrect. Synchrony describes the coordinated interaction between infant and caregiver.

    c. is incorrect. Affiliation describes the tendency of people at any age to seek the companionship of others.

13. b. is the correct answer. (p. 142; video lesson, segment 2; objective 9)

    a. is incorrect. The lesson does not link self-awareness to secure attachment.

    c. is incorrect. On the contrary, secure attachment promotes independence in infants and children.

14. a. is the correct answer. (p. 124; objective 1)

    b., c., & d. are incorrect. As infants become older, they smile more selectively.

15. d (p. 132; objective 11)

True or False Items

16. F Most developmentalists believe that infants are born with a tendency toward sociability as a means of survival. (pp. 124–125; objective 1)
17. F Emotions become more intense and are manifested more quickly and more persistently. (pp. 125–126; objective 2)
18. T (p. 125; objective 2)
19. T (pp. 125–126, 132–134; objective 2)
20. F A securely attached toddler is most likely to explore the environment, the mother's presence being enough to give him or her the courage to do so. (p. 142; video lesson, segment 2; objective 9)
21. F Many researchers believe that high-quality day care is not likely to harm the child. In fact, it is thought to be beneficial to the development of cognitive and social skills. (p. 149; video lesson, segment 3; objective 10)
22. F Temperament is a product of both nature and nurture. (pp. 134–136; video lesson, segment 1; objective 7)
23. T (pp. 126–128; objective 4)
24. T (p. 143; video lesson, segment 2; objective 9)
25. F Experts express the greatest concerns about children who display insecure-disorganized attachment. (p. 143; video lesson, segment 2; objective 9)
26. T (pp. 147–150; video lesson, segment 3; objective 10)
27. T (p. 133; objective 11)

Practice Questions II

Multiple-Choice Questions

1. d. is the correct answer. (p. 124; objective 1)
2. a. is the correct answer. (pp. 129–131; video lesson, segment 2; objectives 5 & 6)
3. c. is the correct answer. (pp. 126–128; objective 4)
4. a. is the correct answer. (pp. 147–150; video lesson, segment 3; objective 10)
5. c. is the correct answer. (pp. 126–128; objective 4)

   a. & b. are incorrect. The social smile, as well as temperamental characteristics, emerge well before the first signs of self-awareness.

   d. is incorrect.
6. c. is the correct answer. (pp. 125–126; objective 2)
7. c. is the correct answer. (pp. 140–145; objectives 8 & 9)
8. d. is the correct answer. (p. 142; video lesson, segment 2; objective 9)
9. a. is the correct answer. (pp. 141–145; video lesson, segment 2; objective 9)

   c. & d. are incorrect. The textbook does not suggest that the consequences of secure and insecure attachment differ in boys and girls.
10. c. is the correct answer. (p. 140; objective 3)

11. a. is the correct answer. (p. 146; objective 5)
12. b. is the correct answer. (video lesson, segment 1; objectives 5 & 6)

    a. & c. Freud would have agreed with both of these statements.

Matching Items

13. h (p. 134; video lesson, segment 1; objective 7)
14. k (p. 131; video lesson, segment 1; objective 6)
15. g (p. 143; video lesson, segment 2; objective 9)
16. j (p. 140; video lesson, segment 2; objective 8)
17. b (p. 131; video lesson, segment 1; objective 6)
18. e (pp. 129–130; objective 5)
19. a (p. 145; video lesson, segment 2; objective 3)
20. c (p. 131; video lesson, segment 1; objective 6)
21. l (p. 126; objective 4)
22. f (pp. 142–143; video lesson, segment 2; objective 9)
23. d (video lesson, segment 2; objective 9)
24. i (video lesson, segment 2; objective 9)
25. m (p. 133; objective 11)

Applying Your Knowledge

1. b. is the correct answer. (p. 142; video lesson, segment 2; objective 9)

   a., c., & d. are incorrect. These responses are more typical of insecurely attached infants.

2. b. is the correct answer. (p. 145; video lesson, segment 2; objective 3)
3. d. is the correct answer. (pp. 141–145; video lesson, segment 2; objective 9)
4. a. is the correct answer. About 40 percent of young infants can be described as "easy." (pp. 134–136; objective 7)

   b. is incorrect. About 15 percent of infants are described as "slow to warm up."

   c. is incorrect. About 10 percent of infants are described as "difficult."

5. a. is the correct answer. (pp. 147–150; objective 10)
6. c. is the correct answer. (pp. 142–143; video lesson, segment 2; objective 9)

   a. & d. are incorrect. When their mothers return following an absence, securely attached infants usually reestablish social contact (with a smile or by climbing into their laps) and then resume playing.

   b. is incorrect. There is no evidence in this example that Ethan is an abused child.

7. c. is the correct answer. (pp. 134–136; objective 7)

   a. & b. are incorrect. There is no evidence in the question that the parents are reinforcing tantrum behavior or failing to meet some biological need of the child's.

   d. is incorrect.

8. d. is the correct answer. (pp. 145–146; video lesson, segment 2; objective 3)

   a. is incorrect. According to Erikson, this is the crisis of toddlerhood.

   b. is incorrect. This describes a moment of coordinated and mutually responsive interaction between a parent and an infant.

   c. is incorrect. Dyssynchrony occurs when the coordinated pace and timing of a synchronous interaction are temporarily lost.

9. c. is the correct answer. (pp. 129–130; objective 5)

   a. & b. are incorrect. In Freud's theory, a person who is fixated in the anal stage exhibits messiness and disorganization or compulsive neatness.

   d. is incorrect. Erikson, rather than Freud, proposed crises of development.

10. c. is the correct answer. (p. 126; objective 4)

11. b. is the correct answer. The fear of being left by a caregiver (separation anxiety) emerges at about 8 or 9 months, and peaks at about 14 months. For this reason, four-month-old Carl can be expected to become less upset than his older sister. (pp. 125–126; objective 2)

12. c. is the correct answer. (pp. 142–144; video lesson, segment 2; objective 9)

Lesson Review

Lesson 7

The First Two Years
Psychosocial Development

Please Note: Use this matrix to guide your study and achieve the learning objectives of this lesson. It will also help you to view the video, which defines and demonstrates important concepts and skills as they relate to everyday life.

Learning Objective	Textbook	Telecourse Student Guide	Video Lesson
1. Describe the basic emotions expressed by infants during the first days and months.	pp. 124–125	Key Terms: 1; Practice Questions I: 1, 2, 14, 16; Practice Questions II: 1.	
2. Describe the main developments in the emotional life of the child between 6 months and 2 years.	pp. 125–126	Key Terms: 2, 3; Practice Questions I: 3, 8, 17, 18, 19; Practice Questions II: 6; 1; Applying Your Knowledge: 11.	
3. Discuss the concept of social referencing, including its development and role in shaping later emotions.	pp. 145–146	Key Terms: 23; Practice Questions I: 4; Practice Questions II: 10, 19; Applying Your Knowledge: 2, 8.	Segment 2: *Attachment*
4. Discuss the links between an infant's emerging self-awareness and his or her continuing emotional development, and explain the connection between the maturing brain, social impulses, and stress.	pp. 126–128	Key Terms: 4; Practice Questions I: 23; Practice Questions II: 3, 5, 21; Applying Your Knowledge: 10.	
5. Describe how Freud's psychosexual stages can be used to explain the origins and development of personality.	pp. 129–130	Practice Questions I: 6; Practice Questions II: 2, 11, 12, 18; Applying Your Knowledge: 9.	Segment 1: *Development through Crises* Segment 2: *Attachment*

Learning Objective	Textbook	Telecourse Student Guide	Video Lesson
6. Describe how Erikson's psychosocial stages can be used to explain the origins and development of personality, and discuss how the concept of social learning fits into the behaviorist model of development.	p. 131	Key Terms: 5, 6, 7; Practice Questions I: 6, 7; Practice Questions II: 2, 12, 14, 17, 20.	Segment 1: *Development through Crises* Segment 2: *Attachment*
7. Define and describe the concept of temperament, discuss its development as an interaction of nature and nurture, and explain the significance of research on temperament for parents and caregivers.	pp. 134–135	Key Terms: 10, 11, 14; Practice Questions I: 5, 9, 22; Practice Questions II: 13; Applying Your Knowledge: 4, 7.	Segment 1: *Development through Crises*
8. Describe the synchrony of parent–infant interaction during the first year, and discuss its significance for the developing person.	pp. 140–141	Key Terms: 15, 16; Practice Questions I: 11; Practice Questions II: 7, 16.	Segment 2: *Attachment*
9. Define attachment, explain how it is measured and how it is influenced by context, and discuss the long-term consequences of secure and insecure attachment.	pp. 141–145	Key Terms: 12, 13, 17, 18, 19, 20, 21, 22, 26, 27, 28; Practice Questions I: 10, 12, 13, 20, 24, 25; Practice Questions II: 7, 8, 9, 15, 22, 23, 24; Applying Your Knowledge: 1, 3, 6, 12.	Segment 2: *Attachment*
10. Discuss the potential effects of day care on a baby's development, and identify the factors that define high-quality day care.	pp. 147–150	Key Terms: 24, 25; Practice Questions I: 21, 26; Practice Questions II: 4; Applying Your Knowledge: 5.	Segment 3: *Attachment and Day Care*
11. Define ethnotheory and the child's "working model" and discuss how cognitive theory is linked to these two concepts.	pp. 132–134	Key Terms: 8, 9; Practice Questions I: 15, 27; Practice Questions II: 25.	

Playing and Growing

Lesson 8

The Play Years: Biosocial Development

Preview

Lesson 8 introduces the developing person between the ages of 2 and 6. This period is called the play years, emphasizing the central importance of play to the biosocial, cognitive, and psychosocial development of preschoolers.

The lesson begins by outlining the changes in size and shape that occur from ages 2 through 6. This is followed by a look at brain growth and development and its role in the development of physical and cognitive abilities. The lesson also addresses the important issues of **injury control** and accidents, the major cause of childhood death in all but the most disease-ridden or war-torn countries. A description of the acquisition of gross and fine motor skills follows, noting that mastery of such skills develops steadily during the play years along with intellectual growth. The lesson concludes with an in-depth exploration of **child maltreatment**, including its prevalence, contributing factors, consequences for future development, treatment, and prevention.

As you move through this lesson, think of children you know in this age range. Consider their size and shape, their eating habits, and their motor skill capabilities—what they can do with their bodies and hands. Also consider any child maltreatment cases you know of or have read about. What were the circumstances? What type of maltreatment occurred? What was the response?

Prior Telecourse Knowledge that Will Be Used in this Lesson

- In this lesson, physical growth and the development of gross and fine motor skills during "The Play Years" will be compared to earlier development during infancy and toddlerhood (Lesson 5/Chapter 5).
- This lesson will return to the topic of brain growth and development, which was introduced in Lesson 6/Chapter 6. In children from ages 2 to 6, the growth of dendrites and axons continues, along with myelination, the insulating process that speeds up the transmission of neural impulses. This brain maturation leads to

many other advances, including development of the visual pathways and eye-hand coordination that will make reading and writing possible.

Learning Objectives

Use this information to guide your reading, viewing, thinking, and studying. After successfully completing this lesson, you should be able to:

1. Describe normal physical growth during the play years, and account for variations in height and weight.
2. Describe changes in eating habits and nutritional needs during the preschool years.
3. Discuss brain growth and development and its effect on other areas of development during the play years.
4. Describe the prevalence of accidental injuries during early childhood, describe some measures that have significantly reduced accidental death rates for children, and identify several factors that contribute to this problem.
5. Distinguish between gross and fine motor skills, discuss the development of each during the play years, and explain how environmental hazards can negatively impact normal development.
6. Identify the various categories and consequences of child maltreatment.
7. Discuss several factors that contribute to maltreatment, and describe current treatment and prevention efforts.

Read Chapter 5, "Early Childhood: Body and Mind," pages 159–170 and 188–195.

View the video for Lesson 8, "Playing and Growing."

Segment 1: *Body and Brain Growth*

Segment 2: *Motor Skills*

Segment 3: *Maltreatment*

Summary

Children grow steadily taller and slimmer during the preschool years, with their genetic background and nutrition being responsible for most of the variation seen in children from various parts of the world. The most significant aspect of growth is the continued maturation of the nervous system and the refinement of the visual, muscular, and cognitive skills that will be necessary for the child to function in school. The brain becomes more specialized as it matures, with the left half usually becoming the center for speech, and the right the center for visual, spatial, and artistic skills.

Gross motor skills, such as running, climbing, jumping, and throwing, improve dramatically between ages 2 and 6, making it essential that children have access to safe play space and guided practice to assist in this developmental process. Fine motor skills, such as pouring, holding a pencil, and using a knife and fork, are much harder for preschoolers to master. This difficulty is due to several factors, including incomplete myelination of the nervous system and incomplete muscular control. Of course, for young children especially, art is not limited to coloring or drawing and often includes using markers, paint brushes, clay, and other vehicles. In fact, very young children (who lack the fine motor skills required to hold a crayon, brush, or pencil) are more likely to use large arm movements (such as those involved in finger painting) in their art. Doing so, of course, is a powerful stimulus to the development of the fine motor skills, as children are drawn to practice these skills in order to produce the artistic results they desire.

Throughout childhood, accidents are the leading cause of death. The accident risk for a particular child depends on several factors. Boys, as a group, and low-socioeconomic status (SES) children suffer more serious injuries and accidental deaths than girls, and high-SES children.

Child maltreatment takes many forms, including physical, emotional, or sexual **abuse**, and emotional or physical **neglect**. Although certain conditions are almost universally harmful, some practices that are considered neglectful or abusive in one culture are acceptable in others. Two environmental aspects have been directly related to potential maltreatment. Maltreatment occurs more frequently as income level falls. Maltreatment is also especially likely to develop in isolated families in which the parents are unusually suspicious or distrustful of outsiders.

The consequences of maltreatment to children include impaired learning, self-esteem, social relationships, and emotional control. Many people erroneously believe that maltreated children automatically become adults who abuse or neglect their own children. The phenomenon of maltreated children invariably growing up to become abusive or neglectful parents themselves (**intergenerational transmission**) is a widely held, and very destructive, misconception. Experts believe that between 30 and 40 percent of children who were abused actually become child abusers themselves. Still, this rate is much higher than that in the general population, so it is safest to conclude that it is a real, although often-exaggerated, problem.

The most effective prevention strategies for maltreatment are those that enhance community support and address the specific material and emotional needs of troubled families. Adoption is the final option when families are inadequate and children are young.

Review all reading assignments for this lesson.

As assigned by your instructor, complete the optional online component for this lesson.

Key Terms

Using your own words, write a brief definition or explanation of each of the following terms on a separate piece of paper.

1. myelination
2. corpus callosum
3. lateralization
4. perseveration
5. amygdala
6. hippocampus
7. hypothalamus
8. injury control/harm reduction
9. primary prevention
10. secondary prevention
11. tertiary prevention
12. child maltreatment
13. child abuse
14. child neglect
15. substantiated maltreatment
16. permanency planning
17. foster care
18. kinship care
19. intergenerational transmission

Practice Questions I

Multiple-Choice Questions

1. During the preschool years, the most common nutritional problem in developed countries is
   a. serious malnutrition.
   b. excessive intake of sweets.
   c. deficiencies in iron, zinc, and calcium.
   d. excessive caloric intake.

2. The brain center for language is usually located in the
   a. right hemisphere.
   b. left hemisphere.
   c. corpus callosum.
   d. space just below the right ear.

3. Childhood height and weight
   a. are consistent throughout the world.
   b. vary from one culture to another.
   c. are more pronounced in Western cultures.
   d. are more pronounced today than in the past.

4. Which of the following is **NOT** true regarding injury control?
   a. Broad-based television announcements do not have a direct impact on children's risk taking.
   b. Unless parents become involved, classroom safety education has little effect on children's actual behavior.
   c. Safety laws that include penalties are more effective than educational measures.
   d. Accidental deaths of one- to five-year-olds have held steady in the United States over the past two decades.

5. Like most U.S. adults, children in the United States tend to have too much ___________ in their diet.
   a. iron
   b. fat
   c. sugar
   d. sodium

6. Skills that involve large body movements, such as running and jumping, are called
   a. activity-level skills.
   b. fine motor skills.
   c. gross motor skills.
   d. left-brain skills.

7. The brain's ongoing myelination during childhood helps children
   a. control their actions more precisely.
   b. react more quickly to stimuli.
   c. focus more easily on printed letters.
   d. do all of the above.

8. The leading cause of death in childhood is
   a. accidents.
   b. untreated diabetes.
   c. malnutrition.
   d. iron deficiency anemia.

9. At age 6, the proportions of a child's body
   a. still retain the "top-heavy" look of infancy.
   b. are more adultlike in girls than in boys.
   c. are not very different from those of an adult.
   d. are influenced more by heredity than by health care or nutrition.

10. Which of the following factors is most responsible for differences in height and weight between children in developed and developing countries?
    a. the child's genetic background
    b. health care
    c. nutrition
    d. age of weaning

11. In which of the following age periods is appetite likely to be the lowest?
    a. infancy
    b. early childhood
    c. adolescence
    d. appetite remains constant across the lifespan

12. The relationship between accident rate and age in childhood can be described as
    a. a positive correlation.
    b. a negative correlation.
    c. curvilinear.
    d. no correlation.

13. Which of the following is true of the corpus callosum?
    a. It enables short-term memory.
    b. It connects the two halves of the brain.
    c. It must be fully myelinated before gross motor skills can be acquired.
    d. All of the above are correct.

14. Physical coordination improves during the play years, in part because
    a. the brain areas associated with this ability become more fully myelinated.
    b. the corpus callosum begins to function.
    c. fine motor skills have matured by age 2.
    d. gross motor skills have matured by age 2.

15. Adoption is most likely to be successful as an intervention for maltreatment when
    a. children are young and biological families are inadequate.
    b. efforts at tertiary prevention have already failed.
    c. children have endured years of maltreatment in their biological family.
    d. foster care and kinship care have failed.

True or False Items

Write T (for true) or F (for false) on the line in front of each statement.

16. _____ Growth between ages 2 and 6 is more rapid than at any other period in the life span.
17. _____ During childhood, the legs develop faster than any other part of the body.
18. _____ For most people, the brain center for language is located in the left hemisphere.
19. _____ The health care, genetic background, and nutrition of the preschool child are major influences on growth.
20. _____ Brain growth during childhood proceeds in spurts and plateaus.
21. _____ Fine motor skills are usually easier for preschoolers to master than are gross motor skills.
22. _____ Most serious childhood injuries truly are "accidents."
23. _____ Children often fare as well in kinship care as they do in conventional foster care.
24. _____ Most child maltreatment does not involve serious physical abuse.

Practice Questions II

Multiple-Choice Questions

1. Each year from ages 2 to 6, the average child gains and grows, respectively
   a. 2 pounds and 1 inch.
   b. 3 pounds and 2 inches.
   c. 4.5 pounds and 3 inches.
   d. 6 pounds and 6 inches.

2. The center for perceiving various types of visual configurations is usually located in the brain's
   a. right hemisphere.
   b. left hemisphere.
   c. right or left hemisphere.
   d. corpus callosum.

3. Which of the following best describes brain growth during childhood?
   a. It proceeds at a slow, steady, linear rate.
   b. The left hemisphere develops more rapidly than the right.
   c. The right hemisphere develops more rapidly than the left.
   d. It involves a nonlinear series of spurts and plateaus.

4. The portion of the brain associated with executive function is the
   a. corpus collosum.
   b. pharyngeal gland.
   c. hippocampus.
   d. prefrontal cortex.

5. Which of the following is an example of secondary prevention of child maltreatment?
   a. removing a child from an abusive home
   b. jailing a maltreating parent
   c. home visitation of families with infants by health professionals
   d. public-policy measures aimed at creating stable neighborhoods

6. When parents or caregivers do not provide adequate food, shelter, attention, or supervision, it is referred to as
   a. abuse.
   b. neglect.
   c. maltreatment.
   d. all of the above.

7. Which of the following is true of a developed nation in which many ethnic groups live together?
   a. Ethnic variations in height and weight disappear.
   b. Ethnic variations in stature persist, but are substantially smaller.
   c. Children of African descent tend to be tallest, followed by Europeans, Asians, and Latinos.
   d. Cultural patterns exert a stronger-than-normal impact on growth patterns.

8. Which of the following is an example of a fine motor skill?
   a. kicking a ball
   b. running
   c. drawing with a pencil
   d. jumping

9. Which of the following reflect the findings of recent research on the dangers posed by various pollutants in the air, food, and water that children are exposed to?
   a. Plastics, pesticides, and lead are known to impair development overall.
   b. Many chemicals in use today impede the growth of the body and brain.
   c. This research has primarily been done on lower animals, not humans.
   d. All of the above are true.

10. Most gross motor skills can be learned by healthy children by about age
   a. 2.
   b. 3.
   c. 6.
   d. 7.

11. Two of the most important factors that affect height during the play years are
   a. socioeconomic status and health care.
   b. gender and health care.
   c. heredity and nutrition.
   d. heredity and activity level.

12. Over the past two decades in the United States, the accidental death rate for children between the ages of 1 and 5 has
   a. decreased, largely as a result of new city, state, and federal safety laws.
   b. decreased, largely because parents are more knowledgeable about safety practices.
   c. increased.
   d. remained unchanged.

13. During the play years, because growth is slow, children's appetites seem ________________ they were in the first two years of life.
   a. larger than
   b. smaller than
   c. about the same as
   d. erratic, sometimes smaller and sometimes larger than

Matching Items

Match each definition or description with its corresponding term.

Terms

14. ________	corpus callosum	19. ________	child neglect
15. ________	gross motor skills	20. ________	primary prevention
16. ________	fine motor skills	21. ________	secondary prevention
17. ________	injury control/harm reduction	22. ________	tertiary prevention
18. ________	child abuse	23. ________	permanency planning

Definitions or Descriptions

a. efforts to find a long-term living situation that will provide stability and support for a maltreated child

b. procedures to prevent child maltreatment from ever occurring

c. running and jumping

d. actions that are deliberately harmful to a child's well-being

e. procedures for spotting and treating the early warning signs of child maltreatment

f. painting a picture or tying shoelaces

g. failure to appropriately meet a child's basic needs

h. an approach emphasizing "accident" prevention

i. procedures to halt maltreatment that has already occurred

j. band of nerve fibers connecting the right and left hemispheres of the brain

Applying Your Knowledge

1. Following an automobile accident, Salma developed severe problems with her language skills. Her doctor believes that the accident injured the ______________ of her brain.

   a. left side

   b. right side

   c. communication pathways

   d. corpus callosum

2. Two-year-old José is quite clumsy, falls down frequently, and often bumps into stationary objects. José most likely

   a. has a neuromuscular disorder.

   b. has an underdeveloped right hemisphere of the brain.

   c. is suffering from iron deficiency anemia.

   d. is a normal two-year-old whose gross motor skills will improve dramatically during the preschool years.

3. Climbing a fence is an example of a

   a. fine motor skill.

   b. gross motor skill.

   c. circular reaction.

   d. launching event.

4. To prevent accidental death in childhood, some experts urge forethought and planning for safety, along with measures to limit the damage of such accidents as do occur. This approach is called

   a. protective analysis.

   b. safety education.

   c. injury control/harm reduction.

   d. childproofing.

5. Young children may be especially likely than older children to be terrified of a "monster hiding under their bed" because

   a. they have increased amygdala activity.

   b. of a lack of brain lateralization.

   c. they use one side of the brain considerably more than the other.

   d. their underdeveloped corpus callosums limit communication between the two brain hemispheres.

6. Which of the following activities would probably be the most difficult for a five-year-old child?

   a. climbing a ladder

   b. catching a ball

   c. throwing a ball

   d. pouring juice from a pitcher without spilling it

7. Most child maltreatment
   a. does not involve serious physical abuse.
   b. involves a rare outburst from the perpetrator.
   c. involves a mentally ill perpetrator.
   d. can be predicted from the victim's personality characteristics.

8. A mayoral candidate is calling for sweeping policy changes to help ensure the well-being of children by promoting home ownership, high-quality community centers, and more stable neighborhoods. If these measures are effective in reducing child maltreatment, they would be classified as
   a. primary prevention.
   b. secondary prevention.
   c. tertiary prevention.
   d. differential response.

9. A factor that would figure very little into the development of fine motor skills, such as drawing and writing, is
   a. strength.
   b. muscular control.
   c. judgment.
   d. short, fat fingers.

10. Three-year-old Kyle's parents are concerned because Kyle, who generally seems healthy, doesn't seem to have the hefty appetite or rate of growth he had as an infant. Should they be worried?
    a. Yes, because both appetite and growth rate normally increase throughout the preschool years.
    b. Yes, because appetite (but not necessarily growth rate) normally increases during the preschool years.
    c. No, because growth rate (and hence caloric need) is less during the preschool years than during infancy.
    d. There is not enough information to determine whether Kyle is developing normally.

Answer Key

Key Terms

1. Myelination is the process by which axons and dendrites become insulated with coating of myelin, a fatty substance that speeds neural communication. (p. 166; video lesson, segment 1; objective 3)

2. The corpus callosum is a band of nerve fibers that connects the right and left sides of the brain. (p. 167; video lesson, segment 1; objective 3)
3. Lateralization refers to the differentiation of the two sides of the brain so that each serves specific, specialized functions. (p. 167; objective 3)
4. Perseveration is the tendency to repeat thoughts or actions, even after they have become unhelpful or inappropriate. In young children, perseveration is a normal product of immature brain functions.

   Memory aid: To persevere is to continue, or persist, at something. (p. 167; objective 3)
5. The amygdala is a brain structure in the limbic system involved in positive and negative emotions. In the play years, activity of the amygdala can overwhelm that of the prefrontal cortex, resulting in strong and sometimes irrational fears. (p. 169; objective 3)
6. The hippocampus is a brain structure in the limbic system that aids in the processing of memories, especially memories related to locations. The hippocampus is also influenced by amygdala activity, helping the child form memories related to emotional experiences. (p. 169; objective 3)
7. The limbic system contains a structure called the hypothalamus, which works in conjunction with the amygdala and the hippocampus to trigger the release of hormones (e.g., stress hormones in response to a frightening experience). (p. 169; objective 3)
8. Injury control/harm reduction refers to practices that are aimed at anticipating, controlling, and preventing dangerous activities; these practices reflect the beliefs that accidents are not random and that injuries can be made less harmful if proper controls are in place. (p. 188; objective 4)
9. Primary prevention refers to public policy measures designed to prevent child maltreatment (or other harm) from ever occurring. (p. 189; objective 7)
10. Secondary prevention involves home visitation and other efforts to spot and treat the early warning signs of maltreatment before problems become severe. (p. 189; objective 7)
11. Tertiary prevention involves efforts to stop child maltreatment after it occurs and to treat the victim. Removing a child from an abusive home, jailing the perpetrator, and providing health care to the victim are examples of tertiary prevention. (p. 189; objective 7)
12. Child maltreatment is intentional harm to, or avoidable endangerment of, anyone under age 18. (p. 190; video lesson, segment 3; objectives 6 & 7)
13. Child abuse refers to deliberate actions that are harmful to a child's well-being. (p. 190; video lesson, segment 3; objectives 6 & 7)
14. Child neglect refers to failure to appropriately meet a child's basic needs. (p. 190; video lesson, segment 3; objectives 6 & 7)

15. Child maltreatment that has been officially reported to authorities, and verified, is called substantiated maltreatment. (p. 191; objective 6)
16. Because repeated changes in caregivers or schools disrupt child development, permanency planning is used to seek a long-term placement for a child where he or she will be able to live until adulthood. (p. 193; objective 7)
17. Foster care is a legally sanctioned, publicly supported arrangement in which children are removed from their biological parents and temporarily given to another adult to nurture. (p. 193; objective 7)
18. Kinship care is a form of foster care in which a relative of a maltreated child becomes the child's legal caregiver. (p. 193; objective 7)
19. Intergenerational transmission is the assumption that mistreated children grow up to become abusive or neglectful parents themselves. (video lesson, segment 3; objective 7)

Practice Questions I

Multiple-Choice Questions

1. c. is the correct answer. (p. 161; objective 2)
2. b. is the correct answer. (p. 168; objective 3)

   a. & d. are incorrect. The right brain is the location of areas associated with recognition of visual configurations.

   c. is incorrect. The corpus callosum helps integrate the functioning of the two halves of the brain; it does not contain areas specialized for particular skills.
3. b. is the correct answer. (p. 160; video lesson, segment 1; objective 1)
4. d. is the correct answer. Accident rates have decreased during this time period. (p. 188; objective 4)
5. c. is the correct answer. (pp. 160–162; objective 2)
6. c. is the correct answer. (pp. 162–163; video lesson, segment 2; objective 5)
7. d. is the correct answer. (pp. 166–167; video lesson, segment 1; objective 3)
8. a. is the correct answer. (p. 188; objective 4)
9. c. is the correct answer. (p. 160; objective 1)

   b. is incorrect. The proportions are more adultlike in both girls and boys.

   d. is incorrect. Nutrition is a bigger factor in growth at this age than either heredity or health care.
10. c. is the correct answer. (pp. 160–161; video lesson, segment 1; objectives 1 & 2)
11. b. is the correct answer. (pp. 160–162; objective 2)
12. b. is the correct answer. Children who are younger have higher accident rates. (pp. 188–190; objective 4)

13. b. is the correct answer. (p. 167; video lesson, segment 1; objective 3)

    a. is incorrect. The corpus callosum is not directly involved in memory.

    c. is incorrect. Myelination of the central nervous system is important to the mastery of fine motor skills.

14. a. is the correct answer. (pp. 166–167; video lesson, segment 1; objective 3)

    b. is incorrect. The corpus callosum begins to function long before the play years.

    c. & d. are incorrect. Neither fine nor gross motor skills have fully matured by age 2.

15. a. is the correct answer. (p. 193; objective 7)

True or False Items

16. F Growth actually slows down during the play years. (p. 160; video lesson, segment 1; objective 1)
17. F During childhood, the brain develops faster than any other part of the body. (video lesson, segment 1; objectives 1 & 3)
18. T (p. 168; objective 3)
19. T (p. 160; video lesson, segment 1; objective 1)
20. T (p. 166; video lesson, segment 1; objective 3)
21. F Fine motor skills are more difficult for preschoolers to master than are gross motor skills. (p. 163; video lesson, segment 2; objective 5)
22. F Most serious accidents involve someone's lack of forethought. (p. 188; objective 4)
23. T (p. 193; objective 7)
24. T (pp. 192–193; video lesson, segment 3; objective 7)

Practice Questions II

Multiple-Choice Questions

1. c. is the correct answer. (p. 160; video lesson, segment 1; objective 1)
2. a. is the correct answer. (p. 168; objective 3)

    b. & c. are incorrect. The left hemisphere of the brain contains areas associated with language development.

    d. is incorrect. The corpus callosum does not contain areas for specific behaviors.

3. d. is the correct answer. (pp. 166–170; video lesson, segment 1; objective 3)

    b. & c. are incorrect. The left and right hemispheres develop at similar rates.

4. d. is the correct answer (pp. 168–169; objective 3)
5. c. is the correct answer. (p. 192; objective 7)

    a. & b. are incorrect. These are examples of tertiary prevention.

    d. is incorrect. This is an example of primary prevention.

6. d. is the correct answer. (p. 190; video lesson, segment 3; objective 7)
7. c. is the correct answer. (p. 160; objective 1)
8. c. is the correct answer. (p. 163; video lesson, segment 2; objective 5)

   a., b., & d. are incorrect. These are gross motor skills.
9. d. is the correct answer. (p. 365; objective 5)
10. c. is the correct answer. (p. 163; video lesson, segment 2; objective 5)
11. c. is the correct answer. (p. 160; objective 1)
12. a. is the correct answer. (pp. 189–190; objective 4)

    b. is incorrect. Although safety education is important, the decrease in accident rate is largely the result of new safety laws.
13. b. is the correct answer. (pp. 160–162; objective 2)

Matching Items

14. j (p. 167; video lesson, segment 1; objective 3)
15. c (pp. 162–163; video lesson, segment 2; objective 5)
16. f (pp. 162–163; video lesson, segment 2; objective 5)
17. h (p. 188; objective 4)
18. d (p. 190; video lesson, segment 3; objectives 6 & 7)
19. g (p. 190; video lesson, segment 3; objectives 6 & 7)
20. b (p. 189; objective 7)
21. e (p. 189; objective 7)
22. i (p. 189; objective 7)
23. a (p. 193; objective 7)

Applying Your Knowledge

1. a. is the correct answer. In most people, the left hemisphere of the brain contains centers for language, including speech. (p. 160; objective 3)
2. d. is the correct answer. (p. 163; objective 3)
3. b. is the correct answer. (p. 163; video lesson, segment 2; objective 5)

   a. is incorrect. Fine motor skills involve small body movements, such as the hand movements used in painting.

   c. & d. are incorrect. These events were not discussed in this chapter.
4. c. is the correct answer. (p. 188; objective 4)
5. a. is the correct answer. (p. 169; objective 3)
6. d. is the correct answer. (p. 163; video lesson, segment 2; objective 5)

   a., b., & c. are incorrect. Preschoolers find these gross motor skills easier to perform than fine motor skills such as that described in d.
7. a. is the correct answer. (pp. 192–193; video lesson, segment 3; objective 7)

8. a. is the correct answer. (p. 192; objective 7)

   b. is incorrect. Had the candidate called for measures to spot the early warning signs of maltreatment, this answer would be true.

   c. is incorrect. Had the candidate called for jailing those who maltreat children or providing greater counseling and health care for victims, this answer would be true.

   d. is incorrect. Differential response is not an approach to prevention of maltreatment; rather, it refers to separate reporting procedures for high- and low-risk families.

9. a. is the correct answer. Strength is a more important factor in the development of gross motor skills. (p. 163; video lesson, segment 2; objective 5)

10. c. is the correct answer. (pp. 160–162; objective 2)

Lesson Review

Lesson 8

The Play Years
Biosocial Development

Please Note: Use this matrix to guide your study and achieve the learning objectives of this lesson. It will also help you to view the video, which defines and demonstrates important concepts and skills as they relate to everyday life.

Learning Objective	Textbook	Telecourse Student Guide	Video Lesson
1. Describe normal physical growth during the play years, and account for variations in height and weight.	p. 160	Practice Questions I: 3, 9, 10, 16, 17, 19; Practice Questions II: 1, 7, 11.	Segment 1: *Body and Brain Growth*
2. Describe changes in eating habits and nutritional needs during the preschool years.	pp. 160–162	Practice Questions I: 1, 5, 10, 11; Practice Questions II: 13; Applying Your Knowledge: 10.	Segment 1: *Body and Brain Growth*
3. Discuss brain growth and development and its effect on other areas of development during the play years.	pp. 166–170	Key Terms: 1, 2, 3, 4, 5, 6, 7; Practice Questions I: 2, 7, 13, 14, 17, 18, 20; Practice Questions II: 2, 3, 4, 14; Applying Your Knowledge: 1, 2, 5.	Segment 1: *Body and Brain Growth*
4. Describe the prevalence of accidental injuries during early childhood, describe some measures that have significantly reduced accidental death rates for children, and identify several factors that contribute to this problem.	pp. 188–190	Key Terms: 8; Practice Questions I: 4, 8, 12, 22; Practice Questions II: 12, 17; Applying Your Knowledge: 4.	
5. Distinguish between gross and fine motor skills, discuss the development of each during the play years, and explain how environmental hazards can negatively impact normal development.	pp. 162–165	Practice Questions I: 6, 21; Practice Questions II: 8, 9, 10, 15, 16; Applying Your Knowledge: 3, 6, 9.	Segment 2: *Motor Skills*
6. Identify the various categories and consequences of child maltreatment.	pp. 190–192	Key Terms: 12, 13, 14, 15; Practice Questions II: 18, 19.	Segment 3: *Maltreatment*

Learning Objective	**Textbook**	**Telecourse Student Guide**	**Video Lesson**
7. Discuss several factors that contribute to maltreatment, and describe current treatment and prevention efforts.	pp. 192–193	Key Terms: 9, 10, 11, 12, 13, 14, 16, 17, 18, 19; Practice Questions I: 15, 23, 24; Practice Questions II: 5, 6, 18, 19, 20, 21, 22, 23; Applying Your Knowledge: 7, 8.	Segment 3: *Maltreatment*

Lesson 9

The Play Years: Cognitive Development

Preview

In countless everyday instances, as well as in the findings of numerous research studies, young children reveal themselves to be remarkably thoughtful, insightful, and perceptive thinkers whose memory of the past and mastery of language are sometimes astonishing. Lesson 9 begins by comparing Jean Piaget's and Lev Vygotsky's views of cognitive development at this age. According to Piaget, young children's thought is prelogical: between the ages of 2 and 6, they are unable to use logical principles and are limited by irreversible and static thinking. Lev Vygotsky, a contemporary of Piaget, saw learning more as a product of social interaction than of individual discovery.

The lesson next focuses on what preschoolers can do, including their competence in understanding number concepts, storing and retrieving memories, and theorizing about the world. This leads into a description of language development during early childhood. Although young children demonstrate rapid improvement in vocabulary and grammar, they have difficulty with abstractions, metaphorical speech, and certain rules of grammar. The lesson concludes with a discussion of preschool education, including a description of "quality" preschool programs and an evaluation of their lifelong impact on children.

As you complete this lesson, consider the cognitive development of any children you know in this age group (2 to 6). Consider what these children understand already and what they have yet to learn. Observe how they think—how they look at the world, interpret events, draw conclusions, and make decisions. Note how these children discover knowledge on their own and how they learn new skills through the guidance of parents, caregivers, and other children. Also, consider the memory skills of these children. For instance, how well can they remember events of their day and how well can they describe them? Consider their language skills—the extent of their vocabulary and their use of grammar. Finally, do any of these children go to day care or preschool? If so, what type of care are they receiving? What sort of learning experiences are they exposed to, and how might that exposure affect their development later in life?

Prior Telecourse Knowledge that Will Be Used in this Lesson

- This lesson will return to Piaget's theory of cognitive development (from Lesson 1/Chapter 2) with a discussion of **preoperational thought**. Recall that Piaget's theory specifies four major periods of cognitive development:
    1. Sensorimotor (birth to 2 years)
    2. **Preoperational (2 to 6 years) ← The Play Years**
    3. Concrete Operational (7 to 11 years)
    4. Formal Operational (12 years through adulthood)
- This lesson will return to the sociocultural theories of Lev Vygotsky (from Lesson 1/Chapter 2). Recall that Vygotsky emphasized the importance of guided participation, a process in which an individual learns through social interaction with a mentor who offers assistance, models strategies, and provides explicit instruction as needed.

Learning Objectives

Use this information to guide your reading, viewing, thinking, and studying. After successfully completing this lesson, you should be able to:

1. Describe the major characteristics of Piaget's stage of preoperational thought/ intelligence, and explain the concept of animism in preoperational thought.
2. Discuss Vygotsky's views on cognitive development, focusing on social learning and guided participation.
3. Explain the significance of the zone of proximal development and scaffolding in promoting cognitive growth.
4. Describe Vygotsky's view of the role of language in cognitive growth.
5. Explain the typical young child's theory of mind, noting how it is affected by culture and context, and relate it to the child's developing ability to understand pretense.
6. Outline the sequence by which vocabulary and grammar develop during the play years, and discuss limitations in the young child's language abilities.
7. Explain the role of fast mapping in children's acquisition of language.
8. Identify the characteristics of a high-quality preschool program, and discuss the long-term benefits of preschool education for the child and his or her family.

Read Chapter 5, "Early Childhood: Body and Mind," pages 171–188.

View the video for Lesson 9, "Playing and Learning."

Segment 1: ***How Preschoolers Think***

Segment 2: ***Words and Memories***

Segment 3: ***Early Childhood Education***

Summary

Symbolic thought, which enables children to form mental representations of things and events they are not immediately experiencing, develops rapidly throughout the preschool years. Both language and imagination become tools of thought, making the typical four-year-old much more verbal and creative than the one-year-old.

Although preschool children can think symbolically, they cannot perform what Jean Piaget called "logical operations." One characteristic of this **preoperational thought/ intelligence** is **irreversibility**: Preschoolers do not generally understand that reversing a process will restore the original conditions. **Egocentrism** also limits the preschooler's ideas about the world to his or her own point of view. Preoperational children also fail to correctly answer problems involving **conservation**, indicating that they do not yet understand the idea that the amount of a substance is unaffected by changes in its shape or placement.

Centration refers to the tendency of preschoolers to focus or center their analysis on one aspect of a problem, for instance, the appearance of liquid in a glass. In tests of conservation, Piaget believed, the problem is that preschoolers center on only the height of the liquid and fail to consider the shape and diameter of the glass it is in. Another example of centration is the preschooler's tendency toward **egocentrism**—to see the world only from his or her perspective.

Piaget focused on the individual child's innate curiosity. In general, he believed that children will find a way to learn when they are ready to do so. In contrast, Lev Vygotsky emphasized the impact of cultural and social factors in learning, including the effects of mentors and teachers. For instance, Vygotsky believed that—for each individual—there is a **zone of proximal development**, which represents the cognitive distance between the child's actual and potential levels of development. To encourage development, mentors can **scaffold** learning—in other words, provide structured assistance to help the child master new skills. Vygotsky also believed that language advances thinking in two ways: through **private speech** that an individual child uses to assist his or her thinking, and as **social mediation**, a tool of verbal interaction between mentor and apprentice. While these approaches are sometimes described as contradictory, a closer examination reveals that they may simply emphasize two different aspects of cognitive development.

Recent experiments have shown that preschoolers are not as illogical as Piaget believed. For example, under certain circumstances, young children can demonstrate the concept of conservation. On the other hand, young children cannot count large amounts, cannot easily add or subtract, and are not skilled at deliberately storing or retrieving memories. By about age 4, however, they do understand basic counting principles. They also develop an elementary **theory of mind** about their own and others' mental processes.

During the play years, children are gaining a better understanding of their own thoughts and feelings. In addition, they are beginning to develop informal theories about why other people act the way they do. In time this develops into what psychologists call a **theory-theory**. This understanding helps children explain basic everyday questions, such as how a person's knowledge and emotions affect his or her actions and how people can have such different perceptions, intentions, and desires.

Language development during the play years includes learning 10,000 words or more, in a predictable sequence according to parts of speech. Words are often learned after only one hearing, through the process called **fast mapping**. By age 3, children demonstrate extensive grammatical knowledge, although they often apply grammatical rules even when they should not (**overregularization**).

Changes in family composition and work patterns have resulted in great increases in early childhood education programs. A high-quality preschool program is characterized by a low teacher-child ratio, a staff with training and credentials in early childhood education, a curriculum geared toward cognitive development rather than behavioral control, and an organization of space that facilitates creative and constructive play.

While children in the play years are developing rapidly, it's important to focus their learning experiences on age-appropriate activities and not force them into tasks that are beyond their capability. For example, before a child's brain develops the ability to link spoken and written language (at about age 5), he or she is not ready to learn to read. That's why formal instruction in reading usually begins at about age 6. (Of course, *preparation* for literacy—such as reading picture books and writing one's name—should begin much earlier.)

Review all reading assignments for this lesson.

As assigned by your instructor, complete the optional online component for this lesson.

Key Terms

Using your own words, write a brief definition or explanation of each of the following terms on a separate piece of paper.

1. preoperational thought/intelligence
2. centration
3. egocentrism
4. focus on appearance
5. static reasoning
6. irreversibility
7. conservation
8. animism
9. apprentice in thinking
10. zone of proximal development
11. scaffold (scaffolding)
12. private speech
13. social mediation
14. theory-theory
15. theory of mind
16. fast mapping
17. overregularization
18. balanced bilingual
19. Reggio Emilia approach
20. Project Head Start
21. symbolic thought

Practice Questions I

Multiple-Choice Questions

1. Piaget believed that children are in the preoperational stage from ages
   a. 6 months to 1 year.
   b. 1 to 3 years.
   c. 2 to 6 years.
   d. 5 to 11 years.

2. Which of the following is **NOT** a characteristic of preoperational thinking?
   a. focus on appearance
   b. static reasoning
   c. lack of imagination
   d. centration

3. Preschoolers sometimes apply the rules of grammar even when they shouldn't. This tendency is called
   a. overregularization.
   b. literal language.
   c. practical usage.
   d. single-mindedness.

4. The Russian psychologist Lev Vygotsky emphasized that
   a. language helps children form ideas.
   b. children form concepts first, then find words to express them.
   c. language and other cognitive developments are unrelated at this stage.
   d. preschoolers learn language only for egocentric purposes.

5. Private speech can be described as
   a. a way of formulating ideas to oneself.
   b. fantasy.
   c. an early learning difficulty.
   d. the beginnings of deception.

6. In later life, high-quality preschool program graduates showed
   a. better report cards, but more behavioral problems.
   b. significantly higher IQ scores.
   c. higher scores on achievement tests.
   d. alienation from their original neighborhoods and families.

7. The child who has not yet grasped the principle of conservation is likely to
   a. insist that a tall, narrow glass contains more liquid than a short, wide glass, even though both glasses actually contain the same amount.
   b. be incapable of egocentric thought.
   c. be able to reverse an event.
   d. do all of the above.

8. The best preschool programs are generally those that provide the greatest amount of
   a. behavioral control.
   b. positive teacher-child social interactions.
   c. instruction in conservation and other logical principles.
   d. demonstration of toys by professionals.

9. Compared with their rate of speech development, children's understanding of language develops
   a. more slowly.
   b. at about the same pace.
   c. more rapidly.
   d. more rapidly in some cultures than in others.

10. Relatively recent experiments have demonstrated that preschoolers can succeed at tests of conservation when
    a. they are allowed to work cooperatively with other children.
    b. the test is presented as a competition.
    c. the children are informed that their parents are observing them.
    d. the test is presented in a simple, gamelike way.

11. Through the process called fast mapping, children
    a. immediately assimilate new words by connecting them through their assumed meaning to categories of words they have already mastered.
    b. acquire the concept of conservation at an earlier age than Piaget believed.
    c. are able to move beyond egocentric thinking.
    d. become skilled in the practical use of language.

True or False Items

Write T (for true) or F (for false) on the line in front of each statement.

12. _____ Piaget's description of cognitive development in early childhood has been universally rejected by contemporary developmentalists.

13. _____ In conservation problems, many preschoolers cannot understand the transformation because they focus exclusively on appearances.

14. _____ Preschoolers who use private speech have slower cognitive growth than those who do not.

15. _____ Whether or not a preschooler demonstrates conservation in an experiment depends in part on the conditions of the experiment.

16. _____ Piaget believed that preschoolers' acquisition of language makes possible their cognitive development.

17. _____ With the beginning of preoperational thought, most preschoolers can understand abstract words.

18. _____ A preschooler who says "You comed up and hurted me" is demonstrating a lack of understanding of English grammar.

19. _____ Successful preschool programs generally have a low teacher-to-child ratio.

20. _____ Vygotsky believed that cognitive growth is largely a social activity.

Practice Questions II

Multiple-Choice Questions

1. During the preschool years, vocabulary increases exponentially, from about 500 words
   a. at age 2 to about 7,000 at age 6.
   b. at age 2 to more than 10,000 at age 6.
   c. at age 3 to more than 20,000 at age 7.
   d. at age 3 to about 25,000 at age 7.

2. Piaget believed that preoperational children fail conservation-of-liquid tests because of their tendency to
   a. focus on appearance.
   b. fast map.
   c. overregularize.
   d. do all of the above.

3. A preschooler who focuses his or her attention on only one feature of a situation is demonstrating a characteristic of preoperational thought called
   a. centration.
   b. overregularization.
   c. reversibility.
   d. egocentrism.

4. One characteristic of preoperational thought is
   a. the ability to categorize objects.

b. the ability to count in multiples of 5.
c. the inability to perform logical operations.
d. difficulty adjusting to changes in routine.

5. The zone of proximal development represents the
   a. skills or knowledge that are within the potential of the learner but are not yet mastered.
   b. influence of a child's peers on cognitive development.
   c. explosive period of language development during the play years.
   d. normal variations in children's language proficiency.

6. According to Vygotsky, language advances thinking through private speech and by
   a. helping children to review privately what they know.
   b. helping children explain events to themselves.
   c. serving as a mediator of the social interaction that is a vital part of learning.
   d. facilitating the process of fast mapping.

7. Irreversibility refers to the
   a. inability to understand that other people view the world from a different perspective than one's own.
   b. inability to think about more than one idea at a time.
   c. failure to understand that changing the arrangement of a group of objects doesn't change their number.
   d. failure to understand that undoing a process will restore the original conditions.

8. According to Piaget
   a. it is impossible for preoperational children to grasp the concept of conservation, no matter how carefully it is explained.
   b. preschoolers fail to solve conservation problems because they center their attention on the transformation that has occurred and ignore the changed appearances of the objects.
   c. with special training, even preoperational children are able to grasp some aspects of conservation.
   d. preschoolers fail to solve conservation problems because they have no theory of mind.

9. In order to scaffold a child's cognitive skills, parents
   a. simplify tasks.
   b. interpret the activity.
   c. solve problems, anticipating mistakes.
   d. do all of the above.

10. Which theorist would be most likely to agree with the statement, "Learning is a social activity more than it is a matter of individual discovery"?
    a. Piaget
    b. Vygotsky
    c. both a and b
    d. neither a nor b

11. Children first demonstrate some understanding of grammar
    a. as soon as the first words are produced.
    b. once they begin to use language for practical purposes.
    c. through the process called fast mapping.
    d. in their earliest two-word sentences.

12. Overregularization indicates that a child
    a. is clearly applying rules of grammar.
    b. persists in egocentric thinking.
    c. has not yet mastered the principle of conservation.
    d. does not yet have a theory of mind.

13. Regarding the value of preschool education, most developmentalists believe that
    a. most disadvantaged children will not benefit from an early preschool education.
    b. most disadvantaged children will benefit from an early preschool education.
    c. because of sleeper effects, the early benefits of preschool education are likely to disappear by grade 3.
    d. the relatively small benefits of antipoverty measures such as Head Start do not justify their huge costs.

Matching Items

Match each definition or description with its corresponding term.

Terms

14. ________	balanced bilingual	19. ________	fast mapping
15. ________	scaffold	20. ________	centration
16. ________	theory of mind	21. ________	conservation
17. ________	zone of proximal development	22. ________	private speech
18. ________	overregularization	23. ________	guided participation

Definitions or Descriptions

a. the idea that amount is unaffected by changes in shape or placement
b. a person who is fluent in two languages
c. the cognitive distance between a child's actual and potential levels of development
d. the tendency to think about one aspect of a situation at a time
e. the process whereby the child learns through social interaction with a "tutor"
f. our understanding of mental processes in ourselves and others
g. the process by which words are learned after only one hearing
h. an inappropriate application of rules of grammar
i. the internal use of language to form ideas
j. to structure a child's participation in learning encounters

Applying Your Knowledge

1. An experimenter first shows a child two rows of checkers that each have the same number of checkers. Then, with the child watching, the experimenter elongates one row and asks the child whether the two rows still have the same number of checkers. This experiment tests the child's understanding of

   a. reversibility.
   b. conservation of matter.
   c. conservation of number.
   d. centration.

2. A preschooler believes that a "party" is the one and only attribute of a birthday. She says that Daddy doesn't have a birthday because he never has a party. This thinking demonstrates the tendency Piaget called

   a. egocentrism.
   b. centration.
   c. conservation of events.
   d. mental representation.

3. A four-year-old tells the teacher that a clown should not be allowed to visit the class because "Pat is 'fraid of clowns." The four-year-old thus shows that he can anticipate how another will feel. This is evidence of the beginnings of

   a. egocentrism.
   b. deception.
   c. a theory of mind.
   d. conservation.

4. Four-year-old Rhana becomes very distressed upon finding pickles on her cheeseburger. Her mother removes the pickles but Rhana still refuses to eat the sandwich, insisting that it is yucky now. Rhana's belief that the pickles permanently damaged her sandwich is consistent with a preoperational child's belief in

   a. tertiary circular reactions.
   b. irreversibility.
   c. explicit memory.
   d. oppositionalism.

5. A nursery school teacher is given the job of selecting holiday entertainment for a group of preschool children. If the teacher agrees with the ideas of Vygotsky, she is most likely to select

   a. a simple television show that every child can understand.
   b. a hands-on experience that requires little adult supervision.
   c. action-oriented play activities that the children and teachers will perform together.
   d. holiday puzzles for children to work on individually.

6. When a child produces sentences that follow rules of word order as "the initiator of an action precedes the verb, the receiver of an action follows it," this development demonstrates a knowledge of

   a. grammar.
   b. semantics.
   c. pragmatics.
   d. phrase structure.

7. The two-year-old child who says, "We goed to the store," is making a grammatical

   a. overextension.
   b. overregularization.
   c. underextension.
   d. script.

8. An experimenter who makes two balls of clay of equal amount, then rolls one into a long, skinny rope and asks the child if the amounts are still the same, is testing the child's understanding of
   a. conservation.
   b. egocentrism.
   c. perspective.
   d. centration.

9. Dr. Jones, who believes that children's language growth greatly contributes to their cognitive growth, evidently is a proponent of the ideas of
   a. Piaget.
   b. Chomsky.
   c. Flavell.
   d. Vygotsky.

10. Jack constantly "talks down" to his three-year-old son's speech level. Jack's speech is
    a. appropriate because three-year-olds have barely begun to comprehend grammatical rules.
    b. commendable, given the importance of scaffolding in promoting cognitive growth.
    c. unnecessary because preschoolers are able to comprehend more complex grammar and vocabulary than they can produce.
    d. clearly within his son's zone of proximal development.

11. In describing the limited logical reasoning of preschoolers, a contemporary developmentalist is least likely to emphasize
    a. irreversibility.
    b. centration.
    c. egocentrism.
    d. private speech.

12. A preschooler fails to complete a difficult puzzle on her own, so her mother encourages her to try again, this time guiding her by asking questions such as, "For this space do we need a big piece or a little piece?" With Mom's help, the child completes the puzzle successfully. Vygotsky would attribute the child's success to
    a. additional practice with the puzzle pieces.
    b. imitation of her mother's behavior.
    c. the social interaction with her mother that restructured the task to make its solution more attainable.
    d. modeling and reinforcement.

13. Mark is answering an essay question that asks him to "discuss the positions of major developmental theorists regarding the relationship between language and cognitive development." To help organize his answer, Mark jots down a reminder that _______________ contended that language is essential to the advancement of thinking, as private speech, and as a _______________ of social interactions.

   a. Piaget; mediator
   b. Vygotsky; mediator
   c. Piaget; theory
   d. Vygotsky; theory

Answer Key

Key Terms

1. According to Piaget, thinking between ages 2 and 6 is characterized by preoperational thought/intelligence, meaning that children cannot yet perform logical operations; that is, they cannot use logical principles. (p. 171; video lesson, segment 1; objective 1)

   Memory aid: Operations are mental transformations involving the manipulation of ideas and symbols. Preoperational children, who lack the ability to perform transformations, are "before" this developmental milestone.
2. Centration is the tendency of young children to focus only on a single aspect of a situation or object. (p. 171; video lesson, segment 1; objective 1)
3. Egocentrism refers to the tendency of young children to view the world exclusively from their own perspective. (p. 171; video lesson, segment 1; objective 1)
4. Focus on appearance refers to the preoperational child's tendency to focus only on physical attributes and ignore all others. (p. 171; video lesson, segment 1; objective 1)
5. Preoperational thinking is characterized by static reasoning, by which is meant that the young child sees the world as unchanging. (p. 171; objective 1)
6. Irreversibility is the characteristic of preoperational thought in which young children fail to recognize that a process can be reversed to restore the original conditions of a situation. (p. 171; video lesson, segment 1; objective 1)
7. Conservation is the understanding that the amount or quantity of a substance or object is unaffected by changes in its shape or configuration. (pp. 171–173; video lesson, segment 1; objective 1)
8. Animism is the belief that natural objects and phenomena are alive. (p. 173; objective 1)
9. According to Vygotsky, a young child is an apprentice in thinking, whose intellectual growth is stimulated by more skilled members of society. (p. 173; video lesson, segment 1; objective 2)
10. According to Vygotsky, for each individual there is a zone of proximal development, which represents the skills that are within the potential of the learner

but cannot be performed independently. (p. 174; video lesson, segment 1; objective 3)

11. Tutors who scaffold structure children's learning experiences by simplifying tasks, maintaining children's interest, solving problems, and anticipating mistakes, among other things. This term can be used as a verb (e.g., "to scaffold") or a noun (e.g., "creating scaffolding"). (p. 174; video lesson, segment 1; objective 3)
12. Private speech is the internal dialogue in which a person talks to himself or herself. Preschoolers' private speech, which often is uttered aloud, helps them think, review what they know, and decide what to do. (p. 175; objective 4)
13. Social mediation is the human interaction that expands and advances understanding, often through words that one person uses to explain something to another. (p. 175; objective 4)
14. Theory-theory refers to the tendency of young children to attempt to construct theories to explain everything they experience. (p. 176; objective 5)
15. A theory of mind is an understanding of mental processes, that is, of one's own or another's emotions, perceptions, intentions, and thoughts. (p. 177; video lesson, segment 2; objective 5)
16. Fast mapping is the process by which children rapidly learn new words by quickly connecting them to words and categories that are already understood. (p. 179; video lesson, segment 2; objective 7)
17. Overregularization occurs when children apply rules of grammar when they should not. It is seen in English, for example, when children add "s" to form the plural even in irregular cases that form the plural in a different way. (p. 180; video lesson, segment 2; objective 6)
18. A balanced bilingual is a person who is so fluent in two languages that there is no audible evidence of which language was learned first. (p. 182; objective 6)
19. Reggio Emilia approach to early childhood education originated in the town of Reggio Emilia, Italy; it encourages each child's creativity in a carefully designed setting. (p. 184; objective 8)
20. Project Head Start is the most widespread early childhood education program in the United States. It began in 1965 and was funded by the federal government. (p. 186; objective 8)
21. Symbolic thought is thinking that involves the use of words, gestures, pictures, or actions to represent other objects, behaviors, or experiences. (video lesson, segment 1; objective 1)

Practice Questions I

Multiple-Choice Questions

1. c. is the correct answer. (p. 171; video lesson, segment 1; objective 1)
2. c. is the correct answer (p. 171; video lesson, segment 1; objective 1)
3. a. is the correct answer. (p. 180; video lesson, segment 2; objective 6)

b. & d. are incorrect. These terms are not identified in the textbook and do not apply to the use of grammar.

c. is incorrect. Practical usage, which also is not discussed in the textbook, refers to communication between one person and another in terms of the overall context in which language is used.

4. a. is the correct answer. (p. 175; objective 4)

   b. is incorrect. This expresses the views of Piaget.

   c. is incorrect. Because he believed that language facilitates thinking, Vygotsky obviously felt that language and other cognitive developments are intimately related.

   d. is incorrect. Vygotsky did not hold this view.

5. a. is the correct answer. (p. 175; objective 4)

6. c. is the correct answer. (pp. 183–184; objective 8)

   b. is incorrect. This is not discussed in the textbook. However, although there was a slight early IQ advantage in Head Start graduates, the difference disappeared by grade 3.

   a. & d. are incorrect. There was no indication of greater behavioral problems or alienation in Head Start guidelines.

7. a. is the correct answer. (pp. 171–172; video lesson, segment 1; objective 1)

   b., c., & d. are incorrect. Failure to conserve is the result of thinking that is centered on appearances. Egocentrism and irreversibility are also examples of centered thinking.

8. b. is the correct answer. (p. 187; video lesson, segment 3; objective 8)

9. c. is the correct answer. (pp. 179–180; video lesson, segment 2; objectives 6 & 7)

10. d. is the correct answer. (video lesson, segment 1; objective 1)

11. a. is the correct answer. (p. 179; video lesson, segment 2; objective 7)

True or False Items

12. F More recent research has found that children may understand conservation earlier than Piaget thought, given a more gamelike presentation. His theory has not been rejected overall, however. (video lesson, segment 1; objective 1)

13. T (p. 172; video lesson, segment 1; objective 1)

14. F In fact, just the opposite is true. Children who have learning difficulties tend to be slower to develop private speech. (p. 175; objective 4)

15. T (p. 172; video lesson, segment 1; objective 1)

16. F Vygotsky believed that preschoolers' language is purely a result of brain development. (p. 175; objective 4)

17. F Preschoolers have difficulty understanding abstract words; their vocabulary consists mainly of concrete nouns and verbs. (pp. 179–180; video lesson, segment 2; objective 6)

18. F In adding "ed" to form a past tense, the child has indicated an understanding of the grammatical rule for making past tenses in English, even though the construction in these two cases is incorrect. (pp. 180–182; video lesson, segment 2; objective 6)
19. T (p. 187; video lesson, segment 3; objective 8)
20. T (pp. 173–174; video lesson, segment 1; objective 2)

Practice Questions II

Multiple-Choice Questions

1. b. is the correct answer (pp. 179–180; objective 6)
2. a. is the correct answer (pp. 171–172; video lesson, segment 1; objective 1)
3. a. is the correct answer. (p. 171; video lesson, segment 1; objective 1)

   b. is incorrect. Overregularization is the child's tendency to apply grammatical rules even when he or she shouldn't.

   c. is incorrect. Reversibility is the concept that reversing an operation, such as addition, will restore the original conditions.

   d. is incorrect. This term is used to refer to the young child's belief that people think as he or she does.
4. c. is the correct answer. This is why the stage is called preoperational. (p. 171; video lesson, segment 1; objective 1)
5. a. is the correct answer. (p. 174; video lesson, segment 1; objective 3)
6. c. is the correct answer. (p. 175; objective 4)

   a. & b. are incorrect. These are both advantages of private speech.

   d. is incorrect. Fast mapping is the process by which new words are acquired, often after only one hearing.
7. d. is the correct answer. (pp. 171–172; video lesson, segment 1; objective 1)

   a. is incorrect. This describes egocentrism.

   b. is incorrect. This is the opposite of centration.

   c. is incorrect. This defines conservation of number.
8. a. is the correct answer. (pp. 171–173; video lesson, segment 1; objective 1)

   b. is incorrect. According to Piaget, preschoolers fail to solve conservation problems because they focus on the appearance of objects and ignore the transformation that has occurred.

   d. is incorrect. Piaget did not relate conservation to a theory of mind.
9. d. is the correct answer. (pp. 174–175; video lesson, segment 1; objective 3)
10. b. is the correct answer. (pp. 173–174; video lesson, segment 1; objective 2)

    a. is incorrect. Piaget believed that learning is a matter of individual discovery.
11. d. is the correct answer. Preschoolers almost always put subject before verb in their two-word sentences. (p. 180; video lesson, segment 2; objective 6)

12. a. is the correct answer. (p. 180; video lesson, segment 2; objective 6)

    b., c., & d. are incorrect. Overregularization is a linguistic phenomenon rather than a characteristic type of thinking (b & d), or a logical principle (c).

13. b. is the correct answer. (p. 187; video lesson, segment 3; objective 8)

Matching Items

14. b (p. 182; objective 6)
15. j (p. 174; video lesson, segment 1; objective 3)
16. f (p. 177; video lesson, segment 2; objective 5)
17. c (p. 174; video lesson, segment 1; objective 3)
18. h (p. 180; video lesson, segment 2; objective 6)
19. g (p. 179; video lesson, segment 2; objective 7)
20. d (p. 171; video lesson, segment 1; objective 1)
21. a (pp. 171–173; video lesson, segment 1; objective 1)
22. i (p. 175; objective 4)
23. e (pp. 173–174; video lesson, segment 1; objective 2)

Applying Your Knowledge

1. c. is the correct answer. (pp. 172–173; video lesson, segment 1; objective 1)

   a. is incorrect. A test of reversibility would ask a child to perform an operation, such as adding 4 to 3, and then reverse the process (subtract 3 from 7) to determine whether the child understood that the original condition (the number 4) was restored.

   b. is incorrect. A test of conservation of matter would transform the appearance of an object, such as a ball of clay, to determine whether the child understood that the object remained the same.

   d. is incorrect. A test of centration would involve the child's ability to see various aspects of a situation.

2. b. is the correct answer. (p. 171; video lesson, segment 1; objective 1)

   a. is incorrect. Egocentrism is thinking that is self-centered.

   c. is incorrect. This is not a concept in Piaget's theory.

   d. is incorrect. Mental representation is an example of symbolic thought.

3. c. is the correct answer. (p. 177; video lesson, segment 2; objective 5)

   a. is incorrect. Egocentrism is self-centered thinking.

   b. is incorrect. Although deception provides evidence of a theory of mind, the child in this example is not deceiving anyone.

   d. is incorrect. Conservation is the understanding that the amount of a substance is unchanged by changes in its shape or placement.

4. b. is the correct answer. (p. 171; video lesson, segment 1; objective 1)

5. c. is the correct answer. In Vygotsky's view, learning is a social activity more than a matter of individual discovery. Thus, social interaction that provides motivation and focuses attention facilitates learning.
   (pp. 173–174; video lesson, segment 1; objective 2)
6. a. is the correct answer. (p. 180; video lesson, segment 2; objective 6)

   b. & d. are incorrect. The textbook does not discuss these aspects of language.

   c. is incorrect. Pragmatics, which is not mentioned in the textbook, refers to the practical use of language in varying social contexts.
7. b. is the correct answer. (p. 180; video lesson, segment 2; objective 6)
8. a. is the correct answer. (pp. 171–173; video lesson, segment 1; objective 1)
9. d. is the correct answer. (p. 175; video lesson, segment 1; objective 4)

   a. is incorrect. Piaget believed that cognitive growth precedes language development.

   b. & c. are incorrect. Chomsky focused on the acquisition of language, and Flavell emphasizes cognition.
10. c. is the correct answer. (pp. 179–180; objective 6)
11. d. is the correct answer. (p. 175; objective 4)
12. c. is the correct answer. (pp. 173–174; video lesson segment 1; objective 2)
13. b. is the correct answer. (p. 175; objective 4)

Lesson Review

Lesson 9

The Play Years
Cognitive Development

Please Note: Use this matrix to guide your study and achieve the learning objectives of this lesson. It will also help you to view the video, which defines and demonstrates important concepts and skills as they relate to everyday life.

Learning Objective	Textbook	Telecourse Student Guide	Video Lesson
1. Describe the major characteristics of Piaget's stage of preoperational thought/intelligence, and explain the concept of animism in preoperational thought.	pp. 171–173	Key Terms: 1, 2, 3, 4, 5, 6, 7, 8, 21; Practice Questions I: 1, 2, 7, 10, 12, 13, 15; Practice Questions II: 2, 3, 4, 7, 8, 20, 21; Applying Your Knowledge: 1, 2, 4, 8.	Segment 1: *How Preschoolers Think*
2. Discuss Vygotsky's views on cognitive development, focusing on social learning and guided participation.	pp. 173–174	Key Terms: 9; Practice Questions I: 20; Practice Questions II: 10, 23; Applying Your Knowledge: 5, 12.	Segment 1: *How Preschoolers Think*
3. Explain the significance of the zone of proximal development and scaffolding in promoting cognitive growth.	pp. 174–175	Key Terms: 10, 11; Practice Questions II: 5, 9, 15, 17.	Segment 1: *How Preschoolers Think*
4. Describe Vygotsky's view of the role of language in cognitive growth.	p. 175	Key Terms: 12, 13; Practice Questions I: 4, 5, 14, 16; Practice Questions II: 6, 22; Applying Your Knowledge: 9, 11, 13.	Segment 1: *How Preschoolers Think*
5. Explain the typical young child's theory of mind, noting how it is affected by culture and context, and relate it to the child's developing ability to understand pretense.	pp. 176–178	Key Terms: 14, 15; Practice Questions II: 16; Applying Your Knowledge: 3.	Segment 2: *Words and Memories*

Learning Objective	Textbook	Telecourse Student Guide	Video Lesson
6. Outline the sequence by which vocabulary and grammar develop during the play years, and discuss limitations in the young child's language abilities.	pp. 179–180	Key Terms: 17, 18; Practice Questions I: 3, 9, 17, 18; Practice Questions II: 1, 11, 12, 14, 18; Applying Your Knowledge: 6, 7, 10.	Segment 2: *Words and Memories*
7. Explain the role of fast mapping in children's acquisition of language.	p. 179	Key Terms: 16; Practice Questions I: 9, 11; Practice Questions II: 19.	Segment 2: *Words and Memories*
8. Identify the characteristics of a high-quality preschool program, and discuss the long-term benefits of preschool education for the child and his or her family.	pp. 182–187	Key Terms: 19, 20; Practice Questions I: 6, 8, 19; Practice Questions II: 13.	Segment 3: *Early Childhood Education*

Lesson 10

The Play Years: Psychosocial Development

Preview

Lesson 10 explores the ways in which young children begin to relate to others in an ever-widening social environment. The lesson begins where social understanding begins, with the emergence of the sense of self. With their increasing social awareness, children become more concerned with how others evaluate them and better able to regulate their emotions.

Next, the lesson explores the origins of helpful, cooperative behaviors in young children, as well as aggression and other hurtful behaviors. These social skills reflect many influences, including the quality of early attachments and learning from playmates through various types of play, as well as from television.

The lesson also describes the increasing complexity of children's interactions with others, paying special attention to the different styles of parenting and how factors such as the cultural, ethnic, and community contexts influence parenting.

The lesson concludes with a description of children's emerging awareness of male-female differences and gender identity. Five major theories of gender-role development are considered.

As you complete this lesson, consider the psychosocial development of one or more preschoolers you know. Consider their self-understanding—what do they think and feel about themselves? How do they interact with adults and other children? What sort of play activities do they engage in, and how might this affect their development? How good are they at controlling their own emotions and behavior? Finally, consider the relationship these children have with their parents. How do the parents support and guide their kids, and how to they handle discipline and punishment?

Prior Telecourse Knowledge that Will Be Used in this Lesson

- This lesson will return to Erik Erikson's theory (introduced in Lesson 1/Chapter 2) that specifies eight stages of psychosocial development, each of which is characterized by a particular challenge, or developmental crisis, which is central to that stage of life and must be resolved:
    1. Trust vs. Mistrust (birth to 1 year)
    2. Autonomy vs. Shame and Doubt (1 to 3 years)
    3. **Initiative vs. Guilt (3 to 6 years) ← The Play Years**
    4. Industry vs. Inferiority (7 to 11 years)
    5. Identity vs. Role Confusion (adolescence)
    6. Intimacy vs. Isolation (adulthood)
    7. Generativity vs. Stagnation (adulthood)
    8. Integrity vs. Despair (adulthood)
- This lesson will use the concept of theory of mind in its discussion of social awareness and the role of play during this period of development. Recall that theory of mind refers to a person's understanding of human mental processes, including the thoughts, feelings, and motivations of others.
- Five major developmental theories (from Lesson 1/Chapter 2) will be used to help explain gender-role development during the play years. Recall that:
    1. Freud's theory specifies stages of psychosexual development, during which the child battles unconscious, biological impulses.
    2. Learning theory emphasizes the effect of conditioning, as the child responds to stimuli, reinforcement, and modeling in his or her immediate environment.
    3. Cognitive theory emphasizes how the child's intellectual processes and thinking affect his or her beliefs and actions.
    4. Sociocultural theory reminds us that development is embedded in a rich cultural context, and is often influenced by the guidance of parents and mentors.
    5. Epigenetic theory emphasizes the interaction of biological and environmental forces that affect each person.

Learning Objectives

Use this information to guide your reading, viewing, thinking, and studying. After successfully completing this lesson, you should be able to:

1. Discuss Erikson's ideas on the initiative vs. guilt stage of development and describe how a child's emerging self-concept and social awareness is influenced by this stage.

2. Discuss the importance of developing a positive self-esteem during the play years and note the connection between guilt and shame and intrinsic and extrinsic motivation.
3. Define emotional regulation and discuss how it is linked to the ability to internalize and externalize problems.
4. Describe prosocial and antisocial behavior, offer examples, and discuss how these two types of behavior could relate to rough-and-tumble and sociodramatic play.
5. Describe the different forms of aggression demonstrated by young children, and discuss the role of television in encouraging these and other maladaptive behaviors.
6. Discuss the pros and cons of physical punishment, and describe the most effective methods for disciplining a child.
7. Compare the three classic styles of parenting, and discuss the factors that might account for variations in parenting style.
8. Distinguish between sex differences and gender differences, and describe the developmental progression of gender awareness in young children.
9. Summarize five theories of gender-role development during the play years, noting important contributions of each.
10. Define empathy and antipathy, and discuss how these feelings could relate to prosocial and antisocial behavior.

Read Chapter 6, "Early Childhood: Psychosocial Development," pages 197–227.

View the video for Lesson 10, "Playing and Socializing."

Segment 1: *Social Awareness*

Segment 2: *Emotional Regulation*

Segment 3: *Parenting Styles*

Summary

During the preschool years, a child's self-confidence, social skills, and social roles become more fully developed. This growth coincides with the child's increased capacity for communication, imagination, and understanding of his or her social context. Much of this development occurs through play activities.

Play provides crucial experiences not only for motor and cognitive development but also for self-understanding and social interaction. This growth is first apparent in mastery play, as children repeatedly practice a skill until they are proficient at it. Other important types of play include **rough-and-tumble play**, in which children mimic aggression but actually have no intent to harm, and **sociodramatic play**, in which children act out various roles and themes in stories of their own creation.

This exploration through play enables children to test their ability to convince others of their ideas and examine personal concerns in a nonthreatening manner.

In Erik Erikson's theory, the crisis of the play years is **initiative versus guilt**. The child is turning away from an exclusive attachment to parents and moving toward membership in the larger culture. A key factor in this developmental progression is learning **emotional regulation**—a key aspect of the child's developing emotional intelligence. Because of brain maturation, children gain a much greater ability to direct or modify their feelings, particularly feelings of fear, frustration, and anger.

Some of the emotions that mature during the preschool years lead to **prosocial behaviors** such as sharing and cooperating, which are performed to benefit other people; for some children, however, **antisocial behaviors** such as hitting or insulting may also emerge. Antisocial behaviors are those that are intended to hurt someone else. Developmental psychologists differentiate among four types of aggression: **instrumental aggression**, **reactive aggression**, **relational aggression**, and **bullying aggression**.

The three classic styles of parenting include **authoritarian** parents, whose word is law and who often show little affection or nurturance; **permissive** parents, who make few demands on their children; and **authoritative** parents, who set limits and enforce rules but do so more democratically by listening to their children's ideas and being willing to make compromises. Among the reasons for parenting variations are culture, religion, ethnicity, and the family's economic well-being. Family size also affects parenting patterns, with large families easier to manage via authoritarian parenting.

Even at age 2, children know whether they are boys or girls and apply gender labels consistently. Each of the major developmental theories has a somewhat different explanation for gender differences. Psychoanalytic theorists focus on fears and fantasies that motivate children to initially adore their opposite-sex parent and then later identify with their same-sex parent. Learning theorists maintain that gender roles are instilled because parents and society provide models and reinforcement for appropriate gender-role behavior and punishment for inappropriate behavior. In explaining gender identity and gender-role development, cognitive theorists focus on children's growing understanding of male-female differences. Sociocultural theorists emphasize the influence of cultural differences, and epigenetic systems theorists point out the biological tendencies that influence the child's brain patterns and behavior.

Review all reading assignments for this lesson.

As assigned by your instructor, complete the optional online component for this lesson.

Key Terms

Using your own words, write a brief definition or explanation of each of the following terms on a separate piece of paper.

1. emotional regulation
2. initiative versus guilt
3. self-esteem
4. self-concept
5. intrinsic motivation
6. extrinsic motivation
7. psychopathology
8. externalizing problems
9. internalizing problems
10. rough-and-tumble play
11. sociodramatic play
12. authoritarian parenting
13. permissive parenting
14. authoritative parenting
15. neglectful/uninvolved parenting
16. empathy
17. antipathy
18. prosocial behavior
19. antisocial behavior
20. instrumental aggression
21. reactive aggression
22. relational aggression
23. bullying aggression
24. psychological control
25. time-out
26. sex differences
27. gender differences
28. phallic stage
29. Oedipus complex
30. superego
31. Electra complex
32. identification
33. gender schema
34. androgyny

Practice Questions I

Multiple-Choice Questions

1. Preschool children have a clear (but not necessarily accurate) concept of self. Typically, the preschooler believes that she or he
   a. owns all objects in sight.
   b. is great at almost everything.
   c. is much less competent than peers and older children.
   d. is more powerful than her or his parents.

2. According to Freud, the third stage of psychosexual development, during which the penis is the focus of psychological concern and pleasure, is the
   a. oral stage.
   b. anal stage.
   c. phallic stage.
   d. latency period.

3. Because it helps children rehearse social roles, work out fears and fantasies, and learn cooperation, an important form of social play is
   a. sociodramatic play.
   b. mastery play.
   c. rough-and-tumble play.
   d. sensorimotor play.

4. The three basic patterns of parenting described by Diana Baumrind are
   a. hostile, loving, and harsh.
   b. authoritarian, permissive, and authoritative.
   c. positive, negative, and punishing.
   d. indulgent, neglecting, and traditional.

5. Authoritative parents are receptive and loving, but they also normally
   a. set limits and enforce rules.
   b. have difficulty communicating.
   c. withhold praise and affection.
   d. encourage aggressive behavior.

6. Acting out emotions in an impulsive, angry way may be indicative of
   a. externalizing problems.
   b. internalizing problems.
   c. neuronal switch.
   d. a developmental disorder.

7. According to Erikson, during the play years, a child's self-concept is defined largely by his or her
   a. expanding range of skills and competencies.
   b. physical appearance.
   c. gender.
   d. relationship with family members.

8. Behaviorists believe that virtually all gender distinctions in the preschool child are a product of ongoing
   a. identification.
   b. reinforcement and punishment.
   c. initiative.
   d. theory of mind.

9. Children apply gender labels, and have definite ideas about how boys and girls behave, as early as age
   a. 3.
   b. 4.
   c. 5.
   d. 7.

10. In chaotic and dangerous environments, _____________ parenting may be most beneficial to children.
    a. authoritative
    b. authoritarian
    c. traditional
    d. permissive

11. Six-year-old Leonardo has superior verbal ability rivaling that of most girls his age. Dr. Laurent believes that although his sex is predisposed to slower language development, Leonardo's upbringing in a linguistically rich home enhanced his biological capabilities. Dr. Laurent is evidently a proponent of
    a. cognitive theory.
    b. gender-schema theory.
    c. sociocultural theory.
    d. modern systems theory.

12. When a child develops an imaginary companion, he or she is thought to be exhibiting
    a. intrinsic motivation.
    b. extrinsic motivation.
    c. psychopathology.
    d. identification.

True or False Items

Write T (for true) or F (for false) on the line in front of each statement.

13. _____ According to Diana Baumrind, only authoritarian parents make maturity demands on their children.

14. _____ Children of authoritative parents tend to be successful, happy with themselves, and generous with others.

15. _____ True sex differences are more apparent in childhood than in adulthood.

16. _____ Spanking is associated with higher rates of aggression toward peers.

17. _____ Many gender differences are genetically based.

18. _____ Children from feminist or nontraditional homes seldom have stereotypic ideas about feminine and masculine roles.

19. _____ Developmentalists do not agree about how children acquire gender roles.

20. _____ Identification was defined by Freud as a defense mechanism in which people identify with others who may be stronger and more powerful than they.

21. _____ Intrinsic motivation is on display when someone does something to gain praise from someone else.

Practice Questions II

Multiple-Choice Questions

1. Children of permissive parents are most likely to lack
   a. social skills.
   b. self-control.
   c. initiative and guilt.
   d. care and concern.

2. Children learn reciprocity, nurturance, and cooperation most readily from their interaction with
   a. their mothers.
   b. their fathers.
   c. friends.
   d. others of the same sex.

3. The neglectful/uninvolved parent
   a. is sometimes mistaken for a permissive parent.
   b. does not usually use physical punishment.
   c. seems not to care what their children are doing.
   d. personifies all of the above.

4. Which of the following best summarizes the current view of developmentalists regarding gender differences?
   a. Some gender differences are biological in origin.
   b. Most gender differences are biological in origin.
   c. Nearly all gender differences are cultural in origin.
   d. There is no consensus among developmentalists regarding the origin of gender differences.

5. According to Freud, a young boy's jealousy of his father's relationship with his mother, and the guilt feelings that result, are part of the
   a. Electra complex.
   b. Oedipus complex.
   c. phallic complex.
   d. penis envy complex.

6. The style of parenting in which the parents make few demands on children, the discipline is lax, and the parents are nurturant and accepting is
   a. authoritarian.
   b. authoritative.
   c. permissive.
   d. rejecting-neglecting.

7. Cooperating with a playmate is to ________________ as insulting a playmate is to ________________.
   a. antisocial behavior; prosocial behavior
   b. prosocial behavior; antisocial behavior
   c. emotional regulation; antisocial behavior
   d. prosocial behavior; emotional regulation

8. Young children are most likely to witness acts of extreme violence
   a. on television.
   b. in their neighborhoods.
   c. while playing with friends.
   d. under none of the above circumstances.

9. Which of the following theories advocates the development of gender identification as a means of avoiding guilt over feelings for the opposite-sex parent?

   a. learning

   b. sociocultural

   c. psychoanalytic

   d. social learning

10. The preschooler's readiness to learn new tasks and play activities reflects his or her

    a. emerging competency and self-awareness.

    b. theory of mind.

    c. relationship with parents.

    d. growing identification with others.

11. Emotional regulation is in part related to maturation of a specific portion of the brain known as the

    a. prefrontal cortex.

    b. parietal cortex.

    c. temporal lobe.

    d. occipital lobe.

12. In which style of parenting is the parents' word law and misbehavior strictly punished?

    a. permissive

    b. authoritative

    c. authoritarian

    d. traditional

13. Erikson noted that preschoolers eagerly begin many new activities, but are vulnerable to criticism and feelings of failure; they experience the crisis of

    a. identity versus role confusion.

    b. initiative versus guilt.

    c. basic trust versus mistrust.

    d. efficacy versus helplessness.

14. Which of the following statements are true regarding feelings of antipathy toward other people?
    a. The child dislikes or even hates the other person.
    b. Antipathy can lead to antisocial behavior.
    c. Antipathy is the ability to understand the emotions of another person.
    d. a and b only

Matching Items

Match each theorist, term, or concept with its corresponding description or definition.

Theorists, Terms, and Concepts

15. __________	rough-and-tumble play	21. __________	Oedipus complex
16. __________	androgyny	22. __________	authoritative
17. __________	sociodramatic play	23. __________	authoritarian
18. __________	prosocial behavior	24. __________	identification
19. __________	antisocial behavior	25. __________	instrumental aggression
20. __________	Electra complex	26. __________	empathy

Descriptions or Definitions

a. aggressive behavior whose purpose is to obtain an object desired by another
b. Freudian theory that every daughter secretly wishes to replace her mother
c. parenting style associated with high maturity demands and low parent-child communication
d. an action performed for the benefit of another person without the expectation of reward
e. Freudian theory that every son secretly wishes to replace his father
f. parenting style associated with high maturity demands and high parent-child communication
g. two children wrestle without serious hostility
h. an action that is intended to harm someone else
i. two children act out roles in a story of their own creation
j. a defense mechanism through which children cope with their feelings of guilt during the phallic stage
k. a balance of traditional male and female characteristics in an individual
j. ability to understand the emotions of another person

Applying Your Knowledge

1. According to Freud, Yolanda eventually copes with the fear and anger she feels over her hatred of her mother and love of her father by
   a. identifying with her mother.
   b. copying her brother's behavior.
   c. adopting her father's moral code.
   d. competing with her brother for her father's attention.

2. A little girl who says she wants her mother to go on vacation so that she can marry her father is voicing a fantasy consistent with the ________________ described by Freud.
   a. Oedipus complex
   b. Electra complex
   c. theory of mind
   d. crisis of initiative versus guilt

3. According to Erikson, *before* the preschool years children are incapable of feeling guilt because
   a. guilt depends on a sense of self, which is not sufficiently established in toddlerhood.
   b. they do not yet understand that they are male or female for life.
   c. this emotion is unlikely to have been reinforced at such an early age.
   d. guilt is associated with the resolution of the Oedipus complex, which occurs later in life.

4. Parents who are strict and aloof are most likely to make their children
   a. cooperative and trusting.
   b. obedient but unhappy.
   c. violent.
   d. withdrawn and anxious.

5. When four-year-old Hai grabs for Tho's beanie baby, Tho slaps her hand away, displaying an example of
   a. bullying aggression.
   b. reactive aggression.
   c. instrumental aggression.
   d. relational aggression.

6. The belief that almost all sexual patterns are learned rather than inborn would find its strongest adherents among
   a. cognitive theorists.
   b. behaviorists.
   c. psychoanalytic theorists.
   d. epigenetic systems theorists.

7. In explaining the origins of gender distinctions, Dr. Christie notes that a child's cognitive concept or general belief about sex differences is based on his or her observation or experiences. Dr. Christie is evidently a proponent of
   a. gender-schema theory.
   b. sociocultural theory.
   c. epigenetic systems theory.
   d. psychoanalytic theory.

8. Positive self-esteem is exhibited when a child
   a. exhibits eagerness to try new things.
   b. gives herself or himself positive evaluations on tasks.
   c. speaks proudly of her or his accomplishments.
   d. all of the above.

9. Which of the following is an example of antisocial behavior?
   a. when a child is helpful and kind
   b. when a child impulsively retaliates for another child's action
   c. when a child deliberately hurts another person, usually without provocation
   d. none of the above

Answer Key

Key Terms

1. Emotional regulation is the ability to manage and modify one's feelings, particularly feelings of fear, frustration, and anger. (p. 197; video lesson, segment 2; objective 3)
2. According to Erikson, the crisis of the preschool years is initiative versus guilt. In this crisis, young children eagerly take on new tasks and play activities and feel guilty when their efforts result in failure or criticism. (p. 198; objective 1)
3. Self-esteem refers to how a child feels about himself or herself; it has to do with how lovable the child feels. (p. 198; video lesson, segment 2; objective 2)

4. Self-concept refers to what a child thinks about him- or herself; it is the child's answer to the question, "who am I?" (p. 198; video lesson, segment 2; objective 1)
5. Intrinsic motivation is the drive to do something because of the pleasure the activity brings. A child who plays with blocks because they simply enjoy doing so is intrinsically motivated. (p. 200; objective 2)
6. When one is motivated to do something because of the promise of some external reward, the individual is acting out of extrinsic motivation. (p. 200; objective 2)
7. An illness or disorder of the mind is referred to as psychopathology. (p. 201; objective 3)
8. Externalizing problems are outwardly expressed emotional problems such as injuring others, destroying property, and defying authority. (p. 201; objective 3)
9. Children who have internalizing problems tend to be fearful and withdrawn as a consequence of their tendencies to keep their emotions bottled up inside themselves. (p. 201; objective 3)
10. Rough-and-tumble play is physical play that often mimics aggression, but involves no intent to harm. (p. 207; video lesson, segment 1; objective 4)
11. In sociodramatic play, children act out roles and themes in stories of their own creation, allowing them to examine personal concerns in a nonthreatening manner. (p. 207; video lesson, segment 1; objective 4)
12. Authoritarian parenting is a style of child rearing in which the parents show little affection or nurturance for their children; maturity demands are high and parent-child communication is low. (p. 210; video lesson, segment 3; objective 7)
13. Permissive parenting is a style of parenting in which the parents make few demands on their children, yet are nurturant and accepting, and communicate well with their children. (p. 210; video lesson, segment 3; objective 7)
14. Authoritative parenting is a style of parenting in which the parents set limits and enforce rules but do so more democratically than do authoritarian parents. (p. 210; video lesson, segment 3; objective 7)

    Memory aid: Authoritative parents act as authorities do on a subject—by discussing and explaining why certain family rules are in place.
15. Neglectful/uninvolved parenting is a style of parenting in which the parents are indifferent toward their children and unaware of what is going on in their children's lives. (p. 210; objective 7)
16. Empathy is a person's ability to understand the emotions of another person. (p. 215; objective 10)
17. Antipathy is referred to as intense dislike or hated of others. (p. 215; objective 10)

18. Prosocial behavior is an action, such as cooperating or sharing, which is performed to benefit another person without the expectation of reward. (p. 215; video lesson, segment 2; objectives 4 & 10)

19. Antisocial behavior is an action, such as hitting or insulting, which is intended to hurt another person. (p. 215; video lesson, segment 2; objectives 4 & 10)

20. Instrumental aggression is an action whose purpose is to obtain or retain an object desired by another. (p. 215; objective 5)

21. Reactive aggression is aggressive behavior that is an angry retaliation for some intentional or incidental act by another person. (p. 215; objective 5)

    Memory aid: Instrumental aggression is behavior that is instrumental in allowing a child to retain a favorite toy. Reactive aggression is a reaction to another child's behavior.

22. Relational aggression involves nonphysical acts, such as insults or social rejection, aimed at harming the social connection between the victim and other people. (p. 215; objective 5)

23. An unprovoked attack on another child is an example of bullying aggression. (p. 215; objective 5)

    Memory aid: Someone who is an authoritarian demands unquestioning obedience and acts in a dictatorial way.

24. Psychological control is exerted by parents when the discipline is meant to provoke a sense of guilt or a fear of the parents' withdrawal of love. (p. 218; objective 6)

25. A time-out is a disciplinary technique in which the child is required to stop all activity and sit in a corner or stay indoors for a few minutes. (p. 218; objective 6)

26. Sex differences are biological differences between females and males. (p. 221; objective 8)

27. Gender differences are cultural differences in the roles and behavior of males and females. (p. 221; objective 8)

28. In psychoanalytic theory, the phallic stage is the third stage of psychosexual development, in which the penis becomes the focus of psychological concerns and physiological pleasure. (p. 222; objective 9)

29. According to Freud, boys in the phallic stage of psychosexual development develop a collection of feelings, known as the Oedipus complex, that center on sexual attraction to the mother and resentment of the father. (p. 222; objective 9)

30. In psychoanalytic theory, the superego is the self-critical and judgmental part of personality that internalizes the moral standards set by parents and society. (p. 222; objective 9)

31. According to Freud, girls in the phallic stage may develop a collection of feelings, known as the Electra complex, that center on sexual attraction to the father and resentment of the mother. (p. 222; objective 9)

32. In Freud's theory, identification is the defense mechanism through which a person takes on the role and attitudes of a person more powerful than himself or herself. (p. 222; objective 9)
33. A gender schema is a child's cognitive understanding of what it means to be a boy or a girl. (p. 224; objective 9)
34. Androgyny is a balance of traditionally female and male gender characteristics in a person. (p. 225; objective 9)

Practice Questions I

Multiple-Choice Questions

1. b. is the correct answer. (pp. 198–199; video lesson, segment 2; objective 1)
2. c. is the correct answer. (p. 222; objective 9)

   a. & b. are incorrect. In Freud's theory, the oral and anal stages are associated with infant and early childhood development, respectively.

   d. is incorrect. In Freud's theory, the latency period is associated with development during the school years.
3. a. is the correct answer. (pp. 207–209; video lesson, segment 1; objective 4)

   b. is incorrect. Mastery play is play that helps children develop new physical and intellectual skills.

   c. is incorrect. Rough-and-tumble play is physical play that mimics aggression.

   d. is incorrect. Sensorimotor play captures the pleasures of using the senses and motor skills.
4. b. is the correct answer. (pp. 209–212; video lesson, segment 3; objective 7)

   d. is incorrect. Traditional is a variation of the basic styles uncovered by later research. Indulgent and neglecting are not discussed in the textbook.
5. a. is the correct answer. (p. 210; video lesson, segment 3; objective 7)

   b. & c. are incorrect. Authoritative parents communicate very well and are quite affectionate.

   d. is incorrect. This is not typical of authoritative parents.
6. a. is the correct answer (pp. 201–202; objective 3)
7. a. is the correct answer. (pp. 198–199; objective 1)
8. b. is the correct answer. (p. 223; objective 9)

   a. is incorrect. This is the focus of Freud's phallic stage.

   c. is incorrect. This is the focus of Erikson's psychosocial theory.

   d. is incorrect. This is the focus of cognitive theorists.
9. a. is the correct answer. (p. 221; objective 8)
10. b. is the correct answer. (p. 210; objective 7)

11. d. is the correct answer. In accounting for Leonardo's verbal ability, Dr. Laurent alludes to both biology and social systems factors, a dead-giveaway for systems theory. (p. 225; objective 9)

    a., b., & c. are incorrect. These theories do not address biological or genetic influences on development.

12. a. is the correct answer. (p. 200; objective 2)

True or False Items

13. F All parents make some maturity demands on their children; maturity demands are high in both the authoritarian and authoritative parenting styles. (pp. 209–212; video lesson, segment 3; objective 7)
14. T (p. 211; video lesson, segment 3; objective 7)
15. F Just the opposite is true. (p. 221; objective 8)
16. T (p. 218; objective 6)
17. T (pp. 221–226; objectives 8 & 9)
18. F Children raised in feminist or nontraditional homes often surprise their parents by expressing stereotypic ideas about feminine and masculine roles. (p. 221; objective 8)
19. T (pp. 221–222; objective 9)
20. T (p. 222; objective 9)
21. F (p. 200; objective 2)

Practice Questions II

Multiple-Choice Questions

1. b. is the correct answer. (p. 211; video lesson, segment 3; objective 7)
2. c. is the correct answer. (pp. 204–205; video lesson, segment 1; objective 4)

    a. & b. are incorrect. Friends often provide better instruction than adults because they are likely to guide, challenge, and encourage a child's social interactions more frequently and intimately.

    d. is incorrect.

3. d. is the correct answer. (p. 210; objective 7)
4. a. is the correct answer. Recent research has found that the sexes are different in part because of subtle differences in brain development. (pp. 221–222, 226–227; objectives 8 & 9)
5. b. is the correct answer. (p. 222; objective 9)

    a. & d. are incorrect. These are Freud's versions of phallic-stage development in little girls.

    c. is incorrect. There is no such thing as the "phallic complex."

6. c. is the correct answer. (p. 210; video lesson, segment 3; objective 7)

    a. & b. are incorrect. Both authoritarian and authoritative parents make high demands on their children.

d. is incorrect. Rejecting-neglecting parents are quite cold and unengaged.

7. b. is the correct answer. (p. 215; video lesson, segment 2; objective 4)
8. a. is the correct answer (pp. 212–213; objective 5)
9. c. is the correct answer. (pp. 222–223; objective 9)

   a. & d. are incorrect. Learning and social learning theories emphasize that children learn about gender by rewards and punishments and by observing others.

   b. is incorrect. Sociocultural theory focuses on the impact of the environment on gender identification.

10. a. is the correct answer. (pp. 198–199; video lesson, segment 1; objective 1)

    b. is incorrect. This viewpoint is associated only with cognitive theory.

    c. is incorrect. Although parent-child relationships are important to social development, they do not determine readiness.

    d. is incorrect. Identification is a Freudian defense mechanism.

11. a. is the correct answer. (p. 197; objective 3)
12. c. is the correct answer. (p. 210; video lesson, segment 3; objective 7)
13. b. is the correct answer. (p. 198; objective 1)

    a. & c. are incorrect. According to Erikson, these are the crises of adolescence and infancy, respectively.

    d. is incorrect. This is not a crisis described by Erikson.

14. d. is the correct answer. (p. 215; objective 10)

Matching Items

15. g (p. 207; video lesson, segment 1; objective 4)
16. k (p. 225; objective 9)
17. i (p. 207; video lesson, segment 1; objective 4)
18. d (p. 215; video lesson, segment 2; objectives 4 & 10)
19. h (p. 215; video lesson, segment 2; objectives 4 & 10)
20. b (p. 222; objective 9)
21. e (p. 222; objective 9)
22. f (pp. 210–211; video lesson, segment 3; objective 7)
23. c (pp. 210–211; video lesson, segment 3; objective 7)
24. j (p. 222; objective 9)
25. a (p. 215; objective 5)
26. l (p. 215; objective 10)

Applying Your Knowledge

1. a. is the correct answer. (p. 222; objective 9)
2. b. is the correct answer. (p. 222; objective 9)

   a. is incorrect. According to Freud, the Oedipus complex refers to the male's sexual feelings toward his mother and resentment toward his father.

   c. & d. are incorrect. These are concepts introduced by cognitive theorists and Erik Erikson, respectively.
3. a. is the correct answer. (p. 198; objective 1)

   b. is incorrect. Erikson did not equate gender constancy with the emergence of guilt.

   c. & d. are incorrect. These reflect the viewpoints of learning theory and Freud, respectively.
4. b. is the correct answer. (pp. 210–211; video lesson, segment 3; objective 7)
5. c. is the correct answer. The purpose of Tho's action is clearly to retain the beanie baby, rather than to retaliate (b, which is incorrect), or bully Hai (a, which is incorrect). (p. 215; objective 5)

   d. is incorrect. Relational aggression takes the form of a verbal insult.
6. b. is the correct answer. (pp. 223–224; objective 9)
7. b. is the correct answer. (p. 224; objective 9)
8. d. is the correct answer. (p. 198; video lesson, segment 2; objective 2)
9. c. is the correct answer. (p. 215; video lesson, segment 2; objectives 4 & 10)

Lesson Review

Lesson 10

The Play Years
Psychosocial Development

Please Note: Use this matrix to guide your study and achieve the learning objectives of this lesson. It will also help you to view the video, which defines and demonstrates important concepts and skills as they relate to everyday life.

Learning Objective	Textbook	Telecourse Student Guide	Video Lesson
1. Discuss Erikson's ideas on the initiative vs guilt stage of development and describe how a child's emerging self-concept and social awareness is influenced by this stage.	pp. 198–199	Key Terms: 2, 4; Practice Questions I: 1, 7; Practice Questions II: 10, 13; Applying Your Knowledge: 3.	Segment 1: *Social Awareness*; Segment 2: *Emotional Regulation*
2. Discuss the importance of developing a positive self-esteem during the play years and note the connection between guilt and shame and intrinsic and extrinsic motivation.	pp. 198–201	Key Terms: 3, 5, 6; Practice Questions I: 12, 21; Applying Your Knowledge: 8.	Segment 2: *Emotional Regulation*
3. Define emotional regulation and discuss how it is linked to the ability to internalize and externalize problems.	pp. 197, 201–204	Key Terms: 1, 7, 8, 9; Practice Questions I: 6; Practice Questions II: 11.	Segment 2: *Emotional Regulation*
4. Describe prosocial and antisocial behavior, offer examples, and discuss how these two types of behaviors could relate to rough-and-tumble and sociodramatic play.	pp. 204–209, 215	Key Terms: 10, 11, 18, 19; Practice Questions I: 3; Practice Questions II: 2, 7, 15, 17, 18, 19; Applying Your Knowledge: 9.	Segment 1: *Social Awareness*; Segment 2: *Emotional Regulation*
5. Describe the different forms of aggression demonstrated by young children, and discuss the role of television in encouraging these and other maladaptive behaviors.	pp. 212–216	Key Terms: 20, 21, 22, 23; Practice Questions II: 8, 25; Applying Your Knowledge: 5.	Segment 2: *Emotional Regulation*
6. Discuss the pros and cons of physical punishment, and describe the most effective methods for disciplining a child.	pp. 216–220	Key Terms: 24, 25; Practice Questions I: 16.	

Learning Objective	Textbook	Telecourse Student Guide	Video Lesson
7. Compare the three classic styles of parenting, and discuss the factors that might account for variations in parenting style.	pp. 209–210	Key Terms: 12, 13, 14, 15; Practice Questions I: 4, 5, 10, 13, 14; Practice Questions II: 1, 3, 6, 12, 22, 23; Applying Your Knowledge: 4.	Segment 3: *Parenting Styles*
8. Distinguish between sex differences and gender differences, and describe the developmental progression of gender awareness in young children.	p. 221	Key Terms: 26, 27; Practice Questions I: 9, 15, 17, 18; Practice Questions II: 4.	
9. Summarize five theories of gender-role development during the play years, noting important contributions of each.	pp. 221–226	Key Terms: 28, 29, 30, 31, 32, 33, 34; Practice Questions I: 2, 8, 11, 17, 19, 20; Practice Questions II: 4, 5, 9, 16, 20, 21, 24; Applying Your Knowledge: 1, 2, 6, 7.	
10. Define empathy and antipathy, and discuss how these feelings could relate to prosocial and antisocial behavior.	pp. 215–216	Key Terms: 16, 17, 18, 19; Practice Questions II: 14, 18, 19, 26; Applying Your Knowledge: 9.	

Lesson 11

The School Years: Biosocial Development

Preview

This lesson introduces biosocial development in middle childhood, the years from age 6 or 7 to age 11. Changes in physical size and shape are described first, and the growing problem of childhood obesity is addressed. The discussion then turns to the continuing development of motor skills during the school years. While growth tends to slow down during this period, children become much better at controlling their bodies.

During the school years, children often take tests. This lesson will discuss different types of tests, including **IQ tests** designed to measure intelligence, and why their use is controversial. As you will find, intelligence is both dynamic and multidimensional, so it is difficult to measure with a single score.

One reason for children to be tested at this age is to identify potential problems or disorders. The final section of this lesson examines the experiences of **children with special needs**, such as those diagnosed with **autism** or **attention-deficit/hyperactivity disorder (ADHD)**. The causes of and treatments for these problems are discussed, with emphasis placed on insights arising from the new **developmental psychopathology** perspective. This perspective makes it clear that "abnormality" is really quite normal in development, and the manifestations of any special childhood problem will change as the child grows older.

As you complete this lesson, think about any children you know in this age range. Consider their height and weight relative to other children of the same age (and younger). Are any of these children overweight? If so, speculate on the possible causes. Also, observe the motor skills of these children—how does their coordination compare with younger and older children? Interview these children or their parents about any tests they've taken recently. Ask them to describe the experience. Have any of these kids taken an IQ test? If so, what was the result? Would you characterize this child as being "intelligent?" Why or why not? Do any of these children have a special problem or disorder, such as autism or ADHD? If so, how are they being treated? What kind of special services or treatment do they receive at school?

Prior Telecourse Knowledge that Will Be Used in this Lesson

- Biosocial development during infancy and toddlerhood (Lesson 5), as well as that during early childhood (Lesson 8), will be referred to as we discuss variations in physique and the development of motor skills during middle childhood.
- This lesson will return to the concept of *self-esteem* (Lesson 10), how a child feels about him- or herself. A child's perception of his or her biological development (especially relative to peers) can affect self-evaluation in both positive and negative ways.

Learning Objectives

Use this information to guide your reading, viewing, thinking, and studying. After successfully completing this lesson, you should be able to:

1. Describe physical growth and health during middle childhood, noting variations and their causes, and discuss the importance of physical activity to children of this age.
2. Describe the problem of childhood obesity, outline its major causes and best approaches for treatment, and discuss the potential effects of obesity on a child's physical and psychological health.
3. Describe the causes of and treatments for childhood asthma, and discuss its potential impact on development.
4. Describe brain development during the school years, focusing on how it relates to motor-skill and cognitive development.
5. Explain how achievement and aptitude tests are used in evaluating individual differences in cognitive growth, and discuss why use of such tests is controversial.
6. Describe Sternberg's and Gardner's theories of multiple intelligences, and explain the significance of these theories.
7. Describe the developmental psychopathology perspective, and discuss its value in treating children with special needs.
8. Identify the symptoms of autism and discuss its possible causes.
9. Discuss the characteristics and possible causes of learning disabilities.
10. Describe the symptoms and possible causes of attention-deficit/hyperactivity disorder (ADHD) and discuss the types of treatment available for children with this disorder.
11. Summarize techniques that have been tried in efforts to educate children with special needs.

Read Chapter 7, "Middle Childhood: Body and Mind," pages 233–239, 242–244, 257–260, and 262–269.

View the video for Lesson 11, "The Golden Years of Childhood."

Segment 1: *Physical Growth*

Segment 2: *Motor-Skill Development*

Segment 3: *Special Needs*

Summary

For most boys and girls, the years of middle childhood are a time when biosocial development is smooth and uneventful. Body maturation coupled with sufficient practice enables school-age children to master many motor skills. Although malnutrition limits the growth of children in some regions of the world, most of the variations in physical development in developed countries are due to heredity. Diet does exert its influence, however, by interacting with heredity, activity level, and other factors. In some cases, the result is obesity—a growing problem in North American children during the school years.

The fact that growth is relatively slow in middle childhood may be part of the reason children become so much more skilled at controlling their bodies. With few exceptions, boys and girls are just about equal in physical abilities during the school years. Boys have somewhat greater upper-arm strength, whereas girls have greater overall flexibility. Expertise in specific skills depends primarily on motivation, guidance, and many hours of practice.

Motor habits that rely on coordinating both sides of the body improve because the corpus callosum between the brain's hemispheres continues to mature. In addition, rough-and-tumble play may help boys overcome their tendencies toward hyperactivity and learning disabilities because it helps with regulation in the frontal lobes of the brain. Motor-skill development is also influenced by culture, national policies, and genetic endowment. Children are said to have a **learning disability** when their difficulty with a particular skill is in surprising contrast with their overall intelligence level. One of the most puzzling problems in childhood is **ADHD (attention-deficit/hyperactivity disorder)**, a behavior problem characterized by excessive activity, an inability to concentrate, and impulsive, sometimes aggressive behavior. ADHD may arise from several factors, including genetic differences, teratogens, and family and environmental influences.

Review all reading assignments for this lesson.

As assigned by your instructor, complete the optional online component for this lesson.

Key Terms

Using your own words, write a brief definition or explanation of each of the following terms on a separate piece of paper.

1. middle childhood
2. asthma
3. body mass index (BMI)
4. overweight
5. obesity
6. selective attention
7. automatization
8. reaction time
9. aptitude
10. IQ tests
11. achievement tests
12. Wechsler Intelligence Scale for Children (WISC)
13. Flynn effect
14. mental retardation
15. children with special needs
16. developmental psychopathology
17. DSM-IV-TR
18. ADHD (attention-deficit/hyperactivity disorder)
19. comorbidity
20. learning disability
21. dyslexia
22. autistic spectrum disorder
23. autism
24. Asperger syndrome
25. dyscalcula
26. mainstreaming

Practice Questions I

Multiple-Choice Questions

1. As children move into middle childhood,
   a. the rate of accidental death increases.
   b. sexual urges intensify.
   c. the rate of weight gain increases.
   d. biological growth slows and steadies.

2. To help obese children, nutritionists usually recommend
   a. strenuous dieting to counteract early overfeeding.
   b. the use of amphetamines and other drugs.
   c. more exercise.
   d. no specific actions.

3. Dyslexia is a learning disability that affects the ability to
   a. do math.
   b. read.
   c. write.
   d. speak.

4. Childhood obesity that continues into adolescence and beyond creates an increased risk for
   a. low blood pressure.
   b. genetic malformation.
   c. muscle injury.
   d. low self-esteem.

5. One developmental psychopathology perspective is that
   a. diagnosis depends on a social context.
   b. emphasis should be on individual therapy.
   c. emphasis should beon the cognitive domain of development.
   d. there is concern with all of the above.

6. The time—usually measured in fractions of a second—it takes for a person to respond to a particular stimulus is called
   a. the interstimulus interval.
   b. reaction time.
   c. the stimulus-response interval.
   d. response latency.

7. The underlying problem in attention-deficit/hyperactivity disorder appears to be
   a. low overall intelligence.
   b. a neurological difficulty in paying attention.
   c. a learning disability in a specific academic skill.
   d. the existence of a conduct disorder.

8. Autistic children generally have severe deficiencies in all but which of the following?
   a. social skills
   b. imaginative play
   c. motor skills
   d. communication ability

9. Psychoactive drugs are most effective in treating attention-deficit/hyperactivity disorder when they are administered
   a. before the diagnosis becomes certain.
   b. for several years after the basic problem has abated.
   c. as part of the labeling process.
   d. with psychological support or therapy.

10. In the earliest aptitude tests, a child's score was calculated by dividing the child's ____________ age by the ____________ age to find the ____________ quotient.
    a. mental; chronological; intelligence
    b. chronological; mental; intelligence
    c. intelligence; chronological; mental
    d. intelligence; mental; chronological

11. Tests that measure a child's potential to learn a new subject are measuring
    a. aptitude.
    b. achievement.
    c. vocational skills.
    d. intelligence.

12. The ability to filter out distractions and concentrate on relevant details is called
    a. metacognition.
    b. information processing.
    c. selective attention.
    d. decentering.

True or False Items

Write T (for true) or F (for false) on the line in front of each statement.

13. _____ Most parents of obese children openly acknowledge that their child is obese.

14. _____ Childhood obesity usually does not correlate with adult obesity.

15. _____ Hours spent watching television and obesity rates in children have both increased during the past 30 to 50 years.

16. _____ The quick reaction time that is crucial in some sports can be readily achieved with practice.

17. _____ Despite the efforts of teachers and parents, most children with learning disabilities can expect their disabilities to persist and even worsen as they enter adulthood.

18. _____ The best way for children to lose weight is through strenuous dieting.

19. _____ Most learning disabilities are caused by a difficult birth or other early trauma to the child.

20. _____ Girls experience symptoms of ADHD more frequently than boys.

21. _____ The drugs sometimes given to children to reduce hyperactive behaviors have a reverse effect on adults.

Practice Questions II

Multiple-Choice Questions

1. During the years from age 6 to 11, the average child
   a. is neither too heavy nor too thin.
   b. gains about 12 pounds a year.
   c. has decreased lung capacity.
   d. is more likely to become obese than at any other period in the life span.

2. Among the factors that are known to contribute to obesity are activity level, quantity and types of food eaten, and
   a. participation in organized sports.
   b. parental occupation.
   c. solitary play.
   d. genetic propensity.

3. A specific learning disability that becomes apparent when a child experiences unusual difficulty in learning to read is
   a. dyslexia.
   b. dyscalcula.
   c. ADHD.
   d. ADHDA.

4. Problems in learning to write, read, and do math are collectively referred to as
   a. learning disabilities.
   b. attention-deficit/hyperactivity disorder.
   c. hyperactivity.
   d. dyscalcula.

5. A measure of obesity in which weight in kilograms is divided by the square of height in meters is the

   a. basal metabolic rate (BMR).

   b. body mass index (BMI).

   c. body fat index (BFI).

   d. basal fat ratio (BFR).

6. The most effective form of help for children with ADHD is

   a. medication.

   b. psychological therapy.

   c. environmental change.

   d. a combination of some or all of the above.

7. A key factor in reaction time is

   a. whether the child is male or female.

   b. brain maturation.

   c. whether the stimulus to be reacted to is an auditory or visual one.

   d. all of the above.

8. Which of the following is true of children with a diagnosed learning disability?

   a. They are, in most cases, average in intelligence.

   b. They often have a specific physical handicap, such as hearing loss.

   c. They often lack basic educational experiences.

   d. All of the above are true.

9. Whether a particular child is considered obese depends on

   a. the child's body type.

   b. the proportion of fat to muscle.

   c. cultural standards.

   d. all of the above.

10. Which approach to education may best meet the needs of children with learning disabilities in terms of both skill remediation and social interaction with other children?

    a. mainstreaming

    b. special education

    c. inclusion

    d. resource rooms

11. Asperger syndrome is a disorder in which
    a. body weight fluctuates dramatically over short periods of time.
    b. verbal skills seem normal, but social perceptions and skills are abnormal.
    c. an autistic child is extremely aggressive.
    d. a child of normal intelligence has difficulty in mastering a specific cognitive skill.

12. Which of the following is **NOT** considered to be a contributing factor of ADHD?
    a. genetic inheritance
    b. dietary sugar and caffeine
    c. prenatal damage
    d. postnatal damage

13. Aptitude and achievement testing are controversial because
    a. most tests are unreliable with respect to the individual scores they yield.
    b. test performance can be affected by many factors other than the child's intellectual potential or academic achievement.
    c. they often fail to identify serious learning problems.
    d. all of the above reasons.

14. Tests that measure what a child has already learned are called ____________________ tests.
    a. aptitude
    b. vocational
    c. achievement
    d. intelligence

15. Which of the following is **NOT** a type of intelligence identified in Robert Sternberg's theory?
    a. academic
    b. practical
    c. achievement
    d. creative

Matching Items

Match each term or concept with its corresponding description or definition.

Terms or Concepts

16. __________ dyslexia
17. __________ automatization
18. __________ autism
19. __________ learning disability
20. __________ asthma
21. __________ Flynn effect
22. __________ individual education plan (IEP)
23. __________ developmental psychopathology
24. __________ *Diagnostic and Statistical Manual of Mental Disorders* (DSM-IV-TR)
25. __________ mainstreaming
26. __________ attention-deficit/hyperactivity disorder

Descriptions or Definitions

a. an unexpected difficulty with one or more academic skills

b. the finding that IQ test scores have increased across the decades suggesting that intelligence is influenced by environmental factors.

c. the diagnostic guide of the American Psychiatric Association

d. legal document that specifies the educational goals for a child with special needs

e. system in which learning-disabled children are taught in general education classrooms

f. disorder characterized by the absence of a theory of mind

g. difficulty in reading

h. chronic inflammation of the airways

i. behavior problem involving difficulty in concentrating, as well as excitability and impulsivity

j. tasks performed repeatedly until the action becomes automatic

k. applies insights from studies of normal development to the study of childhood disorders

Applying Your Knowledge

1. According to developmentalists, the best game for a typical group of eight-year-olds would be
   a. football or baseball.
   b. basketball.
   c. one in which reaction time is not crucial.
   d. a game involving one-on-one competition.

2. Dr. Rutter, who believes that "we can learn more about an organism's normal functioning by studying its pathology and, likewise, more about its pathology by studying its normal condition," evidently is working from which of the following perspectives?
   a. clinical psychology
   b. developmental psychopathology
   c. behaviorism
   d. psychoanalysis

3. Nine-year-old John has difficulty concentrating on his class work for more than a few moments, repeatedly asks his teacher irrelevant questions, and is constantly disrupting the class with loud noises. If his difficulties persist, John is likely to be diagnosed as suffering from
   a. dyslexia.
   b. dyscalcula.
   c. autism.
   d. attention-deficit/hyperactivity disorder.

4. Ten-year-old Jonathan is inattentive, easily frustrated, and highly impulsive. Jonathan may be suffering from
   a. dyslexia.
   b. dyscalcula.
   c. conduct disorder.
   d. attention-deficit/hyperactivity disorder.

5. Because eleven-year-old Christopher is obese, he runs a greater risk of developing
   a. orthopedic problems.
   b. respiratory problems.
   c. psychological problems.
   d. all of the above.

6. Of the following individuals, who is likely to have the fastest reaction time?
   a. a seven-year-old
   b. a nine-year-old
   c. an eleven-year-old
   d. a four-year-old

7. In determining whether an eight-year-old has a learning disability, a teacher looks primarily for
   a. marked poor accomplishment in a particular area.
   b. the exclusion of other explanations.
   c. both a and b.
   d. none of the above.

8. Mary doesn't say "hello," "please," or "thank you" like other children do. However, she has an amazing memory for details about dinosaurs. Mary probably has
   a. attention-deficit/hyperactivity disorder (ADHD).
   b. Asperger syndrome.
   c. dyslexia.
   d. depression.

9. Danny has been diagnosed as having attention-deficit/hyperactivity disorder. Every day, his parents make sure that he takes the proper dose of Ritalin. His parents should
   a. continue this behavior until Danny is an adult.
   b. try different medications when Danny seems to be reverting to his normal overactive behavior.
   c. make sure that Danny also has psychotherapy.
   d. not worry about Danny's condition; he will outgrow it.

10. In concluding her presentation entitled "Facts and falsehoods regarding childhood obesity," Cheryl states that, ______________________ is not a common cause of childhood obesity.
    a. activity level
    b. cultural background
    c. overeating of high-fat foods
    d. a prenatal teratogen

11. Ayme was born in 1984. In 1992, she scored 125 on an intelligence test. Using the original formulation, what was Ayme's mental age when she took the test?
   a. 6
   b. 8
   c. 10
   d. 12

12. Howard Gardner and Robert Sternberg would probably be most critical of traditional aptitude and achievement test because they
   a. inadvertently reflect certain nonacademic competencies.
   b. do not reflect knowledge of cultural ideas.
   c. measure only a limited set of abilities.
   d. underestimate the intellectual potential of disadvantaged children.

Answer Key

Key Terms

1. Middle childhood is generally defined as the period from age 7 to 11. (p. 233; objective 1)
2. Asthma is a disorder in which the airways are chronically inflamed. (p. 234; objective 3)
3. Body mass index (BMI) is a measure of obesity in which a person's weight in kilograms is divided by his or her height squared in meters (p. 236; video lesson, segment 1; objective 2)
4. A person is overweight if they weigh 25–29 percent above the ideal for a person of the same age and height. (p. 236; objective 2)
5. A person is obese if they weigh 30 percent or more above the ideal for a person of the same age and height. (p. 236; objective 2)
6. Focusing one's attention on certain stimuli, while ignoring other stimuli, is referred to as selective attention. (p. 243; objective 4)
7. Automatization is the process by which thoughts and actions are repeated so often that they become almost automatic, requiring little or no conscious thought. (p. 243; objective 4)
8. Reaction time is the length of time it takes a person to respond to a particular stimulus. (p. 243; objective 4)
9. Aptitude refers to potential, what people are capable of, rather than actual accomplishment. (p. 257; objective 5)
10. IQ tests are special aptitude tests designed to measure a person's intelligence, hence the name IQ or intelligence quotient. (p. 257; objective 5)

11. Achievement tests are designed to measure how much a person has learned or achieved in a specific subject area. (p. 257; objective 5)
12. The Wechsler Intelligence Scale for Children (WISC) is an intelligence test created for children. It assesses many areas of knowledge, such as verbal skills, spatial reasoning, and general knowledge. (p. 258; objective 5)
13. The gradual increase in intelligence scores is referred to as the Flynn effect. This suggests that intelligence is influenced by environmental factors. (p. 258; objective 5)
14. Children whose IQ is 70 or below, and whose ability to adapt to daily life is far behind their peers, are considered to have mental retardation. (p. 258; objective 5)
15. A child with special needs requires particular physical, intellectual, or social accommodations in order to learn. (p. 262; video lesson, segment 3; objectives 7 & 11)
16. Developmental psychopathology is a new field that applies the insights from studies of normal development to the study and treatment of childhood disorders, and vice versa. (p. 262; video lesson, segment 3; objective 7)
17. DSM-IV-TR is the fourth edition, text revision, of the *Diagnostic and Statistical Manual of Mental Disorders*, developed by the American Psychiatric Association, the leading means of distinguishing various emotional and behavioral disorders. (p. 263; objective 7)
18. The attention-deficit/hyperactivity disorder (ADHD) is a behavior problem in which the individual has great difficulty concentrating, is often excessively excitable and impulsive, and is sometimes aggressive. (p. 263; video lesson, segment 3; objective 10)
19. Comorbidity occurs when an individual has two or more separate diseases or disorders at the same time. (p. 263; objective 10)
20. A learning disability is a difficulty in a particular cognitive skill that is not attributable to an overall intellectual slowness, a physical handicap, a severely stressful living condition, or a lack of basic education. (p. 265; video lesson, segment 3; objective 9)
21. Dyslexia is a learning disability in reading. (p. 265; video lesson, segment 3; objective 9)
22. Disorders characterized by poor social skills, unusual play patterns, and problems with communication are referred to as autistic spectrum disorder. (p. 265; objective 8)
23. Autism is a severe disturbance of early childhood characterized by inability or unwillingness to communicate, poor social skills, and diminished imagination. (p. 266; objective 8)
24. Asperger syndrome is a disorder in which a person has many symptoms of autism, despite having near normal verbal skills. (p. 266; objective 8)

25. Dyscalcula is a learning disability in math. (video lesson, segment 3; objective 9)
26. Mainstreaming is an educational approach in which children with special needs are included in regular classrooms. (video lesson, segment 3; objective 11)

Practice Questions I

Multiple-Choice Questions

1. d. is the correct answer. (pp. 233–234; video lesson, segment 1; objective 1)
2. c. is the correct answer. (pp. 236–237; video lesson, segment 1; objective 2)

   a. is incorrect. Strenuous dieting can be physically harmful and often makes children irritable, listless, and even sick—adding to the psychological problems of the obese child.

   b. is incorrect. The use of amphetamines to control weight is not recommended at any age.
3. b. is the correct answer. (p. 265; video lesson, segment 3; objective 9)

   a. is incorrect. This is dyscalcula.

   c. & d. are incorrect. The textbook does not give labels for learning disabilities in writing or speaking.
4. d. is the correct answer. (pp. 236–237; video lesson, segment 1; objective 2)
5. a. is the correct answer. (p. 263; video lesson, segment 3; objective 7)

   b. & c. are incorrect. Because of its contextual approach, developmental psychopathology emphasizes group therapy and all domains of development.
6. b. is the correct answer. (p. 243; objective 4)
7. b. is the correct answer. (pp. 263–264; video lesson, segment 3; objective 10)
8. c. is the correct answer. (pp. 265–267; objective 8)
9. d. is the correct answer. (pp. 264–265; video lesson, segment 3; objective 10)
10. a. is the correct answer. (pp. 257–258; objective 5)
11. a. is the correct answer. (p. 257; objective 5)

    b. is incorrect. Achievement tests measure what has already been learned.

    c. is incorrect. Vocational tests, which, as their name implies, measure what a person has learned about a particular trade, are achievement tests.

    d. in incorrect. Intelligence tests measure general aptitude, rather than aptitude for a specific subject.
12. c. is the correct answer. (p. 243; objective 4)

    a. is incorrect. This is the ability to evaluate a cognitive task and to monitor one's performance on it.

b. is incorrect. Information processing is a perspective on cognitive development that focuses on how the mind analyzes, stores, retrieves, and reasons about information.

d. is incorrect. Decentering, which refers to the school-age child's ability to consider more than one aspect of a problem simultaneously, is not discussed in this chapter.

True or False Items

13. F (pp. 236–237; video lesson, segment 1; objective 2)
14. F If obesity is established in middle childhood, it tends to continue into adulthood. (pp. 236–237; video lesson, segment 1; objective 2)
15. T (pp. 236–237; objective 2)
16. F Reaction time depends on brain maturation and is not readily affected by practice. (p. 243; objective 4)
17. F With the proper assistance, many children with learning disabilities develop into adults who are virtually indistinguishable from other adults in their educational and occupational achievements. (p. 265; video lesson, segment 3; objective 9)
18. F Strenuous dieting during childhood can be dangerous. The best way to get children to lose weight is by increasing their activity level. (pp. 236–237; video lesson, segment 1; objective 2)
19. F The causes of learning disabilities are difficult to pinpoint and cannot be specified with certainty. (p. 265; video lesson, segment 3; objective 9)
20. F (pp. 263, 265; video lesson, segment 3; objective 10)
21. T (p. 264; video lesson, segment 3; objective 10)

Practice Questions II

Multiple-Choice Questions

1. a. is the correct answer. (p. 234; video lesson, segment 1; objective 1)

   b. & c. are incorrect. During this period children gain about 5 pounds per year and experience increased lung capacity.

   d. is incorrect. Although childhood obesity is a common problem, the textbook does not indicate that a person is more likely to become obese at this age than at any other.

2. d. is the correct answer. (pp. 236–237; video lesson, segment 1; objective 2)
3. a. is the correct answer. (p. 265; video lesson, segment 3; objective 9)

   b. is incorrect. This learning disability involves math rather than reading.

   c. & d. are incorrect. These disorders do not manifest themselves in a particular academic skill but instead appear in psychological processes that affect learning in general.

4. a. is the correct answer. (p. 265; video lesson, segment 3; objective 9)

   b. & c. are incorrect. ADHD is a general learning disability that usually does not manifest itself in specific subject areas. Hyperactivity is a facet of this disorder.

   d. is incorrect. Dyscalcula is a learning disability in math only.

5. b. is the correct answer. (p. 236; video lesson, segment 1; objective 2)
6. d. is the correct answer. (pp. 263–265; video lesson, segment 3; objective 10)
7. b. is the correct answer. (p. 243; objective 4)
8. a. is the correct answer. (p. 265; video lesson, segment 3; objective 9)
9. d. is the correct answer. (pp. 236–237; video lesson, segment 1; objective 2)
10. c. is the correct answer. (p. 263, Table 7.1; objective 11)

    a. is incorrect. Many general education teachers are unable to cope with the special needs of some children.

    b. & d. are incorrect. These approaches undermined the social integration of children with special needs.

11. b. is the correct answer. (p. 266; objective 8)
12. b. is the correct answer. (pp. 263–264; video lesson, segment 3; objective 10)
13. b. is the correct answer. (pp. 257, 259–260; objective 5)
14. c. is the correct answer. (p. 257; objective 5)
15. c. is the correct answer. (p. 259; objective 6)

Matching Items

16. g (p. 265; video lesson, segment 3; objective 9)
17. j (p. 243; objective 4)
18. f (p. 266; objective 8)
19. a (p. 265; video lesson, segment 3; objective 9)
20. h (p. 234; objective 3)
21. b (p. 258; objective 5)
22. d (p. 263, Table 7.1; video lesson, segment 3; objective 9)
23. k (p. 262; video lesson, segment 3; objective 7)
24. c (p. 263; objective 7)
25. e (p. 263, Table 7.1; video lesson, segment 3; objective 11)
26. i (p. 263; video lesson, segment 3; objective 10)

Applying Your Knowledge

1. c. is the correct answer. (pp. 242–243; objective 4)

   a. & b. are incorrect. Each of these games involves skills that are hardest for schoolchildren to master.

d. is incorrect. Because one-on-one sports are likely to accentuate individual differences in ability, they may be especially discouraging to some children.

2. b. is the correct answer. (p. 262; video lesson, segment 3; objective 7)
3. d. is the correct answer. (p. 263; video lesson, segment 3; objective 10)

   a. & b. are incorrect. Jack's difficulty is in concentrating, not in reading (dyslexia) or math (dyscalcula).

   c. is incorrect. Autism is characterized by a lack of communication skills.
4. d. is the correct answer. (p. 263; video lesson, segment 3; objective 10)
5. d. is the correct answer. (pp. 236–237; video lesson, segment 1; objective 2)
6. c. is the correct answer. (pp. 243–244; objective 4)
7. c. is the correct answer. (p. 265; video lesson, segment 3; objective 9)
8. b. is the correct answer. (p. 266; objective 8)
9. c. is the correct answer. Medication alone cannot ameliorate all the problems of ADHD. (pp. 263–264; video lesson, segment 3; objective 10)
10. d. is the correct answer. There is no evidence that teratogens have anything to do with obesity. (pp. 236–237; objective 2)
11. c. is the correct answer. At the time she took the test, Ayme's chronological age was eight. Knowing that her IQ was 125, we can solve the equation to yield a mental age of ten. (pp. 257–258; objective 5)
12. c. is the correct answer. Both Sternberg and Gardner believe that there are multiple intelligences rather than the narrowly defined abilities measured by traditional aptitude and achievement tests. (pp. 259–260; objective 6)

    a., b., & d. are incorrect. Although these criticisms are certainly valid, they are not specifically associated with Sternberg or Gardner.

Lesson Review

Lesson 11

The School Years
Biosocial Development

Please Note: Use this matrix to guide your study and achieve the learning objectives of this lesson. It will also help you to view the video, which defines and demonstrates important concepts and skills as they relate to everyday life.

Learning Objective	Textbook	Telecourse Student Guide	Video Lesson
1. Describe physical growth and health during middle childhood, noting variations and their causes, and discuss the importance of physical activity to children of this age.	pp. 233–234, 237–239	Key Terms: 1; Practice Questions I: 1; Practice Questions II: 1.	Segment 1: *Physical Growth*
2. Describe the problem of childhood obesity, outline its major causes and best approaches for treatment, and discuss the potential effects of obesity on a child's physical and psychological health.	pp. 236–237	Key Terms: 3, 4, 5; Practice Questions I: 2, 4, 13, 14, 15, 18; Practice Questions II: 2, 5, 9; Applying Your Knowledge: 5, 10.	Segment 1: *Physical Growth*
3. Describe the causes of and treatments for childhood asthma, and discuss its potential impact on development.	pp. 234–236	Key Terms: 2; Practice Questions II: 20.	
4. Describe brain development during the school years, focusing on how it relates to motor-skill and cognitive development.	pp. 242–244	Key Terms: 6, 7, 8; Practice Questions I: 6, 12, 16; Practice Questions II: 7, 17; Applying Your Knowledge: 1, 6.	
5. Explain how achievement and aptitude tests are used in evaluating individual differences in cognitive growth, and discuss why use of such tests is controversial.	pp. 257–262	Key Terms: 9, 10, 11, 12, 13, 14; Practice Questions I: 10, 11; Practice Questions II: 13, 14, 21; Applying Your Knowledge: 11.	
6. Describe Sternberg's and Gardner's theories of multiple intelligences, and explain the significance of these theories.	pp. 259–260	Practice Questions II: 15; Applying Your Knowledge: 12.	

Learning Objective	Textbook	Telecourse Student Guide	Video Lesson
7. Describe the developmental psychopathology perspective, and discuss its value in treating children with special needs.	pp. 262–263	Key Terms: 15, 16, 17; Practice Questions I: 5; Practice Questions II: 23, 24; Applying Your Knowledge: 2.	Segment 3: *Special Needs*
8. Identify the symptoms of autism, and discuss its possible causes.	pp. 265–267	Key Terms: 22, 23, 24; Practice Questions I: 8; Practice Questions II: 11, 18; Applying Your Knowledge: 8.	
9. Discuss the characteristics and possible causes of learning disabilities.	p. 265	Key Terms: 20, 21, 25; Practice Questions I: 3, 17, 19; Practice Questions II: 3, 4, 8, 16, 19, 22; Applying Your Knowledge: 7.	Segment 3: *Special Needs*
10. Describe the symptoms and possible causes of attention-deficit/hyperactivity disorder (ADHD) and discuss the types of treatment available for children with this disorder.	pp. 263–265	Key Terms: 18, 19; Practice Questions I: 7, 9, 20, 21; Practice Questions II: 6, 12, 26; Applying Your Knowledge: 3, 4, 9.	Segment 3: *Special Needs*
11. Summarize techniques that have been tried in efforts to educate children with special needs.	p. 263, Table 7.1	Key Terms: 15, 26; Practice Questions II: 10, 25.	Segment 3: *Special Needs*

The Age of Reason

Lesson 12

The School Years: Cognitive Development

Preview

Lesson 12 looks at the development of cognitive abilities in children from age 7 to 11. The first part of the lesson focuses on changes in the child's processing speed and capacity, memory strategies, **knowledge base**, and problem-solving strategies. Next, we discuss Jean Piaget's view of the child's cognitive development in this period, which involves a growing ability to use logic and reasoning.

The lesson also looks at moral reasoning and language learning in the school years. During this time, children develop a more analytic understanding of words and show a marked improvement in pragmatic skills, such as changing from one form of speech to another when the situation so demands. The linguistic and cognitive advantages of bilingualism are discussed, as are educational and environmental conditions that are conducive to fluency in a second language.

The final part of the lesson describes innovative teaching methods, which emphasize active rather than passive learning and are derived from the developmental theories of Piaget, Vygotsky, and others. Studies that contrast these methods with more traditional approaches have shown their effectiveness in reading and math education. The lesson concludes by examining measures of cognitive growth, such as tests, and variations in cultural standards.

Prior Telecourse Knowledge that Will Be Used in this Lesson

- This lesson will introduce "**concrete operational thought**," the third stage in Jean Piaget's theory of cognitive development (from Chapter 2/Lesson 1). Recall that Piaget's theory specifies four major periods of cognitive development:
    1. Sensorimotor (birth to 2 years)
    2. Preoperational (2 to 6 years)
    3. **Concrete Operational (7 to 11 years)←The School Years**
    4. Formal Operational (12 years through adulthood)

- During its exploration of school learning, this lesson will return to Lev Vygotsky's theory of development (from Chapter 2/Lesson 1). Recall that Vygotsky emphasized the importance of guided participation, a learning process in which an individual learns through social interaction with a mentor.

Learning Objectives

Use this information to guide your reading, viewing, thinking, and studying. After successfully completing this lesson, you should be able to:

1. Describe the components of the information-processing system, noting how they interact.
2. Discuss advances in processing speed and capacity, strategy development, and memory skills during middle childhood.
3. Identify and describe the characteristics of concrete operational thought, give examples of how this type of thinking is demonstrated by schoolchildren, and compare Vygotsky's and Piaget's differing ideas on learning.
4. Outline Kohlberg's stage theory of moral development and describe several criticisms of the theory.
5. Discuss learning in school, teaching values, and hidden curriculum and demonstrate an understanding of the various achievement tests mandated by law to evaluate performance in school.
6. Describe language development during the school years, noting changing abilities in vocabulary, grammar, and code switching.
7. Identify several conditions that foster the learning of a second language, and describe different strategies for teaching another language to school-age children.
8. Describe current controversies in education, and explain how they relate to developmental theories and culture.

Read Chapter 7, "Middle Childhood: Body and Mind," pages 239–257 and 260–262. Also, read page 300 in Chapter 8, "Middle Childhood: Psychosocial Development."

View the video for Lesson 12, "The Age of Reason."

Segment 1: *How School-Age Children Think*

Segment 2: *Language Development*

Summary

Cognitive development between the ages of 7 and 11 is impressive, attested to by children's improved reasoning strategies, mastery of school-related skills, and use of language. For children around the world, the transition into middle childhood marks a passage into a new phase of cognitive development some call the "age of reason." For Piaget, the age of reason begins with the 5-to-7 shift from preoperational to **concrete operational thought**. When this transition is complete, children are much better able to understand logical principles, as long as they are applied to tangible, concrete examples.

Among the logical operations schoolchildren acquire are numerous principles, two of which are the principle that an entity remains the same despite changes in its appearance (**conservation**) and that certain characteristics of an object remain the same when other characteristics are changed (**identity**). Two additional principles acquired are the principle that something that has been changed can be returned to its original state by reversing the process (**reversibility**), and that a change in one object can be compensated for by a corresponding change in another (**reciprocity**).

The **information-processing theory** of cognitive development places more emphasis than Piaget does on the ways in which children process their experiences. The ability to selectively attend to, rehearse, store, organize, and retrieve information improves steadily during middle childhood. Schoolchildren also have a larger processing capacity and **knowledge base** than they did earlier. The ability to evaluate a cognitive task and to monitor one's performance, called **metacognition**, also improves during the school years. The information-processing approach emphasizes that the most effective way to teach is to adapt teaching materials and sequence of instruction to fit the needs of the individual child.

Logical thought processes also foster moral development, as school-age children become better able to grasp moral laws and ethical principles. Moral reasoning also becomes more complex during middle childhood. Lawrence Kohlberg proposed that this reasoning develops through six stages of increasing complexity, from the elemental preconventional stage of moral thinking, in which the individual reasons in terms of his or her own welfare; to conventional moral thinking, in which the individual considers social standards and laws to be the supreme arbiters of moral values; to the recognition of universal ethical principles that characterizes postconventional moral thinking.

Lawrence Kohlberg identified three levels of moral reasoning (each level including two stages):

- Preconventional: Emphasis on avoiding punishment and obtaining rewards. *Stage 1:* Might makes right. *Stage 2*: Look out for number one.
- Conventional: Emphasis on social rules. *Stage 3:* "good girl" and "nice boy." *Stage 4*: "law and order."
- Postconventional: Emphasis on moral principles. *Stage 5:* social contract. *Stage 6:* universal ethical principles.

Language development during these years is also extensive, with children showing improvement in vocabulary, grammar, and pragmatic use of language. This is clearly indicated by their newly found delight in words and their growing sophistication in telling jokes. School-age children can also easily engage in **code-switching**, from the **formal code** used with teachers to the **informal code** used with friends.

Review all reading assignments for this lesson.

As assigned by your instructor, complete the optional online component for this lesson.

Key Terms

Using your own words, write a brief definition or explanation of each of the following terms on a separate piece of paper.

1. concrete operational thought
2. classification
3. knowledge base
4. information-processing theory
5. sensory memory
6. working memory
7. long-term memory
8. metacognition
9. metamemory
10. hidden curriculum
11. English-language learner (ELL)
12. phonics approach
13. whole-language approach
14. No Child Left Behind (NCLB) Act
15. National Assessment of Educational Progress (NAEP)
16. Progress in International Reading Literacy Skills (PIRLS)
17. Trends in Math and Science Study (TIMSS)
18. preconventional moral reasoning
19. conventional moral reasoning
20. postconventional moral reasoning
21. identity
22. reversibility
23. reciprocity
24. conservation
25. storage strategies
26. retrieval strategies
27. output
28. total immersion
29. English as a second language (ESL)
30. bilingual education
31. code-switching
32. formal code
33. informal code

Practice Questions I

Multiple-Choice Questions

1. According to Piaget, the stage of cognitive development in which a person understands specific logical ideas and can apply them to concrete problems is called
   a. preoperational thought.
   b. operational thought.
   c. concrete operational thought.
   d. formal operational thought.

2. The idea that an object that has been transformed in some way can be restored to its original form by undoing the process is
   a. identity.
   b. reversibility.
   c. reciprocity.
   d. automatization.

3. Information-processing theorists contend that major advances in cognitive development occur during the school years because
   a. the child's mind becomes more like a computer as he or she matures.
   b. children become better able to process and analyze information.
   c. most mental activities become automatic by the time a child is about 13 years old.
   d. the major improvements in reasoning that occur during the school years involve increased long-term memory capacity.

4. The term for thc ability to monitor one's cognitive performance—to think about thinking—is
   a. pragmatics.
   b. information processing.
   c. selective attention.
   d. metacognition.

5. Long-term memory is __________ permanent and __________ limited than working memory.
   a. more; less
   b. less; more
   c. more; more
   d. less; less

6. Motivation to read and write may increase when children are allowed to use invented spelling as part of a ____________________ approach to language skills.
   a. whole-language
   b. phonics
   c. bilingual
   d. code-switching

7. The educational emphasis on the importance of active, engaged learning during mathematics instruction is most directly derived from the developmental theory of
   a. Vygotsky and Piaget.
   b. Carl Jung.
   c. information processing.
   d. those who advocate immersion learning.

8. Which of the following statements is true about Piaget and Vygotsky, according to your textbook?
   a. During concrete operational thought, children become more logical, less egocentric.
   b. Vygotsky emphasized the cultural context of learning.
   c. Both Piaget and Vygotsky described children as active, eager learners.
   d. All of the above are true.

9. Billy has just texted George a joke, and George responded with "LOL!" George has just demonstrated
   a. classification.
   b. control process.
   c. informal code.
   d. none of the above.

10. According to Lawrence Kohlberg, the three levels of moral reasoning are
   a. amoral, immoral, and moral.
   b. egocentrism, ethnocentrism, and universality.
   c. preconventional, conventional, and postconventional.
   d. selfishness, law-and-order, and altruistic.

True or False Items

Write T (for true) or F (for false) on the line in front of each statement.

11. _____ Concrete operational thought is Piaget's third stage of development.

12. _____ Learning a second language fosters children's overall linguistic and cognitive development.

13. _____ Children from low-income families have smaller vocabularies and use simpler grammar.

14. _____ Code-switching, especially the occasional use of slang, is a behavior characteristic primarily of children in the lower social strata.

15. _____ Most information that comes into the sensory register is lost or discarded.

16. _____ New standards of math education in many nations emphasize students working collaboratively on proofs and solutions rather than simple memorization of formulas.

Practice Questions II

Multiple-Choice Questions

1. According to Piaget, eight- and nine-year-olds can reason only about concrete things in their lives. "Concrete" means
   a. logical.
   b. abstract.
   c. tangible or specific.
   d. mathematical or classifiable.

2. When psychologists look at the ability of children to receive, store, and organize information, they are examining cognitive development from a view based on
   a. the observations of Piaget.
   b. information processing.
   c. learning theory.
   d. the idea that the key to thinking is the sensory register.

3. The logical operations of concrete operational thought are particularly important to an understanding of the elementary-school subject(s) of
   a. spelling.
   b. reading.
   c. math and science.
   d. social studies.

4. Which of the following Piagetian ideas is **NOT** widely accepted by developmentalists today?
   a. The thinking of school-age children is characterized by a more comprehensive logic than that of preschoolers.
   b. Children are active learners.
   c. How children think is as important as what they know.
   d. Once a certain type of reasoning ability emerges in children, it is evenly apparent in all domains of thinking.

5. Which aspect of the information-processing system stores incoming stimuli for a split second to allow processing?
   a. sensory memory
   b. working memory
   c. long-term memory
   d. control processes

6. An example of schoolchildren's growth in metacognition is their understanding that
   a. transformed objects can be returned to their original state.
   b. rehearsal is a good strategy for memorizing, but outlining is better for understanding.
   c. objects may belong to more than one class.
   d. they can use different language styles in different situations.

7. A new approach to math education focuses on
   a. rote memorization of formulas before problems are introduced.
   b. "hands-on" materials and active discussion of concepts.
   c. one-on-one tutorials.
   d. pretesting children and grouping them by ability.

8. Regarding bilingual education, many contemporary developmentalists believe that
   a. the attempted learning of two languages is confusing to children and delays proficiency in either one or both languages.
   b. bilingual education is linguistically, culturally, and cognitively advantageous to children.
   c. second-language education is most effective when the child has not yet mastered the native language.
   d. bilingual education programs are too expensive to justify the few developmental advantages they confer.

9. In making moral choices, according to Carol Gilligan, females are more likely than males to
   a. score at a higher level in Kohlberg's system.
   b. emphasize the needs of others.
   c. judge right and wrong in absolute terms.
   d. formulate abstract principles.

Matching Items

Match each term or concept with its corresponding description or definition.

Terms or Concepts

10. __________ classification
11. __________ reversibility
12. __________ identity
13. __________ information-processing theory
14. __________ phonics approach
15. __________ metacognition
16. __________ total immersion

Descriptions or Definitions

a. the process of learning language by focusing on the sounds of letters and combinations of letters
b. the idea that a transformation process can be undone to restore the original conditions
c. the idea that certain characteristics of an object remain the same even when other characteristics change
d. developmental perspective that conceives of cognitive development as the result of changes in the processing and analysis of information
e. an educational technique in which instruction occurs entirely in the second language
f. process by which things are organized into groups based on some property they have in common
g. the ability to evaluate a cognitive task and to monitor one's performance on it

Applying Your Knowledge

1. Compared to her four-year-old sister, nine-year-old Shannon is more likely to
   a. steal candy, if she and a friend want it very badly.
   b. judge stealing as wrong, even if the perpetrator is not caught or punished.
   c. use egocentric moral reasoning.
   d. do all of the above.

2. Dr. Larsen believes that the cognitive advances of middle childhood occur because of basic changes in children's thinking speed, knowledge base, and memory retrieval skills. Dr. Larsen evidently is working from the ____________________ perspective.

   a. Piagetian
   b. Vygotskian
   c. information-processing
   d. psychoanalytic

3. Heather has just completed a standardized test of her math skills that will be used to compare the math achievement of students from different nations. Heather has just participated in

   a. No Child Left Behind.
   b. TIMMS.
   c. NAEP.
   d. PIRLS.

4. A child's ability to tell a joke that will amuse his or her audience always depends on

   a. the child's mastery of reciprocity and reversibility.
   b. code-switching.
   c. the child's ability to consider another's perspective.
   d. an expansion of the child's processing capacity.

5. Six-year-old Shannon gives her mother a note reading "I wud lik to pla no." What educational approach encourages invented spelling?

   a. whole language
   b. phonics
   c. Piagetian reasoning
   d. metacognition

6. As compared with her five-year-old brother, seven-year-old Althea has learned to adjust her vocabulary to her audience. This is known as

   a. selective attention.
   b. a retrieval strategy.
   c. code-switching.
   d. classification.

7. Mr. Jones asked the class to tell him the answer to 7 × 2. He called on Bettina, who answered, "16!" Mr. Jones replied, "No. Anyone else?" He then called on Greg who answered "14!" Mr. Jones replied, "Good, Greg. That's right. The answer is 14." Mr. Jones is relying on

   a. math taught by rote.

   b. memorization.

   c. information processing.

   d. a and b only.

Answer Key

Key Terms

1. During Piaget's stage of concrete operational thought, lasting from ages 7 to 11, children can think logically about concrete events and objects but are not able to reason abstractly. (p. 239; video lesson, segment 1; objective 3)
2. Classification is the logical principle by which things are organized into groups, categories, or classes based on some shared feature or property. (p. 239; objective 3)
3. The knowledge base is a body of knowledge in a particular area that has been learned and on which additional learning can be based. (p. 242; video lesson, segment 1; objective 1)
4. According to information-processing theory, human thinking is analogous to a computer in sorting, categorizing, storing, and retrieving stimuli. (p. 242; video lesson, segment 1; objective 1)
5. Sensory memory (or sensory register) is the part of the information-processing system that stores incoming stimuli for a fraction of a second, after which it is passed into working memory, or discarded as unimportant. (p. 244; video lesson, segment 1; objective 1)
6. Working memory is the part of memory that handles current, conscious mental activity. (p. 244; video lesson, segment 1; objective 1)
7. Long-term memory is the part of memory that stores unlimited amounts of information for days, months, or years. (p. 244; video lesson, segment 1; objective 1)
8. Metacognition is the ability to evaluate a cognitive task to determine what to do and to monitor one's performance on that task. (p. 245; objective 1)
9. Metamemory is the ability to understand how memory works in order to use it well; it is an essential element of metacognition. (p. 245; objective 1)
10. A hidden curriculum involves the unofficial, unstated, or implicit rules and priorities that influence the academic curriculum and all aspects of learning in school. (p. 248; objective 5)

11. A child referred to as an English-language learner (ELL) is learning English for the first time. (p. 250; objective 7)
12. The phonics approach is a method of teaching reading by having children learn the sounds of letters before they begin to learn words. (p. 253; objective 8)
13. The whole-language approach is a method of teaching reading by encouraging children to develop all their language skills simultaneously. (p. 257; objective 8)
14. In 2001, the U.S. Congress passed a law referred to as the No Child Left Behind (NCLB) Act. The goal was to increase the quality of schooling by holding schools accountable for their children's progress; however, critics suggest that this federal law has had unintended negative consequences as well. (p. 260; objectives 5 & 8)
15. The National Assessment of Educational Progress (NAEP) is often referred to as "The Nation's Report Card" because it is an ongoing study that tracks children's academic achievement over time. (p. 260; objective 5)
16. The reading ability of fourth graders is the focus of the long-term study referred to as Progress in International Reading Literacy Skills (PIRLS). (p. 261; objective 5)
17. An international assessment of children's achievement in math and science is undertaken by TIMSS (Trends in Math and Science Study), although cross-cultural differences in content validity and test-taking conditions make direct comparisons challenging. (p. 261; objective 5)
18. Kohlberg's first level of moral reasoning, preconventional moral reasoning, emphasizes obedience to authority in order to avoid punishment (stage 1) and being nice to other people so they will be nice to you (stage 2). (p. 300; video lesson, segment 1; objective 4)
19. Kohlberg's second level of moral reasoning, conventional moral reasoning, emphasizes winning the approval of others (stage 3) and obeying the laws set down by those in power (stage 4). (p. 300; video lesson, segment 1; objective 4)
20. Kohlberg's third level, postconventional moral reasoning, emphasizes the social and contractual nature of moral principles (stage 5) and the existence of universal ethical principles (stage 6). (p. 300; video lesson, segment 1; objective 4)
21. In Piaget's theory, identity is the logical principle that certain characteristics of an object remain the same even when other characteristics change. (video lesson, segment 1; objective 3)
22. Reversibility is the logical principle that a transformation process can be reversed to restore the original conditions. (video lesson, segment 1; objective 3)

23. Reciprocity is the logical principle that a transformation in one dimension of an object can be compensated for by a transformation in another. (video lesson, segment 1; objective 3)

    Example: A child who understands reciprocity realizes that rolling a ball of clay into a thin rope makes it longer, but also skinnier, than its original shape.

24. Conservation is the concept that the total quantity, number, or amount of something is the same no matter what the shape or configuration. (video lesson, segment 1; objective 3)
25. Storage strategies are procedures for placing and holding information in memory, such as rehearsal and reorganization. (video lesson, segment 1; objective 1)
26. Retrieval strategies are procedures for accessing previously learned information. (video lesson, segment 1; objective 1)
27. Output refers to the final component of the information processing model, in which the answer—thought, or processing outcome—is somehow communicated, stored, or reprocessed. (video lesson, segment 1; objective 1)
28. Total immersion is an approach to bilingual education in which the child's instruction occurs entirely in the new language. (video lesson, segment 2; objective 7)
29. English as a second language (ESL) is an approach to teaching English in which all instruction is in English, and the teacher does not speak the child's native language. (video lesson, segment 2; objective 7)
30. Bilingual education is an approach to teaching a second language in which the teacher instructs the children in school subjects using their native language as well as the second language. (video lesson, segment 2; objective 7)
31. Code-switching is a pragmatic communication skill involving changing from one form of speech to another. (video lesson, segment 2; objective 6)
32. The formal code is a form of speech used by children in school and other formal situations, characterized by extensive vocabulary, complex syntax, and lengthy sentences. (video lesson, segment 2; objective 6)
33. The informal code is a form of speech used by children in casual situations, characterized by limited vocabulary and syntax. (video lesson, segment 2; objective 6)

Practice Questions I

Multiple-Choice Questions

1. c. is the correct answer. (p. 239; video lesson, segment 1; objective 3)

    a. is incorrect. Preoperational thought is "pre-logical" thinking.

    b. is incorrect. There is no such stage in Piaget's theory.

d. is incorrect. Formal operational thought extends logical reasoning to abstract problems.

2. b. is the correct answer. (video lesson, segment 1; objective 3)

   a. is incorrect. This is the concept that certain characteristics of an object remain the same even when other characteristics change.

   c. is incorrect. This is the concept that a change in one dimension of an object can be compensated for by a change in another dimension.

   d. is incorrect. This is the process by which familiar mental activities become routine and automatic.

3. b. is the correct answer. (pp. 242–243; video lesson, segment 1; objectives 1 & 2)

   a. is incorrect. Information-processing theorists use the mind-computer metaphor at every age.

   c. is incorrect. Although increasing automatization is an important aspect of development, the information-processing perspective does not suggest that most mental activities become automatic by age 13.

   d. is incorrect. Most of the important changes in reasoning that occur during the school years are the result of the improved processing capacity of the person's working memory.

4. d. is the correct answer. (p. 245; objective 1)

   a. is incorrect. Pragmatics refers to the practical use of language to communicate with others.

   b. is incorrect. The information-processing perspective views the mind as being like a computer.

   c. is incorrect. This is the ability to screen out distractions in order to focus on important information.

5. a. is the correct answer. (p. 244; video lesson, segment 1; objective 2)
6. a. is the correct answer (p. 254; objective 6)
7. a. is the correct answer. (p. 255; objective 8)
8. d. is the correct answer. (p. 242; video lesson, segment 1; objective 3)
9. c. is the correct answer. (video lesson, segment 1; objective 6)
10. c. is the correct answer (p. 300; video lesson, segment 1; objective 4)

True or False Items

11. T Most educators agree that the school-age child, like the preschooler, is an active learner. (p. 242; objective 2)
12. T (p. 249; video lesson, segment 2; objective 7)
13. T (p. 250; video lesson, segment 2; objective 6)
14. F Code-switching (including occasional use of slang) is a behavior demonstrated by all children. (p. 249; video lesson, segment 2; objective 6)

15. T (video lesson, segment 1; objective 1)
16. T (pp. 255–256; objectives 5 & 8)

Practice Questions II

Multiple-Choice Questions

1. c. is the correct answer. (p. 239; video lesson, segment 1; objective 3)
2. b. is the correct answer. (p. 242; video lesson, segment 1; objective 1)
3. c. is the correct answer. (video lesson, segment 1; objective 3)
4. d. is the correct answer. (video lesson, segment 1; objective 7)
5. a. is the correct answer. (p. 244; objective 1)

   b. is incorrect. Working memory is the part of memory that handles current, conscious mental activity.

   c. is incorrect. Long-term memory stores information for days, months, or years.
6. b. is the correct answer. (p. 245; objective 2)
7. b. is the correct answer. (pp. 255–256; objective 8)
8. b. is the correct answer. (pp. 249–252; video lesson, segment 2; objective 7)
9. b. is the correct answer. According to Gilligan, males seem to be more concerned with not interfering with the rights of others. (video lesson, segment 1; objective 6)

Matching Items

10. f (p. 239; objective 3)
11. b (video lesson, segment 1; objective 3)
12. c (video lesson, segment 1; objective 3)
13. d (p. 242; video lesson, segment 1; objective 1)
14. a (p. 253; objective 8)
15. g (p. 245; objective 1)
16. e (video lesson, segment 2; objective 7)

Applying Your Knowledge

1. b. is the correct answer. (p. 300; video lesson, segment 1; objective 4)
2. c. is the correct answer. (p. 242; objective 2)

   a. is incorrect. This perspective emphasizes the logical, active nature of thinking during middle childhood.

   b. is incorrect. This perspective emphasizes the importance of social interaction in learning.

   d. is incorrect. This perspective does not address the development of cognitive skills.
3. b. is the correct answer (p. 261; objective 5)

4. c. is the correct answer. Joke-telling is one of the clearest demonstrations of schoolchildren's improved pragmatic skills, including the ability to know what someone else will think is funny. (video lesson, segment 2; objective 6)
5. a. is the correct answer (p. 254; objective 8)
6. c. is the correct answer. (video lesson, segment 2; objective 6)
7. d. is the correct answer. (p. 255; objective 8)

Lesson Review

Lesson 12

The School Years
Cognitive Development

Please Note: Use this matrix to guide your study and achieve the learning objectives of this lesson. It will also help you to view the video, which defines and demonstrates important concepts and skills as they relate to everyday life.

Learning Objective	**Textbook**	**Telecourse Student Guide**	**Video Lesson**
1. Describe the components of the information-processing system, noting how they interact.	p. 242	Key Terms: 3, 4, 5, 6, 7, 8, 9, 25, 26, 27; Practice Questions I: 3, 4, 15; Practice Questions II: 2, 5, 13, 15.	Segment 1: *How School-Age Children Think*
2. Discuss advances in processing speed and capacity, strategy development, and memory skills during middle childhood.	pp. 242–245	Practice Questions I: 3, 5, 11; Practice Questions II: 6; Applying Your Knowledge: 2.	Segment 1: *How School-Age Children Think*
3. Identify and describe the characteristics of concrete operational thought, give examples of how this type of thinking is demonstrated by schoolchildren, and compare Vygotsky's and Piaget's differing ideas on learning.	pp. 239–242	Key Terms: 1, 2, 21, 22, 23, 24; Practice Questions I: 1, 2, 8; Practice Questions II: 1, 3, 10, 11, 12.	Segment 1: *How School-Age Children Think*
4. Outline Kohlberg's stage theory of moral development and describe several criticisms of the theory.	pp. 300–301	Key Terms: 18, 19, 20; Practice Questions I: 10; Applying Your Knowledge: 1.	Segment 1: *How School-Age Children Think*
5. Discuss learning in school, teaching values, and hidden curriculum and demonstrate an understanding of the various achievement tests mandated by law to evaluate performance in school.	pp. 247–248, 260–262	Key Terms: 10, 14, 15, 16, 17; Practice Questions I: 16; Applying Your Knowledge: 3.	
6. Describe language development during the school years, noting changing abilities in vocabulary, grammar, and code switching.	pp. 248–253	Key Terms: 31, 32, 33; Practice Questions I: 6, 9, 13, 14; Practice Questions II: 9; Applying Your Knowledge: 4, 6.	Segment 1: *How School-Age Children Think* Segment 2: *Language Development*

Learning Objective	Textbook	Telecourse Student Guide	Video Lesson
7. Identify several conditions that foster the learning of a second language, and describe different strategies for teaching another language to school-age children.	pp. 249–252	Key Terms: 11, 28, 29, 30; Practice Questions I: 12; Practice Questions II: 4, 8, 16.	Segment 2: *Language Development*
8. Describe current controversies in education, and explain how they relate to developmental theories and culture.	pp. 253–256	Key Terms: 12, 13, 14; Practice Questions I: 7, 16; Practice Questions II: 7, 14; Applying Your Knowledge: 5, 7.	

A Society of Children

Lesson 13

The School Years: Psychosocial Development

Preview

This lesson brings to a close the unit on the school years. We have seen that from ages 7 to 11, the child becomes stronger and more competent, mastering the physical and cognitive abilities that are important in his or her culture. Psychosocial accomplishments are equally impressive.

The lesson begins by exploring the growing social competence of school-age children. Starting with the theories of Freud and Erikson, it moves on to discuss the perspectives of learning, cognitive, sociocultural, and epigenetic systems theorists. The lesson continues with a discussion of the school-age child's growing social awareness and self-understanding.

Children's interaction with peers and others in their ever-widening social world is the subject of the next section. In addition to the changing nature of friendships, the problem of bullies and their victims is discussed.

The lesson also explores the structure and function of families during middle childhood, including the experience of parental divorce and remarriage. The lesson closes with a discussion of the ways in which children cope with stressful situations.

As you complete this lesson, recall some of your own social experiences during this age range (7 to 11). How did you spend a typical day? Who were the friends you spent time with? Did you have a school or neighborhood bully? Did you grow up in a family with both of your biological parents or in some other family structure? What challenges did you face during this period of life and how did you handle them?

Prior Telecourse Knowledge that Will Be Used in this Lesson

- The developmental theory of Erik Erikson (from Lesson 2) will be used to help explain psychosocial development during the school years. Recall that Erikson's theory specifies eight stages of psychosocial development, each of which is characterized by a particular challenge, or developmental crisis, which is central to that stage of life and must be resolved. This lesson will highlight Erikson's fourth stage, "Industry vs. Inferiority":

1. Trust vs. Mistrust (birth to 1 year)
2. Autonomy vs. Shame and Doubt (1 to 3 years)
3. Initiative vs. Guilt (3 to 6 years)
4. **Industry vs. Inferiority (7 to 11 years)** ← **The School Years**
5. Identity vs. Role Confusion (adolescence)
6. Intimacy vs. Isolation (adulthood)
7. Generativity vs. Stagnation (adulthood)
8. Integrity vs. Despair (adulthood)

- This lesson will revisit the concept of *theory of mind* (from Lesson 9), an understanding of human mental processes. During the school years, children gain an increasingly better understanding of the thoughts, emotions, needs, and motivations of others—which allows them to interact more effectively in their social world.

Learning Objectives

Use this information to guide your reading, viewing, thinking, and studying. After successfully completing this lesson, you should be able to:

1. Describe the rising competence and independence of middle childhood from different theoretical perspectives, including Erikson's crisis of "industry vs. inferiority."
2. Define social cognition, and explain how children's theory of mind and emotional understanding evolve during middle childhood.
3. Describe the development of self-understanding during middle childhood and its implications for children's self-esteem.
4. Discuss the importance of peer groups, providing examples of how school-age children develop their own subculture and explaining the importance of this development.
5. Discuss how friendship circles change during the school years.
6. Describe the special problems of unpopular children, of bullies and their victims, and discuss possible ways of helping such children.
7. Identify five essential ways in which families nurture school-age children.
8. Differentiate among various family structures, describe how family structures have changed in recent decades, and discuss their impact on the development of school-age children.
9. Discuss how family problems such as low-income, instability, and divorce influence the psychosocial development of school-age children.
10. Identify the variables that influence the impact of stresses on schoolchildren, and discuss those factors that seem especially important in helping children to cope with stress.

Read Chapter 8, "Middle Childhood: Psychosocial Development," pages 271–303.

View the video for Lesson 13, "A Society of Children."

Segment 1: *Peers*

Segment 2: *Family*

Segment 3: *Coping*

Summary

The major theories of development emphasize similar characteristics in describing the school-age child. They portray an individual who is much more independent, capable, and open to the challenges of the world. Erikson, for example, refers to these years as the time of industry, while Freud says that sexual concerns are latent. Erikson's "industry" refers to children being busy learning all the skills that will make them productive adults. This means that children in the school years should be busy learning how to read, write, calculate, socialize with others, and try things like sports or dance or skill-building hobbies. Learning new skills is the "work" of the school-age child.

As school-age children develop their theory of mind and powers of **social cognition**, they are increasingly aware of the motives, emotions, and personality traits that are the foundation of others' behavior. As their social skills improve, school-age children also become better able to adjust their own behavior to interact appropriately with others.

The expanded social world of children in the school years is full of opportunities for growth, as children create their own subculture or "society"—complete with its own language, values, and codes of behavior—and friendships become more selective and exclusive. This expanded world also presents challenges and special problems. This lesson discusses the impact of low self-esteem, **bullying**, divorce, poverty, and other stresses on children's psychosocial development. Most children, however, are sufficiently **resilient** and resourceful to cope with the stresses they may face during middle childhood. The emotional stability of parents and the amount of attention each child receives are significant factors in their healthy adjustment to environmental stress. How well a family nurtures and supports a child depends on how well it meets the child's basic needs, encourages learning, nurtures peer relationships, provides harmony and stability, and develops the child's self-esteem. While children can thrive in almost any structure, children living with both biological parents (either in nuclear or extended families) tend to have the best opportunity to thrive.

Review all reading assignments for this lesson.

As assigned by your instructor, complete the optional online component for this lesson.

Key Terms

Using your own words, write a brief definition or explanation of each of the following terms on a separate piece of paper.

1. effortful control
2. industry versus inferiority
3. social comparison
4. resilience
5. family function
6. family structure
7. nuclear family
8. blended family
9. single-parent family
10. extended family
11. polygamous family
12. culture of children
13. social cognition
14. aggressive-rejected children
15. withdrawn-rejected children
16. bullying
17. bully-victim
18. peer group

Practice Questions I

Multiple-Choice Questions

1. The best strategy for helping children who are at risk of developing serious psychological problems because of multiple stresses would be to
   a. obtain assistance from a psychiatrist.
   b. change the household situation.
   c. increase the child's competencies or social supports.
   d. reduce the peer group's influence.

2. Compared with preschoolers, older children are more likely to blame
   a. failure on bad luck.
   b. teachers and other authority figures.
   c. their parents for their problems.
   d. themselves for their shortcomings.

3. A bully usually is someone who
   a. has a few friends.
   b. lacks empathy.
   c. finds victims who do not resist.
   d. does all of the above.

4. In regard to popularity, which of the following statements is **FALSE**?
   a. The popularity of school-age children generally stays the same year after year.
   b. Culture, age, and cohort influence popularity.
   c. In North America, most shy children are not popular.
   d. Shy children are popular in China.

5. Divorce and parental remarriage typically prove beneficial to children when they result in
   a. greater stability for the family.
   b. greater role overload.
   c. significant changes in lifestyle.
   d. the inclusion of stepchildren as siblings.

6. Factors that may contribute to a child's bullying behavior may include
   a. brain abnormalities.
   b. insecure attachment to parents.
   c. poor emotional regulation.
   d. all of the above.

7. During the school years, children become ____________ selective about their friends, and their friendship groups become ____________.
   a. less; larger
   c. more; larger
   b. less; smaller
   d. more; smaller

8. Erikson sees the crisis of the school years as that of
   a. industry versus inferiority.
   b. acceptance versus rejection.
   c. initiative versus guilt.
   d. male versus female.

True or False Items

Write T (for true) or F (for false) on the line in front of each statement.

9. _____ As they evaluate themselves according to increasingly complex self-theories, school-age children typically experience a rise in self-esteem.

10. _____ During middle childhood, acceptance by the peer group is valued more than having a close friend.

11. _____ Children from high-incomc homes tend to have more emotional problem than children from middle-income families.

12. _____ Blended families are better for child development than single-parent families.

13. _____ Divorce usually adversely affects the children for at least a year or two.

14. _____ The quality of family interaction seems to be a more powerful predictor of children's development than the actual structure of the family.

15. _____ School-age children are less able than younger children to cope with the chronic stresses that are troublesome at any age.

16. _____ In multiethnic schools, a bully would usually pick on someone from a different ethnic group than his/her own.

17. _____ Friendships become more selective and exclusive as children grow older.

18. ____ In the United States, more than 28% of all school-age children live in a single-parent family.

Practice Questions II

Multiple-Choice Questions

1. Children who are categorized as __________ are particularly vulnerable to bullying.
   a. aggressive-rejected
   b. passive-aggressive
   c. withdrawn-rejected
   d. passive-rejected

2. The main reason for the special vocabulary, dress codes, and behaviors that flourish within the society of children is that they
   a. lead to clubs and gang behavior.
   b. are unknown to or unapproved by adults.
   c. imitate adult-organized society.
   d. provide an alternative to useful work in society.

3. In the area of social cognition, developmentalists are impressed by the school-age child's increasing ability to
   a. identify and take into account other people's viewpoints.
   b. develop an increasingly wide network of friends.
   c. relate to the opposite sex.
   d. resist social models.

4. Typically, children in middle childhood experience a decrease in self-esteem as a result of
   a. a wavering self-theory.
   b. increased awareness of personal shortcomings and failures.
   c. rejection by peers.
   d. difficulties with members of the opposite sex.

5. A ten-year-old's sense of self-esteem is most strongly influenced by his or her
   a. peers.
   b. siblings.
   c. mother.
   d. father.

6. Which of the following most accurately describes how friendships change during the school years?
   a. Friendships become more casual and less intense.
   b. Older children demand less of their friends.
   c. Older children change friends more often.
   d. Close friendships increasingly involve members of the same sex, ethnicity, and socioeconomic status.

7. Which of the following is an accurate statement about school-age bullies?
   a. They are unapologetic about their aggressive behavior.
   b. They usually have friends who abet, fear, and admire them.
   c. Their popularity fades over the years.
   d. All of the above are accurate statements.

8. Two factors that most often help the child cope well with multiple stresses are social support and
   a. social comparison.
   b. competence in a specific area.
   c. remedial education.
   d. referral to mental health professionals.

9. Family ____________________ is more crucial to children's well-being than family ____________________ is.
   a. structure; socioeconomic status (SES)
   b. socioeconomic status (SES); stability
   c. socioeconomic status (SES); structure
   d. functioning; structure

10. According to Freud, the period between ages 7 and 11 when a child's sexual drives are relatively quiet is the
    a. phallic stage.
    b. genital stage.
    c. period of latency.
    d. period of industry versus inferiority.

11. Research studies have found that children who are forced to cope with ongoing stress (for example, poverty or large family size) are
    a. more likely to develop serious psychiatric problems than children with none of these stresses.
    b. able to cope much better when provided with a consistent daily routine.
    c. more likely to develop intense, destructive friendships than other children.
    d. less likely to be accepted by their peer group.

12. The culture of children includes
    a. rules passed down from older to younger children.
    b. rhymes.
    c. insults.
    d. all of the above.

Matching Items

Match each term or concept with its corresponding description or definition.

Terms or Concepts

13. __________ social cognition
14. __________ peer group
15. __________ society of children/culture of children
16. __________ bullying
17. __________ aggressive-rejected
18. __________ withdrawn-rejected

Descriptions or Definitions

a. the games, vocabulary, dress codes, and culture of children
b. a perspective that highlights how schoolchildren advance in learning, cognition, and culture by building on maturation and experience to become more articulate, insightful, and competent
c. children who are disliked because of their confrontational nature
d. a group of individuals of roughly the same age and social status who play, work, or learn together
e. children who are disliked because of their timid, anxious behavior
f. repeated efforts by a single child or group of children to inflict harm on another child through physical, verbal, or social attacks

Applying Your Knowledge

1. As an advocate of Freud's psychoanalytic theory, Dr. Wayans is most likely to explain a ten-year-old child's new independence as the result of
   a. sexual urges being submerged.
   b. the acquisition of new skills.
   c. greater self-understanding.
   d. the child's need to join the wider community and the parents' need to focus on younger children.

2. Dr. Ferris believes that skill mastery is particularly important because children develop views of themselves as either competent or incompetent in skills valued by their culture. Dr. Ferris is evidently working from the perspective of
   a. behaviorism.
   b. social learning theory.
   c. Erik Erikson's theory of development.
   d. Freud's theory of development.

3. Bonnie, who is low achieving, shy, and withdrawn, is rejected by most of her peers. Her teacher, who wants to help Bonnie increase her self-esteem and social acceptance, encourages her parents to
   a. transfer Bonnie to a different school.
   b. help their daughter improve her motor skills.
   c. help their daughter learn to accept more responsibility for her academic failures.
   d. help their daughter improve her skills in relating to peers.

4. Jorge, who has no children of his own, is worried about his twelve-year-old niece because she wears unusual clothes and uses vocabulary unknown to him. What should Jorge do?
   a. Tell his niece's parents that they need to discipline their daughter more strictly.
   b. Convince his niece to find a new group of friends.
   c. Recommend that his niece's parents seek professional counseling for their daughter, because such behaviors often are the first signs of a lifelong pattern of antisocial behavior.
   d. Jorge need not necessarily be worried because children typically develop their own subculture of speech, dress, and behavior.

5. Compared with her seven-year-old brother Walter, ten-year-old Felicity is more likely to describe their cousin
   a. in terms of physical attributes.
   b. as feeling exactly the same way she does when they are in the same social situation.
   c. in terms of personality traits.
   d. in terms of their cousin's outward behavior.

6. Seven-year-old Chantal fumes after a friend compliments her new dress, thinking that the comment was intended to be sarcastic. Chantal's reaction is an example of
   a. egocentrism.
   b. feelings of inferiority.
   c. the distorted thought processes of an emotionally disturbed child.
   d. lack of prosocial skills.

7. In contrast to younger children discussing friendship, nine-year-old children will
   a. deny that friends are important.
   b. state that they prefer same-sex playmates.
   c. stress the importance of help and emotional support in friendship.
   d. be less choosy about whom they call a friend.

8. Social cognition
   a. is the ability to understand human interactions.
   b. is usually well established by late adulthood.
   c. can be impaired in children but they usually become very successful anyway.
   d. involves none of the above.

9. Of the following children, who is likely to have the lowest overall self-esteem?
   a. Karen, age 5
   b. David, age 7
   c. Carl, age 9
   d. Cindy, age 10

10. Ten-year-old Benjamin is less optimistic and self-confident than his five-year-old sister. This may be explained in part by the tendency of older children to
    a. evaluate their abilities by comparing them with their own competencies a year or two earlier.
    b. evaluate their competencies by comparing them with those of others.
    c. be less realistic about their own abilities.
    d. do both b and c.

Answer Key

Key Terms

1. Effortful control is a cognitive ability to inhibit impulses, and gains in this ability help foster a child's growing ability to understand social situations. (p. 273; objectives 1 & 2)
2. According to Erikson, the crisis of middle childhood is that of industry versus inferiority, in which children try to master many skills and develop views of themselves as either competent or incompetent and inferior. (p. 273; video lesson, introduction; objective 1)
3. Social comparison is the tendency to assess one's abilities, achievements, and social status by measuring them against those of others, especially those of one's peers. (p. 274; objective 3)
4. Individuals who are able to cope with stress and very difficult situations demonstrate a high degree of resilience. (p. 276; objective 10)
5. Family function refers to how a family works to meet the needs of its members, which vary with age. Schoolchildren need their families to provide such basic necessities as food, clothing, and shelter; to encourage them to learn; to develop their self-esteem; to nurture their friendships with peers; and to provide harmony and stability at home. (p. 281; video lesson, segment 2; objective 7)
6. Family structure refers to the legal and genetic relationships that exist between members of a particular family. (p. 282; video lesson, segment 2; objective 6)
7. A nuclear family consists of two parents and their mutual biological offspring. (p. 283; video lesson, segment 2; objective 6)
8. A blended family consists of two adults, at least one with biological children from another union, and any children the adults have together. (p. 284; objective 8)
9. A single-parent family consists of one parent and his or her (usually biological) children. (p. 285; video lesson, segment 2; objective 8)
10. An extended family is one that includes grandparents, aunts, cousins, or other relatives in addition to parents and their children. (p. 285; objective 8)
11. A family consisting of one man and several wives and the biological children of the man and his wives is a polygamous family. (p. 285; objective 8)
12. Children in middle childhood develop and transmit their own subculture, called the culture of children, which has its own games, vocabulary, dress codes, and rules of behavior. (p. 291; video lesson, introduction; objective 4)
13. Social cognition involves being able to understand social interaction, including the causes and consequences of behavior. (p. 293; video lesson, segment 1; objective 2)

14. The peer group shuns aggressive-rejected children because they are overly confrontational. (p. 294; video lesson, segment 1; objective 6)
15. Withdrawn-rejected children are shunned by the peer group because of their withdrawn and anxious demeanor. (p. 294; video lesson, segment 1; objective 6)
16. Bullying is the repeated, systematic effort to inflict harm on a child through physical, verbal, or social attack. (p. 294; video lesson, segment 1; objective 6)
17. A bully-victim (also known as a provocative victim) is a bully who is or has been a victim of bullying. (p. 295; video lesson, segment 1; objective 6)
18. A peer group is a group of individuals of roughly the same age and social status that play, work, or learn together. (video lesson, segment 1; objective 4)

Practice Questions I

Multiple-Choice Questions

1. c. is the correct answer. (pp. 276–279; video lesson, segment 3; objective 10)
2. d. is the correct answer. (video lesson, segment 1; objective 3)
   a., b., & c. Compared with preschool children, schoolchildren are more self-critical, and their self-esteem dips, so they blame themselves.
3. d. is the correct answer. (p. 295; video lesson, segment 1; objective 6)
4. a. is the correct answer. (pp. 292–293; video lesson, segment 1; objective 6)
5. a. is the correct answer. (video lesson, segment 3; objective 9)
   b., c., & d. are incorrect. These factors are likely to increase, rather than decrease, stress, and therefore to have an adverse effect on children.
6. d. is the correct answer (pp. 295–296; objective 6)
7. d. is the correct answer. (p. 292; objective 5)
8. a. is the correct answer. (p. 273; video lesson, segment 1; objective 1)

True or False Items

9. F In fact, just the opposite is true. (p. 275; objective 3)
10. F In fact, just the opposite is true. (p. 292; video lesson, segment 1; objectives 4 & 5)
11. T (p. 287; objective 8)
12. F (pp. 284–285; objectives 8 & 9)
13. T (video lesson, segment 2; objective 9)
14. T (pp. 281–286; video lesson, segment 2; objectives 7 & 8)
15. F Because of the coping strategies that school-age children develop, they are better able than younger children to cope with stress. (p. 276; objective 9)
16. F (p. 294; video lesson, segment 1; objective 6)
17. T (p. 292; video lesson, segment 1; objective 5)
18. T (p. 285; objective 8)

Practice Questions II

Multiple-Choice Questions

1. c. is the correct answer. (p. 294; video lesson, segment 1; objective 6)
   a. is incorrect. These are usually bullies.
   b. & d. are incorrect. These are not subcategories of rejected children.
2. b. is the correct answer. (video lesson, introduction; objective 4)
3. a. is the correct answer. (p. 293; objective 2)
   b. is incorrect. Friendship circles typically become smaller during middle childhood, as children become more choosy about their friends.
   c. & d. are incorrect. These issues are not discussed in the textbook.
4. b. is the correct answer. (p. 275; objective 3)
   a. is incorrect. This tends to promote, rather than reduce, self-esteem.
   c. is incorrect. Only 10 percent of schoolchildren experience this.
   d. is incorrect. This issue becomes more important during adolescence.
5. a. is the correct answer. (video lesson, segment 1; objective 3)
6. d. is the correct answer. (p. 292; objective 5)
   a., b., & c. are incorrect. In fact, just the opposite is true of friendship during the school years.
7. d. is the correct answer. (pp. 294–295; objective 6)
8. b. is the correct answer. (video lesson, segment 3; objective 10)
9. d. is the correct answer. (pp. 281–286; video lesson, segment 2; objectives 7 & 8)
10. c. is the correct answer. (pp. 273–274; objective 1)
11. b. is the correct answer. (pp. 276–277; objective 10)
    c. & d. are incorrect. The textbook did not discuss how stress influences friendship or peer acceptance.
12. d. is the correct answer (p. 291; objective 4)

Matching Items

13. b (p. 293; video lesson, segment 2; objective 2)
14. d (video lesson, segment 1; objective 4)
15. a (p. 291; video lesson, introduction; objective 4)
16. f (p. 294; video lesson, segment 1; objective 6)
17. c (p. 294; video lesson, segment 1; objective 6)
18. e (p. 294; video lesson, segment 1; objective 6)

Applying Your Knowledge

1. a. is the correct answer. (pp. 273–274; objective 1)
   d. is incorrect. This describes the epigenetic systems perspective.
   b. is incorrect. This is the viewpoint of a learning theorist.
   c. is incorrect. This is the viewpoint of a cognitive theorist.

2. c. is the correct answer. The question describes what is, for Erikson, the crisis of middle childhood: industry versus inferiority. (p. 273; video lesson, segment 1; objective 1)
3. d. is the correct answer. (p. 294; video lesson, segment 1; objective 6)

   a. is incorrect. Because it would seem to involve "running away" from her problems, this approach would likely be more harmful than helpful.

   b. is incorrect. Improving motor skills is not a factor considered in the textbook and probably has little value in raising self-esteem in such situations.

   c. is incorrect. If Bonnie is like most school-age children, she is quite self-critical and already accepts responsibility for her failures.
4. d. is the correct answer. (video lesson, segment 1; objective 3)
5. c. is the correct answer. (p. 274; objective 5)

   a., b., & d. are incorrect. These are more typical of preschoolers.
6. d. is the correct answer. (p. 292; objective 5)

   a. is incorrect. Egocentrism is self-centered thinking. In this example, Chantal is misinterpreting her friend's comment.

   b. & c. are incorrect. There is no reason to believe that Chantal is suffering from an emotional disturbance or that she is feeling inferior.
7. b. is the correct answer. (video lesson, segment 1; objective 5)
8. a. is the correct answer. (p. 293; video lesson, segment 1; objective 2)
9. d. is the correct answer. Self-esteem decreases throughout middle childhood. (pp. 274–275; objective 3)
10. b. is the correct answer. (pp. 274–276; objective 3)

    a. & c. are incorrect. These are more typical of preschoolers than school-age children.

Lesson Review

Lesson 13

The School Years
Psychosocial Development

Please Note: Use this matrix to guide your study and achieve the learning objectives of this lesson. It will also help you to view the video, which defines and demonstrates important concepts and skills as they relate to everyday life.

Learning Objective	Textbook	Telecourse Student Guide	Video Lesson
1. Describe the rising competence and independence of middle childhood from different theoretical perspectives, including Erikson's crisis of "industry vs. inferiority."	pp. 272–274	Key Terms: 1, 2; Practice Questions I: 8; Practice Questions II: 10; Applying Your Knowledge: 1, 2.	Introduction; Segment 1: *Peers*
2. Define social cognition, and explain how children's theory of mind and emotional understanding evolve during middle childhood.	p. 293	Key Terms: 1, 13; Practice Questions II: 3, 13; Applying Your Knowledge: 8.	Segment 1: *Peers* Segment 2: *Family*
3. Describe the development of self-understanding during middle childhood and its implications for children's self-esteem.	pp. 274–276	Key Terms: 3; Practice Questions I: 2, 9; Practice Questions II: 4, 5; Applying Your Knowledge: 4, 9, 10.	Segment 1: *Peers*
4. Discuss the importance of peer groups, providing examples of how school-age children develop their own subculture and explaining the importance of this development.	pp. 291–292	Key Terms: 12, 18; Practice Questions I: 10; Practice Questions II: 2, 12, 14, 15.	Introduction; Segment 1: *Peers*
5. Discuss how friendship circles change during the school years.	p. 292	Practice Questions I: 7, 10, 17; Practice Questions II: 6; Applying Your Knowledge: 5, 6, 7.	Segment 1: *Peers;* Segment 3: *Coping*
6. Describe the special problems of unpopular children, of bullies and their victims, and discuss possible ways of helping such children.	pp. 292–297	Key Terms: 6, 7, 14, 15, 16, 17; Practice Questions I: 3, 4, 6, 16; Practice Questions II: 1, 7, 16, 17, 18; Applying Your Knowledge: 3.	Segment 1: *Peers;* Segment 2: *Family*
7. Identify five essential ways in which families nurture school-age children.	pp. 281–282	Key Terms: 5; Practice Questions I: 14; Practice Questions II: 9.	Segment 2: *Family*

Learning Objective	Textbook	Telecourse Student Guide	Video Lesson
8. Differentiate among various family structures, describe how family structures have changed in recent decades, and discuss their impact on the development of school-age children.	pp. 282–286	Key Terms: 8, 9, 10, 11; Practice Questions I: 11, 12, 14, 18; Practice Questions II: 9.	Segment 2: *Family*
9. Discuss how family problems such as low income, instability, and divorce influence the psychosocial development of school-age children.	pp. 286–290	Practice Questions I: 5, 12, 13, 15.	Segment 3: *Coping*
10. Identify the variables that influence the impact of stresses on schoolchildren, and discuss those factors that seem especially important in helping children to cope with stress.	pp. 276–279	Key Terms: 4; Practice Questions I: 1; Practice Questions II: 8, 11.	Segment 3: *Coping*

Explosions

Lesson 14

Adolescence: Biosocial Development

Preview

Between the ages of 11 and 20, young people cross the great divide between childhood and adulthood that we call **adolescence**. This crossing encompasses all three domains of development—biosocial, cognitive, and psychosocial. Lesson 14 focuses on the dramatic changes that occur in the biosocial domain, beginning with **puberty** and the **growth spurt**. The biosocial metamorphosis of the adolescent is discussed in detail, with emphasis on sexual maturation, nutrition, and the effects of the timing of puberty, including possible problems arising from early or late maturation.

Although adolescence is, in many ways, a healthy time of life, this lesson addresses three health hazards that too often affect children of this age: sexual abuse, poor nutrition, and use of alcohol, tobacco, and other drugs.

As you begin this lesson, reflect on your own experience in adolescence. Recall your physical growth and development during this period (i.e., height, weight, voice changes, hair growth, developing curves/shoulders). Did you develop any earlier or later than your peers? How did these changes make you feel? How well did you eat and take care of yourself physically? What pressures did you feel regarding drugs and alcohol?

Prior Telecourse Knowledge that Will Be Used in this Lesson

- Biosocial development during infancy (Lesson 5), early childhood (Lesson 8), and middle childhood (Lesson 11) will be referred to as we discuss physical developments during adolescence. As you'll learn, the rate of growth in adolescence is second only to the rapid growth experienced prenatally (in the womb) and postnatally (during the first year of life).
- Five theories of development introduced in Lesson 1/Chapter 2 (psychoanalytic, learning, cognitive, sociocultural, and epigenetic) will be used to offer alternative explanations for eating disorders in adolescence.

Learning Objectives

Use this information to guide your reading, viewing, thinking, and studying. After successfully completing this lesson, you should be able to:

1. Identify and describe the biological events of puberty.
2. Identify several factors that influence the onset of puberty, and explain gender differences in the influence of early or late maturation on adolescent development.
3. Describe the growth spurt experienced during adolescence by both boys and girls, including changes in weight, height, and the body's internal organ system.
4. Describe the development of sexual characteristics in males and females during puberty, and describe influences on adolescents' sexual activity.
5. Discuss the emotional and psychological impact of pubertal hormones and how puberty can alter biorhythms.
6. Describe cultural, social, and individual factors that have an impact on the adolescent's development of a positive body image.
7. Describe potential sex-related problems in adolescence, including the prevalence and consequences of child sexual abuse.
8. Discuss the nutritional needs and nutritional deficiencies in adolescents.
9. Discuss the use and abuse of alcohol, tobacco, and other drugs among adolescents today, including prevalence, significance for development, and the best methods of prevention.

Read Chapter 9, "Adolescence: Body and Mind," pages 309–324 and 344–345.

View the video for Lesson 14, "Explosions."

Segment 1: *Puberty*

Segment 2: *Body Image*

Segment 3: *Health*

Summary

Puberty begins when a hormonal signal from the hypothalamus stimulates hormone production in the pituitary gland, which, in turn, triggers hormone production by the adrenal glands and by the **gonads** (sex glands). The major physical changes of puberty generally occur in the same sequence for everyone and are usually complete three or four years after they have begun. Variation in growth is related to sex, genetic inheritance, nutrition, and other factors.

The sequence of growth during puberty is from the extremities inward, making many adolescents temporarily big-footed, long-legged, and short-waisted. Internal organs also grow, including the lungs (which triple in weight) and the heart (which doubles in size and slows in rate). These changes give the adolescent increased physical endurance. The lymphoid system—including the tonsils and adenoids—decreases in size at adolescence, making teenagers less susceptible than children to respiratory ailments. The growth and maturation of the sex organs, called **primary sex characteristics**, that result in the development of reproductive potential are signaled by the first menstrual period (**menarche**) in girls and by the first ejaculation (**spermarche**) in boys.

Attitudes toward menarche and spermarche have changed over the past two decades, and—for the most part—fewer young people face these events with anxiety, embarrassment, or guilt. Young people who experience puberty at the same time as their friends tend to view the experience more positively than those who do not. The effects of early and late maturation differ for boys and girls. Girls find *early* maturation more difficult because of the added pressures that accompany sexual maturation. Boys find *late* maturation more difficult because of the correlation between peer status and a mature build.

Parents who are in conflict with each other, immature, socially isolated, alcoholic, or drug-abusing are more likely to be sexually abusive or so neglectful that their children are vulnerable to abuse from others. The psychological effects of **child sexual abuse** depend on the extent and duration of the abuse, the age of the child, and the reactions of family members and authorities once the abuse is known. Unlike younger victims of abuse, adolescents are prone to becoming self-destructive through substance abuse or eating disorders, running away from home, risking AIDS through unsafe sex, or even attempting suicide.

Drug abuse always harms physical and psychological development. **Drug use** may or may not be harmful, depending in part on how mature the drug user is and his or her reason for using the drug. Drug use is also increasing among younger adolescents. This is cause for particular concern because research has shown that early drug use is likely to disrupt the brain and body growth that occur during adolescence and can lead to long-term problems.

Review all reading assignments for this lesson.

As assigned by your instructor, complete the optional online component for this lesson.

Key Terms

Using your own words, write a brief definition or explanation of each of the following terms on a separate piece of paper.

1. puberty
2. menarche
3. spermarche
4. hormone
5. pituitary gland
6. adrenal glands
7. HPA (hypothalamus-pituitary-adrenal) axis
8. gonads
9. estradiol
10. testosterone
11. leptin
12. body image
13. anorexia nervosa
14. bulimia nervosa
15. growth spurt
16. primary sex characteristics
17. secondary sex characteristics
18. sexually transmitted infection (STI)
19. child sexual abuse
20. drug use
21. drug abuse
22. drug addiction
23. adolescence

Practice Questions I

Multiple-Choice Questions

1. Which of the following most accurately describes the sequence of pubertal development in girls?
   a. breast buds and pubic hair; growth spurt in which fat is deposited on hips and buttocks; first menstrual period; ovulation
   b. growth spurt; breast buds and pubic hair; first menstrual period; ovulation
   c. first menstrual period; breast buds and pubic hair; growth spurt; ovulation
   d. breast buds and pubic hair; growth spurt; ovulation; first menstrual period

2. When it comes to hormonal changes during adolescence,
   a. girls are only a few months, not years, ahead of boys.
   b. boys are a year earlier than girls.
   c. boys and girls reach sexual maturity at the same time.
   d. girls are about two years ahead of boys.

3. The first readily observable sign of the onset of puberty is
   a. the voice lowers.
   b. the appearance of facial, body, and pubic hair.
   c. a change in the shape of the eyes.
   d. a lengthening of the torso.

4. More than any other group in the population, adolescent girls are likely to have
   a. asthma.
   b. acne.
   c. iron-deficiency anemia.
   d. osetoporosis

5. The first set of changes during puberty is
   a. the growth spurt.
   b. menarche in girls/spermarche in boys.
   c. nutritional deficiencies.
   d. none of the above.

6. For girls, the specific event that is taken to indicate sexual maturity is ____________________; for boys, it is _________________.
   a. the growth of breast buds; voice deepening
   b. menarche; spermarche
   c. an ovulation; the testosterone surge
   d. the growth spurt; pubic hair

7. The most significant hormonal changes of puberty include a marked increase of ___________________ in ___________________ and a marked increase of ___________________ in ___________________.
   a. progesterone; boys; estradiol; girls
   b. estradiol; boys; testosterone; girls
   c. progesterone; girls; estradiol; boys
   d. estradiol; girls; testosterone; boys

8. In general, adolescents are
   a. overweight.
   b. satisfied with their appearance.
   c. dissatisfied with their appearance.
   d. unaffected by cultural attitudes about beauty.

9. The damage caused by sexual abuse depends on all of the following factors **EXCEPT**
   a. repeated incidence.
   b. the gender of the perpetrator.
   c. distorted adult-child relationships.
   d. impairment of the child's ability to develop normally.

10. The HPA axis leads from
   a. gonads to body to behavior.
   b. brain to behavior to body.
   c. brain to behavior to gonads.
   d. brain to body to behavior.

True or False Items

Write T (for true) or F (for false) on the line in front of each statement.

11. ____ Nutritional deficiencies in minerals is grater than deficiencies in vitamins during adolescence.

12. ____ The first indicator of reproductive potential in males is menarche.

13. ____ Lung capacity, heart size, and total volume of blood increase significantly during adolescence.

14. ____ Puberty generally begins sometime between ages 8 and 14.

15. ____ Worldwide, sexually active teens have higher rates of the most common STIs.

16. ____ The strong emphasis on physical appearance is unique to adolescents and finds little support from teachers, parents, and the larger culture.

17. ____ The hormone leptin affects appetite and has been implicated in the onset of puberty.

18. ____ Hormones from the pituitary gland often cause a "phase-delay" in sleep/wake patterns; many teens are wide awake at 8 a.m.

Practice Questions II

Multiple-Choice Questions

1. Which of the following is the correct sequence of pubertal events in boys?
   a. growth spurt; pubic hair; first ejaculation; lowering of voice
   b. pubic hair; first ejaculation; growth spurt; lowering of voice
   c. lowering of voice; pubic hair; growth spurt; first ejaculation
   d. growth spurt; lowering of voice; pubic hair; first ejaculation

2. Which of the following statements about adolescent physical development is NOT true?

   a. Hands and feet generally lengthen before arms and legs.
   b. Facial features usually grow before the head itself reaches adult size and shape.
   c. Oil, sweat, and odor glands become more active.
   d. The lymphoid system increases slightly in size, and the heart increases by nearly half.

3. In puberty, a hormone that increases markedly in girls (and only somewhat in boys) is

   a. estrogen.
   b. testosterone.
   c. androgen.
   d. menarche.

4. In females, puberty is typically marked by a(n)

   a. significant widening of the shoulders.
   b. significant widening of the hips.
   c. enlargement of the torso and upper chest.
   d. decrease in the size of the eyes and nose.

5. Nonreproductive sexual characteristics, such as the deepening of the voice and the development of breasts, are called

   a. gender-typed traits.
   b. primary sex characteristics.
   c. secondary sex characteristics.
   d. pubertal prototypes.

6. Puberty is initiated when hormones are released from the ______________, then from the ___________________, and then from the adrenal glands and the ____________________.

   a. hypothalamus; pituitary; gonads
   b. pituitary; gonads; hypothalamus
   c. gonads; pituitary; hypothalamus
   d. pituitary; hypothalamus; gonads

7. With regard to appearance, adolescent girls are most commonly dissatisfied with
   a. timing of maturation.
   b. eyes and other facial features.
   c. weight.
   d. legs.

8. Individuals who experiment with drugs early are
   a. typically affluent teenagers who are experiencing an identity crisis.
   b. more likely to have multiple drug-abuse problems later on.
   c. less likely to have alcohol-abuse problems later on.
   d. usually able to resist later peer pressure leading to long-term addiction.

9. Because of brain-related hormonal changes, adolescents
   a. are on a later sleep–wake cycle than adults.
   b. are skilled at using logical thinking during emotional situations.
   c. can withstand long periods of sleep deprivation with little to no effect on their health and school performance.
   d. experience a slowing down of reaction time.

10. Puberty is most accurately defined as the period
    a. of rapid physical growth that occurs during adolescence.
    b. during which sexual maturation is attained.
    c. of rapid physical growth and sexual maturation that ends childhood.
    d. during which adolescents establish identities separate from their parents.

11. Which of the following does **NOT** typically occur during puberty?
    a. The lungs increase in size and capacity.
    b. The heart's size and rate of beating increase.
    c. Blood volume increases.
    d. The lymphoid system decreases in size.

12. Teenagers' susceptibility to respiratory ailments typically ________________ during adolescence, as a result of a(n) ________________ in the size of the lymphoid system.
    a. increases; increase
    b. increases; decrease
    c. decreases; increase
    d. decreases; decrease

Matching Items

Match each definition or description with its corresponding term.

Terms

13. __________	puberty	18. __________	primary sex characteristics
14. __________	HPA axis	19. __________	menarche
15. __________	testosterone	20. __________	spermarche
16. __________	estradiol	21. __________	secondary sex characteristics
17. __________	growth spurt	22. __________	body image

Definitions or Descriptions

a. onset of menstruation
b. period of rapid physical growth and sexual maturation that ends childhood
c. hormone that increases dramatically in boys during puberty
d. route followed by many hormones to trigger puberty and to regulate other bodily changes
e. hormone that increases dramatically in girls during puberty
f. first sign is increased bone length and density
g. attitude toward one's physical appearance
h. physical characteristics not involved in reproduction
i. the sex organs involved in reproduction
j. first ejaculation containing sperm

Applying Your Knowledge

1. Fifteen-year-old Latoya is preoccupied with her "disgusting appearance" and seems depressed most of the time. The best thing her parents could do to help her through this difficult time would be to
   a. ignore her self-preoccupation, since their attention would only reinforce it.
   b. encourage her to "shape up" and not give in to self-pity.
   c. kid her about her appearance in the hope that she will see how silly she is acting.
   d. offer practical advice, such as clothing suggestions, to improve her body image.

2. Thirteen-year-old Rosa, an avid runner and dancer, is worried because most of her friends have begun to menstruate regularly. Her doctor tells her

   a. that she should have a complete physical exam, because female athletes usually menstruate earlier than average.

   b. not to worry, since female athletes usually menstruate later than average.

   c. that she must stop running immediately, because the absence of menstruation is a sign of a serious health problem.

   d. that the likely cause of her delayed menarche is an inadequate diet.

3. Twelve-year-old Kwan is worried because his twin sister has suddenly grown taller and more physically mature than he. His parents should

   a. reassure him that the average boy is one or two years behind the average girl in the onset of the growth spurt.

   b. tell him that within a year or less he will grow taller than his sister.

   c. tell him that one member of each fraternal twin pair is always shorter.

   d. encourage him to exercise more to accelerate the onset of his growth spurt.

4. Regarding the effects of early and late maturation on boys and girls, which of the following is **NOT** true?

   a. Early maturation is usually easier for boys to manage than it is for girls.

   b. Late maturation is usually easier for girls to manage than it is for boys.

   c. Late-maturing girls may be drawn into older peer groups and may exhibit problem behaviors, such as early sexual activity.

   d. Late-maturing boys may not "catch up" physically, or in terms of their self-images, for many years.

5. Which of the following adolescents is likely to begin puberty at the earliest age?

   a. Aretha, an African-American teenager who hates exercise

   b. Todd, a football player of European ancestry

   c. Kyu, an Asian-American honors student

   d. There is too little information to make a prediction.

6. Of the following teenagers, those most likely to be distressed about their physical development are

   a. late-maturing girls.

   b. late-maturing boys.

   c. early-maturing boys.

   d. girls or boys who masturbate.

7. Thirteen-year-old Kristin seems apathetic and lazy to her parents. You tell them
   a. that Kristin is showing signs of chronic depression.
   b. that Kristin may be experiencing psychosocial difficulties.
   c. that Kristin has a poor attitude and needs more discipline.
   d. to have Kristin's iron level checked.

8. I am a hormone that causes the gonads to increase sex hormone production during puberty in both males and females. What am I?
   a. estradiol
   b. testosterone
   c. GnRH
   d. menarche

9. Eleven-year-old Linda, who has just begun to experience the first signs of puberty, laments, "When will the agony of puberty be over?" You tell her that the major events of puberty typically end about _______________ after the first visible signs appear.
   a. 6 years
   b. 3 or 4 years
   c. 2 years
   d. 1 year

Answer Key

Key Terms

1. Puberty is the period of rapid physical growth and sexual maturation that ends childhood and brings the young person to adult size, shape, and sexual potential. (p. 310; video lesson, segment 1; objective 1)
2. Menarche, which refers to the first menstrual period, is the specific event that is taken to indicate fertility in adolescent girls. (p. 310; video lesson, segment 1; objective 1)
3. Spermarche, which refers to the first ejaculation of seminal fluid containing sperm, is the specific event that is taken to indicate fertility in adolescent boys. (p. 310; video lesson, segment 1; objective 1)
4. Hormones are substances created by a body tissue and transmitted through the bloodstream to other body tissues to influence a psychological function. (p. 310; objective 1)
5. The pituitary gland, under the influence of the hypothalamus, produces hormones that regulate growth and control other glands. (p. 310; objectives 1 & 2)

6. The adrenal glands secrete epinephrine and norephinephrine, hormones that prepare the body to deal with emergencies or stress. (p. 310; objectives 1 & 2)
7. The HPA axis (hypothalamus/pituitary/adrenal axis) is the route followed by many hormones to trigger puberty and to regulate stress, growth, and other bodily changes. (p. 311; objectives 1 & 2)
8. The gonads are the pair of sex glands in humans—the ovaries in girls and the testes or testicles in boys. (p. 311; video lesson, segment 1; objectives 2 & 5)
9. Estradiol is a sex hormone that is secreted in greater amounts by females than males. (p. 311; objective 2)
10. Testosterone is a sex hormone that is secreted more by males than by females. (p. 311; video lesson, segment 1; objective 2)
11. Leptin is a hormone that affects appetite and is believed to be involved in the onset of puberty. Leptin levels increase during childhood and peak at around age 12. (p. 314; objective 2)
12. Body image refers to adolescents' mental conception of, and attitude toward, their physical appearance. (p. 317; video lesson, segment 2; objective 6)
13. Anorexia nervosa is an eating disorder characterized by self-starvation. Affected individuals voluntarily undereat and often overexercise, depriving their vital organs of nutrition. Anorexia can be fatal. (p. 318; objectives 3, 6, & 8)
14. Bulimia nervosa is an eating disorder characterized by binge eating and subsequent purging usually by induced vominting and/or the use of laxatives. (p. 318; objectives 3, 6, & 8)
15. The growth spurt, which begins with an increase in bone length and density and includes rapid weight gain and organ growth, is one of the many observable signs of puberty. (p. 319; video lesson, segment 1; objective 3)
16. During puberty, changes in the primary sex characteristics involve those sex organs that are directly involved in reproduction. (p. 320; video lesson, segment 1; objective 4)
17. During puberty, changes in the secondary sex characteristics involve parts of the body that are not directly involved in reproduction but that signify sexual development. (p. 320; video lesson, segment 1; objective 4)
18. Diseases such as HIV, chlamydia, syphilis, and others transmitted through sexual contact are referred to as sexually transmitted infections (STIs). (p. 322; objective 7)
19. Child sexual abuse is any activity in which an adult uses a child for his or her own sexual stimulation or pleasure—even if the use does not involve physical contact. (p. 323; objective 7)

20. Drug use is the ingestion of a drug, regardless of the amount or affect of ingestion. (video lesson, segment 3; objective 9)
21. Drug abuse is the ingestion of a drug to the extent that it impairs the user's well-being. (video lesson, segment 3; objective 9)
22. Drug addiction is a person's dependence on a drug or a behavior in order to feel physically or psychologically at ease. (video lesson, segment 3; objective 9)
23. Adolescence is the period of biological, cognitive, and psychosocial transition from childhood to adulthood. (video lesson, segment 1; objective 1)

Practice Questions I

Multiple-Choice Questions

1. a. is the correct answer. (p. 310; video lesson, segment 1; objective 1)
2. a. is the correct answer. (p. 313; video lesson, segment 1; objectives 1 & 2)
3. b. is the correct answer. (p. 310; video lesson, segment 1; objective 1)
4. c. is the correct answer. (pp. 316–317; objective 8)
5. a. is the correct answer. (p. 319; video lesson, segment 1; objective 3)
6. b. is the correct answer. (p. 310; video lesson, segment 1; objective 1)
7. d. is the correct answer. (p. 311; video lesson, segment 1; objectives 1 & 2)
8. c. is the correct answer. (p. 317; video lesson, segment 2; objective 6)

   a. is incorrect. Although some adolescents become overweight, many diet and lose weight in an effort to attain a desired body image.

   d. is incorrect. On the contrary, cultural attitudes about beauty are an extremely influential factor in the formation of a teenager's body image.
9. b. is the correct answer. (pp. 323–324; objective 7)
10. d. is the correct answer. (p. 311; objective 5)

True or False Items

11. T (p. 316; objective 8)
12. F The first indicator of reproductive potential in males is ejaculation of seminal fluid containing sperm (spermarche). Menarche (the first menstrual period) is the first indication of reproductive potential in females. (p. 310; video lesson, segment 1; objective 1)
13. T (p. 320; objective 3)
14. T (p. 310; video lesson, segment 1; objectives 1 & 2)
15. T (p. 322; objective 7)
16. F The strong emphasis on appearance is reflected in the culture as a whole; for example, teachers (and, no doubt, prospective employers) tend to judge people who are physically attractive as being more competent than those who are less attractive. (video lesson, segment 2; objective 6)

17. T (p. 314; objective 2)
18. F (p. 312; objective 5)

Practice Questions II

Multiple-Choice Questions

1. b. is the correct answer. (p. 310; objective 1)
2. d. is the correct answer. During adolescence, the lymphoid system decreases in size and the heart doubles in size. (p. 320; objective 3)
3. a. is the correct answer. (pp. 310–311; video lesson, segment 1; objective 1)

   b. is incorrect. Testosterone increases markedly in boys.

   c. is incorrect. Androgen is another name for testosterone.

   d. is incorrect. Menarche is the first menstrual period.
4. b. is the correct answer. (p. 310; objective 1)
5. c. is the correct answer. (p. 320; video lesson, segment 1; objective 4)

   a. is incorrect. Although not a term used in the textbook, a gender-typed trait is one that is typical of one sex but not of the other.

   b. is incorrect. Primary sex characteristics are those involving the reproductive organs.

   d. is incorrect. This is not a term used by developmental psychologists.
6. a. is the correct answer. (p. 311; video lesson, segment 1; objectives 1 & 2)
7. c. is the correct answer. (video lesson, segment 2; objective 6)

   a. is incorrect. If the timing of maturation differs substantially from that of the peer group, dissatisfaction is likely; however, this is not the most common source of dissatisfaction in teenage girls.

   b. & d. are incorrect. Although teenage girls are more likely than boys to be dissatisfied with certain features, which body parts are troubling varies from girl to girl.
8. b. is the correct answer. (video lesson, segment 3; objective 9)
9. a. is the correct answer. (p. 312; objective 5)
10. c. is the correct answer. (p. 310; video lesson, segment 1; objective 1)
11. b. is the correct answer. Although the size of the heart increases during puberty, heart rate decreases. (pp. 319–320; objective 3)
12. d. is the correct answer. (p. 320; objective 3)

Matching Items

13. b (p. 310; video lesson, segment 1; objective 1)
14. d (p. 311; objectives 1 & 2)
15. c (p. 311; video lesson, segment 1; objectives 1 & 2)
16. e (p. 311; objectives 1 & 2)

17. f (p. 319; video lesson, segment 1; objective 3)
18. i (p. 320; video lesson, segment 1; objective 4)
19. a (p. 310; video lesson, segment 1; objective 1)
20. j (p. 310; video lesson, segment 1; objective 1)
21. h (p. 320; video lesson, segment 1; objective 4)
22. g (p. 317; video lesson, segment 2; objective 6)

Applying Your Knowledge

1. d. is the correct answer. (video lesson, segment 2; objective 6)

   a., b., & c. are incorrect. These would likely make matters worse.

2. b. is the correct answer. (p. 314; objective 2)

   a. is incorrect. Because they typically have little body fat, female dancers and athletes menstruate later than average.

   c. is incorrect. Delayed maturation in a young dancer or athlete is usually quite normal.

   d. is incorrect. The textbook does not indicate that the age of menarche varies with diet.

3. a. is the correct answer. (p. 313; objective 2)

   b. is incorrect. It usually takes longer than one year for a prepubescent male to catch up with a female who has begun puberty.

   c. is incorrect. This is not true.

   d. is incorrect. The textbook does not suggest that exercise has an effect on the timing of the growth spurt.

4. c. is the correct answer. It is early maturing girls who are often drawn into involvement with older boys. (pp. 315–316; objective 2)

5. a. is thc correct answer. African Americans often begin puberty earlier than Asian Americans or Americans of European ancestry. Furthermore, females who are inactive menstruate earlier than those who are more active. (p. 315; objective 2)

6. b. is the correct answer. (p. 316; video lesson, segment 2; objective 2)

   a. is incorrect. Late maturation is typically more difficult for boys than for girls.

   c. is incorrect. Early maturation is generally a positive experience for boys.

   d. is incorrect. Adolescent masturbation is no longer the source of guilt or shame that it once was.

7. d. is the correct answer. Kristin's symptoms are typical of iron-deficiency anemia, which is more common in teenage girls than in any other agc group. (pp. 316–317; objective 8)

8. c. is the correct answer. (p. 311; objectives 1 & 2)

   a. is incorrect. Only in girls do estradiol levels rise markedly during puberty.

   b. is incorrect. Only in boys do testosterone levels rise markedly during puberty.

   d. is incorrect. Menarche is the first menstrual period.

9. b. is the correct answer. (video lesson, segment 1; objective 1)

Lesson Review

Lesson 14

Adolescence
Biosocial Development

Please Note: Use this matrix to guide your study and achieve the learning objectives of this lesson. It will also help you to view the video, which defines and demonstrates important concepts and skills as they relate to everyday life.

Learning Objective	Textbook	Telecourse Student Guide	Video Lesson
1. Identify and describe the biological events of puberty.	pp. 310–312	Key Terms: 1, 2, 3, 4, 5, 6, 7, 23; Practice Questions I: 1, 2, 3, 6, 7, 12, 14; Practice Questions II: 1, 3, 4, 6, 10, 13, 14, 15, 16, 19, 20; Applying Your Knowledge: 8, 9.	Segment 1: *Puberty*
2. Identify several factors that influence the onset of puberty, and explain gender differences in the influence of early or late maturation on adolescent development.	pp. 312–316	Key Terms: 5, 6, 7, 8, 9, 10, 11; Practice Questions I: 2, 7, 14, 17; Practice Questions II: 6, 14, 15, 16; Applying Your Knowledge: 2, 3, 4, 5, 6, 8.	Segment 1: *Puberty*
3. Describe the growth spurt experienced during adolescence by both boys and girls, including changes in weight, height, and the body's internal organ system.	pp. 319–320	Key Terms: 13, 14, 15; Practice Questions I: 5, 13; Practice Questions II: 2, 11, 12, 17.	Segment 1: *Puberty;* Segment 2: *Body Image*
4. Describe the development of sexual characteristics in males and females during puberty, and describe influences on adolescents' sexual activity.	pp. 320–324	Key Terms: 16, 17; Practice Questions II: 5, 18, 21.	Segment 1: *Puberty*
5. Discuss the emotional and psychological impact of pubertal hormones and how puberty can alter biorhythms.	pp. 311–312	Key Terms: 8; Practice Questions I: 10, 18; Practice Questions II: 9.	Segment 1: *Puberty*

Learning Objective	**Textbook**	**Telecourse Student Guide**	**Video Lesson**
6. Describe cultural, social, and individual factors that have an impact on the adolescent's development of a positive body image.	pp. 317–319	Key Terms: 12, 13, 14; Practice Questions I: 8, 16; Practice Questions II: 7, 22; Applying Your Knowledge: 1.	Segment 2: *Body Image*
7. Describe potential sex-related problems in adolescence, including the prevalence and consequences of child sexual abuse.	pp. 321–324	Key Terms: 18, 19; Practice Questions I: 9, 15.	Segment 1: *Puberty*
8. Discuss the nutritional needs and nutritional deficiencies of adolescents.	pp. 316–317	Key Terms: 13, 14; Practice Questions I: 4, 11; Applying Your Knowledge: 7.	
9. Discuss the use and abuse of alcohol, tobacco, and other drugs among adolescents today, including prevalence, significance for development, and the best methods of prevention.	*	Key Terms: 20, 21, 22; Practice Questions II: 8.	Segment 3: *Health*

* The video for this lesson provides a useful exploration of these topics.

What If?

Lesson 15

Adolescence: Cognitive Development

Preview

Lesson 15 begins by describing the cognitive advances of adolescence, especially the emerging ability to think in an adult way, that is, to be logical, to think in terms of possibilities, and to reason scientifically and abstractly.

Not all adolescents attain this level of reasoning ability, however, and even those who do spend much of their time thinking at less advanced levels. For instance, adolescents may have difficulty thinking rationally about themselves and their immediate experiences, often seeing themselves as psychologically unique and more socially significant than they really are.

The lesson also addresses the question, "What kind of school best fosters adolescent intellectual growth?" Many adolescents enter secondary school feeling less motivated and more vulnerable to self-doubt than they did in elementary school. The rigid behavioral demands and intensified competition of most secondary schools do not, unfortunately, provide a supportive learning environment for adolescents.

Throughout this lesson, recall your own cognitive development during adolescence. In what ways was your thinking more like an adult's, and it what ways was it still "youthful"? Did you think about yourself, about your interests and your future? Reflect on your experiences in middle and secondary school. Did you get what you consider to be a good education? Why or why not? Was there much academic competition in your school(s)?

Prior Telecourse Knowledge that Will Be Used in this Lesson

- This lesson will return to Piaget's theory of cognitive development (from Lesson 1/Chapter 2). Recall that Piaget's theory specifies four major periods of development, the fourth and final stage being *formal operational thought*:
    1. Sensorimotor (birth to 2 years)
    2. Preoperational (2 to 6 years)
    3. Concrete Operational (7 to 11 years)
    4. **Formal Operational (12 years through adulthood)**

Learning Objectives

Use this information to guide your reading, viewing, thinking, and studying. After successfully completing this lesson, you should be able to:

1. Describe Piaget's concept of formal operational thinking and provide examples of adolescents' emerging ability to reason deductively and inductively.
2. Discuss adolescent egocentrism and give three examples of egocentric fantasies or fables.
3. Describe the concept of person–environment fit, explain how schools can be organized to more effectively meet adolescents' cognitive needs, and identify the main challenges adolescents face in middle school.
4. Describe the major ethnic and cultural factors that can affect adolescent schooling, and discuss factors that influence school engagement.
5. Discuss the dual-process model of adolescent thinking, and describe how it can explain common errors in adolescent reasoning.
6. Discuss the emergence of computer technology and its influence on adolescent thinking and learning.

Read Chapter 9, "Adolescence: Body and Mind," pages 324–345.

View the video for Lesson 15, "What If?"

Segment 1: *Formal Operational Thought*

Segment 2: *Educating Adolescents*

Segment 3: *Adolescent Decision-Making*

Summary

The basic skills of thinking, learning, and remembering continue to be refined during the adolescent years. According to most developmentalists, the distinguishing feature of adolescent thought is the capacities to think in terms of possibility rather than only in terms of reality.

Piaget described the reasoning that characterizes adolescence as **formal operational thought**, which arises from maturation and experience. On the whole, adolescents are able to fantasize, speculate, and hypothesize much more readily and on a much grander scale than younger children are. With this capacity for **hypothetical thought**, the adolescent is able to consider the here and now as one among many alternative possibilities. In addition, the capacities for **deductive reasoning** (deriving conclusions from premises) and **inductive reasoning** (reasoning from one or more specific experiences or facts to a general conclusion) become refined.

Developmental psychologists have described **adolescent egocentrism** as a stage of development in which young people typically consider their own psychological experiences (love and anger, for example) to be unique. The **invincibility fable** that they are somehow immune to common dangers and the **personal fable** that their lives are unique or heroic are further examples of adolescents' egocentrism. As another part of their egocentrism, adolescents often create for themselves an **imaginary audience** that allows them to fantasize about how others will react to their appearance and behavior.

With regard to education, the optimum **person–environment fit** depends not only on the individual's developmental stage, cognitive abilities, and learning style, but also on the society's traditions, educational objectives, and future needs, which vary substantially from place to place and time to time. Many educational settings rely on ego-involvement learning, in which grades are based solely on individual test performance and students are ranked against each other. In such competitive conditions, many students—especially girls and minority students—find it easier and psychologically safer not to compete. Some may perform better in settings based on task-involvement learning, which encourages cooperative (group) learning and measures a student's performance based on his or her mastery of the material.

Because they often think about possibilities rather than practicalities, and because egocentrism makes it difficult to plan ahead, adolescents tend not to make major decisions about their future plans on their own. On matters of personal lifestyle, however, they do make decisions, sometimes ones that involve considerable risk. Because of their sense of personal invincibility, many teens underestimate the chances of getting pregnant or of contracting a sexually transmitted infection (STI). In addition, teens often fail to think through all the possible consequences of their behavior, focusing instead on immediate concerns only. Many school systems have begun to develop sex education programs that encourage thinking, role playing, and discussion about sexuality instead of focusing only on biological facts. Such programs help adolescents to understand and consider the consequences of teen sexual activity and its impact on their future.

Review all reading assignments for this lesson.

As assigned by your instructor, complete the optional online component for this lesson.

Key Terms

Using your own words, write a brief definition or explanation of each of the following terms on a separate piece of paper.

1. adolescent egocentrism
2. personal fable
3. invincibility fable
4. imaginary audience
5. formal operational thought
6. hypothetical thought
7. deductive reasoning
8. inductive reasoning
9. dual-process model
10. intuitive thought
11. analytic thought
12. secondary education
13. middle school
14. digital divide
15. cyberbullying
16. high-stakes test
17. person–environment fit
18. volatile mismatch

Practice Questions I

Multiple-Choice Questions

1. Many psychologists consider the distinguishing feature of adolescent thought to be the ability to think in terms of
   a. moral issues.
   b. concrete operations.
   c. possibility, not just reality.
   d. logical principles.

2. Piaget's last stage of cognitive development is
   a. formal operational thought.
   b. concrete operational thought.
   c. universal ethical principles.
   d. symbolic thought.

3. The adolescent who takes risks and feels immune to the laws of mortality is showing evidence of the
   a. invincibility fable.
   b. personal fable.
   c. imaginary audience.
   d. death instinct.

4. Imaginary audiences, invincibility fables, and personal fables are expressions of adolescent
   a. morality.
   b. thinking games.
   c. decision making.
   d. egocentrism.
5. In their egocentrism, adolescents regard themselves as
   a. unique.
   b. special.
   c. socially significant.
   d. all of the above.
6. When adolescents enter middle school, many
   a. experience a drop in their academic self-confidence.
   b. are more disconnected from teachers.
   c. are less conscientious than they were in elementary school.
   d. experience all of the above.
7. Thinking that begins with a general premise and then draws logical conclusions from it is called
   a. inductive reasoning.
   b. deductive reasoning.
   c. "the game of thinking."
   d. hypothetical reasoning.
8. Serious reflection on important issues is a wrenching process for many adolescents because of their newfound ability to reason
   a. inductively.
   b. deductively.
   c. hypothetically.
   d. symbolically.
9. Many adolescents seem to believe that their own sexual behaviors will not lead to pregnancy. This belief is an expression of the
   a. personal fable.
   b. invincibility fable.
   c. imaginary audience.
   d. "game of thinking."

10. While the United States is increasing the use of high-stakes testing in education, East Asian countries are
    a. testing students on an ever-widening array of subjects.
    b. reducing high-stakes testing and encouraging innovation.
    c. discontinuing the use of high-stakes tests entirely.
    d. doing none of the above.

11. Which of the following characteristics is the most important characteristic to ensure high school graduation?
    a. intelligence
    b. persistence
    c. creativity
    d. social skills

12. Which statement is **TRUE** in regard to attending middle school?
    a. Academic achievement slows down.
    b. Personal relationships grow.
    c. Bonding with teachers is common.
    d. Students are not concerned with body image at this age.

True or False Items

Write T (for true) or F (for false) on the line in front of each statement.

13. _____ Adolescents are generally better able than eight-year-olds at recognizing the validity of arguments that clash with their own beliefs.

14. _____ Everyone attains the stage of formal operational thought by adulthood.

15. _____ The transition from primary to secondary school is stressful only when it brings about negative changes in the adolescent's life.

16. _____ Adolescents often create an imaginary audience as they envision how others will react to their appearance and behavior.

17. _____ One potential unintended consequence of high-stakes tests is an increase in the high school dropout rate.

18. _____ Inductive reasoning is a hallmark of formal operational thought.

19. _____ The digital divide refers to the gap between those who have computer access and those who do not.

Practice Questions II

Multiple-Choice Questions

1. Adolescents who fall prey to the invincibility fable may be more likely to
   a. engage in risky behaviors.
   b. suffer from depression.
   c. have low self-esteem.
   d. drop out of school.

2. Thinking that extrapolates from a specific experience to form a general premise is called
   a. inductive reasoning.
   b. deductive reasoning.
   c. "the game of thinking."
   d. hypothetical reasoning.

3. Recent research regarding Piaget's theory has found that
   a. many adolescents arrive at formal operational thinking later than Piaget predicted.
   b. formal operational thinking is more likely to be demonstrated in certain domains than in others.
   c. individuals often demonstrate formal operational thinking in some domains while failing to demonstrate it in other domains.
   d. all of the above are true.

4. When young people overestimate their significance to others, they are displaying
   a. concrete operational thought.
   b. adolescent egocentrism.
   c. a lack of cognitive growth.
   d. immoral development.

5. The personal fable refers to adolescents imagining that
   a. they are immune to the dangers of risky behaviors.
   b. they are always being scrutinized by others.
   c. their own lives are unique, heroic, or even mythical.
   d. the world revolves around their actions.

6. The typical middle school environment
   a. has school schedules that inhibit making friends.
   b. inhibits striving for good grades because of harsher grading practices.
   c. provides scarce extra curricular activities that interest students.
   d. includes all of the above.

7. As compared to elementary schools, most secondary schools exhibit all of the following **EXCEPT**
   a. a more flexible approach to education.
   b. intensified competition.
   c. more punitive grading practices.
   d. less individualized attention.

8. Thought that arises from an emotion or a hunch is
   a. analytic reasoning.
   b. intuitive thought.
   c. egocentrism.
   d. none of the above.

9. Which of the following is one of the hallmarks of formal operational thought?
   a. egocentrism
   b. deductive thinking
   c. symbolic thinking
   d. all of the above

10. During the 1980s, Germany was a major innovator in _______________ programs.
    a. home schooling
    b. study abroad
    c. apprenticeships
    d. none of the above

11. Which of the following statements is **TRUE** regarding computer use in education?
    a. Children with and without computers do equally well in math.
    b. Most teen computer use is educational in nature, not social.
    c. One study found that 16% of secondary school children have engaged in cyberbullying.
    d. Only a and c are true.

Matching Items

Match each definition or description with its corresponding term.

Terms

12. __________ invincibility fable
13. __________ imaginary audience
14. __________ person–environment fit
15. __________ hypothetical thought
16. __________ deductive reasoning
17. __________ inductive reasoning
18. __________ formal operational thought
19. __________ volatile mismatch
20. __________ adolescent egocentrism
21. __________ cyberbullying

Definitions or Descriptions

a. the tendency of adolescents to focus on themselves to the exclusion of others
b. adolescents feel immune to the consequences of dangerous behavior
c. a creation of adolescents, who are preoccupied with how others react to their appearance and behavior
d. the match or mismatch between an adolescent's needs
e. reasoning about propositions that may or may not reflect reality
f. the last stage of cognitive development, according to Piaget
g. thinking that moves from premise to specific conclusion
h. thinking that moves from a specific experience to a general conclusion
i. a clash between a teenager's needs and the structure
j. insults and rumors, and video embarrassment over the Internet

Applying Your Knowledge

1. A 13-year-old can create and solve logical problems on the computer but is not usually reasonable, mature, or consistent in his or her thinking when it comes to people and social relationships. This supports the finding that
   a. some children reach the stage of formal operational thought earlier than others.
   b. the stage of formal operational thought is not attained by age 13.
   c. formal operational thinking may be demonstrated in certain domains and not in other domains.
   d. older adolescents and adults often do poorly on standard tests of formal operational thought.

2. An experimenter hides a ball in her hand and says, "Either the ball in my hand is red or it is not red." Most preadolescent children say
   a. the statement is true.
   b. the statement is false.
   c. they cannot tell if the statement is true or false.
   d. they do not understand what the experimenter means.

3. Fourteen-year-old Monica is very idealistic and often develops crushes on people she doesn't even know. This reflects her newly developed cognitive ability to
   a. deal simultaneously with two sides of an issue.
   b. take another person's viewpoint.
   c. imagine possible worlds and people.
   d. see herself as others see her.

4. Which of the following is the **BEST** example of a personal fable?
   a. Adriana imagines that she is destined for a life of fame and fortune.
   b. Ben makes up stories about his experiences to impress his friends.
   c. Kalil questions his religious beliefs when they seem to offer little help for a problem he faces.
   d. Julio believes that every girl he meets is attracted to him.

5. Which of the following is the **BEST** example of adolescents' ability to think hypothetically?
   a. Twelve-year-old Stanley feels that people are always watching him.
   b. Fourteen-year-old Mindy engages in many risky behaviors, reasoning that "nothing bad will happen to me."
   c. Fifteen-year-old Philip believes that no one understands his problems.
   d. Thirteen-year-old Josh delights in finding logical flaws in virtually everything his teachers and parents say.

6. Frustrated because of the dating curfew her parents have set, Melinda exclaims, "You just don't know how it feels to be in love!" Melinda's thinking demonstrates
   a. the invincibility fable.
   b. the personal fable.
   c. the imaginary audience.
   d. adolescent egocentrism.

7. Compared to her 13-year-old brother, 17-year-old Yolanda is likely to
   a. be more critical about herself.
   b. be more egocentric.
   c. have less confidence in her abilities.
   d. be more capable of reasoning hypothetically.

8. Nathan's fear that his friends will ridicule him because of a pimple that has appeared on his nose reflects a preoccupation with
   a. his personal fable.
   b. the invincibility fable.
   c. an imaginary audience.
   d. preconventional reasoning.

9. Thirteen-year-old Malcolm, who lately is very sensitive to the criticism of others, feels significantly less motivated and capable in middle school than when he was in elementary school. Malcolm is probably
   a. experiencing a sense of vulnerability that is common in adolescents.
   b. a lower-track student.
   c. a student in a task-involvement classroom.
   d. all of the above.

10. In presenting an argument for why her religion is the best, 14-year-old Janice is likely to emphasize ________________ thought over ________________ thought.
    a. intuitive; analytic
    b. analytic; intuitive
    c. deductive; inductive
    d. inductive; deductive

11. After hearing that an unusually aggressive child has been in full-time day care since he was a toddler, 16-year-old Keenan concludes that nonparental care leads to behavior problems. Keenan's conclusion is an example of
    a. inductive reasoning.
    b. deductive reasoning.
    c. hypothetical thinking.
    d. adolescent egocentrism.

12. In which of the following schools are students likely to feel most engaged?
    a. Adams High School, which has a population of 1,000 students
    b. Jasper High School, where students are encouraged to participate in extracurricular activities
    c. Franklin High School, where most teachers have a graduate degree in the topic they teach
    d. Anderson High School, where students must take an exit exam before they can graduate

Answer Key

Key Terms

1. Adolescent egocentrism refers to the tendency of adolescents to see themselves as much more socially significant than they actually are. (p. 326; video lesson, segment 1; objective 2)
2. Another example of adolescent egocentrism is the personal fable, through which adolescents imagine their own lives as unique, heroic, or even mythical. (p. 327; video lesson, segment 1; objective 2)

   Memory aid: A fable is a mythical story.
3. Adolescents who experience the invincibility fable feel that they are immune to the dangers of risky behaviors. (p. 327; video lesson, segment 1; objective 2)
4. Adolescents often create an imaginary audience for themselves, as they assume that others are as intensely interested in them as they themselves are. (p. 328; video lesson, segment 1; objective 2)
5. In Piaget's theory, the last stage of cognitive development, which arises from a combination of maturation and experience, is called formal operational thought. A hallmark of formal operational thinking is the capacity for hypothetical, logical, and abstract thought. (p. 328; video lesson, segment 1; objective 1)
6. Hypothetical thought involves reasoning about propositions and possibilities that may or may not reflect reality. (p. 330; video lesson, segment 1; objective 1)
7. Deductive reasoning is thinking that moves from the general to the specific, or from a premise to a logical conclusion. (p. 330; video lesson, segment 1; objective 1)
8. Inductive reasoning is thinking that moves from one or more specific experiences to a general conclusion. (p. 331; video lesson, segment 1; objective 1)
9. The dual-process model suggests that there are two thought processes that develop and influence one another: the emotional/intuitive process and the analytical/logical process. (p. 331; objective 5)

10. Intuitive thought is similar to having a "hunch"; it is based more on emotion and experience than on logic. (p. 332; objective 5)
11. Analytic thought stems from the careful and logical analysis of a problem. (p. 332; objective 5)
12. Secondary education begins after the completion of elementary education. It typically includes middle school and high school. (p. 334; objective 3)
13. Middle schools exist to educate students who have entered adolescence, but are not yet prepared for high school. This school experience usually begins with grade 5 or 6 and ends with grade 8. (p. 334; objective 3)
14. The gap between students who have access to computers and those who do not, often a gap between rich and poor, is called the digital divide. In the United States and most developed nations, this gap has been bridged because of the prevalence of computers in schools. (p. 335; objective 6)
15. Bullying that occurs via Internet insults and rumors, texting, anonymous phone calls, and video embarrassment. (p. 337; objective 6)
16. A high-stakes test is a test that determines whether a student will graduate or be promoted. It is referred to as "high-stakes" because the test is expected to measure whether the student has succeeded or failed in some aspect of his or her education. (p. 339; objective 4)
17. The term person–environment fit refers to the best setting for personal growth, as in the optimum educational setting. (video lesson, segment 2; objective 3)
18. When teenagers' individual needs do not match the size, routine, and structure of their schools, a volatile mismatch may occur. (video lesson, segment 2; objective 3)

Practice Questions I

Multiple-Choice Questions

1. c. is the correct answer. (pp. 328–329; video lesson, segment 1; objective 1)

   a. is incorrect. Although moral reasoning becomes much deeper during adolescence, it is not limited to this stage of development.

   b. & d. are incorrect. Concrete operational thought, which is logical, is the distinguishing feature of childhood thinking.

2. a. is the correct answer. (p. 328; video lesson, segment 1; objective 1)

   b. is incorrect. In Piaget's theory, this stage precedes formal operational thought.

   c. & d. are incorrect. These are not stages in Piaget's theory.

3. a. is the correct answer. (pp. 327–328; video lesson, segment 1; objective 2)

   b. is incorrect. This refers to adolescents' tendency to imagine their own lives as unique, heroic, or even mythical.

   c. is incorrect. This refers to adolescents' tendency to fantasize about how others will react to their appearance and behavior.

   d. is incorrect. This is a concept in Freud's theory.

4. d. is the correct answer. These thought processes are manifestations of adolescents' tendency to see themselves as being much more central and important to the social scene than they really are. (pp. 326–328; video lesson, segment 1; objective 2)
5. d. is the correct answer. (p. 326; video lesson, segment 1; objective 2)
6. d. is the correct answer. (p. 334; objective 3)
7. b. is the correct answer. (p. 330; video lesson, segment 1; objective 1)

   a. is incorrect. Inductive reasoning moves from specific facts to a general conclusion.

   c. & d. are incorrect. The "game of thinking," which is an example of hypothetical reasoning, involves the ability to think creatively about possibilities.
8. c. is the correct answer. (p. 330; video lesson, segment 3; objective 1)
9. b. is the correct answer. (p. 327; objective 2)

   a. is incorrect. This refers to adolescents' tendency to imagine their own lives as unique, heroic, or even mythical.

   c. is incorrect. This refers to adolescents' tendency to fantasize about how others will react to their appearance and behavior.

   d. is incorrect. This is the adolescent ability to suspend knowledge of reality in order to think playfully about possibilities.
10. b. is the correct answer. Japanese schools are placing less emphasis on high-stakes testing than they used to. (pp. 339–340; objective 4)
11. b. is the correct answer. (p. 342; objective 4)
12. a. is the answer. (p. 334; objective 3)

True or False Items

13. T (p. 330; video lesson, segment 1; objective 1)
14. F Some people never reach the stage of formal operational thought. (video lesson, segment 1; objective 1)
15. F Even positive changes during school transition produce stress. (pp. 334–335; objective 3)
16. T (p. 328; video lesson, segment 1; objective 2)
17. T (p. 341; objective 4)
18. F Deductive reasoning is a hallmark of formal operational thought, although adolescents continue to improve their inductive reasoning skills as well. (pp. 330–331; video lesson, segment 1; objective 1)
19. T (p. 335; objective 6)

Practice Questions II

Multiple-Choice Questions

1. a. is the correct answer. (p. 327; video lesson, segment 1; objective 2)

   b., c., & d. are incorrect. The invincibility fable leads some teens to believe that they are immune to the dangers of risky behaviors; it is not necessarily linked to depression, low self-esteem, or the likelihood that an individual will drop out of school.

2. a. is the correct answer. (p. 331; video lesson, segment 1; objective 1)

   b. is incorrect. Deductive reasoning begins with a general premise and then draws logical conclusions from it.

   c. & d. are incorrect. The "game of thinking," which is an example of hypothetical reasoning, involves the ability to think creatively about possibilities.

3. d. is the correct answer. (pp. 328–329; video lesson, segment 1; objective 1)
4. b. is the correct answer. (p. 326; video lesson, segment 1; objective 2)
5. c. is the correct answer. (p. 327; video lesson, segment 1; objective 2)

   a. is incorrect. This describes the invincibility fable.

   b. is incorrect. This describes the imaginary audience.

   d. is incorrect. This describes adolescent egocentrism in general.

6. d. is the correct answer. (p. 335; objective 3)
7. a. is the correct answer. (p. 335; objective 3)
8. b. is the correct answer. (p. 332; objective 5)
9. d. is the correct answer. (p. 330; video lesson, segment 1; objective 1)
10. c. is the correct answer. (p. 340; objective 4)

    a., b., & d. are incorrect. These are more likely to be emphasized by information-processing theorists, Piagetian theorists, or epigenetic theorists.

11. d. is the correct answer. (pp. 336–337; objective 6)

Matching Items

12. b (p. 327; video lesson, segment 1; objective 2)
13. c (p. 328; video lesson, segment 1; objective 2)
14. d (video lesson, segment 2; objective 3)
15. e (p. 330; video lesson, segment 1; objective 1)
16. g (p. 330; video lesson, segment 1; objective 1)
17. h (p. 331; video lesson, segment 1; objective 1)
18. f (p. 328; video lesson, segment 1; objective 1)
19. i (video lesson, segment 2; objective 3)
20. a (p. 326; video lesson, segment 1; objective 2)
21. j (p. 337; objective 6)

Applying Your Knowledge

1. c. is the correct answer. (pp. 328, 331; video lesson, segment 1; objectives 1 & 5)
2. c. is the correct answer. Although this statement is logically verifiable, preadolescents who lack formal operational thought cannot prove or disprove it. (pp. 328–329; objective 1)
3. c. is the correct answer. (video lesson, segment 1; objective 1)
4. a. is the correct answer. (p. 327; video lesson, segment 1; objective 2)

   b. & d. are incorrect. These behaviors are more indicative of a preoccupation with the imaginary audience.

   c. is incorrect. Kalil's questioning attitude is a normal adolescent tendency that helps foster moral reasoning.
5. d. is the correct answer. (p. 330; video lesson, segment 1; objective 1)

   a. is incorrect. This is an example of the imaginary audience.

   b. is incorrect. This is an example of the invincibility fable.

   c. is incorrect. This is an example of adolescent egocentrism.
6. d. is the correct answer. (p. 326; video lesson, segment 1; objective 2)
7. d. is the correct answer. (p. 333; video lesson, segment 1; objective 1)
8. c. is the correct answer. (p. 328; video lesson, segment 1; objective 2)

   a. is incorrect. In this fable, adolescents see themselves destined for fame and fortune.

   b. is incorrect. In this fable, young people feel that they are somehow immune to the consequences of common dangers.

   d. is incorrect. This is a stage of moral reasoning in Kohlberg's theory.
9. a. is the correct answer. (pp. 333–335; objective 3)
10. a. is the correct answer. (pp. 331–333; objective 5)
11. a. is the correct answer. (p. 331; video lesson, segment 1; objective 1)

    b. is incorrect. Keenan is reasoning from the specific to the general, rather than vice versa.

    c. is incorrect. Keenan is thinking about an actual observation, rather than a hypothetical possibility.

    d. is incorrect. Keenan's reasoning is focused outside himself, rather than being self-centered.
12. b. is the correct answer. (pp. 342–343; objective 4)

Lesson Review

Lesson 15

Adolescence
Cognitive Development

Please Note: Use this matrix to guide your study and achieve the learning objectives of this lesson. It will also help you to view the video, which defines and demonstrates important concepts and skills as they relate to everyday life.

Learning Objective	Textbook	Telecourse Student Guide	Video Lesson
1. Describe Piaget's concept of formal operational thinking and provide examples of adolescents' emerging ability to reason deductively and inductively.	pp. 328–331	Key Terms: 5, 6, 7, 8; Practice Questions I: 1, 2, 7, 8, 13, 14, 18; Practice Questions II: 2, 3, 9, 15, 16, 17, 18; Applying Your Knowledge: 1, 2, 3, 5, 7, 11.	Segment 1: *Formal Operational Thought* Segment 3: *Adolescent Decision-Making*
2. Discuss adolescent egocentrism and give three examples of egocentric fantasies or fables.	pp. 326–328	Key Terms: 1, 2, 3, 4; Practice Questions I: 3, 4, 5, 9, 16; Practice Questions II: 1, 4, 5, 12, 13, 20; Applying Your Knowledge: 4, 6, 8.	Segment 1: *Formal Operational Thought*
3. Describe the concept of person–environment fit, explain how schools can be organized to more effectively meet adolescents' cognitive needs, and identify the main challenges adolescents face in middle school.	pp. 333–335	Key Terms: 12, 13, 17, 18; Practice Questions I: 6, 12, 15; Practice Questions II: 6, 7, 14, 19; Applying Your Knowledge: 9.	Segment 2: *Educating Adolescents*
4. Describe the major ethnic and cultural factors that can affect adolescent schooling, and discuss factors that influence school engagement.	pp. 339–343	Key Terms: 16; Practice Questions I: 10, 11, 17; Practice Questions II: 10; Applying Your Knowledge: 12.	Segment 3: *Adolescent Decision-Making*
5. Discuss the dual-process model of adolescent thinking, and describe how it can explain common errors in adolescent reasoning.	pp. 331–333	Key Terms: 9, 10, 11; Practice Questions II: 8; Applying Your Knowledge: 1, 10.	Segment 1: *Formal Operational Thought*

Learning Objective	Textbook	Telecourse Student Guide	Video Lesson
6. Discuss the emergence of computer technology and its influence on adolescent thinking and learning.	pp. 335–338	Key Terms: 14, 15; Practice Question I: 19; Practice Question II: 11, 21.	

Who Am I?

Lesson 16

Adolescence: Psychosocial Development

Preview

Adolescence brings a heightened quest for self-understanding, a crucial process in the transition from childhood to adulthood. This lesson focuses on the psychosocial development required for attainment of adult status and maturity, particularly the formation of **identity**, which is a consistent definition of one's self. The influences of family, peers, and society on this development are examined in some detail.

During adolescence, biological changes make reproduction possible, and cognitive changes make teenagers more capable of mature decision making. In simpler cultures, the plan of life often allows for an early transition into adult life. But, in technologically advanced societies, a decade of preparation is needed before self-reliance becomes practical. The resulting conflict can be difficult to manage.

This lesson also explores the issue of adolescent suicide and the special problem of adolescent lawbreaking. Suggestions for alleviating or treating these problems are given. While no other period of life except infancy is characterized by so many changes, for most young people, the teenage years are happy ones. In addition, serious problems in adolescence do not necessarily lead to lifelong problems.

As you complete this lesson, consider your own psychosocial development during adolescence. How would you define your identity at that time? What kind of person were you? What was your relationship with your parents like? Was there much friction or bickering? If so, over what kind of issues? Describe your social circles, your peers and friends. Did these people have a positive or negative influence on your development? Did you have any romantic relationships? What were they like? Did you or someone you know ever think about suicide during this time? What were the circumstances? Did you know someone who broke the law or got arrested? What was the situation?

Prior Telecourse Knowledge that Will Be Used in this Lesson

- This lesson will return to Erik Erikson's theory from Lesson 1 that specifies eight stages of *psychosocial development,* each of which is characterized by a particular challenge, or *developmental crisis,* which is central to that stage of life and must be resolved. This lesson will focus on Erikson's fifth stage, called "identity vs. role confusion":
  1. Trust vs. Mistrust (birth to 1 year)
  2. Autonomy vs. Shame and Doubt (1 to 3 years)
  3. Initiative vs. Guilt (3 to 6 years)
  4. Industry vs. Inferiority (7 to 11 years)
  5. **Identity vs. Role Confusion (adolescence)**
  6. Intimacy vs. Isolation (adulthood)
  7. Generativity vs. Stagnation (adulthood)
  8. Integrity vs. Despair (adulthood)
- In a discussion of family influences during adolescence, this lesson will return to the concept of "parenting styles" introduced in Lesson 13. Recall that three basic styles include *authoritarian* (parents expect unquestioning obedience and offer little affection), *permissive* (affectionate but with few demands), and *authoritative* (parents expect obedience, set appropriate limits, and offer affection).

Learning Objectives

Use this information to guide your reading, viewing, thinking, and studying. After successfully completing this lesson, you should be able to:

1. Define the concept of identity and describe the development of identity during adolescence, incorporating Erikson's crisis of "identity versus role confusion."
2. Describe the five major identity statuses or conditions and give an example of each.
3. Describe the four main domains of identity development.
4. Discuss parent-child relationships during adolescence, including typical conflicts.
5. Discuss the influence of peers, friends, and romantic relationships in adolescence.
6. Discuss the causes and consequences of sadness, anger, and depression among adolescents, including the factors that contribute to adolescent suicide.
7. Discuss delinquency among adolescents today, noting its incidence and prevalence, significance for later development, and best approaches for prevention and treatment.
8. Describe adolescents' sexual development, and explain how parents, peers, and schools influence adolescent sexual behavior.
9. Discuss drug use and abuse, describe how drug use can affect development in regard to gender, age, cohort, and national differences, and identify some harmful consequences of specific substances.

10. Define generational forgetting and discuss what works in the area of drug prevention.

Read Chapter 10, "Adolescence: Psychosocial Development," pages 347–379.

View the video for Lesson 16, "Who Am I?"

Segment 1: *Identity*

Segment 2: *Friends and Family*

Summary

Adolescence heightens the search for self-understanding because of the momentous changes that occur during the teenage years. Many adolescents experience the emergence of **possible selves**, or diverse perceptions of identity in different groups or settings.

According to Erik Erikson, the psychosocial challenge of adolescence is **identity versus role confusion**. The specific task of this challenge is the search for identity, both as an individual and as a member of the larger community. The ultimate goal, **identity achievement**, occurs when adolescents establish their own goals and values by abandoning some of those set by parents and society while accepting others.

Some adolescents form an identity prematurely, a process called **foreclosure**. Other adolescents, unable to find alternative roles that are truly their own, simply rebel and become the opposite of what is expected of them, adopting a **negative identity**. Others experience identity diffusion, with few commitments to goals or values, whether those of parents, peers, or the larger society. Many adolescents declare an **identity moratorium**, often by using an institutionalized time-out such as college or voluntary military service as a means of postponing final decisions about career or marriage. While identity formation is a major task of adolescence, many people don't reach identity achievement until early adulthood (or later), and most continue to shape and refine their identities throughout the life span.

For immigrants and minority adolescents, identity formation is particularly complex because they must find the right balance between their ethnic background and the values of the society at large. This may cause them to embrace a negative identity or, as is more often the case, to foreclose on identity prematurely.

Research studies demonstrate that the **generation gap** is not as wide as it is popularly assumed to be. Indeed, studies have found substantial agreement between parents and adolescents on political, religious, educational, and vocational opinions and values. However, there is a **generational stake**, which refers to the particular needs and concerns of each generation in the parent-adolescent relationship, as well as the natural tendency to see the family in a certain way.

The adolescent's peer group is a social institution that eases the transition from childhood to adulthood by functioning in a variety of ways. Peer groups function as a source of information and social support, a group of contemporaries who are experiencing similar struggles. As adolescents associate themselves with a particular subgroup, peers help them define who they are by helping them define who they are not. Peer groups also serve as a sounding board for exploring and defining one's values and aspirations.

While the search for identity brings with it certain difficulties, most adolescents reach adulthood safe and secure. Others have special problems, including delinquent behavior and depression that may lead to suicide. Thinking about suicide (**suicidal ideation**) is quite common among high school students. Fortunately, most suicide attempts in adolescence do not result in death. Deliberate acts of self-destruction that do not cause death are referred to as **parasuicide**. Whether or not suicidal ideation leads to parasuicide or suicide depends on **parental monitoring**, the availability of lethal methods, the use of alcohol and other drugs, and the attitudes about suicide held by the adolescent's family, friends, and culture.

Review all reading assignments for this lesson.

As assigned by your instructor, complete the optional online component for this lesson.

Key Terms

Using your own words, write a brief definition or explanation of each of the following terms on a separate piece of paper.

1. identity versus role confusion/diffusion
2. identity
3. identity achievement
4. role confusion
5. foreclosure
6. identity moratorium
7. gender identity
8. sexual orientation
9. bickering
10. parental monitoring
11. clique
12. crowd
13. peer pressure
14. deviancy training
15. clinical depression
16. rumination
17. suicidal ideation
18. cluster suicide
19. parasuicide
20. juvenile delinquent
21. life-course-persistent offender
22. adolescent-limited offender
23. generational forgetting
24. possible selves
25. negative identity
26. generation gap
27. generational stake

Practice Questions I

Multiple-Choice Questions

1. According to Erikson, the primary task of adolescence is that of establishing
   a. basic trust.
   b. an identity.
   c. intimacy.
   d. integrity.

2. According to developmentalists who study identity formation, foreclosure involves
   a. accepting an identity prematurely, without exploration.
   b. taking time off from school, work, and other commitments.
   c. opposing parental values.
   d. failing to commit oneself to a vocational goal.

3. When adolescents adopt an identity that is the opposite of the one they are expected to adopt, they are considered to be taking on a
   a. foreclosed identity.
   b. diffused identity.
   c. negative identity.
   d. reverse identity.

4. The main sources of emotional support for most young people who are establishing independence from their parents are
   a. older adolescents of the opposite sex.
   b. older siblings.
   c. teachers.
   d. peer groups.

5. For members of minority ethnic groups, identity achievement may be particularly complicated because
   a. their cultural ideal clashes with the Western emphasis on adolescent self-determination.
   b. democratic ideology espouses a color-blind, multiethnic society in which background is irrelevant.
   c. parents and other relatives tend to emphasize ethnicity and expect teens to honor their roots.
   d. of all of the above reasons.

6. In a crime-ridden neighborhood, parents can protect their adolescents by keeping close watch over activities, friends, and so on. This practice is called
   a. generational stake.
   b. foreclosure.
   c. peer screening.
   d. parental monitoring.

7. Increased parent–adolescent conflict is likely to occur in ________________ and to center on issues of ____________.
   a. early adolescence; morality
   b. late adolescence; self-discipline
   c. early adolescence; self-control
   d. late adolescence; politics

8. Which of the following did Erikson identify as an area of identity development?
   a. political identity
   b. religious identity
   c. sexual/gender identity
   d. all of the above

9. Suicide is _____________ common among adults than adolescents. Parasuicide is _____________ common among adults than adolescents.
   a. less; less
   b. more; less
   c. less; more
   d. more; more

10. The early signs of life-course-persistent offenders include all of the following **EXCEPT**
    a. signs of brain damage early in life.
    b. antisocial school behavior.
    c. delayed sexual intimacy.
    d. use of alcohol and tobacco at an early age.

11. Regarding gender differences in self-destructive acts, the rate of parasuicide is ____________________ and the rate of suicides ____________________.
    a. higher in males; higher in females
    b. higher in females; higher in males
    c. the same in males and females; higher in males
    d. the same in males and females; higher in females

12. Conflict between parents and adolescent offspring is
    a. most likely to involve fathers and their late-maturing sons.
    b. more frequent in single-parent homes.
    c. more likely to involve mothers and daughters.
    d. not likely in any of the above situations.

13. Compared to adolescents 10 years ago, teens today
    a. have sex with more partners.
    b. are more likely to become pregnant.
    c. are more likely to use contraception.
    d. are more influenced by biology.

14. Inhalants are the only drug category used more by
    a. eighth grade boys.
    b. high-school seniors.
    c. adults.
    d. girls between the ages of 15 and 18.

15. Overall, drug use among adolescents has
    a. decreased in the United States since 1976.
    b. decreased worldwide since 1976.
    c. increased in the United States since 1976.
    d. increased worldwide since 1976.

True or False Items

Write T (for true) or F (for false) on the line in front of each statement.

16. _____ Both gay men and lesbian women report realizing their sexual orientation during adolescence.

17. _____ Most adolescents have political views and educational values that are markedly different from those of their parents.

18. _____ Peer pressure is inherently destructive to the adolescent seeking an identity.

19. _____ For most adolescents, group socializing and dating precede the establishment of true intimacy with one member of the opposite sex.

20. _____ Suicidal ideation is common in adolescence.

21. _____ The rate of youth suicide in the United States has doubled since 1960.

22. _____ In finding themselves, teens try to find an identity that is stable, consistent, and mature.

23. _____ Parents who exert extreme psychological control over their teens have the most successful adolescents.

24. _____ Completed suicides are more common among boys.

25. _____ Generational forgetting is the idea that each new generation forgets the lessons of the previous generations.

26. _____ When parents forbid smoking in their homes, fewer adolescents smoke.

Practice Questions II

Multiple-Choice Questions

1. Which of the following was **NOT** identified as a factor that influences the likelihood of parasuicide or suicide?
   a. availability of lethal means
   b. lack of parental supervision
   c. use of alcohol and other drugs
   d. increased arguing with parents

2. Sex education in U.S. schools
   a. typically provides referrals for STI treatment.
   b. encourages increased sexual activity.
   c. often encourage abstinence.
   d. is rarely presented in classrooms.

3. The adolescent experiencing identity diffusion is typically
   a. very apathetic.
   b. a risk-taker, anxious to experiment with alternative identities.
   c. willing to accept parental values wholesale, without exploring alternatives.
   d. one who rebels against all forms of authority.

4. Crime statistics show that during adolescence
   a. males and females are equally likely to be arrested.
   b. males are more likely to be arrested than females.
   c. females are more likely to be arrested than males.
   d. males commit more crimes than females but are less likely to be arrested.

5. Major crimes are more frequent during
   a. adolescence and emerging adulthood.
   b. early adolescence.
   c. late adulthood.
   d. none of the above.

6. A period during which a young person experiments with different identities, postponing important choices, is called a(n)
   a. identity foreclosure.
   b. negative identity.
   c. identity diffusion.
   d. identity moratorium.

7. When adolescents' political, religious, educational, and vocational opinions are compared with those held by their own parents, the so-called "generation gap" is
   a. much smaller than when the younger and older generations are compared overall.
   b. much wider than when the younger and older generations are compared overall.
   c. wider between parents and sons than between parents and daughters.
   d. wider between parents and daughters than between parents and sons.

8. Parent–teen conflict tends to center on issues related to
   a. politics and religion.
   b. education.
   c. vacations.
   d. daily details, such as musical tastes.

9. Researchers have found that among high school students, suicidal ideation is
   a. not as common among high school students as is popularly believed.
   b. more common among males than females.
   c. more common among females than among males.
   d. quite common among both males and females.

10. The best way to limit adolescent law-breaking in general would be to
   a. strengthen the family, school, and community fabric.
   b. increase the number of police officers in the community.
   c. improve the criminal justice system.
   d. establish rehabilitative facilities for law-breakers.

11. Adolescents help each other in many ways, including the development of
    a. identity.
    b. independence.
    c. social skills.
    d. all of the above.

12. In the United States, occasional drug use such as trying marijuana is
    a. more common in boys than girls.
    b. more common in girls than boys.
    c. equally common in both sexes.
    d. none of the above.

Matching Items

Match each definition or description with its corresponding term.

Terms

13. __________	identity achievement	18. __________	generation gap
14. __________	foreclosure	19. __________	generational stake
15. __________	negative identity	20. __________	parental monitoring
16. __________	identity diffusion	21. __________	suicidal ideation
17. __________	identity moratorium	22. __________	parasuicide

Definitions or Descriptions

a. premature identity formation
b. contemplation of suicide
c. the adolescent has few commitments to goals or values
d. differences between the younger and older generations
e. self-destructive act that does not result in death
f. awareness of where children are and what they are doing
g. an individual's self-definition
h. a period during which adolescents experiment with alternative identities
i. family members in different developmental stages see the family in different ways
j. an identity opposite of the one an adolescent is expected to adopt

Applying Your Knowledge

1. From childhood, Sharon thought she wanted to follow in her mother's footsteps and be a homemaker. Now, at age 40 with a home and family, she admits to herself that what she really wanted to be was a medical researcher. Erik Erikson would probably say that Sharon
   a. adopted a negative identity when she was a child.
   b. experienced identity foreclosure at an early age.
   c. never progressed beyond the obvious identity diffusion she experienced as a child.
   d. took a moratorium from identity formation.

2. Fifteen-year-old David is rebelling against his devoutly religious parents by taking drugs, stealing, and engaging in other antisocial behaviors. Evidently, David has
   a. foreclosed on his identity.
   b. declared an identity moratorium.
   c. adopted a negative identity.
   d. experienced identity diffusion.

3. Fourteen-year-old Sean, who is fiercely proud of his Irish heritage, is prejudiced against members of several other ethnic groups. It is likely that, in forming his identity, Sean
   a. attained identity achievement.
   b. foreclosed on his identity.
   c. declared a lengthy moratorium.
   d. experienced identity diffusion.

4. An adolescent exaggerates the importance of differences in her values and those of her parents. Her parents see these differences as smaller and less important. This phenomenon is called the
   a. generation gap.
   b. generational stake.
   c. family enigma.
   d. parental imperative.

5. In modern society, the most obvious examples of institutionalized moratoria on identity formation are
   a. the Boy Scouts and the Girl Scouts.
   b. college and the peacetime military.
   c. marriage and divorce.
   d. bar mitzvahs and baptisms.

6. First-time parents Norma and Norman are worried that, during adolescence, their healthy parental influence will be undone as their children are encouraged by peers to become sexually promiscuous, drug-addicted, or delinquent. Their wise neighbor, who is a developmental psychologist, tells them that
   a. during adolescence, peers are generally more likely to complement the influence of parents than they are to pull their friends in the opposite direction.
   b. research suggests that peers provide a negative influence in every major task of adolescence.
   c. only through authoritarian parenting can parents give children the skills they need to resist peer pressure.
   d. unless their children show early signs of learning difficulties or antisocial behavior, parental monitoring is unnecessary.

7. Thirteen-year-old Cassandra is constantly experimenting with different behaviors and possible identities. It is likely that she
   a. has low self-esteem.
   b. foreclosed prematurely on her identity.
   c. has great self-understanding.
   d. comes from a home environment in which there is considerable tension and conflict.

8. In forming an identity, the young person seeks to make meaningful connections with his or her past. This seeking is described as an unconscious striving for
   a. individual uniqueness.
   b. peer-group membership.
   c. continuity of experience.
   d. vocational identity.

9. Ray was among the first of his friends to have sex, drink alcohol, and smoke cigarettes. These attributes, together with his having been hyperactive and having poor emotional control, would suggest that Ray is at high risk of
   a. becoming an adolescent-limited offender.
   b. becoming a life-course-persistent offender.
   c. developing an antisocial personality.
   d. foreclosing his identity prematurely.

10. Carl is a typical sixteen-year-old adolescent who has no special problems. It is likely that Carl has
    a. contemplated suicide.
    b. engaged in some minor illegal act.
    c. struggled with "who he is."
    d. done all of the above.

11. Coming home from work, Malcolm hears a radio announcement warning parents to be alert for possible cluster suicide signs in their teenage children. What might have precipitated such an announcement?

   a. government statistics that suicide has been on the rise since the 1990s
   b. the highly publicized suicide of a famous rock singer
   c. the recent crash of an airliner, killing all on board
   d. any of the above

Answer Key

Key Terms

1. Erikson's term for the psychosocial crisis of adolescence, identity versus role confusion (also referred to as identity versus diffusion), refers to adolescents' need to combine their self-understanding and social roles into a coherent identity. (p. 348; video lesson, segment 1; objective 1)
2. Identity, as used by Erikson, refers to a person's self-definition as a separate individual in terms of roles, attitudes, beliefs, and aspirations. (p. 348; video lesson, segment 1; objective 1)
3. In Erikson's theory, identity achievement occurs when adolescents attain their new identity by establishing their own goals and values and abandoning some of those set by their parents and culture and accepting others. (p. 348; video lesson, segment 1; objective 2)
4. Adolescents who experience role confusion, according to Erikson, have few commitments to goals or values and are often apathetic about trying to find an identity. (p. 348; video lesson, segment 1; objective 2)
5. In identity foreclosure, according to Erikson, the adolescent forms an identity prematurely, accepting earlier roles and parental values wholesale, without truly forging a unique personal identity. (p. 348; video lesson, segment 1; objective 2)
6. According to Erikson, in the process of finding a mature identity, many young people seem to declare an identity moratorium, a kind of time-out during which they experiment with alternative identities without trying to settle on any one. (p. 349; video lesson, segment 1; objective 2)
7. Gender identity is a person's self-identification of being female or male, including the roles and behaviors that society assigns to that sex. (p. 350; objective 3)
8. An individual's sexual orientation is based on whether they are romantically attached to the same sex, opposite sex, or both sexes. (p. 350; objective 3)
9. Bickering refers to the repeated, petty arguing that typically occurs in early adolescence about common, daily life activities. (p. 354; objective 4)

10. Parental monitoring is parental watchfulness about where one's child is and what he or she is doing, and with whom. (p. 356; objective 4)
11. A small group of close friends who are loyal to each other and exclude outsiders is referred to as a clique. (p. 356; objective 5)
12. A large group of individuals who have something in common (e.g., they are all members of sports teams) is referred to as a crowd. Members of a crowd may or may not be friends. (p. 356; objective 5)
13. Peer pressure refers to the social pressure to conform to one's friends in behavior, dress, and attitude. It may be positive or negative in its effects. (p. 357; video lesson, segment 2; objective 5)
14. Deviancy training is negative support provided among friends, encouraging dangerous, antisocial, or otherwise maladapative behavior. (p. 357; objective 5)
15. Clinical depression is defined by overwhelming feelings of sadness and worthlessness that last for at least two weeks. (p. 366; objective 6)
16. Rumination occurs when we think or talk about the same (usually negative) experience over and over again, which can lead to feelings of depression. (p. 366; objective 6)
17. Suicidal ideation refers to thinking about committing suicide, usually with some serious emotional and intellectual overtones. (p. 366; objective 6)
18. A cluster suicide refers to a series of suicides or suicide attempts that are precipitated by one initial suicide, usually that of a famous person or a well-known peer. (p. 367; objective 6)
19. Parasuicide is a deliberate act of self-destruction that does not result in death. (p. 367; objective 6)
20. A person under the age of 18 who breaks the law is referred to as a juvenile delinquent. (p. 370; objective 7)
21. Life-course-persistent offenders are adolescent lawbreakers who later become career criminals. (p. 371; objective 7)
22. Adolescent-limited offenders are juvenile delinquents, whose criminal activity stops by age 21. (p. 372; objective 7)
23. Generational forgetting is the idea that each new generation forgets what the previous generation learned. As used in your textbook, the term refers to knowledge about the harm drugs can do. (p. 377; objective 10)
24. Many adolescents try out possible selves, or variations on who they are and who they might like to become. (video lesson, segment 1; objective 1)
25. Adolescents who take on a negative identity, according to Erikson, adopt an identity that is the opposite of the one they are expected to adopt. (video lesson, segment 1; objective 2)
26. The generation gap refers to the alleged distance between generations in values, behaviors, and knowledge. (video lesson, segment 2; objective 4)

27. The generational stake refers to the tendency of each family member, because of that person's different developmental stage, to see the family in a certain way. (video lesson, segment 2; objective 4)

Practice Questions I

Multiple-Choice Questions

1. b. is the correct answer. (p. 348; video lesson, segment 1; objective 1)

   a. is incorrect. According to Erikson, this is the crisis of infancy.

   c. & d. are incorrect. In Erikson's theory, these crises occur later in life.

2. a. is the correct answer. (pp. 348–349; video lesson, segment 1; objective 2)

   b. is incorrect. This describes an identity moratorium.

   c. is incorrect. This describes a negative identity.

   d. is incorrect. This describes identity diffusion.

3. c. is the correct answer. (video lesson, segment 1; objective 2)

4. d. is the correct answer. (pp. 356–357; video lesson, segment 2; objective 5)

5. d. is the correct answer. (pp. 351–352; video lesson, segments 1 & 2; objective 3)

6. d. is the correct answer. (p. 356; objective 4)

   a. is incorrect. The generational stake refers to differences in how family members from different generations view the family.

   b. is incorrect. Foreclosure refers to the premature establishment of identity.

   c. is incorrect. Peer screening is an aspect of parental monitoring, but it was not specifically discussed in the text.

7. c. is the correct answer. (video lesson, segment 2; objective 4)

8. d. is the correct answer. (pp. 349–353; objective 3)

   b. is incorrect. This was not discussed in the textbook.

   c. is incorrect. This is true of girls.

9. b. is the correct answer. (pp. 366–367; objective 6)

10. c. is the correct answer. Most life-course-persistent offenders are among the earliest of their cohort to have sex. (pp. 371–372; objective 7)

11. b. is the correct answer. (pp. 367–368; objective 6)

12. c. is the correct answer. (p. 354; objective 4)

    a. is incorrect. In fact, parent-child conflict is more likely to involve mothers and their early maturing offspring.

13. c. is the correct answer. (p. 365; objective 8)

14. a. is the correct answer. (p. 373; objective 9)
15. a. is the correct answer. (p. 374; objective 9)

True or False Items

16. F Gay men reporting knowing their sexual orientation around the age of 11, but lesbian women most often report realizing their sexual orientation during the years of emerging adulthood. (p. 362; objective 8)
17. F Numerous studies have shown substantial agreement between parents and their adolescent children on political opinions and educational values. (p. 352; video lesson, segment 2; objective 3)
18. F Just the opposite is true. (p. 356; video lesson, segment 2; objective 5)
19. T (video lesson, segment 2; objective 5)
20. T (p. 366; objective 6)
21. T (p. 368; objective 6)
22. T (p. 348; objective 1)
23. F (p. 356; objective 4)
24. T (p. 368; objective 6)
25. T (p. 377; objective 10)
26. T (p. 378; objective 10)

Practice Questions II

Multiple-Choice Questions

1. d. is the correct answer. (p. 368; objective 6)
2. c. is the correct answer. For this reason, autonomy in their offspring tends to be delayed. (p. 363; objective 8)
3. a. is the correct answer. (p. 348; video lesson, segment 1; objective 2)

   b. is incorrect. This describes an adolescent undergoing an identity moratorium.

   c. is incorrect. This describes identity foreclosure.

   d. is incorrect. This describes an adolescent who is adopting a negative identity.
4. b. is the correct answer. (p. 370; objective 7)
5. a. is the correct answer. (p. 370; objective 7)
6. d. is the correct answer. (p. 349; video lesson, segment 1; objective 2)

   a. is incorrect. Identity foreclosure occurs when the adolescent prematurely adopts an identity, without fully exploring alternatives.

   b. is incorrect. Adolescents who adopt an identity that is opposite to the one they are expected to develop have taken on a negative identity.

   c. is incorrect. Identity diffusion occurs when the adolescent is apathetic and has few commitments to goals or values.
7. a. is the correct answer. (video lesson, segment 2; objective 4)

8. d. is the correct answer. (p. 354; objective 4)

   a., b., & c. are incorrect. In fact, on these issues parents and teenagers tend to show substantial agreement.

9. d. is the correct answer. (p. 366; objective 6)
10. a. is the correct answer. (p. 372; objective 7)
11. d. is the correct answer. (p. 356; objective 5)
12. c. is the correct answer. (p. 375; objective 9)

Matching Items

13. g (p. 348; video lesson, segment 1; objective 1)
14. a (p. 348; video lesson, segment 1; objective 2)
15. j (video lesson, segment 1; objective 2)
16. c (p. 348; video lesson, segment 1; objective 2)
17. h (p. 349; video lesson, segment 1; objective 2)
18. d (video lesson, segment 2; objective 4)
19. i (video lesson, segment 2; objective 4)
20. f (p. 356; objective 4)
21. b (p. 366; objective 6)
22. e (p. 367; objective 6)

Applying Your Knowledge

1. b. is the correct answer. Apparently, Sharon never explored alternatives or truly forged a unique personal identity. (p. 348; video lesson, segment 1; objective 2)

   a. is incorrect. Individuals who rebel by adopting an identity that is the opposite of the one they are expected to adopt have taken on a negative identity.

   c. is incorrect. Individuals who experience identity diffusion have few commitments to goals or values. This was not Sharon's problem.

   d. is incorrect. Had she taken a moratorium on identity formation, Sharon would have experimented with alternative identities and perhaps would have chosen that of a medical researcher.

2. c. is the correct answer. (video lesson, segment 1; objective 2)
3. b. is the correct answer. (p. 348; video lesson, segment 1; objective 2)

   a. is incorrect. Identity achievers often have a strong sense of ethnic identification but usually are low in prejudice.

   c. & d. are incorrect. The textbook does not present research that links ethnic pride and prejudice with either identity diffusion or moratorium.

4. b. is the correct answer. (video lesson, segment 2; objective 4)

   a. is incorrect. The generation gap refers to actual differences in attitudes and values between the younger and older generations. This example is concerned with how large these differences are perceived to be.

   c. & d. is incorrect. These terms are not used in the textbook in discussing family conflict.

5. b. is the correct answer. (p. 349; objective 2)

6. a. is the correct answer. (p. 357; video lesson, segment 2; objective 5)

   b. is incorrect. In fact, just the opposite is true.

   c. is incorrect. Developmentalists recommend authoritative, rather than authoritarian, parenting.

   d. is incorrect. Parental monitoring is important for all adolescents.

7. c. is the correct answer. (video lesson, segment 1; objective 1)

   a., b., & d. are incorrect. Experimenting with possible selves is a normal sign of adolescent identity formation.

8. c. is the correct answer. (p. 348; objective 1)

9. b. is the correct answer. (p. 371; objective 7)

10. d. is the correct answer. (pp. 348, 370, 376; objectives 1, 6, & 7)

11. b. is the correct answer. (p. 367; objective 6)

    a., c., & d. are incorrect. Cluster suicides occur when the suicide of a well-known person leads others to attempt suicide.

Lesson Review

Lesson 16

Adolescence
Psychosocial Development

Please Note: Use this matrix to guide your study and achieve the learning objectives of this lesson. It will also help you to view the video, which defines and demonstrates important concepts and skills as they relate to everyday life.

Learning Objective	**Textbook**	**Telecourse Student Guide**	**Video Lesson**
1. Define the concept of identity and describe the development of identity during adolescence, incorporating Erikson's crisis of "identity versus role confusion."	p. 348	Key Terms: 1, 2, 24; Practice Questions I: 1, 22; Practice Questions II: 13; Applying Your Knowledge: 7, 8, 10.	Segment 1: *Identity*
2. Describe the five major identity statuses or conditions and give an example of each.	pp. 348–349	Key Terms: 3, 4, 5, 6, 25; Practice Questions I: 2, 3; Practice Questions II: 3, 6, 14, 15, 16, 17; Applying Your Knowledge: 1, 2, 3, 5.	Segment 1: *Identity*
3. Describe the four main domains of identity development.	pp. 349–353	Key Terms: 7, 8; Practice Questions I: 5, 8, 17.	Segment 1: *Identity;* Segment 2: *Friends and Family*
4. Discuss parent-child relationships during adolescence, including typical conflicts.	pp. 353–356	Key Terms: 9, 10, 26, 27; Practice Questions I: 6, 7, 12, 23; Practice Questions II: 7, 8, 18, 19, 20; Applying Your Knowledge: 4.	Segment 2: *Friends and Family*
5. Discuss the influence of peers, friends, and romantic relationships in adolescence.	pp. 356–360, 361–362	Key Terms: 11, 12, 13, 14; Practice Questions I: 4, 18, 19; Practice Questions II: 11; Applying Your Knowledge: 6.	Segment 2: *Friends and Family*

Learning Objective	Textbook	Telecourse Student Guide	Video Lesson
6. Discuss the causes and consequences of sadness, anger, and depression among adolescents, including the factors that contribute to adolescent suicide.	pp. 365–369	Key Terms: 15, 16, 17, 18, 19; Practice Questions I: 9, 11, 20, 21, 24; Practice Questions II: 1, 9, 21, 22; Applying Your Knowledge: 10, 11.	
7. Discuss delinquency among adolescents today, noting its incidence and prevalence, significance for later development, and best approaches for prevention and treatment.	pp. 369–372	Key Terms: 20, 21, 22; Practice Questions I: 10; Practice Questions II: 4, 5, 10; Applying Your Knowledge: 9, 10.	
8. Describe adolescents' sexual development, and explain how parents, peers, and schools influence adolescent sexual behavior.	pp. 360–361, 362–365	Practice Questions I: 13, 16; Practice Questions II: 2.	
9. Discuss drug use and abuse, describe how drug use can affect development in regard to gender, age, cohort, and national differences, and identify some harmful consequences of specific substances.	pp. 373–377	Practice Questions I: 14, 15; Practice Questions II: 12.	
10. Define generational forgetting and discuss what works in the area of drug prevention.	pp. 377–378	Key Terms: 23; Practice Questions I: 25, 26.	

Choices

Lesson 17

Early Adulthood: Biosocial Development

Preview

In this lesson, we encounter the developing person in the prime of life. The early adult years are the best time for hard physical labor—because strength is at a peak—and for reproduction—because overall health is good and fertility is generally high. With the attainment of full maturity, however, a new aspect of physical development comes into play—that is, decline. Lesson 17 takes a look at how people perceive changes that occur as the body ages as well as how lifestyle choices can affect the course of their overall development.

The lesson begins with a description of the growth, strength, and health of the individual during adulthood—both visible age-related changes, such as wrinkling, and less obvious changes, such as declines in the efficiency of the body's systems. Sexual-reproductive health, a matter of great concern to young adults, is also discussed, with particular attention paid to trends in sexual responsiveness during adulthood and fertility problems that may develop. The final section looks at three problems that are more prevalent during young adulthood than at any other period of the life span: drug abuse, compulsive eating and destructive dieting, and violence.

As you complete this lesson, consider some of your own biophysical changes during emerging adulthood and early adulthood (ages 18 to 35). Has (or did) your body become stronger, more capable of extended activity? If you're old enough, when did you first notice signs of aging, such as wrinkles, declines in eyesight, graying hair, or a reduction in energy or endurance? Has anyone you know had trouble conceiving a child? What were the circumstances? Consider your use of alcohol, cigarettes, and other drugs during this time. Do you know anyone who has abused these substances? What effect has this had on his or her health? Has anyone you know developed an eating disorder? Did she or he seek treatment?

Prior Telecourse Knowledge that Will Be Used in This Lesson

- This lesson will return to the subject of drug use, drug abuse, and drug addiction introduced in Lesson 14 (Adolescence: Biosocial Development). Most of those who use drugs begin in adolescence. This use tends to increase through a person's mid-20s, then decreases with age and maturity.
- Recall the concept of *body image* (also from Lesson 14). If a person has a distorted view of his or her appearance, serious eating disorders can result. These disorders often have their start in late adolescence and—if not treated—worsen in early adulthood. Also in this lesson, psychoanalytic, learning, cognitive, sociocultural, and epigenetic systems theories (from Lesson 1) will be used to offer possible causes for eating disorders.

Learning Objectives

Use this information to guide your reading, viewing, thinking, and studying. After successfully completing this lesson, you should be able to:

1. Describe the changes in growth, strength, and overall health that occur during early adulthood.
2. Discuss the meaning of the phrase, "health is interdependent," and describe the dynamic systems concept of health, including a definition of "homeostasis."
3. Identify age-related trends in the norms for sexual activity, and describe potential consequences of sexual activity during emerging adulthood.
4. Discuss changes in substance abuse during early adulthood, and describe the causes and consequences of this abuse.
5. Discuss the affinity for risk taking in emerging adulthood and define the term "edgework" in regard to risk taking.
6. Describe the typical victims of anorexia nervosa and bulimia nervosa, and discuss possible explanations for these disorders.
7. Explain how social norms and gender socialization may be related to self-destructive behavior among emerging adults.
8. Discuss the factors that may determine whether a young male adult will suffer a violent death.

Read Chapter 11, "Emerging Adulthood: Body, Mind, and Social World," pages 385–395 and 417.

View the video for Lesson 17, "Choices"

Segment 1: *Growth, Strength, and Health*
Segment 2: *Health Problems*
Segment 3: *Gender Socialization and Violence*

Summary

In terms of overall health, the years of early adulthood are the prime of life. While signs of decline appear in every body system, most changes go unnoticed because physical strength and **organ reserve** are at a peak. Even athletic performance can remain high.

Biosocial development during early adulthood is not without potential problems, however. For example, drug abuse, eating disorders, and violent death are also more likely during early adulthood than at any other time. A genetic temperament that includes attraction to excitement, intolerance of frustration, and vulnerability to depression and a social context that encourages drug use and abuse are major factors in determining an individual's propensity to use and respond to a given drug. Fortunately, many young adults stop abusing alcohol and illicit drugs before middle age, partly because their social context changes and partly because they become more mature.

Cultural norms and the specifics of the social context may undermine the body's natural tendency to maintain a healthy weight. Some dieters, especially those who are young and well educated, develop an obsession with food and weight control that turns into a serious eating disorder. **Anorexia nervosa** and **bulimia nervosa** can be life threatening. Young college women are especially likely to diet, take diet pills, binge, and purge.

Stereotypes about "masculine" behavior may promote violent death through suicide, homicide, and fatal accidents, particularly in young adult men. While genetic factors are important causes of masculine violence, researchers believe that social factors are at the root of the problem. Living up to the ideals of masculinity makes it hard for young men to avoid conflicts, back away from challenges, or admit that they need help.

Review all reading assignments for this lesson.

As assigned by your instructor, complete the optional online component for this lesson.

Key Terms

Using your own words, write a brief definition or explanation of each of the following terms on a separate piece of paper.

1. emerging adulthood
2. homeostasis
3. replacement rate
4. edgework
5. extreme sports
6. drug abuse
7. drug addiction
8. social norms approach
9. organ reserve
10. senescence
11. anorexia nervosa
12. bulimia nervosa
13. gender socialization

Practice Questions I

Multiple-Choice Questions

1. Senescence refers to
   a. a loss of efficiency in the body's regulatory systems.
   b. age-related decline.
   c. decreased physical strength.
   d. vulnerability to disease.

2. When do noticeable increases in height stop?
   a. at about the same age in men and women
   b. at an earlier age in women than in men
   c. at an earlier age in men than in women
   d. There is such diversity in physiological development that it is impossible to generalize regarding this issue.

3. A difference between men and women during early adulthood is that men have
   a. a higher percentage of body fat.
   b. lower metabolism.
   c. proportionately more muscle.
   d. greater organ reserve.

4. The majority of young adults rate their own health as
   a. very good or excellent.
   b. average or fair.
   c. poor.
   d. worse than it was during adolescence.

5. The automatic adjustment of the body's systems to keep physiological functions in a state of equilibrium, even during heavy exertion, is called
   a. organ reserve.
   b. homeostasis.
   c. stress.
   d. muscle capacity.

6. Which of the following temperamental characteristics was **NOT** identified as being associated with a tendency to seek out risks?
   a. being male
   b. having a predisposition to be impulsive
   c. being extroverted
   d. being an emerging adult

7. Regarding sex, most emerging adults believe that
   a. extramarital sex is acceptable.
   b. marriage is not an important goal for their future.
   c. there is nothing wrong with premarital sex.
   d. all of the above statements are true.

8. Serial monogamy
   a. is practiced by most emerging adults in the United States.
   b. is rare among emerging adults in European nations.
   c. prevents emotional entanglements resulting from casual sex.
   d. helps explain decreasing rates of sexually transmitted infections.

9. Which of the following statements best describes rates of sexual activity for young women in North America and Europe?
   a. They are close to those for young men.
   b. They are far less than those for young men.
   c. They are far more than those for young men.
   d. none of the above

10. Serious disease is uncommon in emerging adults **EXCEPT** for
    a. tuberculosis (TB).
    b. malnutrition.
    c. parasitic infestations.
    d. sexually transmitted infections (STIs).

11. According to sociocultural explanations, the development of eating disorders such as anorexia nervosa is encouraged by
    a. societal pressures to be thin.
    b. evolutionary pressures to reproduce.
    c. the rising rates of obesity.
    d. conflict with mothers.

12. The leading cause of death among young adult African-American men is
    a. cancer.
    b. homicide.
    c. fatal accidents.
    d. suicide.

13. Which of the following was **NOT** suggested as a reason for the high rate of drug use and abuse during emerging adulthood?
    a. Young adults tend to ignore the lesson learned about drug use and abuse from older generations.
    b. Young adults are trying to imitate their parents' behavior.
    c. Young adults may use drugs as a way of relieving job or educational stress.
    d. Young adults make decisions based on delay discounting.

True or False Items

Write T (for true) or F (for false) on the line in front of each statement.

14. _____ Health is interdependent, which means that health in one part of the body does not affect the other parts.

15. _____ Employment almost never requires physical strength these days.

16. _____ The older a person is, the more likely they are to notice declines in homeostasis and organ reserve.

17. _____ Risky occupations attract young adults.

18. _____ Adolescents use and abuse drugs more than emerging adults.

19. _____ The incidence of sexually transmitted disease is lower than ever before.

20. _____ Most young adults rate their health as average or below average.

21. _____ College women and athletes are at particular risk for eating disorders.

22. _____ Emerging adults sometime subvert their natural homeostasis because of odd eating habits.

23. _____ Drug addiction is particularly common among those who die violently.

Practice Questions II

Multiple-Choice Questions

1. The early 20s are the peak years for
   a. hard physical work.
   b. problem-free reproduction.
   c. athletic performance.
   d. all of the above.

2. Approaches to reducing drug use include
   a. making them illegal.
   b. increasing supervision of emerging adults.
   c. social norms approach.
   d. all of the above.

3. Violent death rates in Canada, New Zealand, Mexico, and Australia are
   a. far below those in the United States.
   b. far above those in the United States.
   c. almost as high as the United States.
   d. none of the above.

4. Lung capacity
   a. remains stable throughout the 20s.
   b. is as large as it will ever be during the 20s.
   c. begins to decline during the 30s.
   d. declines significantly at about age 30.

5. Replacement rate means
   a. two parents are replacing themselves when they have children.
   b. two parents are replacing their parents who will die before them.
   c. two parents are replacing their grandparents who are most likely already dead.
   d. none of the above.

6. Emerging adults enjoy taking risks. In the Berger textbook, this behavior is called
   a. risky behavior.
   b. gender socialization.
   c. edgework.
   d. stupid and irresponsible.

7. Which of the following is **NOT** a characteristic of sexual behavior in young adulthood?
   a. fewer orgasms
   b. strong sex drive
   c. high fertility
   d. high testosterone

8. The typical bulimic patient is a
   a. college-age woman.
   b. woman who starves herself to the point of emaciation.
   c. woman in her late 40s.
   d. woman who suffers from life-threatening obesity.

9. A diagnosis of anorexia nervosa may be warranted if a woman
   a. intensely fears gaining weight.
   b. has a disturbed body perception.
   c. does not menstruate.
   d. experiences all of the above.

10. Relative to all other age groups, young adult males are at increased risk for virtually every kind of
    a. eating disorder.
    b. violence.
    c. acute disease.
    d. chronic disease.

11. The heaviest use of most drugs in the United States occurs during
    a. adolescence.
    b. emerging adulthood.
    c. the 30s.
    d. late adulthood.

12. Which of the following factors has resulted in the development of effective contraception?
    a. modern medicine
    b. globalization
    c. advanced technology
    d. all of the above

Matching Items

Match each definition or description with its corresponding term.

Terms

13. __________ senescence
14. __________ homeostasis
15. __________ organ reserve
16. __________ emerging adults
17. __________ social norms approach
18. __________ extreme sports
19. __________ drug abuse
20. __________ edgework
21. __________ anorexia nervosa
22. __________ bulimia nervosa

Definitions or Descriptions

a. jobs or activities that involve significant risk or danger

b. young people between the ages of 18–25

c. sports that involve significant risk of injury or death

d. extra capacity for responding to stressful events

e. a state of physiological equilibrium

f. an affliction characterized by binge-purge eating

g. age-related decline

h. using a drug to the extent that it impairs a user's biological or psychological well-being

i. an affliction characterized by self-starvation

j. publicizing surveys to prevent risky behavior

Applying Your Knowledge

1. Your instructor asks you to summarize, in one sentence, the extent and cause of biosocial decline during early adulthood. You wisely respond

   a. "Any difficulties experienced by young adults in biosocial development are usually related to factors other than aging per se."

   b. "Significant declines in all aspects of physical well-being become apparent by the mid-20s."

   c. "With the attainment of full maturity, development is released from the constraints of heredity."

   d. "The first signs of aging are usually not apparent until middle adulthood."

2. When we are hot, we perspire in order to give off body heat. This is an example of the way our body functions maintain
   a. senescence.
   b. homeostasis.
   c. endometriosis.
   d. motility.

3. Because of a decline in organ reserve, 28-year-old Brenda
   a. has a higher resting heart rate than she did when she was younger.
   b. needs longer to recover from strenuous exercise than she did when she was younger.
   c. has a higher maximum heart rate than her younger sister.
   d. has all of the above.

4. Summarizing the results of cross-sectional research on attitudes, the lecturer states that "More young adults than older adults believe that casual sex is normal and acceptable behavior." The most likely explanation for the lecturer's statement is
   a. decreases in the desire to get married.
   b. increases in availability of effective contraception.
   c. decreases in moral reasoning.
   d. increases in rates of sexually transmitted infections.

5. If Benny is like most men, as he grows older, he will
   a. experience an increase in sexual activity.
   b. become more interested in edgework.
   c. engage in more risky behavior.
   d. become less likely to die a violent death.

6. Sheila dieted for several weeks until she lost ten pounds. Upon returning to a normal diet, she is horrified to find that she has gained some of the weight back. It is likely that Sheila's weight gain was caused by
   a. overconsumption of high-fat foods.
   b. too little exercise in her daily routine.
   c. her homeostatic mechanism returning to her natural set point.
   d. a low body set point.

7. Of the following, who is most likely to suffer from anorexia nervosa?
   a. Bill, a 23-year-old professional football player
   b. Florence, a 30-year-old account executive
   c. Lynn, a 20-year-old college student
   d. Carl, a professional dancer

8. As a psychoanalyst, Dr. Mendoza is most likely to believe that eating disorders are caused by
   a. the reinforcing effects of fasting, bingeing, and purging.
   b. low self-esteem and depression, which act as a stimulus for destructive patterns of eating.
   c. unresolved conflicts with parents.
   d. the desire of working women to project a strong, self-controlled image.

9. Michael, who is in his mid-20s, is most likely to seek medical attention for
   a. a common cold.
   b. a sports- or drug-related injury.
   c. a life-threatening chronic illness.
   d. infertility.

10. Lucretia, who has a body mass index of 24, has been trying unsuccessfully to lose ten pounds. It is likely that her difficulty has occurred because
    a. she has a glandular disorder.
    b. she suffers from bulimia nervosa.
    c. her natural weight set point is higher than she would like.
    d. her obesity is accompanied by a very low metabolic rate.

11. The automobile death rate is highest between the ages of
    a. 18–25.
    b. 25–27.
    c. 15–20.
    d. none of the above.

Answer Key

Key Terms

1. Emerging adulthood is the period between the ages of 18–25, which is now widely thought of as a separate developmental stage. It is also called "young adulthood" or "youth." (p. 385; objective 1)
2. Homeostasis refers to the process by which body functions are automatically adjusted to keep our physiological functioning in a state of balance. (p. 388; video lesson, segment 1; objective 2)
3. Replacement rate is the number of births per woman that would be required to maintain a nation's (or the world's) population with no increases or decreases. The current replacement rate is considered to be about 2.1 births per woman. (p. 389; objective 3)
4. Work that involves a significant risk of harm is referred to as edgework because the person is "living on the edge" between safety and harm while engaged in these activities. (p. 391; objectives 5 & 7)
5. Extreme sports, such as motorcross, involve a significant risk of danger or even death. (p. 392; objectives 5 & 7)
6. When a drug is ingested to such a degree that biological and/or psychological well-being is impaired, drug abuse has occurred. (p. 392; objective 4)
7. Drug addiction is evident in a person when the absence of a drug in his or her body produces the drive to ingest more of the drug. (p. 392; video lesson, segment 2; objective 4)
8. The social norms approach aims to reduce risky behavior by showing individuals how common certain behaviors actually are in a given population. For example, if college students learned that most of their peers do not engage in binge drinking, this might create a social norm against binge drinking (p. 395; objective 7)
9. Organ reserve is the extra capacity of each body organ for responding to unusually stressful events or conditions that demand intense or prolonged effort. (video lesson, segment 1; objective 2)
10. Senescence is age-related decline throughout the body. (video lesson, segment 1; objective 1)
11. Anorexia nervosa is an affliction characterized by self-starvation that is most common in high-achieving college-age women. (video lesson, segment 2; objective 6)
12. Bulimia nervosa is an eating disorder that involves compulsive binge eating followed by purging through vomiting or taking massive doses of laxatives. (video lesson, segment 2; objective 6)
13. Gender socialization refers to the process by which an individual acquires a masculine or feminine social role. (video lesson, segment 3; objective 7)

Practice Questions I

Multiple-Choice Questions

1. b. is the correct answer. (video lesson, segment 1; objective 1)

   a., c., & d. are incorrect. Each of these is a specific example of the more general process of senescence.

2. b. is the correct answer. (p. 386; objective 1)
3. c. is the correct answer. (p. 386; objective 1)

   a. & b. are incorrect. These are true of women.

   d. is incorrect.

4. a. is the correct answer. (p. 387; video lesson, segment 1; objective 1)
5. b. is the correct answer. (p. 388; video lesson, segment 1; objective 2)

   a. is incorrect. This is the extra capacity that each organ of the body has for responding to unusually stressful events or conditions that demand intense or prolonged effort.

   c. is incorrect. Stress, which is not defined in this lesson, refers to events or situations that tax the body's resources.

   d. is incorrect. This simply refers to a muscle's potential for work.

6. c. is the correct answer. (pp. 391–392; objective 5)
7. c. is the correct answer. (p. 391; objective 3)
8. a. is the correct answer. (p. 390; objective 3)
9. a. is the correct answer. (p. 390; objective 3)
10. d. is the correct answer. (p. 391; objective 1)
11. a. is the correct answer. (video lesson, segment 2; objective 6)
12. b. is the correct answer. (p. 394, Figure 11.4; video lesson, segment 3; objective 8)

    a. is incorrect. Although this is the most common fatal disease in early adulthood, it certainly is not the most common cause of death.

    c. is incorrect. This is the leading cause of death for young European-American men.

    d. is incorrect. Suicide is much less frequently a cause of death for African-American men, partly because they tend to have extensive family and friendship networks that provide social support.

13. b. is the correct answer. In fact, just the opposite is true. Young adults may use drugs to express independence from their parents. (pp. 392–393; objective 4)

True or False Items

14. F (p. 387; video lesson, segment 1; objective 2)
15. T (p. 386; objective 1)
16. T (p. 388; video lesson, segment 1; objective 2)
17. T (p. 391; objective 5)
18. F Just the opposite is true. (p. 392; objective 4)
19. F (p. 391; objective 3)
20. F (p. 387; objective 1)
21. T (video lesson, segment 2; objective 6)
22. T (p. 388; objective 2)
23. T Among young European-American men, accidents are the number one cause of death. (p. 393; video lesson, segment 3; objective 8)

Practice Questions II

Multiple-Choice Questions

1. d. is the correct answer. (pp. 386–387; video lesson, segment 1; objectives 1 & 2)
2. d. is the correct answer. (p. 395; objective 7)
3. c. is the correct answer. (p. 394; objective 8)
4. b. is the correct answer. (p. 387; objective 2)
5. a. is the correct answer. (p. 389; objective 3)
6. c. is the correct answer. (p. 391; objective 5)
7. a. is the correct answer. (p. 388; objective 3)
8. a. is the correct answer. (video lesson, segment 2; objective 6)

   b. is incorrect. This describes a woman suffering from anorexia nervosa.

   c. is incorrect. Eating disorders are much more common in younger women.

   d. is incorrect. Most women with bulimia nervosa are usually close to normal in weight.
9. d. is the correct answer. (video lesson, segment 2; objective 6)
10. b. is the correct answer. (pp. 393–395; video lesson, segment 3; objectives 5 & 8)

    a. is incorrect. Eating disorders are more common in women than men.

    c. & d. are incorrect. Disease is relatively rare at this age.
11. b. is the correct answer. (p. 392; video lesson, segment 2; objective 4)
12. d. is the correct answer. (p. 389; objective 3)

Matching Items

13. g (video lesson, segment 1; objective 1)
14. e (p. 388; video lesson, segment 1; objective 2)

15. d (video lesson, segment 1; objective 2)
16. b (p. 385; objective 1)
17. j (p. 395; objective 7)
18. c (p. 392; objectives 5 & 7)
19. h (p. 392; objective 4)
20. a (p. 391; objective 5)
21. i (video lesson, segment 2; objective 6)
22. f (video lesson, segment 2; objective 6)

Applying Your Knowledge

1. a. is the correct answer. (pp. 385–387; video lesson, segment 1; objective 1)

   b. is incorrect. Physical declines during the 20s are usually of little consequence.

   c. is incorrect. This is not true nor does it address the instructor's request.

   d. is incorrect. The first signs of aging become apparent at an earlier age.

2. b. is the correct answer. (p. 388; video lesson, segment 1; objective 2)

   a. is incorrect. This is age-related decline.

   c. is incorrect. This is a common fertility problem for women.

   d. is incorrect. This refers to the swimming ability of sperm.

3. b. is the correct answer. (video lesson, segment 1; objective 2)

   a. is incorrect. Resting heart rate remains stable throughout adulthood.

   c. is incorrect. Maximum heart rate declines with age.

4. b. is the correct answer. (p. 390; objective 3)
5. d. is the correct answer. (pp. 393–394; objective 8)
6. c. is the correct answer. (p. 388; objective 2)
7. c. is the correct answer. (video lesson, segment 2; objective 6)

   a. & d. are incorrect. Eating disorders are more common in women than men.

   b. is incorrect. Eating disorders are more common in younger women.

8. c. is the correct answer. (video lesson, segment 2; objective 6)

   a. & b. are incorrect. Those who emphasize learning theory or cognitive theory would more likely offer these explanations.

   d. is incorrect. This is a sociocultural explanation of eating disorders.

9. b. is the correct answer. (video lesson, segment 1; objectives 1 & 2)
10. c. is the correct answer. (p. 388; objective 2)

    a. & d. are incorrect. There is no evidence that Lucretia has a glandular disorder or is obese. In fact, a BMI of 24 is well within the normal weight range.

    b. is incorrect. There is no evidence that Lucretia is bingeing and purging.

11. a. is the correct answer. (p. 392; objective 5)

Lesson Review

Lesson 17

Early Adulthood
Biosocial Development

Please Note: Use this matrix to guide your study and achieve the learning objectives of this lesson. It will also help you to view the video, which defines and demonstrates important concepts and skills as they relate to everyday life.

Learning Objective	Textbook	Telecourse Student Guide	Video Lesson
1. Describe the changes in growth, strength, and overall health that occur during early adulthood.	pp. 385–387	Key Terms: 1, 10; Practice Questions I: 1, 2, 3, 4, 10, 15, 20; Practice Questions II: 1, 13, 16; Applying Your Knowledge: 1, 9.	Segment 1: *Growth, Strength, and Health*
2. Discuss the meaning of the phrase "health is interdependent" and describe the dynamic systems concept of health, including a definition of "homeostasis."	pp. 387–388	Key Terms: 2, 9; Practice Questions I: 5, 14, 16, 22; Practice Questions II: 1, 4, 14, 15; Applying Your Knowledge: 2, 3, 6, 9, 10.	Segment 1: *Growth, Strength, and Health*
3. Identify age-related trends in the norms for sexual activity, and describe potential consequences of sexual activity during emerging adulthood.	pp. 388–391	Key Terms: 3; Practice Questions I: 7, 8, 9, 19; Practice Questions II: 5, 7, 12; Applying Your Knowledge: 4.	
4. Discuss changes in substance abuse during early adulthood, and describe the causes and consequences of this abuse.	pp. 392–393	Key Terms: 6, 7; Practice Questions I: 13, 18; Practice Questions II: 11, 19.	Segment 2: *Health Problems*
5. Discuss the affinity for risk taking in emerging adulthood and define the term "edgework" in regard to risk taking.	pp. 391–392	Key Terms: 4, 5; Practice Questions I: 6, 17; Practice Questions II: 6, 10, 18, 20; Applying Your Knowledge: 11.	Segment 3: *Gender Socialization and Violence*

Learning Objective	**Textbook**	**Telecourse Student Guide**	**Video Lesson**
6. Describe the typical victims of anorexia nervosa and bulimia nervosa, and discuss possible explanations for these disorders.	*	Key Terms: 11, 12; Practice Questions I: 11, 21; Practice Questions II: 8, 9, 21, 22; Applying Your Knowledge: 7, 8.	Segment 2: *Health Problems*
7. Explain how social norms and gender socialization may be related to self-destructive behavior among emerging adults.	p. 395	Key Terms: 4, 5, 8, 13; Practice Questions II: 2, 17, 18.	Segment 2: *Health Problems*; Segment 3: *Gender Socialization and Violence*
8. Discuss the factors that may determine whether a young male adult will suffer a violent death.	pp. 393–395	Practice Questions I: 12, 23; Practice Questions II: 3, 10; Applying Your Knowledge: 5.	Segment 3: *Gender Socialization and Violence*

* The video for this lesson provides a useful exploration of these topics.

Decisions, Decisions

Lesson 18

Early Adulthood: Cognitive Development

Preview

During the course of adulthood, there are many shifts in cognitive development—in the speed and efficiency with which we process information, in the focus and depth of our cognitive processes, and perhaps in the quality, or wisdom, of our thinking. Developmental psychologists use different approaches in explaining these shifts, with each approach providing insights into the nature of adult cognition. This chapter takes a *postformal approach*, describing age-related changes in an attempt to uncover patterns or predictable stages.

The lesson begins by describing how adult thinking differs from adolescent thinking. The experiences and challenges of adulthood result in a new, postformal thought, evidenced by more practical and adaptive thinking—the dynamic cognitive style that adults typically use to solve the problems of daily life.

Next, the lesson explores how the events of emerging adulthood and early adulthood can affect moral development and thinking about faith and religious matters.

The lesson also examines the effect of the college experience on cognitive growth; findings here indicate that years of education correlate positively with virtually every measure of cognition, as thinking becomes progressively more flexible and tolerant. A final section discusses the importance of life events—such as parenthood, job promotion, or illness—in triggering cognitive growth during young adulthood.

As you complete this lesson, consider your own cognitive development during emerging adulthood and early adulthood (or that of someone you know in this age range, 18 to 35). In what ways have your thinking and cognitive skills advanced during this period? How has your perspective on religion, faith, and morality changed (if at all)? What particular life events or experiences have been the most significant in changing the way you approach problems and think about life?

Prior Telecourse Knowledge that Will Be Used in this Lesson

- This lesson will return to the theories of Jean Piaget (from Lessons 2 and 12). Recall that Piaget specified four age-related periods of cognitive development:
  1. Sensorimotor (birth to 2 years)
  2. Preoperational (2 to 6 years)
  3. Concrete Operational (7 to 11 years)
  4. Formal Operational (12 years through adulthood)
- Piaget described formal operational thought as the last stage of cognitive development, beginning in adolescence and extending into adulthood. But, as you will learn in this lesson, adults often develop a more complex, practical, and flexible type of cognition called *postformal thought*.
- For its discussion of adult moral reasoning and the development of faith, this lesson will briefly return to the ideas of Lawrence Kohlberg and Carol Gilligan (from Lesson 12). Recall that Kohlberg described three levels of moral reasoning: preconventional, conventional, and postconventional.

Learning Objectives

Use this information to guide your reading, viewing, thinking, and studying. After successfully completing this lesson, you should be able to:

1. Describe the cognitive maturity of the emerging adult and contrast it to the cognitive processes of adolescence (formal operational thought), reflecting on the value of experience.
2. Describe the main characteristics of postformal thought, and discuss the concept of stereotype threat.
3. Define and describe dialectical thought, and give examples of its usefulness.
4. Discuss whether postformal thought (cognitive maturity, dialectical thought) represents a separate stage of development.
5. Discuss the relationship between cognitive growth and higher education.
6. Identify and evaluate differences between contemporary colleges and college students and their counterparts of a decade or two ago.
7. Discuss how life events may trigger new patterns of thinking and result in cognitive growth.

Read Chapter 11, "Emerging Adulthood: Body, Mind, and Social World," pages 396–404.

View the video for Lesson 18, "Decisions, Decisions."

Segment 1: *Postformal Thought*

Segment 2: *Life Experiences and Their Effects*

Segment 3: *Moral Reasoning*

Summary

As people grow from adolescence into adulthood, the commitments, demands, and responsibilities of adult life can produce a new type of thinking that is better suited than formal operations to solving the practical problems of daily life. Adult cognition has been studied in three major ways: from a postformal perspective, from a psychometric perspective, and from an information-processing perspective. The lesson focuses on the postformal perspective. Postformal thought is more adaptive, flexible, and dialectical. **Dialectical thought**, which some developmental psychologists consider the most advanced form of cognition, recognizes that most of life's important questions do not have single, unvarying, correct answers. It is grounded in the ability to consider both sides of an issue simultaneously.

Thinking about questions of faith and ethics may also progress during adulthood, especially in response to significant life experiences, such as participating in higher education and becoming a parent. Carol Gilligan suggests that men and women come to recognize the limitations of moral reasoning based solely on abstract principles and personal concerns and attempt to integrate the two with life experiences to forge a more reflective, less absolute moral awareness. James Fowler has bridged the fields of psychology and religion by creating a model in which faith is broadly conceived. Building on the cognitive and personality theories of Jean Piaget and Erik Erikson, Fowler's model extends the concept of faith beyond religious faith to include whatever each person really cares about—his or her "ultimate concern." Fowler's theory describes six stages, each of which has distinct features and is classified as typical of a certain age.

Level of education is strongly correlated with virtually every measure of adult cognition. College education leads people to become more tolerant of differing views, more flexible and realistic in their attitudes, and dialectical in their reasoning. Throughout the world, the number of college students has increased, and more students are female, ethnic minorities, part-time, commuter, and older than ever before. Young adults are developing the ability to reason about emotionally charged issues, a skill that peaks in middle adulthood.

Review all reading assignments for this lesson.

As assigned by your instructor, complete the optional online component for this lesson.

Key Terms

Using your own words, write a brief definition or explanation of each of the following terms on a separate piece of paper.

1. stereotype threat
2. postformal thought
3. objective thought
4. subjective thought
5. dialectical thought

Practice Questions I

Multiple-Choice Questions

1. Differences in the reasoning maturity of adolescents and young adults are most likely to be apparent when
   a. groups with low socioecomic status and high socioecomic status are compared.
   b. ethnic-minority adolescents and adults are compared.
   c. ethnic-majority adolescents and adults are compared.
   d. emotionally charged issues are involved.

2. Which of the following self-descriptions had not been reached by people under 20 in Labouvie-Vief's study of adolescents in 2006?
   a. dysregulated
   b. self-protected
   c. integrated
   d. complex

3. Compared to adolescent thinking, adult thinking tends to be
   a. more flexible.
   b. more practical.
   c. more integrative.
   d. all of the above.

4. Experts have shown that the hallmark of adult adaptive thought is the
   a. ability to engage in dialectical thinking.
   b. reconciliation of both objective and subjective approaches to real-life problems.
   c. adoption of conjunctive faith.
   d. all of the above.

5. Most contemporary students attend college primarily to
   a. secure their vocational and financial futures.
   b. learn marketable skills.
   c. secure a broad general education so they can understand events in their complex world.
   d. obtain a and b only.

6. The thinking of college students changes as they progress through the academic process. Which of the following statements is **TRUE** of college freshmen?
   a. They do not believe clear and perfect truths exist.
   b. They generally believe questions have specific answers.
   c. They accept the fact some questions have no answers.
   d. none of the above

7. Postformal thinking is most useful for solving ____________________ problems.
   a. science
   b. mathematics
   c. everyday
   d. abstract, logical

8. The kind of thinking that involves the consideration of both poles of an idea and their reconciliation, or synthesis, in a new idea is
   a. subjective thinking.
   b. postformal thought.
   c. adaptive reasoning.
   d. dialectical thinking.

9. Thesis is to antithesis as __________________ is to ____________________.
   a. a new idea; an opposing idea
   b. abstract; concrete
   c. concrete; abstract
   d. provisional; absolute

10. Which of the following pairs of adjectives best describes cognitive development during adulthood?
    a. multidirectional and multicontextual
    b. unidirectional and linear
    c. straightforward and stable
    d. random and patternless

11. Which of the following most accurately describes postformal thought?
    a. subjective thinking that arises from the personal experiences and perceptions of the individual
    b. objective reasoning that follows abstract, impersonal logic
    c. a form of reasoning that combines subjectivity and objectivity
    d. thinking that is rigid, inflexible, and fails to recognize the existence of other potentially valid views

12. An important factor in determining whether college students learn to think deeply is
    a. the particular influence between fellow students, faculty, books, and class discussion.
    b. the college's overall religious or secular philosophy.
    c. the college's size.
    d. all of the above.

13. Research has revealed that a typical outcome of college education is that students become
    a. very liberal politically.
    b. less committed to any particular ideology.
    c. less tolerant of others' views.
    d. more tolerant of others' views.

True or False Items

Write T (for true) or F (for false) on the line in front of each statement.

14. _____ Research shows that the main reason most young adults today attend college is to improve their thinking and reasoning skills.

15. _____ Adult cognitive growth is more straightforward than that of childhood and adolescence.

16. _____ Objective, logical thinking is "adaptive" for the school-age child and adolescent who is in the process of categorizing and organizing his or her experiences.

17. _____ Because they recognize the changing and subjective nature of beliefs and values, dialectical thinkers avoid making personal or intellectual commitments.

18. _____ In recent years, the number of female college students has dropped significantly.

19. _____ Postformal thought is less absolute and less abstract than formal thought.

20. _____ In the United States, of those earning advanced degrees today, 57% are women.

Practice Questions II

Multiple-Choice Questions

1. Which approach to adult cognitive development "picks up where Piaget left off"?
   a. psychometric
   b. information-processing
   c. postformal
   d. dialectical

2. As adult thinking becomes more focused on occupational and interpersonal demands, it also becomes less inclined toward
   a. formal operational thought.
   b. dialectical thought.
   c. adaptive thought.
   d. all of the above.

3. The result of dialectical thinking is a view that
   a. one's self is an unchanging constant.
   b. few of life's important questions have single, correct answers.
   c. "everything is relative."
   d. all of the above are true.

4. Formal operational thinking is most useful for solving problems that
   a. involve logical relationships or theoretical possibilities.
   b. require integrative skills.
   c. involve the synthesis of diverse issues.
   d. require seeing perspectives other than one's own.

5. College seems to make people more accepting of other people's attitudes because it

   a. boosts self-esteem.

   b. makes new ideas less threatening.

   c. promotes extroversion.

   d. does all of the above.

6. Stereotype threat can

   a. make people doubt their ability to succeed.

   b. increase anxiety.

   c. negatively impact grades in college.

   d. all of the above.

7. Formal operational thinking is to postformal thinking as ________________ is to ____________________.

   a. psychometric; information-processing

   b. adolescence; adulthood

   c. thesis; antithesis

   d. self-esteem; extroversion

8. Many of the problems of adult life are characterized by ambiguity, partial truths, and extenuating circumstances, and therefore are often best solved using ___________ thinking.

   a. formal

   b. reintegrative

   c. postformal

   d. executive

9. Which aspect of college is the primary catalyst for cognitive growth?

   a. academic work

   b. the encounter with new ideas

   c. the discussion with peers

   d. all of the above

10. Research examining adult cognition has found that when adults of various ages are asked to come up with solutions to common life dilemmas, emerging adults
    a. imagine a single solution and stick to it.
    b. are unable to suggest a plausible solution.
    c. typically think of several solutions and then select the best one.
    d. are inflexible and do not consider their own life experiences.

Applying Your Knowledge

1. Concluding her comparison of postformal thinking with Piaget's cognitive stages, Lynn notes that
    a. not every adult thinks in a postformal manner.
    b. dialectical thinking is more evident in some contexts than in others.
    c. not everyone who thinks in a postformal way is also capable of formal operational thought.
    d. all of the above are true.

2. Research suggests that a college sophomore or junior is most likely to have reached a phase in which he or she
    a. believes that there are clear and perfect truths to be discovered.
    b. questions personal and social values, and even the idea of truth itself.
    c. rejects opposing ideas in the interest of finding one right answer.
    d. accepts a simplistic either/or dualism.

3. In his scheme of cognitive and ethical development (seen in Table 11.3 on page 402), researcher William Perry describes a position in which the college student says, "I see I am going to have to make my own decisions in an uncertain world with no one to tell me I'm right." This position marks the culmination of a phase of
    a. either/or dualism.
    b. modified dualism.
    c. relativism.
    d. commitments in relativism.

4. After suffering a heart attack in his 30s, Rob begins to think differently about life and its deeper meaning. This is an example of
    a. the effect of a mentor on cognitive development.
    b. having reached the reintegrative stage of adult cognition.
    c. a life event that results in cognitive growth.
    d. a biological or age-related change in intelligence.

5. Dr. Polaski studies how thinking during adulthood builds on the earlier formal thinking skills of adolescence. Evidently, Dr. Polaski follows the ______________________ approach to the study of development.

   a. postformal
   b. psychometric
   c. cognitive
   d. information-processing

6. When she was younger, May-Ling believed that "Honesty is always the best policy." She now realizes that although honesty is desirable, it is not always the best policy. May-Ling's current thinking is an example of

   a. formal thought.
   b. dialectical thinking.
   c. mythic-literal thinking.
   d. conjunctive thinking.

7. In concluding her presentation on "The College Student of Today," Coretta states that

   a. "The number of students in higher education has increased significantly in virtually every country worldwide."
   b. "There are more low-income and ethnic-minority students today than ever before."
   c. "More students choose specific career-based majors rather than a liberal arts education."
   d. all of the above are true.

8. In concluding his paper on postformal thinking, Stanley notes that

   a. postformal thinking is not the same kind of universal, age-related stage that Piaget described for earlier cognitive growth.
   b. very few adults attain this highest stage of reasoning.
   c. most everyday problems require sensitivity to subjective feelings and therefore do not foster postformal thinking.
   d. all of the above are true.

9. Despite the challenges posed by the hidden curriculum, students who are ________________ find that college represents an especially transforming element in their lives.

   a. technologically savvy
   b. working part-time
   c. the first in their families to attend college
   d. from families with high socioeconomic status

10. According to a 1991 research study, which of the following statements is true about college seniors, in comparison to college freshmen?

   a. They are better able to understand more than one side of a complex issue.
   b. They are more skilled at using reason and evidence to address problems that are not supported by verifiable evidence.
   c. They show no greater reasoning ability than freshmen.
   d. a and b

Answer Key

Key Terms

1. The possibility that one's appearance or behavior will be misused to confirm another person's oversimplified, prejudiced attitude is called stereotype threat. (p. 398; objective 2)
2. Proposed by some developmentalists as an additional level of cognitive development, postformal thought is suited to solving real-world problems and is less abstract, less absolute, and more integrative and synthetic than formal thought. (video lesson, segment 1; objective 2)
3. Objective thought is a kind of thinking that follows abstract, impersonal logic. (video lesson, segment 1; objective 2)
4. Subjective thought is a kind of thinking that arises from the personal experiences and perceptions of an individual. (video lesson, segment 1; objective 2)
5. Dialectical thought is thinking that involves considering both poles of an idea (thesis and antithesis) simultaneously and then forging them into a synthesis. (video lesson, segment 1; objectives 2 & 3)

Practice Questions I

Multiple-Choice Questions

1. d. is the correct answer. (p. 396; video lesson, segment 1; objectives 1 & 2)

   a., b., & c. are incorrect. Socioeconomic status and ethnicity do not predict reasoning maturity.

2. c. is the correct answer. (p. 396; objective 1)

3. d. is the correct answer. (pp. 396–398; video lesson, segment 1; objectives 1 & 2)
4. b. is the correct answer. (p. 396; video lesson, segment 1; objective 1)
5. d. is the correct answer. (p. 401; objective 5)
6. d. is the correct answer. (p. 402; objective 5)
7. c. is the correct answer. (video lesson, segment 1; objective 1)

   a., b., & d. are incorrect. Because of its more analytical nature, formal thinking is most useful for solving these types of problems.
8. d. is the correct answer. (p. 396; video lesson, segment 1; objective 3)

   a. is incorrect. Thinking that is subjective relies on personal reflection rather than objective observation.

   b. is incorrect. Although dialectical thinking is characteristic of postformal thought, this question refers specifically to dialectical thinking.

   c. is incorrect. Adaptive reasoning, which also is characteristic of postformal thought, goes beyond mere logic in solving problems to also explore real-life complexities and contextual circumstances.
9. a. is the correct answer. (p. 396; objectives 1 & 3)
10. a. is the correct answer. (pp. 396–404; objective 4)
11. c. is the correct answer. (p. 396; video lesson, segment 1; objectives 1, 2, & 3)
12. a. is the correct answer. (p. 403; objective 5)
13. d. is the correct answer. (pp. 402–403; video lesson, segment 2; objective 5)

True or False Items

14. F Most people today attend college primarily to secure better jobs. (p. 401; video lesson, segment 2; objective 5)
15. F Adult cognitive growth is multidirectional. (pp. 396–404; video lesson, introduction; objectives 2 & 4)
16. T (pp. 396–398; objectives 1, 2, & 3)
17. F Dialectical thinkers recognize the need to make commitments to values even though these values will change over time. (p. 396; video lesson, segment 1; objectives 1 & 3)
18. F (p. 403; objective 6)
19. T (pp. 396–404; video lesson, segment 1; objectives 2 & 4)
20. T (p. 403; objective 6)

Practice Questions II

Multiple-Choice Questions

1. c. is the correct answer. (p. 328; video lesson, segment 1; objectives 1 & 2)
2. a. is the correct answer. (pp. 328, 396–398; video lesson, segment 1; objectives 1 & 2)

b. & c. are incorrect. During adulthood, thinking typically becomes more dialectical and adaptive.

3. b. is the correct answer. (video lesson, segment 1; objective 3)
4. a. is the correct answer. (pp. 396–401; video lesson, segment 1; objectives 1 & 2)

   b., c., & d. are incorrect. Postformal thought is most useful for solving problems such as these.
5. b. is the correct answer. (pp. 401–404; video lesson, segment 2; objective 5)

   a. & c. are incorrect. The impact of college on self-esteem and extroversion were not discussed. Moreover, it is unclear how such an impact would make a person more accepting of others.
6. d. is the correct answer. (pp. 398–399; video lesson, segment 1; objective 2)

   a. is incorrect. A thesis is a new idea.

   b. is incorrect. An antithesis is an idea that opposes a particular thesis.

   d. is incorrect. Hypotheses, which are testable predictions about behavior, are not an aspect of dialectical thinking.
7. b. is the correct answer. (pp. 396–398; video lesson, segment 1; objectives 1 & 2)
8. c. is the correct answer. (pp. 396–398; video lesson, segment 1; objectives 1 & 2)

   a. is incorrect. Formal thinking is best suited to solving problems that require logic and analytical thinking.

   b. & d. are incorrect. These terms are not discussed in the textbook.
9. d. is the correct answer. Research has no conclusive answer. (p. 403; video lesson, segment 2; objective 5)

   a. is incorrect by itself.

   c. is incorrect by itself.

   d. is incorrect by itself.
10. c. is the correct answer. (p. 398; objective 7)

Applying Your Knowledge

1. d. is the correct answer. (pp. 396–401; video lesson, introduction & segment 1; objectives 2, 3, & 4)
2. b. is the correct answer. (p. 402; objective 5)

   a. is incorrect. First-year college students are more likely to believe this is so.

   c. & d. are incorrect. Over the course of their college careers, students become less likely to do either of these.
3. c. is the correct answer. (p. 402; objective 5)
4. c. is the correct answer. (video lesson, segment 2; objective 7)

5. a. is the correct answer. (pp. 396–398; video lesson, segment 1; objectives 1 & 2)

   b. is incorrect. This approach analyzes components of intelligence such as those measured by IQ tests.

   c. is incorrect. Each of these approaches is cognitive in nature.

   d. is incorrect. This approach studies the encoding, storage, and retrieval of information throughout life.

6. b. is the correct answer. May-Ling has formed a synthesis between the thesis that honesty is the best policy and its antithesis. (video lesson, segment 1; objective 3)

   a. is incorrect. This is an example of postformal rather than formal thinking.

   c. & d. are incorrect. These are stages in the development of faith as proposed by James Fowler.

7. d. is the correct answer. (pp. 403–404; objective 6)

8. a. is the correct answer. (pp. 396–401; video lesson, introduction & segment 1; objectives 2 & 4)

   b. is incorrect. Because postformal thinking is typical of adult thought, this is untrue.

   c. is incorrect. It is exactly this sort of problem that fosters postformal thinking.

9. c. is the correct answer. (p. 403; objective 5)

10. d. is the correct answer. (p. 401; objective 5)

Lesson Review

Lesson 18

Early Adulthood
Cognitive Development

Please Note: Use this matrix to guide your study and achieve the learning objectives of this lesson. It will also help you to view the video, which defines and demonstrates important concepts and skills as they relate to everyday life.

Learning Objective	Textbook	Telecourse Student Guide	Video Lesson
1. Describe the cognitive maturity of the emerging adult and contrast it to the cognitive processes of adolescence (formal operational thought), reflecting on the value of experience.	p. 396 & review p. 328 in Chapter 9 (Lesson 15)	Practice Questions I: 1, 2, 3, 4, 7, 9, 11, 16, 17; Practice Questions II: 1, 2, 4, 7, 8; Applying Your Knowledge: 5.	Segment 1: *Postformal Thought*
2. Describe the main characteristics of postformal thought and discuss the concept of stereotype threat.	pp. 396–401	Key Terms: 1, 2, 3, 4, 5; Practice Questions I: 1, 3, 11, 15, 16, 19; Practice Questions II: 1, 2, 4, 6, 7, 8; Applying Your Knowledge: 1, 5, 8.	Introduction; Segment 1: *Postformal Thought*
3. Define and describe dialectical thought, and give examples of its usefulness.	*	Key Terms: 5; Practice Questions I: 8, 9, 11, 16, 17; Practice Questions II: 3; Applying Your Knowledge: 1, 6.	Segment 1: *Postformal Thought*
4. Discuss whether postformal thought (cognitive maturity, dialectical thought) represents a separate stage of development.	pp. 396–404	Practice Questions I: 10, 15, 19; Applying Your Knowledge: 1, 8.	Introduction; Segment 1: *Postformal Thought*
5. Discuss the relationship between cognitive growth and higher education.	pp. 401–404	Practice Questions I: 5, 6, 12, 13, 18; Practice Questions II: 5, 9; Applying Your Knowledge: 2, 3, 9, 10.	Segment 2: *Life Experiences and Their Effects*

* The video for this lesson provides a useful exploration of these topics.

Learning Objective	Textbook	Telecourse Student Guide	Video Lesson
6. Identify and evaluate differences between contemporary colleges and college students and their counterparts of a decade or two ago.	pp. 403–404	Practice Questions I: 18, 20; Applying Your Knowledge: 7.	Segment 2: *Life Experiences and Their Effects*
7 . Discuss how life events may trigger new patterns of thinking and result in cognitive growth.	pp. 396–398	Practice Questions II: 10; Applying Your Knowledge: 4.	Segment 2: *Life Experiences and Their Effects*

Love and Work

Lesson 19

Early Adulthood: Psychosocial Development

Preview

Biologically mature and no longer bound by parental authority, the young adult typically is now free to choose a particular path of development. Today, the options are incredibly varied. Not surprisingly, then, the hallmark of psychosocial development during early adulthood is diversity. Nevertheless, developmentalists have identified several themes or patterns that help us understand the course of development between the ages of 18 and 35.

After describing the task of identity development, the lesson turns next to the two basic psychosocial needs of adulthood, love and work. No matter what terminology is used, these two needs are recognized by almost all developmentalists.

Next, the lesson discusses the need for **intimacy** in adulthood, focusing on the development of friendship, love, and marriage. The impact of divorce is also discussed.

The final section of the lesson is concerned with **generativity**, or the motivation to be productive during adulthood, highlighting the importance of work and parenthood and addressing the special challenges facing stepparents, adoptive parents, and foster parents.

As you complete this lesson, consider your own psychosocial development during early adulthood (or that of someone you know in this age range). How strong is (was) your need to make friends, fall in love, get married, build a career, and have children? Have these needs grown over time? Have you felt any family or social pressure to move ahead in these areas? How have your friendships changed in young adulthood compared to adolescence? Consider your romantic relationships. What does intimacy mean to you? What role does it play in your life? Consider your marriage (or, if you're not married, your idea of marriage). In your opinion, what are the characteristics of a successful marriage? Do you know anyone who has been divorced? How do you think this might have affected their development? Consider your career. How important is work to you, and why? Do you or does someone you know have children? How might parenthood affect his or her development?

Prior Telecourse Knowledge that Will Be Used in this Lesson

- Erik Erikson's theory (from Lesson 2) will be used to help explain psychosocial development during young adulthood. Recall that Erikson specifies eight stages of psychosocial development, each of which is characterized by a particular challenge, which is central to that stage of life and must be resolved:
    1. Trust vs. Mistrust (birth to 1 year)
    2. Autonomy vs. Shame and Doubt (1 to 3 years)
    3. Initiative vs. Guilt (3 to 6 years)
    4. Industry vs. Inferiority (7 to 11 years)
    5. Identity vs. Role Confusion (adolescence)
    6. **Intimacy vs. Isolation (adulthood)**
    7. **Generativity vs. Stagnation (adulthood)**
    8. Integrity vs. Despair (Adulthood)
- This lesson will also return to Erikson's challenge of "identity vs. role confusion" (from Lesson 16). Experts agree that many young adults grapple with identity issues well into their 20s (sometimes later), as they continue to work out "who they are." In other words, this challenge may not be resolved in adolescence.

Learning Objectives

Use this information to guide your reading, viewing, thinking, and studying. After successfully completing this lesson, you should be able to:

1. Describe the psychosocial tasks of identity, intimacy, and generativity, and explain how the viewpoint of most developmentalists regarding adult stages has shifted.
2. Explain how the social clock influences the timing of important events during early adulthood.
3. Review the changing nature of friendships during adulthood, noting factors that promote friendship and gender differences in friendship patterns.
4. Describe common young adult experiences with romantic relationships and identify and discuss Sternberg's three components of love.
5. Discuss the role of serious relationships and marriage in adulthood, describe the impact of cohabitation on relationships, and identify at least three factors that influence relationship success.
6. Discuss the importance of work to the individual and how the experiences of today's workers differ from those of past generations.
7. Discuss the myths, challenges, and opportunities of dual-earner family life.
8. Describe the changing relationship between emerging adults and their parents.
9. Explain variation in well-being during emerging adulthood, and identify characteristics of psychopathology.

Read Chapter 11, "Emerging Adulthood: Body, Mind, and Social World," pages 404–417.

View the video for Lesson 19, "Love and Work."

Segment 1: *The Tasks of Adulthood*

Segment 2: *Intimacy*

Segment 3: *Generativity*

Summary

Although psychosocial development in early adulthood is marked by diversity, two basic needs or "tasks" drive its evolution: *intimacy,* achieved through friendships and love relationships; and *generativity,* usually achieved through work and/or parenting.

The **social clock** is a culturally set timetable that establishes when various events and behaviors in life typically take place. The "settings" of the social clock still influence behavior, but less rigidly than in the past. For example, our current social clock would suggest that adolescents are too young to be getting married; our cultural timetable places marriage sometime during early adulthood.

Young adults typically form extensive and varied social networks. Whereas friendships for women may be important as a way of coping with problems, for men friendship may include elements of competition and may serve as a way of maintaining a favorable self-concept.

For most people, the deepest source of intimacy is found through an intimate relationship with a mate, typically when they **cohabit** or marry. In general, the younger marriage partners are when they wed, the less likely the marriage is to succeed. Marriages between partners with similar interests and backgrounds (homogamy) are more likely to endure than those between dissimilar partners (heterogamy). The extent to which partners perceive equality in their relationship, or **marital equity**, also affects the fate of marriage.

For many adults, working is central to living for reasons that extend beyond financial security. Work is an outlet for self-expression, a source of esteem and status, and a context for mentoring. The shift from a manufacturing to a service-based economy means that workers today must acquire more flexible job skills than ever before. That most parents today are part of dual-earner families, or dual caregiving relationships, is another shift that brings both benefits and problems that traditional families in the past did not have.

Review all reading assignments for this lesson.

As assigned by your instructor, complete the optional online component for this lesson.

Key Terms

Using your own words, write a brief definition or explanation of each of the following terms on a separate piece of paper.

1. diathesis–stress model
2. cohabit
3. intimacy versus isolation
4. generativity versus stagnation
5. social clock
6. homogamy
7. marital equity
8. dual-earner family
9. identity

Practice Questions I

Multiple-Choice Questions

1. According to Erik Erikson, a basic task of adulthood is to establish
   a. a residence apart from parents.
   b. intimacy with others.
   c. generativity through work or parenthood.
   d. a career commitment.

2. Most social scientists who study adulthood emphasize that
   a. intimacy and generativity take various forms throughout adulthood.
   b. adult lives are less orderly and predictable than stage models suggest.
   c. each culture has a somewhat different social clock.
   d. all of the above are true.

3. In the past, males and females preferred friends of their own sex, and engaged in sex-specific activities with them. Today, the difference between males and females are such that
   a. the differences are less apparent among emerging adults.
   b. most emerging adults also have one or two friends of the opposite sex.
   c. most also have nonsexual, same-sex friendships.
   d. all of the above are true.

4. The concept of linked lives helps explain why
   a. adult children benefit from continued connections to their parents.
   b. it can be detrimental to young adults' well-being to achieve complete independence from their parents.
   c. parents remain invested in their adult child's development.
   d. all of the above are true.

5. According to Erikson, the failure to achieve intimacy during early adulthood is most likely to result in
   a. generativity.
   b. stagnation.
   c. role diffusion.
   d. isolation.
6. Regarding friendships, most young adults tend to
   a. be very satisfied.
   b. be very dissatisfied.
   c. find it difficult to form social networks.
   d. be without close friends.
7. According to Robert Sternberg, consummate love emerges
   a. as a direct response to passion.
   b. as a direct response to physical intimacy.
   c. when commitment is added to passion and intimacy.
   d. during the early years of parenthood.
8. An arrangement in which two unrelated, unmarried adults of the opposite sex live together is called
   a. cross-sex friendship.
   b. a passive-congenial pattern.
   c. cohabitation.
   d. affiliation.
9. Differences in religious customs or rituals are most likely to arise in a
   a. homogamous couple.
   b. heterogamous couple (a couple who are not homogamous).
   c. cohabiting couple.
   d. very young married couple.
10. In regard to identity achievement, which of the following statements is true?
   a. The search begins at puberty.
   b. Most emerging adults are still seeking their identity.
   c. Religious commitments, gender roles, political loyalties, and career options all play a part in identity achievement.
   d. All of the above statements are true.

11. Adults who combine the roles of spouse, parent, and employee tend to report
    a. less overall happiness than other adults.
    b. more overall happiness than other adults.
    c. regrets over parental roles.
    d. problems in career advancement.

12. Hikikomori is a(n) ________________________ disorder.
    a. anxiety
    b. mood
    c. substance abuse
    d. psychotic

True or False Items

Write T (for true) or F (for false) on the line in front of each statement.

13. _____ According to Erikson, adults experience a crisis of intimacy versus isolation and, after that, a crisis of generativity versus stagnation.

14. _____ Erikson's stages may not be applicable to all adults because of cultural and social changes.

15. _____ According to Sternberg, early in a relationship, emotional intimacy is at its highest.

16. _____ Good communication, marital equity, and homogamy are factors that increase the chances for marital success.

17. _____ Gender diversity in the workplace is decreasing.

18. _____ A high level of marital homogamy is extremely rare.

19. _____ It is best for the development of emerging adults to eliminate their emotional and financial dependence on their parents.

20. _____ Because of the complexity of the high-tech work world, most young adults can expect to remain at the same job throughout their careers.

21. _____ Contributing to society through work and/or having a family are ways to avoid feelings of stagnation.

22. _____ The social clock is set according to prevailing cultural values.

23. _____ Psychological disorders are more likely to emerge during young adulthood than at any other time in the life span.

Practice Questions II

Multiple-Choice Questions

1. Erikson theorizes that if generativity is not attained, an adult is most likely to experience
   a. lack of advancement in his or her career.
   b. infertility or childlessness.
   c. feelings of emptiness and stagnation.
   d. feelings of profound aloneness or isolation.

2. Which of the following statements is true regarding contemporary friendships?
   a. Most emerging adults have friends of both sexes.
   b. Online connections foster close friendships.
   c. Friends are chosen and earned, not a given benefit of growing up.
   d. all of the above

3. The prime effect of the social clock is to make an individual aware of
   a. his or her socioeconomic status.
   b. the diversity of psychosocial paths during early adulthood.
   c. the means of fulfilling affiliation and achievement needs.
   d. the "right" or "best" time for assuming adult roles.

4. Which of the following statements about ethnic identity development is **FALSE**?
   a. It is a reciprocal process, involving responses to others and personal choices.
   b. It is typically established only once, during emerging adulthood.
   c. It is influenced by context, such as life circumstances.
   d. It is multifaceted, meaning that one can accept certain aspects and reject others.

5. Cross-sex friendships provide several advantages to both men and women. These advantages include
   a. allowing men to assist women in solving problems.
   b. expanding each partner's perspective.
   c. making it acceptable for men and women to engage in good-natured teasing.
   d. allowing men and women to develop sexual relationships without the bonds of marriage.

6. In the past, men's friendships tended to be based on ____________________, and friendships between women tended to be based on ____________________.
   a. shared confidences; shared interests
   b. cooperation; competition
   c. shared interests; shared confidences
   d. finding support for personal problems; discussion of practical issues

7. According to Robert Sternberg, the three dimensions of love are
   a. passion, intimacy, and consummate love.
   b. physical intimacy, emotional intimacy, and consummate love.
   c. passion, commitment, and consummate love.
   d. passion, intimacy, and commitment.

8. Research on cohabitation in the United States suggests that
   a. relatively few young adults ever live with an unrelated partner of the other sex.
   b. adults who cohabit and then marry experience lower rates of divorce.
   c. adults who cohabit tend to be happier and healthier than married people are.
   d. none of the above are true.

9. A homogamous marriage is best defined as a marriage between
   a. people who are physically similar to each other.
   b. people of similar social backgrounds.
   c. people of dissimilar socioeconomic backgrounds.
   d. two caring people of the same sex.

10. The strongest motivation to attend college is to resolve one's
   a. social homogamy.
   b. exclusion criteria.
   c. ethnic identity.
   d. vocational identity.

11. Today's workforce
   a. is less predictable than in previous years.
   b. should not expect to remain in a single career for their entire working lives.
   c. is characterized by more dual-earner couples than in previous years.
   d. is characterized by all of the above.

12. Over the years of adulthood, people who balance marital, parental, and vocational loads
    a. inevitably suffer from the stress of role overload.
    b. are far more likely to divorce.
    c. generally are happier than those who function in only one or two of these roles.
    d. experience both a and b.

13. One potential, unintended outcome of the quest for vocational identity is
    a. remaining in the same job for the majority of the adulthood years.
    b. unrealistic expectations regarding how self-fulfilling one will find one's work to be.
    c. failing to recognize the importance of education.
    d. burnout from focusing so intently on building one's résumé.

14. According to research, which of the following factors does **NOT** contribute to a happy marriage?
    a. cohabitation before marriage
    b. the degree to which a couple is homogamous or heterogamous
    c. the degree of marital equity
    d. whether identity needs have been met before marriage

Matching Items

Match each definition or description with its corresponding term.

Terms

15. ________	social clock	19. ________	marital equity
16. ________	cohabitation	20. ________	generativity vs. stagnation
17. ________	dual-earner family	21. ________	homogamy
18. ________	intimacy vs. isolation		

Descriptions or Definitions

a. a family in which both parents work outside the home
b. the extent to which partners perceive equality in their relationship
c. a marriage between people with similar interests and backgrounds
d. Erikson's sixth stage of development
e. the culturally set timetable at which key life events are deemed appropriate
f. Erikson's idea that adults need to be productive in meaningful ways
g. arrangement in which two unrelated adults of the opposite sex live together

Applying Your Knowledge

1. Jack is in his mid-20s. Compared to his father, who was 25 during the late 1950s, Jack is
   a. more likely to have settled on a career.
   b. less likely to have settled on a career.
   c. likely to feel more social pressure to make decisions regarding career, marriage, and so forth.
   d. more likely to be concerned with satisfying his need for achievement at a younger age.

2. Marie is 24 years old. Compared to past generation, what is likely to be true about Marie's relationship with her parents?
   a. It is a more important and crucial influence on her development.
   b. It is not as close.
   c. It is less likely to involve financial support.
   d. None of the above are likely to be true.

3. To determine ways to lower the high rate of divorce, Dr. Wilson is conducting research on marital satisfaction and the factors that contribute to it. Which of the following would he consider to be important factors?
   a. homogamy
   b. having similar social backgrounds
   c. marital equity
   d. All of the above contribute to marital satisfaction.

4. Rwanda and Rodney have been dating for about a month. Their relationship is most likely characterized by
   a. strong feelings of commitment.
   b. consummate love.
   c. physical intimacy without true emotional intimacy.
   d. all of the above.

5. I am 25 years old. It is most likely that I
   a. am married.
   b. am divorced.
   c. have never been married.
   d. am divorced and remarried.

6. If asked to explain the high failure rate of marriages between young adults, Erik Erikson would most likely say that
   a. achievement goals are often more important than intimacy in early adulthood.
   b. intimacy is difficult to establish until identity is formed.
   c. divorce has almost become an expected stage in development.
   d. today's cohort of young adults has higher expectations of marriage than did previous cohorts.

7. Which of the following employer initiatives would be most likely to increase employee job satisfaction?
   a. offering higher wages
   b. offering improved worker benefits
   c. the opportunity to develop personal skills
   d. All of the above have about the same impact on employee satisfaction.

8. Which of the following would be the worst advice for a young adult entering the job market today?
   a. Seek education that fosters a variety of psychosocial and cognitive skills.
   b. Expect that educational requirements for work will shift every few years.
   c. To avoid diluting your skills, concentrate your education on preparing for one specific job.
   d. Be flexible and willing to adjust to the varied pacing and timing of today's jobs.

9. Arthur and Mabel have been married for 5 years. According to Sternberg, if their relationship is a satisfying one, which of the following best describes their relationship?
   a. They are strongly committed to each other.
   b. They are passionately in love.
   c. They are in the throes of establishing intimacy.
   d. They are beginning to wonder why the passion has left their relationship.

10. Hamah and Oliver are recent college graduates who have been dating for three years and are considering living with each other before they get married. They should be informed that
    a. their experience of cohabitation will be very similar to their experience as a married couple.
    b. they will be unusual because most of their friends will not live together before marriage.
    c. cohabitation does not appear to solve problems in the relationship previous to marriage.
    d. cohabitation relationships tend to be more harmonious than married relationships.

11. Which of the following best summarizes the research on psychological well-being during emerging adulthood?

   a. Overall, emerging adulthood is a time of declining psychological well-being.

   b. Because well-being is determined by genetics, there are no clear patterns of development regarding well-being during emerging adulthood.

   c. The challenges and opportunities of emerging adulthood can lead to enhanced well-being or increased vulnerability toward psychological disorders.

   d. Emerging adults are most likely to thrive if they are encouraged to become as independent as possible.

12. Which of the following would be the best advice to give a new college counselor regarding the mental health of emerging adults?

   a. The students with a genetic predisposition toward psychological disorders are at highest risk of psychological problems because of the stresses of emerging adulthood.

   b. Emerging adulthood is a relatively calm time for mental health because most disorders do not emerge until middle adulthood.

   c. Schizophrenia is the most common psychological disorders during emerging adulthood.

   d. Young adults are less likely than middle-aged adults to develop post-traumatic stress disorder after experiencing a traumatic event.

Answer Key

Key Terms

1. The view that psychological disorders, such as schizophrenia, are produced by the interaction of genetic vulnerability (the diathesis) and stressful environmental factors and life events is referred to as the diathesis-stress model. (p. 406; objective 9)
2. Increasingly common among young adults in all industrialized countries is the living pattern called cohabitation in which two unrelated adults of the opposite sex live together. (p. 414; objective 5)
3. According to Erik Erikson, the first crisis of adulthood is intimacy versus isolation, which involves the need to share one's personal life with someone else or risk profound loneliness. (p. 408, Table 11.4; video lesson, segment 1; objective 1)
4. In Erikson's theory, the second crisis of adulthood is generativity versus stagnation, which involves the need to be productive in some meaningful way, usually through work or parenthood. (p. 408, Table 11.4; video lesson, segment 1; objective 1)

5. The social clock represents the culturally set timetable that establishes when various events and behaviors in life are appropriate and called for. (video lesson, segment 1; objective 2)
6. Homogamy refers to marriage between people who are similar in attitudes, socioeconomic background, interests, ethnicity, religion, and the like. (video lesson, segment 2; objective 5)
7. An important factor in a successful marriage, marital equity involves how much each partner perceives that the other is contributing to the relationship to help make it work. (video lesson, segment 2; objective 5)
8. Dual-earner families are those in which both spouses work at jobs outside the home. (video lesson, segment 3; objective 7)
9. In Erikson's theory, the developmental stage that begins in late adolescence and may extend into young adulthood is identity (vs. role confusion), which involves the need to find out who we are and how we fit into the adult world. (video lesson, segment 1; objective 1)

Practice Questions I

Multiple-Choice Questions

1. b. is the correct answer. (p. 411; video lesson, segment 1; objective 1)
2. d. is the correct answer. (video lesson, segment 1; objectives 1 & 2)
3. d. is the correct answer. (p. 412; objectives 3 & 4)
4. d. is the correct answer. (pp. 415–416; objective 8)
5. d. is the correct answer. (p. 411; video lesson, segment 3; objective 1)

   a. is incorrect. Generativity is a characteristic of the crisis following the intimacy crisis.

   b. is incorrect. Stagnation occurs when generativity needs are not met.

   c. is incorrect. Erikson's theory does not address this issue.
6. a. is the correct answer. (pp. 411–412; objective 3)

   c. is incorrect. Because they are mobile and tend to have fewer commitments, young adults find it relatively easy to form friendships.

   d. is incorrect. Almost never do young adults feel bereft of friendship.
7. c. is the correct answer. (pp. 412–413; objective 4)

   d. is incorrect. Sternberg's theory is not concerned with the stages of parenthood.
8. c. is the correct answer. (p. 414; objective 5)
9. b. is the correct answer. (video lesson, segment 2; objective 5)

   a. is incorrect. By definition, homogamous couples share values, background, and the like.

   c. & d. are incorrect. These may or may not be true, depending on the extent to which such a couple is homogamous.
10. d. is the correct answer. (p. 408; objective 1)

11. b. is the correct answer. (video lesson, segment 3; objective 7)

    c. is incorrect. Most parents report that they are pleased that they have had children.

12. a. is the correct answer. (p. 407; objective 9)

True or False Items

13. T (p. 411; video lesson, segment 1; objective 1)
14. T (video lesson, segment 1; objective 2)
15. F Physical intimacy and feelings of closeness are highest in the earliest stages of a relationship. (p. 412; objective 4)
16. T (video lesson, segment 2; objective 5)
17. F (video lesson; segment 3; objective 6)
18. T (video lesson, segment 2; objective 5)
19. F (pp. 415–416; objective 8)
20. F Most young adults should learn basic skills so that they have the flexibility to move into different jobs. (video lesson, segment 3; objective 6)
21. T (video lesson, segment 3; objective 6)
22. T (video lesson, segment 1; objective 2)
23. T (p. 407; objective 9)

Practice Questions II

Multiple-Choice Questions

1. c. is the correct answer. (p. 408, Table 11.4; video lesson, segment 3; objective 1)

    a. is incorrect. Lack of career advancement may prevent generativity.

    b. is incorrect. Erikson's theory does not address these issues.

    d. is incorrect. Such feelings are related to the need for intimacy rather than generativity.

2. d. is the correct answer. (pp. 411–412; objective 3)
3. d. is the correct answer. (video lesson, segment 1; objective 2)
4. b. is the correct answer. (p. 409; objective 1)
5. b. is the correct answer. (pp. 411–412; objective 3)

    a. is incorrect. Men are frustrated that women won't allow them to do this.

    c. is incorrect. Women become upset by such teasing.

    d. is incorrect. Men may try to make a platonic relationship sexual, women are offended when they do so.

6. c. is the correct answer. (p. 412; objective 3)
7. d. is the correct answer. (p. 412; objective 4)

    a., b., & c. are incorrect. According to Sternberg, consummate love emerges when commitment is added to passion and intimacy.

8. b. is the correct answer. (p. 414; objective 5)

   a. is incorrect. Slightly more than half of all women aged 25 to 40 in the United States cohabit before their first marriage.

   c. is incorrect. In fact, a large study of adults found that cohabitants were much less happy and healthy than married people were.

9. b. is the correct answer. (video lesson, segment 2; objective 5)

   a. & d. are incorrect. These characteristics do not pertain to homogamy.

   c. is incorrect. This describes a heterogamous marriage.

10. d. is the correct answer. (p. 410; objectives 1 & 6)
11. d. is the correct answer. (video lesson, segment 3; objective 6)
12. c. is the correct answer. (video lesson, segment 3; objective 7)
13. b. is the correct answer. (p. 411; objectives 1 & 6)
14. a. is the correct answer. Cohabitation before marriage does not strengthen the relationship. (p. 414; video lesson, segment 2; objective 5)

Matching Items

15. e (video lesson, segment 1; objective 2)
16. g (p. 414; objective 5)
17. a (video lesson, segment 3; objective 7)
18. d (p. 408, Table 11.4; video lesson, segment 1; objective 1)
19. b (video lesson, segment 2; objective 5)
20. f (p. 408, Table 11.4; video lesson, segment 1; objective 1)
21. c (video lesson, segment 2; objective 5)

Applying Your Knowledge

1. b. is the correct answer. (video lesson, segment 1; objectives 1 & 6)

   c. & d. are incorrect. The video lesson does not indicate that there are cohort effects in these areas.

2. a. is the correct answer. (pp. 415–416; objective 8)
3. d. is the correct answer. The most successful relationships are between people of similar backgrounds and similar interests. The partners' perceptions of marital equity are also important. (pp. 510–512; video lesson, segment 2; objective 5)
4. c. is the correct answer. (p. 412; objective 4)

   a. & b. are incorrect. These feelings emerge more gradually in relationships.

5. c. is the correct answer. (p. 414; objective 5)
6. b. is the correct answer. (p. 411; video lesson, segment 1; objective 1)

   a. is incorrect. In Erikson's theory, the crisis of intimacy precedes the need to be productive through work.

   c. & d. are incorrect. Although these items are true, Erikson's theory does not address these issues.

7. c. is the correct answer. (video lesson, segment 3; objective 6)
8. c. is the correct answer. (video lesson, segment 3; objective 6)

   a., b., & d. are incorrect. These would all be good pieces of advice for new workers today.
9. a. is the correct answer. (pp. 412–413; objective 4)
10. c. is the correct answer. (p. 414; objective 5)
11. c. is the correct answer. (pp. 405–407; objective 9)
12. a. is the correct answer. (pp. 405–407; objective 9)

Lesson Review

Lesson 19

Early Adulthood
Psychosocial Development

Please Note: Use this matrix to guide your study and achieve the learning objectives of this lesson. It will also help you to view the video, which defines and demonstrates important concepts and skills as they relate to everyday life.

Learning Objective	**Textbook**	**Telecourse Student Guide**	**Video Lesson**
1. Describe the psychosocial tasks of identity, intimacy and generativity, and explain how the viewpoint of most developmentalists regarding adult stages has shifted.	pp. 408–411	Key Terms: 3, 4, 9; Practice Questions I: 1, 2, 5, 10, 13; Practice Questions II: 1, 4, 10, 13, 18, 20; Applying Your Knowledge: 1, 6.	Segment 1: *The Tasks of Adulthood*; Segment 2: *Intimacy*; Segment 3: *Generativity*
2. Explain how the social clock influences the timing of important events during early adulthood.	*	Key Terms: 5; Practice Questions I: 2, 14, 22; Practice Questions II: 3, 15.	Segment 1: *The Tasks of Adulthood*
3. Review the changing nature of friendships during adulthood, noting factors that promote friendship and gender differences in friendship patterns.	pp. 411–412	Practice Questions I: 3, 6; Practice Questions II: 2, 5, 6.	
4. Describe common young adult experiences with romantic relationships and identify and discuss Sternberg's three components of love.	pp. 412–414	Practice Questions I: 3, 7, 15; Practice Questions II: 7; Applying Your Knowledge: 4, 9.	
5. Discuss the role of serious relationships and marriage in adulthood, describe the impact of cohabitation on relationships, and identify at least three factors that influence relationship success.	pp. 413–414	Key Terms: 2, 6, 7; Practice Questions I: 8, 9, 16, 18; Practice Questions II: 8, 9, 14, 16, 19, 21; Applying Your Knowledge: 3, 5, 10.	Segment 2: *Intimacy*

* The video for this lesson offers a useful exploration of this concept.

Learning Objective	Textbook	Telecourse Student Guide	Video Lesson
6. Discuss the importance of work to the individual and how the experiences of today's workers differ from those of past generations.	*	Practice Questions I: 17, 20, 21; Practice Questions II: 10, 11, 13; Applying Your Knowledge: 1, 7, 8.	Segment 3: *Generativity*
7. Discuss the myths, challenges, and opportunities of dual-earner family life.	*	Key Terms: 8; Practice Questions I: 11; Practice Questions II: 12, 17.	Segment 3: *Generativity*
8. Describe the changing relationship between emerging adults and their parents.	pp. 415–416	Practice Questions I: 4, 19; Applying Your Knowledge: 2.	
9. Explain variation in well-being during emerging adulthood, and identify characteristics of psychopathology.	pp. 404–408	Key Terms: 1; Practice Questions I: 12, 23; Applying Your Knowledge: 11, 12.	

* The video for this lesson offers a useful exploration of this concept.

Thriving in Midlife

Lesson 20

Middle Adulthood: Biosocial Development

Preview

This lesson deals with biosocial development between the ages of 25 and 64. It begins by describing changes in appearance and in the functioning of the sense organs and vital body systems. The potential impact of these changes for women and men is discussed. Although declines in all the body's senses and systems occur, for most adults these changes have no significant health consequences and do not interfere with daily living. Indeed, today's cohort of middle-aged adults is healthier than cohorts from previous years.

This lesson further explores health-related behaviors of the middle-aged, focusing on smoking, drinking, eating habits, and exercise. By middle age, most adults understand how lifestyle choices and health habits can affect their well-being. There is a decline in the number of smokers, as well as a tendency toward moderation in alcohol consumption. However, for a number of adults, risky lifestyle behaviors remain serious health hazards.

The lesson continues with a discussion of reasons for individual variations in health. These variations arise from a combination of many factors, including race, ethnicity, socioeconomic status, and gender. The lesson concludes with a discussion of the changes in the sexual-reproductive system that occur during adulthood and shows why many individuals find these changes less troubling than they anticipated.

Prior Telecourse Knowledge that Will Be Used in this Lesson

- Biosocial development during the school years (Lesson 11), adolescence (Lesson 14), and early adulthood (Lesson 17) will be referred to as we discuss normal changes in adulthood and reasons for variations in health.
- Body Mass Index (Lesson 17) will be referred to as we discuss obesity as a risk factor for diabetes and other chronic illnesses.

Learning Objectives

Use this information to guide your reading, viewing, thinking, and studying. After successfully completing this lesson, you should be able to:

1. Identify typical physical changes of middle adulthood and discuss their impact.
2. Describe how the functions of the sense organs and vital body systems change during middle adulthood.
3. Describe the relationship between certain lifestyle factors—smoking, alcohol use, nutrition, weight, and exercise—and health.
4. Differentiate four measures of health, and explain why disability is more damaging to society than morbidity and mortality.
5. Explain how variations in health are related to gender, socioeconomic status, and cultural differences.
6. Identify the typical changes that occur in the sexual-reproductive system during adulthood, explain the potential positive and negative outcomes of these changes, and discuss assisted reproductive technology (ART) and hormone replacement therapy (HRT).

Read Chapter 12, "Adulthood: Body and Mind," pages 419–434 and 453.

View the video for Lesson 20, "Thriving in Midlife."

Segment 1: *Normal Physical Changes*

Segment 2: *Health Habits*

Segment 3: *Variations in Health*

Segment 4: *The Sexual Reproductive System*

Summary

Although the biological clock does not program a series of specific events to mark midlife, for most women and men, the years of middle adulthood bring about signs of aging that cannot be ignored. For example, the bodies of middle-aged adults have been aging for decades, but so imperceptibly that it takes years for some declines to become apparent. These signs include the graying and thinning of the hair, drying and wrinkling of the skin, and other changes in appearance. They also include noticeable losses in hearing and vision, and a reduction in organ reserve in the lungs, heart, and digestive and immune systems.

In general, middle-aged persons are healthier today than were earlier cohorts. Variations in health—measured in terms of **mortality**, **morbidity**, **disability**, and **vitality**—are related to genetic, educational, and socioeconomic factors, among others. The most important reason for individual variations in health, however, is personal lifestyle. Risk factors include cigarette smoking, alcohol consumption, poor nutrition, obesity, and lack of exercise.

Ethnicity, with its attendant genetic and cultural factors, is also a powerful influence on all four measures of health in middle age. Gender is also an important factor. Beginning at midlife, women have higher morbidity and disability rates than men, due in part to a gender bias in medical research that has paid insufficient attention to arthritis, **osteoporosis**, and other common chronic illnesses that affect far more women than men.

Most women find **menopause**, with its accompanying cessation of menstruation and decline in estrogen, much less troubling than they expected it to be. Although men do not experience sudden age-related drops in hormone levels or fertility, sexual response does slow down over time. Some experts suggest that the term **andropause** should be used to refer to these changes in the reproductive capabilities of men. Because of wide individual variations, however, past experience is a better predictor of sexual activity during middle adulthood than is aging.

Review all reading assignments for this lesson.

As assigned by your instructor, complete the optional online component for this lesson.

Key Terms

Using your own words, write a brief definition or explanation of each of the following terms on a separate piece of paper.

1. senescence
2. presbycusis
3. in vitro fertilization (IVF)
4. menopause
5. hormone replacement therapy (HRT)
6. andropause
7. mortality
8. morbidity
9. disability
10. vitality
11. osteoporosis

Practice Questions I

Multiple-Choice Questions

1. During the years from age 25 to age 64, the average adult
   a. becomes proportionally slimmer.
   b. gains about 5 pounds per year.
   c. gains about 1 pound per year.
   d. is more likely to be overweight.

2. Some outward signs of senescence can include

   a. fine wrinkles around the eyes and lips as collagen decreases.

   b. "middle-age spread."

   c. full, thick, abundant hair in both men and women.

   d. a and b only.

3. Which of the following have been listed in the Berger textbook as age-related deficits in eyesight?

   a. Peripheral vision narrows faster than frontal vision.

   b. Color vision shifts and becomes less acute.

   c. Nearsightedness increases.

   d. All of the above have been listed.

4. Level of disability is determined in part by

   a. the impact on a person's normal functioning.

   b. the origin of the condition.

   c. whether the person is able to engage in vigorous exercise.

   d. none of the above.

5. At midlife, individuals who ______________________ tend to live longer and have fewer chronic illnesses or disabilities.

   a. are relatively well educated

   b. are financially secure

   c. live in or near cities

   d. are or do all of the above

6. The term that refers to diseases of all kinds is

   a. mortality.

   b. morbidity.

   c. disability.

   d. vitality.

7. On average, women reach menopause at age

   a. 39.

   b. 42.

   c. 46.

   d. 51.

8. In explaining ethnic variations in health and illness during middle age, ________________ factors are more important than ________________ factors.

   a. genetic; social and psychological

   b. social and psychological; genetic

   c. intrinsic; cultural

   d. cultural; extrinsic

9. In middle age, ________________ rates are higher for men than for women, whereas ________________ rates are higher for women than men.

   a. mortality; morbidity

   b. morbidity; mortality

   c. vitality; disability

   d. disability; vitality

10. According to the video for this lesson, factors that affect an adult's physical health can include

    a. ethnicity.

    b. daily health habits.

    c. lifestyle.

    d. all of the above.

11. Which of the following terms refers to how energetic and healthy a person feels?

    a. morbidity

    b. libidinous

    c. vitality

    d. mortality

12. Menopause

    a. is the cessation of ovulation and menstruation in women.

    b. occurs in women between the ages of 42–58 years of age.

    c. can cause uncomfortable physical symptoms for a number of years.

    d. all of the above are true regarding menopause.

13. Which of the following is true in regard to smoking?

    a. Smoking diseases are a natural result of smoking for ten years or more, whether or not the person eventually quits.

    b. Smoking-related cancers throughout the world are increasing.

    c. Smoking diseases are all incurable.

    d. None of the above statements are true.

True or False Items

Write T (for true) or F (for false) on the line in front of each statement.

14. _____ Some men take hormone replacement to combat the natural decline in testosterone.

15. _____ The Women's Health Initiative study of 2002 found that taking hormone replacement therapy (HRT) increases the risk of heart disease, cancer, and stroke in women.

16. _____ Sixty-six percent of all middle-aged Americans are overweight.

17. _____ Moderate users of alcohol are more likely than nondrinkers to have heart attacks.

18. _____ Those who exercise regularly have lower rates of serious illness than do sedentary people.

19. _____ Middle-aged adults are less likely to improve their health habits than are members of any other age group.

20. _____ During middle adulthood, sexual responses slow down, particularly in men.

21. _____ During middle adulthood, sexual responses slow down, in both men and women.

22. _____ Scientists agree that there is no "male menopause."

23. _____ A woman's culture can determine her psychological reaction to menopause.

Practice Questions II

Multiple-Choice Questions

1. The normal physical changes that occur during middle age have an impact on
   a. physical appearance.
   b. flexibility.
   c. sense organs.
   d. all of the above.

2. Age-related deficits in the sense organs are most obvious in
   a. taste and touch.
   b. vision and hearing.
   c. smell and balance.
   d. balance and hearing.

3. Which of the following is true?
   a. If younger adults experience sight problems, they are either nearsighted or farsighted.
   b. If older adults experience sight problems, they can be both nearsighted and farsighted.
   c. Neither a nor b are correct.
   d. Both a and b are correct.

4. It is estimated that in the United States, infertility affects
   a. at least half of all married couples in which the woman is in her early 30s.
   b. men more than women.
   c. about one-third of all married couples.
   d. about 15 percent of all couples.

5. To be a true index of health, morbidity rates must be refined in terms of which of the following health measures?
   a. mortality rate
   b. disability and mortality rates
   c. vitality
   d. disability and vitality

6. A measure of obesity in which weight in kilograms is divided by the square of height in meters is the
   a. basal metabolic rate (BMR).
   b. body mass index (BMI).
   c. body fat index (BFI).
   d. basal fat ratio (BFR).

7. A technique that involves fertilization of the ovum outside the uterus is referred to as
   a. endometriosis.
   b. artificial insemination.
   c. in vitro fertilization.
   d. in vivo fertilization.

8. Which of the following is **NOT** true regarding alcohol consumption?
   a. Alcohol decreases the blood's supply of high-density lipoprotein.
   b. Alcohol dependence is more common in middle adulthood.
   c. Alcohol is implicated in about half of all accidents, suicides, and homicides.
   d. Alcohol abuse is the main cause of cirrhosis of the liver.

9. Which of the following is true of sexual expressiveness in middle age?
   a. Menopause impairs a woman's sexual relationship.
   b. Men's frequency of ejaculation increases until approximately age 55.
   c. Signs of arousal in a woman are as obvious as they were at age 20.
   d. Men and women can experience fulfilling sex lives throughout this time period.

Matching Items

Match each definition or description with its corresponding term.

Terms

10. __________ mortality
11. __________ morbidity
12. __________ vitality
13. __________ osteoporosis
14. __________ disability
15. __________ menopause
16. __________ presbycusis
17. __________ andropause
18. __________ hormone replacement therapy (HRT)

Definitions or Descriptions

a. disease of all kinds
b. what some scientist argue to be the "male menopause," characterized by declining levels of testosterone
c. an age-related decline in hearing, usually not noticeable until the 60s
d. sometimes prescribed to treat the symptoms of menopause
e. a condition of thin and brittle bones
f. death; as a measure of health, it usually refers to the number of deaths each year per thousand individuals
g. the cessation of ovulation and menstruation
h. more important to quality of life than any other measure of health
i. the inability to perform normal activities

Applying Your Knowledge

1. Which of the following types of exercise would be most beneficial in promoting general health and reducing risk of disease?
   a. walking around the block once a week
   b. shooting hoops occasionally with friends
   c. using the stairs instead of the elevator whenever you think of it
   d. cycling regularly at an intensity that raises the heart rate to 75 percent of its maximum

2. Fifty-five-year-old Harvey is concerned because sexual stimulation seems to take longer and needs to be more direct than earlier. As a friend, you should tell him
   a. "You should see a therapist. It is not normal."
   b. "See a doctor if your 'sexual prowess' doesn't improve soon. You may have some underlying physical problem."
   c. "Don't worry. This is normal for middle-aged men."
   d. "You're too old to have sex, so just give it up."

3. Coretta and Vernon Castle have been trying to conceive a baby for more than a year. Because they are both in their 40s, their physician suspects that
   a. Vernon is infertile.
   b. Coretta is infertile.
   c. neither Vernon nor Coretta is infertile.
   d. Vernon and Coretta are equally likely to be infertile.

4. Forty-five-year-old Cindy is the same weight she has been since college and continues to eat the same types and amounts of food she has always eaten. In order to maintain her weight through middle age, Cindy should
   a. continue to eat the same amounts and types of foods.
   b. reduce her caloric intake.
   c. eat more foods high in LDL.
   d. reduce her intake of foods high in HDL.

5. Fifty-year-old Peggy has a college degree and a good job and lives near Seattle, Washington. Compared to her sister, who dropped out of high school and is struggling to survive on a dairy farm in rural Wisconsin, Peggy is most likely to
   a. live longer.
   b. have fewer chronic illnesses.
   c. have fewer disabilities.
   d. do or have all of the above.
6. Morbidity is to mortality as __________________ is to __________________.
   a. disease; death
   b. death; disease
   c. inability to perform normal daily activities; disease
   d. disease; subjective feeling of being healthy
7. If Edgar is like most men, as he grows older, he will require
   a. less direct stimulation to become sexually excited.
   b. a shorter refractory period following each orgasm.
   c. a longer time between erection and ejaculation.
   d. all of the above.
8. Compared to his identical twin brother, 48-year-old Jerry has lower blood pressure, better circulation, a lower ratio of body fat to body weight, and higher HDL in his blood. The most probable explanation for these differences is that Jerry
   a. doesn't smoke.
   b. eats a high-fiber diet.
   c. engages in regular aerobic exercise.
   d. does all of the above.

Answer Key

Key Terms

1. The gradual age-related decline in the physical body is referred to as senescence. (p. 420; objective 1)
2. The loss of hearing that occurs as a result of senescence is referred to as presbycusis. (p. 421; objective 2)
3. In vitro fertilization (IVF) is a technique in which ova are surgically removed from the ovaries and fertilized by sperm in the laboratory. (p. 423; objective 6)

4. At menopause, ovulation and menstruation stop and the production of estrogen, progesterone, and testosterone hormones drops. (p. 424; video lesson, segment 3; objective 6)
5. Hormone replacement therapy (HRT) is intended to help relieve menopausal symptoms, especially in women who experience an abrupt drop in hormone levels because their ovaries are surgically removed. (p. 424; video lesson, segment 3; objective 6)
6. Andropause is a term used to describe "male menopause," a drop in testosterone that is thought to relate to a decrease in sex drive, sexual performance, and muscle mass. However, use of this term is controversial because testosterone decrease is very gradual, and other factors—such as stress or anxiety—can influence levels of testosterone as well. (p. 425; objective 6)
7. Mortality means death. As a measure of health, it usually refers to the number of deaths each year per thousand individuals. (p. 430; video lesson, segment 3; objective 4)
8. Morbidity means disease. As a measure of health, it refers to the rate of diseases of all kinds, which can be sudden and severe (acute) or extend over a long time period (chronic). (p. 430; video lesson, segment 3; objective 4)
9. Disability refers to a person's inability to perform activities that most others can. (p. 430; video lesson, segment 3; objective 4)
10. Vitality refers to how healthy and energetic—physically, intellectually, and socially—an individual actually feels. (p. 431; video lesson, segment 3; objective 4)
11. Osteoporosis is a condition of porous and brittle bones leading to increased fractures and frailty in old age for which women who are thin, Caucasian, and postmenopausal are at increased risk. (video lesson, segment 3; objectives 1 & 6)

Practice Questions I

Multiple-Choice Questions

1. d. is the correct answer. (pp. 427–428; video lesson, segment 1; objective 3)
2. d. is the correct answer. (p. 420; video lesson, segment 2; objective 1)
3. a. is the correct answer. (pp. 420–421; video lesson, segment 3; objective 2)
4. a. is the correct answer. (p. 430; video lesson, segment 3; objectives 2 & 4)
5. d. is the correct answer. (video lesson, segment 1; objective 5)
6. b. is the correct answer. (p. 430; video lesson, segment 3; objective 4)

   a. is incorrect. This is the overall death rate.

   c. is incorrect. This refers to a person's inability to perform activities that most others can.

d. is incorrect. This refers to how physically, intellectually, and socially healthy an individual feels.

7. d. is the correct answer. (p. 424; video lesson, segment 3; objective 6)
8. b. is the correct answer. (video lesson, segment 2; objective 5)

   c. & d. are incorrect. Genes and culture are intrinsic and extrinsic factors, respectively.
9. a. is the correct answer. (pp. 431–432; video lesson, segment 3; objective 5)
10. d. is the correct answer. (video lesson, segment 3; objectives 3 & 5)
11. c. is the correct answer. (p. 431; video lesson, segment 3; objective 4)
12. d. is the correct answer. (p. 424; objective 6)
13. b. is the correct answer. (p. 426; objective 3)

True or False Items

14. T (p. 425; objective 6)
15. T (p. 424; video lesson, segment 4; objective 6)
16. T About two of every three Americans are overweight, and 2 percent of men and 1 percent of women are obese. (p. 428; video lesson, segment 2; objective 3)
17. F Moderate use of alcohol is associated with reduced risk of heart attacks. (p. 427; objective 3)
18. T (p. 429; video lesson, segment 2; objective 3)
19. F Middle-aged adults are much more likely to improve their health habits than younger adults. (video lesson, segment 2; objective 3)
20. T (pp. 424–425; video lesson, segment 4; objective 6)
21. F (p. 422; objective 6)
22. F (p. 425; objective 6)
23. T (p. 424; objectives 5 & 6)

Practice Questions II

Multiple-Choice Questions

1. d. is the correct answer. (p. 420; video lesson, segment 1; objective 1)

   a., b., & c. are incorrect. For the most part, the normal physical changes of middle adulthood have no significant health consequences.
2. b. is the correct answer. (pp. 420–421; objective 2)
3. d. is the correct answer. (p. 421; objective 2)

   c. & d. are incorrect. Although overall health is an important factor in all aspects of aging, the textbook does not compare the relative influences of overall health and heredity on visual acuity.
4. d. is the correct answer. (p. 422; objective 6)
5. d. is the correct answer. (p. 430; video lesson, segment 3; objective 4)

6. b. is the correct answer. (p. 428, Table 12.1; video lesson, segment 2; objective 3)
7. c. is the correct answer. (p. 423; objective 6)
8. a. is the correct answer. Alcohol increases the blood's supply of HDL, which is one possible reason that adults who drink in moderation may live longer than "nondrinkers." (p. 427; objective 3)
9. d. is the correct answer. (p. 422; video lesson, segment 4; objective 6)

Matching Items

10. f (p. 430; video lesson, segment 3; objective 4)
11. a (p. 430; video lesson, segment 3; objective 4)
12. h (p. 431; video lesson, segment 3; objective 4)
13. e (video lesson, segment 3; objectives 1 & 6)
14. i (p. 430; video lesson, segment 3; objective 4)
15. g (p. 424; video lesson, segment 3; objective 6)
16. c (p. 421; objective 2)
17. b (p. 425; objective 6)
18. d (p. 424; video lesson, segment 3; objective 6)

Applying Your Knowledge

1. d. is the correct answer. (p. 429; video lesson, segment 2; objective 3)

   a., b., & c. are incorrect. These forms of exercise will not produce the beneficial effects of regular aerobic exercise.
2. c. is the correct answer. (p. 425; video lesson, segment 4; objective 6)
3. d. is the correct answer. (p. 422; objective 6)
4. b. is the correct answer. (pp. 427–429; video lesson, segment 2; objective 3)

   a. is incorrect. As Cindy ages, her metabolism will slow down, so she should reduce her caloric intake.

   c. & d. are incorrect. Just the opposite is true. She should decrease her intake of foods high in LDL and increase her intake of foods high in HDL.
5. d. is the correct answer. People who are relatively well-educated, financially secure, and live in or near cities tend to receive all these benefits. (pp. 431–432; objective 5)
6. a. is the correct answer. (pp. 430–431; video lesson, segment 3; objective 4)

   b. is incorrect. This answer would be correct if the statement were "Mortality is to morbidity."

   c. is incorrect. This answer would be correct if the statement were "Disability is to morbidity."

   d. is incorrect. This answer would be correct if the statement were "Morbidity is to vitality."

7. c. is the correct answer. (p. 425; objective 6)
8. c. is the correct answer. (pp. 426–429; objective 3)

   a. & b. are incorrect. Although these behaviors promote health, only regular aerobic exercise produces all the health benefits that Jerry is experiencing.

Lesson Review

Lesson 20

Middle Adulthood
Biosocial Development

Please Note: Use this matrix to guide your study and achieve the learning objectives of this lesson. It will also help you to view the video, which defines and demonstrates important concepts and skills as they relate to everyday life.

Learning Objective	Textbook	Telecourse Student Guide	Video Lesson
1. Identify typical physical changes of middle adulthood and discuss their impact.	p. 420	Key Terms: 1, 11; Practice Questions I: 2; Practice Questions II: 1, 13.	Segment 1: *Normal Physical Changes;* Segment 2: *Health Habits;* Segment 3: *Variations in Health*
2. Describe how the functions of the sense organs and vital body systems change during middle adulthood.	pp. 420–421	Key Terms: 2; Practice Questions I: 3, 4; Practice Questions II: 2, 3, 16.	Segment 1: *Normal Physical Changes;* Segment 3: *Variations in Health*
3. Describe the relationship between certain lifestyle factors—smoking, alcohol use, nutrition, weight, and exercise—and health.	pp. 426–429	Practice Questions I: 1, 10, 13, 16, 17, 18, 19; Practice Questions II: 6, 8; Applying Your Knowledge: 1, 4, 8.	Segment 1: *Normal Physical Changes;* Segment 2: *Health Habits;* Segment 3: *Variations in Health*
4. Differentiate four measures of health, and explain why disability is more damaging to society than morbidity and mortality.	pp. 430–431	Key Terms: 7, 8, 9, 10; Practice Questions I: 4, 6, 11; Practice Questions II: 5, 10, 11, 12, 14; Applying Your Knowledge: 6.	Segment 3: *Variations in Health*
5. Explain how variations in health are related to gender, socioeconomic status, and cultural differences.	pp. 431–434	Practice Questions I: 5, 8, 9, 10, 23; Applying Your Knowledge: 5.	Segment 1: *Normal Physical Changes;* Segment 2: *Health Habits;* Segment 3: *Variations in Health*

Learning Objective	Textbook	Telecourse Student Guide	Video Lesson
6. Identify the typical changes that occur in the sexual-reproductive system during adulthood, explain the potential positive and negative outcomes of these changes, and discuss assisted reproductive technology (ART) and hormone replacement therapy (HRT).	pp. 422–425	Key Terms: 3, 4, 5, 6, 11; Practice Questions I: 7, 12, 14, 15, 20, 21, 22, 23; Practice Questions II: 4, 7, 9, 13, 15, 17, 18; Applying Your Knowledge: 2, 3, 7.	Segment 3: *Variations in Health*; Segment 4: *The Sexual Reproductive System*

Use It or Lose It

Lesson 21

Middle Adulthood: Cognitive Development

Preview

This lesson examines cognitive development between the ages of 25 and 65. Cognitive development was once thought to be an ability that could be measured as a single aptitude. However, as psychologists began to study intelligence, they discovered that it was much more complex. It is now considered to consist of many different abilities.

The lesson then examines the multidirectional nature of intelligence, noting that some abilities (such as short-term memory) decline with age, while others (such as vocabulary) generally increase. It also includes a discussion of the debate over whether all cognitive abilities inevitably decline during adulthood, or if some abilities may remain stable or even increase.

The lesson next focuses on the fact that intelligence is characterized more by variability among people than by consistency from person to person. Each person's cognitive development occurs in a unique context influenced by variations in genes, life experiences, and cohort effects.

The lesson also discusses cognitive expertise that often comes with experience, pointing out the ways in which expert thinking differs from that of the novice. Expert thinking is more specialized, flexible, and intuitive and is guided by more and better problem-solving strategies.

The lesson concludes with the message that during middle adulthood, individual differences are much more critical in determining the course of cognitive development than is chronological age alone.

Prior Telecourse Knowledge that Will Be Used in this Lesson

- Cognitive development during the school years (Lesson 12) and adolescence (Lesson 15), as well as that during early adulthood (Lesson 18), will be referred to as we discuss normal changes in middle adulthood and the multidirectional and multidimensional nature of intelligence.

- Longitudinal and cross-sectional research studies (Lesson 1) will be referred to as we discuss the apparently contradictory findings of research using these methods to investigate age-related changes in intelligence.

Learning Objectives

Use this information to guide your reading, viewing, thinking, and studying. After successfully completing this lesson, you will be able to:

1. Discuss the psychometric approach to adult cognition, distinguish between fluid (mechanics) and crystallized (pragmatics) intelligence, and explain how each is affected by age.
2. Differentiate the three fundamental forms of intelligence described by Robert Sternberg, and discuss how each tends to vary over the life span.
3. Explain the concept of selective optimization with compensation.
4. Outline Howard Gardner's theory of intelligence, noting the impact of culture and aging on the various dimensions of intelligence.
5. Discuss the multidirectionality of intelligence.
6. Briefly trace the history of the controversy regarding adult intelligence, including the findings of cross-sectional and longitudinal research and how cross-sequential research compensates for their shortcomings.
7. Explain how and why context and cohort affect intellectual development during adulthood.
8. Discuss the plasticity of intelligence, and describe how the cognitive processes of experts differ from those of novices.

Read Chapter 12, "Adulthood: Body and Mind," pages 435–453.

View the video for Lesson 21, "Use It or Lose It."

Segment 1: *Psychometric Approach*

Segment 2: *Dimensions and Directions of Intelligence*

Segment 3: *Contextual Influences*

Segment 4: *Plastic Intellectual Change*

Summary

Psychologists' views of the nature and development of intelligence have changed considerably in recent years. Psychologists often use the psychometric approach to measure ability, aptitude, or skill in a variety of ways that are scientifically sound. Neuropsychological tests are also used—often in medical settings—to examine and diagnose individuals who appear to have memory problems or other problems that impair their cognitive functioning.

Historically, psychologists have considered intelligence to be a single ability, what Spearman referred to as ***g***, or general intelligence. In the 1960s, researchers differentiated fluid intelligence and crystallized intelligence. **Fluid intelligence** is flexible reasoning and is made up of the basic mental abilities such as inductive reasoning, abstract thinking, and speed of thinking required for understanding any subject. **Crystallized intelligence** refers to the accumulation of facts, information, and knowledge that comes with education and experience within a particular culture.

Robert Sternberg has developed a theory regarding the **multidimensional nature of intelligence**, proposing that intelligence is composed of three distinct parts: 1) an analytic or academic aspect consisting of mental processes that foster efficient learning, remembering, and thinking; 2) a creative aspect involving the capacity to be flexible and innovative when dealing with new situations; and 3) a practical aspect that enables the person to adapt his or her abilities to contextual demands. An additional perspective on cognition suggests that the ability to strategically use one's cognitive strengths to compensate for the declining capacities associated with age (**selective optimization with compensation**) is a hallmark of successful aging.

Howard Gardner believes that there are at least eight distinct intelligences: linguistic, musical, logical-mathematical, spatial, bodily-kinesthetic, naturalistic, self-understanding, and social-understanding. The value placed on each dimension depends on the particular cultural environment and, therefore, on the training of the individual and on those evaluating him or her. Thus, differences associated with age in cross-sectional studies may reflect the experience of growing up during a particular time period rather than actual age-related developmental phenomena.

For most of the twentieth century, researchers believed that intellectual ability peaks during adolescence, then declines steadily as age advances. More recently, researchers have begun to doubt whether there is an inevitable decline in cognitive functioning with age. The earlier evidence of a decline in cognitive ability may be attributable to the shortcomings of **cross-sectional** research. Because it is impossible to match subjects in every aspect except age, cohort effects are inevitable.

Contemporary researchers also believe that since intellectual abilities are multidirectional, it is misleading to ask whether intelligence, in general, either increases or decreases. Intellectual development is greatly influenced by genetic heritage and life experiences, including changes in family and career responsibilities, cohort, educational level, income, marital status, and physical and mental health. Intellectual abilities are also characterized by their plasticity, which means that abilities can become enhanced or diminished, depending on how, when, and why a person uses them. Some researchers believe that as we age, our intelligence increases in specific areas that are of importance to us; that is, each of us develops an area of expertise.

Review all reading assignments for this lesson.

As assigned by your instructor, complete the optional online component for this lesson.

Key Terms

Using your own words, write a brief definition or explanation of each of the following terms on a separate piece of paper.

1. general intelligence (*g*)
2. Seattle Longitudinal Study
3. fluid intelligence
4. crystallized intelligence
5. selective optimization with compensation
6. selective expert
7. psychometric approach
8. multidimensional
9. multidirectional
10. analytic intelligence
11. creative intelligence
12. practical intelligence
13. cross-sectional study
14. plasticity
15. expertise

Practice Questions I

Multiple-Choice Questions

1. Most of the evidence for an age-related decline in intelligence came from
   a. cross-sectional research.
   b. longitudinal research.
   c. cross-sequential research.
   d. random sampling.

2. The major flaw in cross-sectional research is the virtual impossibility of
   a. selecting subjects who are similar in every aspect except age.
   b. tracking all subjects over a number of years.
   c. finding volunteers with high IQs.
   d. testing concept mastery.

3. Because of the limitations of other research methods, K. Warner Schaie developed a new research design based on
   a. observer-participant methods.
   b. in-depth questionnaires.
   c. personal interviews.
   d. both cross-sectional and longitudinal methods.

4. Why don't traditional intelligence tests reveal age-related declines in processing speed and short-term memory during adulthood?
   a. They measure only fluid intelligence.
   b. They measure only crystallized intelligence.
   c. They separate verbal and nonverbal IQ scores, obscuring these declines.
   d. They yield a single IQ score, allowing adulthood increases in crystallized intelligence to mask these declines.
5. Which of the following is most likely to decrease with age?
   a. vocabulary
   b. accumulated facts
   c. speed of thinking
   d. practical intelligence
6. The basic mental abilities that go into learning and understanding any subject have been classified as
   a. crystallized intelligence.
   b. plastic intelligence.
   c. fluid intelligence.
   d. rote memory.
7. Some psychologists contend that intelligence consists of fluid intelligence, which ____________________ during adulthood, and crystallized intelligence, which ____________________.
   a. remains stable; declines
   b. declines; remains stable
   c. increases; declines
   d. declines; increases
8. Charles Spearman argued for the existence of a single general intelligence factor, which he referred to as
   a. *g*.
   b. practical intelligence.
   c. analytic intelligence.
   d. creative intelligence.

9. The plasticity of adult intellectual abilities refers primarily to the effects of
   a. fluid intelligence.
   b. experience.
   c. genetic inheritance.
   d. crystallized intelligence.

10. The shift from conscious, deliberate processing of information to a more unconscious, effortless performance requires
    a. automatic processing.
    b. subliminal execution.
    c. plasticity.
    d. encoding.

11. Concerning expertise, which of the following is true?
    a. In performing tasks, experts tend to be more set in their ways, preferring to use strategies that have worked in the past.
    b. The reasoning of experts is usually more formal, disciplined, and stereotyped than that of the novice.
    c. In performing tasks, experts tend to be more flexible and to enjoy experimentation more than novices do.
    d. Experts often have difficulty adjusting to situations that are exceptions to the rule.

12. Which of the following scientists famously proposed that there is a single entity, general intelligence, which is called *g*?
    a. Charles Spearman
    b. Howard Gardner
    c. Robert Sternberg
    d. K. Warner Schaie

13. Which of the following describes the results of Nancy Bayley's follow-up study of members of the Berkeley Growth Study?
    a. Most subjects reached a plateau in intellectual functioning at age 21.
    b. The typical person at age 36 improved on two of ten subtests of the Wechsler Adult Intelligence Scale: Picture Completion and Arithmetic.
    c. The typical person at age 36 was still improving on the most important subtests of the intelligence scale.
    d. No conclusions could be reached because the sample of subjects was not representative.

14. Which of the following is **NOT** one of the general conclusions of research about intellectual changes during adulthood?

    a. In general, most intellectual abilities increase or remain stable throughout early and middle adulthood until the 60s.

    b. Cohort differences have a powerful influence on intellectual differences in adulthood.

    c. Intellectual functioning is affected by educational background.

    d. Intelligence becomes less specialized with increasing age.

15. The psychologist who has proposed that intelligence is composed of analytic, creative, and practical aspects is

    a. Charles Spearman.

    b. Howard Gardner.

    c. Robert Sternberg.

    d. K. Warner Schaie.

16. Paul Baltes and his colleagues believe that the strategy of selective optimization with compensation accounts for

    a. the ability of most middle-aged adults to increase performance levels.

    b. the ability of many older adults to maintain the performance levels of their younger years.

    c. the ability to remain physically fit.

    d. the increase in analytic intelligence.

True or False Items

Write T (for true) or F (for false) on the line in front of each statement.

17. _____ A person's IQ is unaffected by years of schooling.

18. _____ To date, cross-sectional research has shown a gradual increase in intellectual ability.

19. _____ Longitudinal research usually shows that intelligence in most abilities increases throughout early and middle adulthood.

20. _____ By age 60, most people decline in even the most basic cognitive abilities.

21. _____ IQ scores have shown a steady upward drift over most of the twentieth century.

22. _____ All people reach an intellectual peak in adolescence.

23. _____ Historically, most psychologists have considered intelligence to be composed of several distinct abilities.

24. _____ Today, most researchers studying cognitive abilities believe that intelligence is multidimensional.

25. _____ Compared to novices, experts tend to be more intuitive and less stereotyped in their work performance.

26. _____ Many researchers believe that a hallmark of successful aging is the ability to use intellectual strengths strategically to compensate for declining capacities.

Practice Questions II

Multiple-Choice Questions

1. The debate over the status of adult intelligence focuses on the question of its inevitable decline and on
   a. pharmacological deterrents to that decline.
   b. the accompanying decline in moral reasoning.
   c. its possible continuing growth.
   d. the validity of longitudinal versus personal-observation research.

2. The accumulation of facts that comes about with education and experience has been classified as
   a. crystallized intelligence.
   b. plastic intelligence.
   c. fluid intelligence.
   d. rote memory.

3. Thinking that is more intuitive, flexible, specialized, and automatic is characteristic of
   a. fluid intelligence.
   b. crystallized intelligence.
   c. expertise.
   d. plasticity.

4. The ________________ nature of intelligence was attested to by Howard Gardner, who proposed the existence of nine different intelligences.
   a. multidirectional
   b. multidimensional
   c. plastic
   d. practical

5. The _________________ nature of intelligence refers to the fact that each intellectual ability may rise, fall, or remain stable, according to its own unique developmental trajectory.

   a. multidirectional

   b. multidimensional

   c. plastic

   d. practical

6. At the present stage of research in adult cognition, which of the following statements has the most research support?

   a. Intellectual abilities inevitably decline from adolescence onward.

   b. Each person's cognitive development occurs in a unique context influenced by variations in genes, life experiences, and cohort effects.

   c. Some 90 percent of adults tested in cross-sectional studies show no decline in intellectual abilities until age 40.

   d. Intelligence becomes crystallized for most adults between ages 32 and 41.

7. Research on expertise indicates that during adulthood, intelligence

   a. increases in most primary mental abilities.

   b. increases in specific areas of interest to the person.

   c. increases only in those areas associated with the individual's career.

   d. shows a uniform decline in all areas.

8. Research indicates that during adulthood, declines occur in

   a. crystallized intelligence.

   b. fluid intelligence.

   c. both crystallized and fluid intelligence.

   d. neither crystallized nor fluid intelligence.

9. Fluid intelligence is based on all of the following **EXCEPT**

   a. short-term memory.

   b. abstract thinking.

   c. speed of thinking.

   d. general knowledge.

10. In recent years, researchers are more likely than before to consider intelligence as

    a. a single entity.

    b. primarily determined by heredity.

    c. entirely the product of learning.

    d. made up of several abilities.

11. One of the drawbacks of longitudinal studies of intelligence is that
    a. they are especially prone to the distortion of cohort effects.
    b. people who are retested may show improved performance as a result of practice.
    c. the biases of the experimenter are more likely to distort the results than is true of other research methods.
    d. all of the above are true.

12. To a developmentalist, an expert is a person who
    a. is extraordinarily gifted at a particular task.
    b. is significantly better at a task than people who have not put time and effort into performing that task.
    c. scores at the ninetieth percentile or better on a test of achievement.
    d. is none of the above.

13. One reason for the variety in patterns in adult intelligence is that during adulthood
    a. intelligence is fairly stable in some areas.
    b. intelligence increases in some areas.
    c. intelligence decreases in some areas.
    d. people develop specialized competencies in activities that are personally meaningful.

14. Selective optimization with compensation is crucial most of all in _____________, where there's so much you have to compensate for, but _____________ is the time when most people first start noticing that they can't do everything quite as well as they used to.
    a. late adulthood; middle adulthood
    b. middle adulthood; late adulthood
    c. middle adulthood; adolescence
    d. middle adulthood; early adulthood

Matching Items

Match each definition or description with its corresponding term.

Terms

15. ____	fluid intelligence	20. ____	plasticity
16. ____	crystallized intelligence	21. ____	practical intelligence
17. ____	multidimensional	22. ____	expertise
18. ____	multidirectional	23. ____	selective optimization with compensation
19. ____	creative intelligence	24. ____	analytic intelligence

Definitions or Descriptions

a. intellectual skills used in everyday problem solving

b. intelligence that involves the capacity to be intellectually flexible and innovative

c. intelligence is made up of several different abilities

d. specialized competence

e. flexible reasoning used to draw inferences

f. intellectual flexibility

g. cognitive abilities can follow different trajectories with age

h. the accumulation of facts, information, and knowledge

i. mental processes that foster efficient learning

j. theory that people look for the best way to compensate for physical and cognitive losses and to become more proficient at activities they can do well

Applying Your Knowledge

1. In identifying the multiple aspects of intelligence, Gardner explains that
   a. intelligence appears in three fundamental forms.
   b. a general intelligence can be inferred from these various abilities.
   c. each intelligence has its own neurological network in a particular section of the brain.
   d. fluid intelligence declines with age, while crystallized intelligence increases.

2. In Sternberg's theory, which aspect of intelligence is most similar to the abilities constituting fluid intelligence?
   a. analytic
   b. creative
   c. practical
   d. None of the above is part of Sternberg's theory.

3. Concerning the acquisition of fluid and crystallized intelligence, most experts agree that
   a. both fluid and crystallized intelligence are primarily determined by heredity.
   b. both fluid and crystallized intelligence are primarily acquired through learning.
   c. fluid intelligence is primarily genetic, whereas crystallized intelligence is primarily learned.
   d. intelligence is age-sensitive.

4. Regarding the multidirectionality of intelligence, which of the following statements has the most empirical support?
   a. Most intellectual abilities remain stable with age.
   b. Most intellectual abilities decline with age.
   c. Each intellectual ability may increase, decrease, or remain stable with age.
   d. There is a single mental capacity underlying all intellectual skills, and this capacity may rise or fall with age.

5. A psychologist has found that the mathematical ability of adults born in the 1920s is significantly different from that of those born in the 1950s. She suspects that this difference is a reflection of the different educational emphases of the two historical periods. This is an example of
   a. longitudinal research.
   b. sequential research.
   c. a cohort effect.
   d. all of the above.

6. Sharetta knows more about her field of specialization now at age 45 than she did at age 35. This increase is most likely the result of
   a. an increase in crystallized intelligence.
   b. an increase in fluid intelligence.
   c. increases in both fluid and crystallized intelligence.
   d. a cohort difference.

7. A contemporary developmental psychologist is most likely to disagree with the statement that
   a. many people show increases in intelligence during middle adulthood.
   b. for many behaviors, the responses of older adults are slower than those of younger adults.
   c. intelligence peaks during adolescence and declines thereafter.
   d. intelligence is multidimensional and multidirectional.

8. Regarding their accuracy in measuring adult intellectual decline, cross-sectional research is to longitudinal research as ______________________ is to ______________________.
   a. underestimate; overestimate
   b. overestimate; underestimate
   c. accurate; inaccurate
   d. inaccurate; accurate

9. Dr. Hatfield wants to analyze the possible effects of retesting, cohort differences, and aging on adult changes in intelligence. Which research method should she use?

   a. cross-sectional
   b. longitudinal
   c. cross-sequential
   d. case study

10. Joseph has remained associated with interesting and creative people throughout his life. In contrast, James has become increasingly isolated as he has aged. Given these lifestyle differences, which aspect of intelligence will be most affected in Joseph and James?

   a. fluid intelligence
   b. crystallized intelligence
   c. overall IQ
   d. It is impossible to predict how their intelligence will be affected.

11. When Merle retired from teaching, he had great difficulty adjusting to the changes in his lifestyle. Robert Sternberg would probably say that Merle was somewhat lacking in which aspect of his intelligence?

   a. analytic
   b. creative
   c. practical
   d. plasticity

12. Compared to her 20-year-old daughter, 40-year-old Wendy is likely to perform better on measures of what type of intelligence?

   a. fluid
   b. practical
   c. analytic
   d. none of the above

13. Most developmentalists would agree with which of the following statements?

   a. Faster thinking is deeper thinking.
   b. Slower thinking is deeper thinking.
   c. Speed of thinking is a critical element of fluid intelligence.
   d. Speed of thinking is a critical element of crystallized intelligence.

Answer Key

Key Terms

1. General intelligence (*g*) is the idea that intelligence is one basic trait, underlying all cognitive abilities, according to Spearman. (p. 436; video lesson, segment 1; objective 1)
2. The Seattle Longitudinal Study, an ongoing project begun by researcher K. Warner Schaie, is the first cross-sequential study of adult intelligence. (p. 438; objective 6)
3. Fluid intelligence is made up of those basic mental abilities—inductive reasoning, abstract thinking, speed of processing, and the like—required for understanding any subject matter. (p. 440; video lesson, segment 2; objective 1)
4. Crystallized intelligence is the accumulation of facts, information, and knowledge that comes with education and experience within a particular culture. (p. 440; video lesson, segment 2; objective 1)
5. A hallmark of successful aging, selective optimization with compensation is the ability to strategically use one's intellectual strengths to compensate for the declining capacities that are associated with aging. (p. 443; video lesson, segment 2; objective 3)
6. According to developmentalists, a selective expert is someone who is notably more skilled and knowledgeable about a specific intellectual topic or practical ability than the average person is. (p. 444; objective 8)
7. The psychometric approach to intelligence focuses on measuring a person's ability, aptitude, or skill in a variety of ways that are scientifically sound. (video lesson, segment 1; objective 1)
8. The multidimensional nature of intelligence is the fact that intelligence is made up of several distinct abilities, rather than a single, general ability. (video lesson, segment 2; objectives 1, 2, & 4)
9. The multidirectional nature of intelligence is the fact that cognitive abilities often follow different trajectories with age. (video lesson, segment 2; objective 5)
10. Analytic intelligence refers to mental processes that foster efficient learning, remembering, and thinking. (video lesson, segment 2; objective 2)
11. Creative intelligence refers to the capacity to be flexible and innovative when dealing with new situations. (video lesson, segment 2; objective 2)
12. Practical intelligence refers to a person's ability to adapt his or her abilities to changing contextual demands. (video lesson, segment 2; objective 2)
13. A cross-sectional study is a research design in which groups of people, each group different from the others in age but similar to them in other important ways, are compared. (video lesson, segment 3; objective 6)

14. Intelligence is characterized by plasticity, meaning that abilities can become enhanced or diminished, depending on how, when, and why a person uses them. (video lesson, segment 4; objective 8)
15. A hallmark of adulthood is the development of expertise, or specialized competencies, in activities that are personally meaningful to us. (video lesson, segment 4; objective 8)

Practice Questions I

Multiple-Choice Questions

1. a. is the correct answer. (p. 437; video lesson, segment 3; objective 6)

   b. is incorrect. Although results from this type of research may also be misleading, longitudinal studies often demonstrate age-related increases in intelligence.

   c. is incorrect. Cross-sequential research is the technique devised by K. Warner Schaie that combines the strengths of the cross-sectional and longitudinal methods.

   d. is incorrect. Random sampling refers to the selection of subjects for a research study.

2. a. is the correct answer. (p. 437; video lesson, segment 3; objectives 6 & 7)

   b. is incorrect. This is a problem in longitudinal research.

   c. & d. are incorrect. Neither of these is particularly troublesome in cross-sectional research.

3. d. is the correct answer. (p. 438; video lesson, segment 3; objectives 6 & 7)

   a., b., & c. are incorrect. Cross-sequential research as described in this chapter is based on objective intelligence testing.

4. d. is the correct answer. (pp. 440–441; video lesson, segment 2; objective 1)

   a. & b. are incorrect. Traditional IQ tests measure both fluid and crystallized intelligence.

5. c. is the correct answer. (pp. 440–441; video lesson, segment 4; objective 1)

   a., b., & d. are incorrect. These often increase with age.

6. c. is the correct answer. (p. 440; video lesson, segment 2; objective 1)

   a. is incorrect. Crystallized intelligence is the accumulation of facts and knowledge that comes with education and experience.

   b. is incorrect. Although intelligence is characterized by plasticity, "plastic intelligence" is not discussed as a specific type of intelligence.

   d. is incorrect. Rote memory is memory that is based on the conscious repetition of to-be-remembered information.

7. d. is the correct answer. (pp. 440–441; video lesson, segment 2; objective 1)

8. a. is the correct answer. (p. 436; video lesson, segment 1; objectives 1 & 6)

   b. is incorrect. Practical intelligence refers to the intellectual skills used in everyday problem solving.

   c. & d. are incorrect. These are two aspects of intelligence identified in Robert Sternberg's theory.

9. b. is the correct answer. Life experiences give intelligence its flexibility and account for the variety of patterns of adult cognitive development. (video lesson, segment 2; objective 8)

10. a. is the correct answer. (p. 445; objective 8)

    b. is incorrect. This was not discussed in the chapter.

    c. is incorrect. Plasticity refers to the flexible nature of intelligence.

    d. is incorrect. Encoding refers to the placing of information into memory.

11. c. is the correct answer. (p. 447; video lesson, segment 4; objective 8)

    a., b., & d. are incorrect. These are more typical of novices than experts.

12. a. is the correct answer. (p. 436; video lesson, segment 1; objective 1)

13. c. is the correct answer. (p. 437; objectives 5 & 6)

    b. is incorrect. In fact, these were the only two subtests on which performance did not improve.

    d. is incorrect. No such criticism was made of Bayley's study.

14. d. is the correct answer. In fact, intelligence often becomes more specialized with age. (pp. 442, 436–439; objectives 4 & 5)

15. c. is the correct answer. (p. 441; video lesson, segment 2; objective 2)

    a. is incorrect. Charles Spearman proposed the existence of an underlying general intelligence, which he called *g*.

    b. is incorrect. Howard Gardner proposed that intelligence consists of eight autonomous abilities.

    d. is incorrect. K. Warner Schaie was one of the first researchers to recognize the potentially distorting cohort effects on cross-sectional research.

16. b. is the correct answer. (pp. 443–444; objective 3)

True or False Items

17. F Intellectual functioning as measured by IQ tests is powerfully influenced by years of schooling. (pp. 437–438; video lesson, segment 1; objectives 4 & 7)

18. F Cross-sectional research shows a decline in intellectual ability. (p. 437; video lesson, segment 3; objective 6)

19. T (pp. 437–438; video lesson, segment 3; objectives 1 & 6)

20. F Many adults show intellectual improvement over most of adulthood, with no decline, even by age 60. (pp. 436–439; video lesson, segment 2; objectives 5 & 7)

21. T (pp. 438–439; objective 7)

22. F There is agreement that intelligence does not peak in adolescence and decline thereafter. (pp. 436–439; video lesson, segment 2; objective 5)
23. F Historically, psychologists have conceived of intelligence as a single entity. (p. 436; video lesson, segment 1; objectives 5 & 6)
24. T (p. 442; video lesson, segment 1; objective 4)
25. T (pp. 444–445; objective 8)
26. T (pp. 443–444; video lesson, segment 2; objective 3)

Practice Questions II

1. c. is the correct answer. (video lesson, segment 3; objective 6)
2. a. is the correct answer. (pp. 440–441; video lesson, segment 2; objective 1)

   b. is incorrect. Although intelligence is characterized by plasticity, "plastic intelligence" is not discussed as a specific type of intelligence.

   c. is incorrect. Fluid intelligence consists of the basic abilities that go into the understanding of any subject.

   d. is incorrect. Rote memory is based on the conscious repetition of to-be-remembered information.
3. c. is the correct answer. (pp. 444–448, 450–451; video lesson, segment 4; objective 8)
4. b. is the correct answer. (p. 442; objective 4)
5. a. is the correct answer. (pp. 436–439, 443–448, 450–451; video lesson, segment 2; objective 5)

   b. is incorrect. This refers to the fact that intelligence consists of multiple abilities.

   c. is incorrect. This characteristic suggests that intelligence can be molded in many ways.

   d. is incorrect. Practical intelligence refers to the skills used in everyday problem solving.
6. b. is the correct answer. (pp. 436–439; video lesson, segment 3; objectives 5 & 7)

   a. is incorrect. There is agreement that intelligence does not peak during adolescence.

   c. is incorrect. Cross-sectional research usually provides evidence of declining ability throughout adulthood.

   d. is incorrect. Crystallized intelligence refers to the accumulation of knowledge with experience; intelligence does not "crystallize" at any specific age.
7. b. is the correct answer. (p. 444; objective 8)
8. b. is the correct answer. (pp. 439–441; video lesson, segment 2; objectives 1 & 6)

a., c., & d. are incorrect. Crystallized intelligence typically increases during adulthood.

9. d. is the correct answer. This is an aspect of crystallized intelligence. (p. 440; video lesson, segment 2; objective 1)

10. d. is the correct answer. (pp. 436–442; video lesson, segment 2; objectives 1, 2, 4, & 6)

    a. is incorrect. Contemporary researchers emphasize the multidimensional nature of intelligence.

    b. & c. are incorrect. Contemporary researchers see intelligence as the product of both heredity and learning.

11. b. is the correct answer. (pp. 437–438; video lesson, segment 3; objective 6)

    a. is incorrect. This is a drawback of cross-sectional research.

    c. is incorrect. Longitudinal studies are no more sensitive to experimenter bias than other research methods.

12. b. is the correct answer. (p. 444; objective 8)

13. d. is the correct answer. (pp. 436–439; video lesson, segment 3; objective 7)

14. a. is the correct answer. (pp. 443–444; objective 3)

Matching Items

15. e (p. 440; video lesson, segment 2; objective 1)
16. h (p. 440; video lesson, segment 2; objective 1)
17. c (video lesson, segment 2; objectives 1, 2, & 4)
18. g (video lesson, segment 2; objective 5)
19. b (video lesson, segment 2; objective 2)
20. f (video lesson, segment 4; objective 8)
21. a (video lesson, segment 2; objective 2)
22. d (video lesson, segment 4; objective 8)
23 j (p. 443; video lesson, segment 2; objective 3)
24. i (video lesson, segment 2; objective 2)

Applying Your Knowledge

1. c. is the correct answer. (p. 442; video lesson, segment 2; objective 4)

   a. is incorrect. This is Sternberg's theory.

   b. is incorrect. This refers to Spearman's view of a *g* factor.

   d. is incorrect. While this is true, it is not part of Gardner's theory.

2. a. is the correct answer. This aspect consists of mental processes fostering efficient learning, remembering, and thinking. (pp. 441–442; video lesson, segment 2; objective 2)

   b. is incorrect. This aspect enables the person to accommodate successfully to changes in the environment.

c. is incorrect. This aspect concerns the extent to which intellectual functions are applied to situations that are familiar or novel in a person's history.

3. d. is the correct answer. This is so in part because the acquisition of crystallized intelligence is affected by the quality of fluid intelligence. (p. 441; objective 1)
4. c. is the correct answer. (video lesson, segment 2; objective 5)
5. c. is the correct answer. (pp. 436–439; video lesson, segment 1; objective 7)

   a. & b. are incorrect. From the information given, it is impossible to determine which research method the psychologist used.
6. a. is the correct answer. (pp. 440–441; video lesson, segment 2; objective 1)

   b. & c. are incorrect. According to the research, fluid intelligence declines markedly during adulthood.

   d. is incorrect. Cohort effects refer to generational differences in life experiences.
7. c. is the correct answer. (p. 437; video lesson, segment 1; objective 6)
8. b. is the correct answer. (p. 437; video lesson, segment 3; objective 6)

   c. & d. are incorrect. Both cross-sectional and longitudinal research are potentially misleading.
9. c. is the correct answer. (pp. 438–439; video lesson, segment 3; objectives 1 & 6)

   a. & b. are incorrect. Schaie developed the cross-sequential research method to overcome the drawbacks of the cross-sectional and longitudinal methods, which were susceptible to cohort and retesting effects, respectively.

   d. is incorrect. A case study focuses on a single subject and therefore could provide no information on cohort effects.
10. b. is the correct answer. Because the maintenance of crystallized intelligence depends partly on how it is used, the consequences of remaining socially involved or of being socially isolated become increasingly apparent in adulthood. (pp. 436–441; video lesson, segment 2; objective 7)
11. b. is the correct answer. Creative intelligence enables the person to accommodate successfully to changes in the environment, such as those accompanying retirement. (p. 441; video lesson, segment 2; objective 2)

    a. is incorrect. This aspect of intelligence consists of mental processes that foster efficient learning, remembering, and thinking.

    c. is incorrect. This aspect of intelligence concerns the extent to which intellectual functions are applied to situations that are familiar or novel in a person's history.

    d. is incorrect. Plasticity refers to the flexible nature of intelligence; it is not an aspect of Sternberg's theory.
12. b. is the correct answer. (p. 441; video lesson, segment 2; objectives 1 & 2)
13. c. is the correct answer. (pp. 439–440; video lesson, segment 2; objective 1)

Lesson Review

Lesson 21

Middle Adulthood
Cognitive Development

Please Note: Use this matrix to guide your study and achieve the learning objectives of this lesson. It will also help you to view the video, which defines and demonstrates important concepts and skills as they relate to everyday life.

Learning Objective	Textbook	Telecourse Student Guide	Video Lesson
1. Discuss the psychometric approach to adult cognition, distinguish between fluid (mechanics) and crystallized (pragmatics) intelligence, and explain how each is affected by age.	pp. 439–441	Key Terms: 1, 3, 4, 7, 8; Practice Questions I: 4, 5, 6, 7, 8, 12, 19; Practice Questions II: 2, 8, 9, 10, 15, 16, 17; Applying Your Knowledge: 3, 6, 9, 12, 13.	Segment 1: *Psychometric Approach;* Segment 2: *Dimensions & Directions of Intelligence;* Segment 4: *Plastic Intellectual Change*
2. Differentiate the three fundamental forms of intelligence described by Robert Sternberg, and discuss how each tends to vary over the life span.	pp. 441–442	Key Terms: 8, 10, 11, 12; Practice Questions I: 15; Practice Questions II: 10, 17, 19, 21, 24; Applying Your Knowledge: 2, 11, 12.	Segment 2: *Dimensions & Directions of Intelligence*
3. Explain the concept of selective optimization with compensation.	pp. 443–444	Key Terms: 5; Practice Questions I: 16, 26; Practice Questions II: 14, 23.	Segment 2: *Dimensions & Directions of Intelligence*
4. Outline Howard Gardner's theory of intelligence, noting the impact of culture and aging on the various dimensions of intelligence.	p. 442	Key Terms: 8; Practice Questions I: 14, 17, 24; Practice Questions II: 4, 10, 17; Applying Your Knowledge: 1.	Segment 2: *Dimensions & Directions of Intelligence*
5. Discuss the multidirectionality of intelligence.	pp. 436–439, 443–448, 450–451	Key Terms: 9; Practice Questions I: 13, 14, 20, 22, 23; Practice Questions II: 5, 6, 18; Applying Your Knowledge: 4.	Segment 2: *Dimensions & Directions of Intelligence*

Learning Objective	Textbook	Telecourse Student Guide	Video Lesson
6. Briefly trace the history of the controversy regarding adult intelligence, including the findings of cross-sectional and longitudinal research and how cross-sequential research compensates for their shortcomings.	pp. 436–439	Key Terms: 2, 13; Practice Questions I: 1, 2, 3, 8, 12, 13, 18, 19, 23; Practice Questions II: 1, 8, 10, 11; Applying Your Knowledge: 7, 8, 9.	Segment 1: *Psychometric Approach;* Segment 2: *Dimensions & Directions of Intelligence;* Segment 3: *Contextual Influences*
7. Explain how and why context and cohort affect intellectual development during adulthood.	pp. 436–439	Practice Questions I: 2, 3, 17, 20, 21; Practice Questions II: 6, 13, 19; Applying Your Knowledge: 5, 10.	Segment 2: *Dimensions & Directions of Intelligence;* Segment 3: *Contextual Influences*
8. Discuss the plasticity of intelligence, and describe how the cognitive processes of experts differ from those of novices.	pp. 444–448, 450–451	Key Terms: 6, 14, 15; Practice Questions I: 9, 10, 11, 25; Practice Questions II: 3, 7, 12, 20, 22.	Segment 2: *Dimensions & Directions of Intelligence;* Segment 4: *Plastic Intellectual Change*

Making Lemonade

Lesson 22

Middle Adulthood:
Psychosocial Development

Preview

Lesson 22 is concerned with midlife, commonly believed to be a time of crisis and transition, when self-doubt, reevaluation of career goals, changes in family responsibilities, and a growing awareness of one's mortality lead to turmoil. The lesson begins with an examination of the changes that occur at midlife, showing that although middle adulthood may have its share of pressures and stress, a crisis is not inevitable.

Next, this lesson examines the question of whether there is stability of personality throughout adulthood, identifying five basic clusters of personality traits that remain fairly stable throughout adulthood. One personality trend attributed to middle age is that gender roles become less rigid; both sexes tend to take on characteristics typically reserved for the opposite sex. For instance, middle-aged women tend to become more assertive, whereas men of this age are likely to become more expressive.

The lesson then turns to a consideration of the changing dynamics between middle-aged adults and their adult children and aging parents, showing why the various demands of the younger and older generations have led the middle-aged to be called the "sandwich generation." Changes in the marital relationship are also examined.

The lesson ends with an examination of the evolution of work in the individual's life during middle adulthood. Many women and men place greater emphasis on balancing their work lives with parenthood and other life concerns by scaling back on their efforts in the workplace.

Prior Telecourse Knowledge that Will Be Used in this Lesson

- Erik Erikson's theory (from Lesson 2) will be used to help explain psychosocial development during young adulthood. Recall that Erikson specifies eight stages of psychosocial development, each of which is characterized by a particular challenge, which is central to that stage of life and must be resolved:

1. Trust vs. Mistrust (birth to 1 year)
2. Autonomy vs. Shame and Doubt (1 to 3 years)
3. Initiative vs. Guilt (3 to 6 years)
4. Industry vs. Inferiority (7 to 11 years)
5. Identity vs. Role Confusion (adolescence)
6. **Intimacy vs. Isolation (adulthood)**
7. **Generativity vs. Stagnation (adulthood)**
8. Integrity vs. Despair (Adulthood)

Learning Objectives

Use this information to guide your reading, viewing, thinking, and studying. After successfully completing this lesson, you should be able to:

1. Discuss Erikson's and Maslow's ideas on the stages of adulthood and explain how the social clock influences the timing of important events during adulthood.
2. Describe the caregiving roles of middle-aged adults and explain why middle-aged adults are considered the "sandwich generation."
3. Describe the Big Five clusters of personality traits, and discuss reasons for their relative stability during adulthood.
4. Explain the concept of an ecological niche, noting how it interacts with personality.
5. Explain the tendency toward gender role convergence during middle age.
6. Discuss how and why marital relationships tend to change during middle adulthood.
7. Discuss the impact of divorce and remarriage during middle adulthood, including reasons for the high divorce rate among the remarried.
8. Describe the components of the social convoy, and explain this convoy's increasing importance during middle adulthood.
9. Describe how the balance among work, family, and self often shifts during middle adulthood.
10. Define allostatic load, discuss the affects of stress in middle adulthood, and explain some measures that can be employed to reduce it.

Read Chapter 13, "Adulthood: Psychosocial Development," pages 455–491.

View the video for Lesson 22, "Making Lemonade."

Segment 1: *Personality Throughout Adulthood*
Segment 2: *Family Relationships*
Segment 3: *Work and Life*

Summary

Many personal changes occur during middle age. These include the awareness that one is beginning to grow old, the need to make adjustments in parental roles as children enter adolescence and subsequently adulthood, the reaching of a plateau in one's career, and the tendency to question choices that have been made in life thus far. Few developmentalists, however, believe that the challenges of midlife inevitably bring on a midlife crisis. How people react to midlife has more to do with their overall developmental history than with age.

Longitudinal and cross-sectional research finds five basic clusters of personality traits (the Big Five) that remain stable throughout adulthood. These include extroversion, agreeableness, neuroticism, conscientiousness, and openness. In pinpointing the reasons for the apparent consistency of some traits, researchers note the importance of genes, culture, early child rearing, and the experiences and choices made during late adolescence and early adulthood. The manifestation of these traits is usually stable by age 30, when most people have settled into an **ecological niche**—a life that they have crafted for themselves by making decisions about vocations, mates, neighborhood, and lifestyles—that evokes and reinforces their personality.

Middle-aged adults have been referred to as the **sandwich generation**, because they are often believed to be caught between or squeezed by the needs of both the older and younger generations. Recent research shows that this is largely a myth. The middle-aged adults who provide extensive help to their parents and children tend to enjoy providing assistance and may be particularly generous individuals. Although the typical contemporary American family is less likely to consist of several generations living under the same roof, this does not mean that family links have weakened. Close contact is still maintained by visits, telephone conversations, or regular correspondence.

The relationship between most middle-aged adults and their parents improves with time. This may occur because as adult children mature, they develop a more balanced view of the relationship. In addition, today's elderly are generally healthy, active, and independent, enhancing the relationship between themselves and their grown families. The middle generation, particularly women, tend to be the **kinkeepers**, maintaining the links between the generations. Parents generally maintain close relationships with their children, even when the latter are full-grown and independent. Typically, financial help and other support flows from the middle-aged parents to the young adults.

While grandparents today are usually peripheral, some are called upon to become surrogate parents, taking over the work of raising their children's children. This is especially likely when the parents are poor, young, unemployed, addicted, or newly divorced. Grandparents are most likely to provide surrogate care for children who need intensive involvement, such as infants who are drug-affected or rebellious.

Throughout adulthood, marriage is the family relationship that seems most clearly linked to personal happiness, health, and companionship. After the first ten years or so, the longer a couple has been married, the happier they are. Several reasons have been suggested for this improvement: greater financial security of families at the empty-nest stage, the increasing sense of equity in the relationship, and increased time for shared activities once children have left home.

Review all reading assignments for this lesson.

As assigned by your instructor, complete the optional online component for this lesson.

Key Terms

Using your own words, write a brief definition or explanation of each of the following terms on a separate piece of paper.

1. social clock
2. midlife crisis
3. ecological niche
4. gender convergence
5. social convoy
6. familism
7. fictive kin
8. empty nest
9. kinkeeper
10. sandwich generation
11. relative deprivation
12. extrinsic rewards of work
13. intrinsic rewards of work
14. mentor (mentoring)
15. flextime
16. telecommuting
17. stressor
18. allostatic load
19. organ reserve
20. problem-focused coping
21. emotion-focused coping
22. scaling back

Practice Questions I

Multiple-Choice Questions

1. The most important factor in how a person adjusts to middle age is his or her
   a. gender.
   b. personality history.
   c. age.
   d. race.

2. The Big Five personality factors are
   a. emotional stability, openness, introversion, sociability, locus of control.
   b. neuroticism, extroversion, openness, emotional stability, sensitivity.
   c. extroversion, agreeableness, conscientiousness, neuroticism, openness.
   d. neuroticism, gregariousness, extroversion, impulsiveness, openness.

3. Concerning the prevalence of midlife crises, which of the following statements has the greatest empirical support?
   a. Virtually all men, and most women, experience a midlife crisis.
   b. Virtually all men, and about 50 percent of women, experience a midlife crisis.
   c. Women are more likely to experience a midlife crisis than are men.
   d. Few contemporary developmentalists believe that the midlife crisis is a common experience.

4. Middle-age shifts in personality often reflect
   a. the particular traits that are valued within the culture at that time.
   b. rebellion against earlier life choices.
   c. the tightening of gender roles.
   d. all of the above.

5. During middle age, gender roles tend to
   a. become more distinct.
   b. reflect patterns established during early adulthood.
   c. converge.
   d. be unpredictable.

6. Middle-aged adults who are providing care or assistance to adult children *and* aging parents are
   a. said to be in the sandwich generation.
   b. especially likely to suffer burnout.
   c. especially likely to suffer alienation.
   d. all of the above.

7. Which of the following statements best describes the relationship of most middle-aged adults to their aging parents?
   a. The relationship tends to improve with time.
   b. During middle adulthood, the relationship tends to deteriorate.
   c. For women, but not men, the relationship tends to improve with time.
   d. The relationship usually remains as good or as bad as it was in the past.

8. In families, middle-aged adults tend to function as the ________________, celebrating family achievements, keeping the family together, and staying in touch with distant relatives.
   a. sandwich generation
   b. nuclear bond
   c. intergenerational gatekeepers
   d. kinkeepers

9. In stress responses, older adults are most likely to use which form of coping?
   a. allostatic load
   b. intrinsic
   c. problem-focused
   d. emotion-focused

10. During middle adulthood, scaling back refers to the tendency of both men and women to
   a. limit their involvement in activities that take away from their careers.
   b. deliberately reduce workload in order to meet their family needs.
   c. pull away from their spouses as they reevaluate their life's accomplishments.
   d. explore the "shadow sides" of their personalities.

11. According to research conducted by the U.S. Bureau of the Census, the jump in the number of homosexual couples between 2000 and 2006 is likely the result of

    a. legalization of same-sex marriage.
    b. prior undercounting of same-sex couples.
    c. an increase in the divorce rate.
    d. none of the above.

12. Concerning the degree of stability of personality traits, which of the following statements has the greatest research support?

    a. There is little evidence that personality traits remain stable during adulthood.
    b. In women, but less so in men, there is notable continuity in many personality characteristics.
    c. In men, but less so in women, there is notable continuity in many personality characteristics.
    d. In both men and women, there is notable continuity in many personality characteristics.

13. People who exhibit the personality dimension of ________________ tend to be outgoing, active, and assertive.

    a. extroversion
    b. agreeableness
    c. conscientiousness
    d. neuroticism

14. Developmentalists have found that over the course of adulthood, the two sexes become more alike in their behaviors and attitudes. This phenomenon is called

    a. gender divergence.
    b. midlife crises.
    c. gender convergence.
    d. none of the above.

15. Which of the following personality traits was **NOT** identified in the Berger textbook as tending to remain stable throughout adulthood?

    a. neuroticism
    b. introversion
    c. openness
    d. conscientiousness

True or False Items

Write T (for true) or F (for false) on the line in front of each statement.

16. _____ At least 75 percent of American men experience a significant midlife crisis between ages 38 and 43.
17. _____ Better than age as a predictor of whether a midlife crisis will occur is an individual's personality history.
18. _____ By age 30, most of an individual's basic personality traits become stable.
19. _____ The current cohort of middle-aged adults is notable for the marked convergence of their sex roles.
20. _____ The extended family is typical of modern societies, such as those in North America today.
21. _____ Today's parents are less likely to maintain close relationships with their aging parents.
22. _____ After stressful periods early in marriage, marital happiness often rebounds once couples understand each other better.
23. _____ Second marriages end in divorce more often than first marriages.
24. _____ According to the Berger textbook, children of African-American couples who divorce are less troubled by it than children of white couples who divorce.
25. _____ Women with children are less likely to remarry than women without children.

Practice Questions II

Multiple-Choice Questions

1. Society recognizes midlife as beginning around the age of ________________ and lasting until about age ________________.

   a. 35; 64

   b. 40; 70

   c. 30; 45

   d. 50; 75

2. By what age have most people settled into a particular ecological niche?

   a. 20

   b. 25

   c. 30

   d. 40

3. Which of the following factors play a role in whether grandparents will become surrogate parents?
   a. Both parents are full-time college students.
   b. Both parents have been deemed unfit by the courts.
   c. One parent is busy establishing a career and the other does not want to assume the burden of raising a child.
   d. All of the above factors are true.

4. Which of the following is true regarding the ecological niche of a middle-aged adult?
   a. It is determined by the person's characteristic traits.
   b. It depends almost entirely on the person's life experiences.
   c. It is shaped by and might interact with his or her personality traits.
   d. It prevents the person from changing during adulthood.

5. Whether a person ranks high or low in each of the Big Five personality factors is determined by
   a. heredity.
   b. temperament.
   c. his or her lifestyle.
   d. the interaction of genes, culture, and early experiences.

6. Regarding the strength of the contemporary family bond, most developmentalists believe that
   a. family links are considerably weaker in the typical contemporary American family than in earlier decades.
   b. family links are considerably weaker in the typical contemporary American family than in other cultures.
   c. both a and b are true.
   d. despite the fact that extended families are less common, family links are not weaker today.

7. Most families have a kinkeeper. This role is usually filled by
   a. older women.
   b. younger women.
   c. older men who are retired.
   d. younger men because of gender convergence.

8. Which of the following statements explains why couples are particularly likely to report an increase in marital satisfaction during middle adulthood?

   a. Marital satisfaction is closely tied to financial security, which tends to improve during middle adulthood.

   b. The successful launching of children is a source of great pride and happiness.

   c. There often is improvement in marital equity during this period.

   d. For all of the above reasons, couples are likely to report improvement in their marriages during middle adulthood.

9. Besides caregiving, the other major avenue for generativity is

   a. social networking.

   b. volunteering for a favorite organization.

   c. employment.

   d. none of the above.

10. Sociologist Thorstein Veblen first described a behavior in which people buy things for the express purpose of showing them off. He referred to this behavior as

   a. conspicuous consumption.

   b. relative deprivation.

   c. intrinsic consumption.

   d. none of the above.

11. Research shows that average income has doubled in the United States, and relative to this, research also shows that

   a. as income rises, happiness levels increase.

   b. as income rises, happiness levels have not increased.

   c. people don't correlate income with happiness.

   d. none of the above.

12. The total burden on a person's body from all stressors experienced both physical and emotional is known as

   a. allostatic load.

   b. work/life outcome.

   c. midlife crisis.

   d. relative deprivation.

13. Age differences are apparent in strategies for coping with stress. Younger adults tend to use
    a. problem-focused coping.
    b. emotion-focused coping.
    c. talk therapy.
    d. physical activity in the form of regular exercise.

Matching Items

Match each definition or description with its corresponding term.

Terms

14. ________	allostatic load	20. ________	agreeableness
15. ________	kinkeeper	21. ________	conscientiousness
16. ________	sandwich generation	22. ________	neuroticism
17. ________	social clock	23. ________	openness
18. ________	fictive kin	24. ________	extrinsic rewards of work
19. ________	extroversion	25. ________	social convoy

Definitions or Descriptions

a. tendency to be outgoing
b. the total combined burden of stress and disease that an individual must cope with
c. tendency to be imaginative
d. used to describe someone who becomes accepted as part of a family to whom he or she has no blood relationship.
e. tendency to be organized
f. those who focus more on the family
g. tendency to be helpful
h. tangible rewards (e.g., payment) that one receives for employment
i. those pressured by the needs of the older and younger generations
j. tendency to be moody
k. stages of life are set by social standards rather than by biological maturation
l. group of people who form relationships with an individual through which they guide and socialize that person over the course of his or her life

Applying Your Knowledge

1. Which developmentalist formulated the "hierarchy of needs"?
   a. Erik Erikson
   b. Carl Jung
   c. Jean Piaget
   d. Abraham Maslow

2. For her class presentation, Christine plans to discuss the Big Five personality factors. Which of the following is **NOT** a factor that Christine will discuss?
   a. extroversion
   b. openness
   c. independence
   d. agreeableness

3. It has long been researched that, for biological reasons, I will inevitably experience a midlife crisis. I am
   a. a middle-aged man.
   b. a middle-aged woman.
   c. either a middle-age man or a middle-aged woman.
   d. neither a nor b.

4. Compared to when they were younger, middle-aged Sarah is likely to become more _________________, while middle-aged Donald becomes more _________________.
   a. introverted; extroverted
   b. assertive; emotionally expressive
   c. disappointed with life; satisfied with life
   d. extroverted; introverted

5. The parents of Rebecca and her middle-aged twin, Josh, have become frail and unable to care for themselves. It is likely that
   a. Rebecca and Josh will play equal roles as caregivers for their parents.
   b. Rebecca will play a larger role in caring for their parents.
   c. Josh will play a larger role in caring for their parents.
   d. If Rebecca and Josh are well educated, their parents will be placed in a professional caregiving facility.

6. In the United States, the happiness of a middle-aged adult
   a. tends to decrease.
   b. strongly correlates with his or her marital happiness.
   c. tends to increase.
   d. is most strongly related to his or her career satisfaction.

7. Ben and Nancy have been married for 10 years. Although they are very happy, Nancy worries that with time this happiness will decrease. Research would suggest that Nancy's fear
   a. may or may not be reasonable, depending on whether she and her husband are experiencing a midlife crisis.
   b. is reasonable, since marital discord is most common in couples who have been married 6 months to 3 years or more.
   c. is reasonable, since after the first 10 years or so, happiness dips as children reach puberty and rises when children leave the nest.
   d. is probably a sign of neuroticism.

8. Fifty-year-old Kenneth remarried this year following his divorce 3 years ago. It is likely that Kenneth will
   a. become healthier.
   b. become more social.
   c. have improved relationships with his children.
   d. experience all of the above.

9. After a painful phone call with her unhappy middle-aged mother, your college roommate confides her fear that she will not be able to handle the burdens of children, career, and caring for her aging parents. Your response is that
   a. she's right to worry, since middle-aged women who juggle these roles simultaneously almost always feel unfairly overburdened.
   b. her mother's unhappiness is a warning sign that she herself may be genetically prone toward developing a midlife crisis.
   c. Both a and b are true.
   d. If these roles are important to her, if her relationships are satisfying, and if the time demands are not overwhelming, filling these roles is likely to be a source of satisfaction.

10. Bill suffers from the effects of allostatic load. He has lost his job, he is divorced, his children are estranged from him, he has heart trouble, and he is severely overweight. His stress levels can be eased if he

 a. checks himself into a mental hospital.
 b. calls his children regularly to ask them why they don't call him.
 c. seek social support from sympathetic friends and family.
 d. none of the above.

11. Jan and her sister Sue have experienced similar frequent changes in careers, residences, and spouses. Jan has found these upheavals much less stressful than Sue and so is probably characterized by which of the following personality traits?

 a. agreeableness
 b. conscientiousness
 c. openness
 d. extroversion

Answer Key

Key Terms

1. Social clock refers to the idea that the stages of life are set by social standards and not by biological maturation. (p. 457; objective 1)
2. The midlife crisis is a period of unusual anxiety, radical reexamination, and sudden transformation that is widely associated with middle age. (p. 459; video lesson, segment 1; objective 1)
3. Ecological niche refers to the lifestyle and social context adults settle into that are compatible with their individual personality needs and interests. (p. 460; video lesson, segment 1; objective 4)
4. Gender convergence is the tendency for men and women to become more similar as they move through middle age. (p. 463; objective 5)
5. A social convoy is a group of people who form relationships with an individual through which they guide and socialize that person as he or she moves through life. (p. 464; objective 8)
6. Familism is the idea that family members should support each other because family unity is more important than individual freedom and success. (p. 466; objective 8)
7. The term used to describe someone who becomes accepted as part of a family to which he or she has no blood relation is fictive kin. (p. 467; objective 8)
8. The time in the lives of parents when their children have left the family home to pursue their own lives is referred to as empty nest. (p. 469; objective 6)

9. Because women tend to focus more on family than men do, they are the kinkeepers, the people who celebrate family achievements, gather the family together, and keep in touch with family members who have moved away. (p. 474; objective 2)
10. Middle-aged adults are commonly referred to as the sandwich generation because they are often squeezed by the needs of the younger and older generations. (p. 477; video lesson, segment 2; objective 2)
11. Relative deprivation is the idea that people compare themselves to others in their group and are satisfied if they are no worse off than the group norm. (p. 479; objective 9)
12. The tangible benefits of work, usually in the form of compensation such as salary, health insurance and pension are referred to as the extrinsic rewards of work. (p. 480; objective 9)
13. The intangible gratifications of work, such as job satisfaction, self-esteem and pride, are referred to as the intrinsic rewards of work. (p. 480; objective 9)
14. A mentor is a guide or teacher who helps an inexperienced person. (p. 482; video lesson, segment 3; objective 9)
15. An arrangement in which work schedules are flexible so that employees can balance personal and occupational responsibilities is referred to as flextime. (p. 484; objective 9)
16. Telecommuting is working at home and keeping in touch with the office via computer, telephone and fax. (p. 484; objective 9)
17. A stressor is any situation, event, experience or other stimulus that causes a person to feel stressed. (p. 485; objective 10)
18. Allostatic load is the load of stress and disease that people carry with them throughout life. A large allostatic load increases the risk of disease, premature aging, and death. (p. 486; objective 10)
19. The capacity of human organs to allow the body to cope with unusual stress is referred to as organ reserve. (p. 487; objective 10)
20. A strategy that is often used by younger adults to deal with stress in which they tackle a stressful issue directly is referred to as problem-focused coping. (p. 487; objective 10)
21. A strategy that is often used by older adults to deal with stress in which they change their feelings about the stressor rather than changing the stressor itself is called emotion-focused coping. (p. 487; objective 10)
22. Scaling back refers to the tendency of many middle-aged adults to deliberately put less than full effort into their work. (video lesson, segment 3; objective 9)

Practice Questions I

Multiple-Choice Questions

1. b. is the correct answer. (p. 459; video lesson, segment 1; objective 3)
2. c. is the correct answer. (p. 460; video lesson, segment 1; objective 3)
3. d. is the correct answer. (p. 459; video lesson, introduction; objective 1)

   a. & b. are incorrect. Recent studies have shown that the prevalence of the midlife crisis has been greatly exaggerated.

   c. is incorrect. The textbook does not suggest a gender difference in terms of the midlife crisis.
4. a. is the correct answer. (pp. 460–462; video lesson, segment 1; objective 4)

   b. is incorrect. This answer reflects the notion of a midlife crisis—a much rarer event than is popularly believed.

   c. is incorrect. Gender roles tend to loosen in middle adulthood.
5. c. is the correct answer. (p. 463; objective 5)

   a. is incorrect. Gender roles become less distinct during middle adulthood.

   b. is incorrect. Gender roles often are most distinct during early adulthood, after which they tend to loosen.

   d. is incorrect. Although there is diversity from individual to individual, gender-role shifts during middle adulthood are nevertheless predictable.
6. a. is the correct answer. (p. 477; video lesson, segment 2; objective 2)

   b. & c. are incorrect. These are job-related problems.
7. a. is the correct answer. (pp. 465–466; video lesson, segment 2; objective 2)

   c. is incorrect. The relationship improves for both men and women.

   d. is incorrect. Most of today's elderly are healthy, active, and independent, and this gives them and their grown children a measure of freedom and privacy that enhances the relationship between them.
8. d. is the correct answer. (p. 474; objective 2)

   a. is incorrect. This term describes middle-aged women and men, who are pressured by the needs of both the younger and older generations.

   b. & c. are incorrect. These terms are not used in the textbook.
9. d. is the correct answer. (p. 487; objective 10)
10. b. is the correct answer. (video lesson, segment 3; objective 9)
11. b. is the correct answer. (p. 470; objective 6)

    a. is incorrect. Though some states have legalized same-sex marriage, this has not affected national census rates.

    c. is incorrect. The divorce rate is unrelated.

    d. is incorrect. This pattern was common a century ago.

12. d. is the correct answer. (pp. 459–460; video lesson, segment 1; objective 3)

13. a. is the correct answer. (p. 460; video lesson, segment 1; objective 3)

    b. is incorrect. This is the tendency to be kind and helpful.

    c. is incorrect. This is the tendency to be organized, deliberate, and conforming.

    d. is incorrect. This is the tendency to be anxious, moody, and self-punishing.

14. c. is the correct answer. (p. 463; objective 5)

15. b. is the correct answer. (p. 461; video lesson, segment 1; objective 4)

True or False Items

16. F Studies have found that crises at midlife are not inevitable. (p. 459; video lesson, introduction; objective 1)

17. T (p. 459; video lesson, segment 1; objective 1)

18. T (p. 460; video lesson, segment 1; objective 3)

19. F In fact, the current cohort is less marked in their convergence of sex roles because male and female roles are already less sharply defined than before. (p. 463; objective 5)

20. F The extended family is typical of traditional societies, but not those in North America. (p. 466; objective 8)

21. F Just the opposite is true. (pp. 465–466; objective 8)

22. T (p. 470; objective 6)

23. T (p. 473; objective 7)

24. T (p. 472; objective 7)

25. F (p. 472; video lesson, segment 1; objective 7)

Practice Questions II

1. a. is the correct answer. (video lesson, introduction; objective 1)

2. c. is the correct answer. (p. 460; video lesson, segment 1; objective 4)

3. d. is the correct answer. Grandparents are most likely to act as surrogate parents if the parents are poor, young, unemployed, drug or alcohol addicted, or single or newly divorced, or if the child needs intensive involvement or is rebellious (as in b.). (p. 476; objective 2)

4. c. is the correct answer. (pp. 460–461; video lesson, segment 1; objective 4)

5. d. is the correct answer. (pp. 459–460; video lesson, segment 1; objective 3)

6. d. is the correct answer. (pp. 465–467; objective 8)

7. a. is the correct answer. (p. 474; objective 2)

   c. is incorrect. The relationship improves for both men and women.

d. is incorrect. It generally improves, especially if the children have emerged from adolescence successfully. Most of today's elderly are healthy, active, and independent, and this gives them and their grown children a measure of freedom and privacy that enhances the relationship between them.

8. d. is the correct answer. (pp. 468–470; video lesson, segments 2 & 3; objective 6)
9. c. is the correct answer. (p. 478; video lesson, segment 3; objective 9)
10. a. is the correct answer. (p. 479; objective 9)
11. b is the correct answer. (p. 479; video lesson, segment 1; objective 9)
12. a. is the correct answer. (p. 486 objective 10)
13. a. is the correct answer. (p. 487; video lesson, segment 1; objective 10)

Matching Items

14. b (p. 486; objective 10)
15. f (p. 474; objectives 2)
16. i (p. 477; video lesson, segment 2; objective 2)
17. k (p. 457; objective 1)
18. d (p. 467; objective 8)
19. a (p. 460; video lesson, segment 1; objective 3)
20. g (p. 460; video lesson, segment 1; objective 3)
21. e (p. 460; video lesson, segment 1; objective 3)
22. j (p. 460; video lesson, segment 1; objective 3)
23. c (p. 460; video lesson, segment 1; objective 3)
24. h (p. 480; objective 9)
25. l (p. 464; objective 8)

Applying Your Knowledge

1. d. is the correct answer. (p. 457; video lesson, segment 3; objective 1)

   b. & c. are incorrect. Ken's feelings are common in middle-aged male workers, and are not necessarily indicative of neuroticism.

   d. is incorrect. The sandwich generation refers to middle-aged adults being squeezed by the needs of the younger and older generations.
2. c. is the correct answer. (p. 460; video lesson, segment 1; objective 3)
3. d. is the correct answer. Researchers have found no evidence that a midlife crisis is inevitable in middle adulthood. (p. 459; video lesson, introduction; objective 1)
4. b. is the correct answer. This is an example of the convergence of gender roles during middle adulthood. (p. 463; objective 5)

a. & d. are incorrect. Extroversion is a relatively stable personality trait. Moreover, there is no gender difference in the developmental trajectory of this trait.

c. is incorrect. There is no gender difference in life satisfaction at any age.

5. b. is the correct answer. Because women tend to be kinkeepers, Rebecca is likely to play a larger role than her brother. (pp. 474–477; objective 2)

   d. is incorrect. The relationship of education to care of frail parents is not discussed in the textbook.

6. b. is the correct answer. (p. 468; video lesson, introduction; objective 6)

7. c. is the correct answer. (pp. 468–471; objective 6)

   a. is incorrect. Marital satisfaction can be an important buffer against midlife stress.

   d. is incorrect. There is no reason to believe Nancy's concern is abnormal, or neurotic.

8. d. is the correct answer. (p. 472; video lesson, segment 2; objective 7)

9. d. is the correct answer. (pp. 477–478; video lesson, segments 2 & 3; objectives 2 & 9)

10. c. is the correct answer. (p. 488; video lesson, segment 1; objective 10)

11. c. is the correct answer. Openness to new experiences might make these life experiences less threatening. (p. 460; video lesson, segment 1; objective 3)

Lesson Review

Lesson 22

Middle Adulthood
Psychosocial Development

Please Note: Use this matrix to guide your study and achieve the learning objectives of this lesson. It will also help you to view the video, which defines and demonstrates important concepts and skills as they relate to everyday life.

Learning Objective	Textbook	Telecourse Student Guide	Video Lesson
1. Discuss Erikson's and Maslow's ideas on the stages of adulthood and explain how the social clock influences the timing of important events during adulthood.	pp. 456–459	Key Terms: 1, 2; Practice Questions I: 3, 16, 17; Practice Questions II: 1, 17; Applying Your Knowledge: 1, 3.	Introduction; Segment 1: *Personality Throughout Adulthood*
2. Describe the caregiving roles of middle-aged adults and explain why middle-aged adults are considered the "sandwich generation."	pp. 473–478	Key Terms: 9, 10; Practice Questions I: 6, 7, 8; Practice Questions II: 3, 7, 15, 16; Applying Your Knowledge: 5, 9.	Segment 2: *Family Relationships*
3. Describe the Big Five clusters of personality traits, and discuss reasons for their relative stability during adulthood.	pp. 459–460	Practice Questions I: 1, 2, 12, 13, 18; Practice Questions II: 5, 19, 20, 21, 22, 23; Applying Your Knowledge: 2, 11.	Segment 1: *Personality Throughout Adulthood*
4. Explain the concept of an ecological niche, noting how it interacts with personality.	pp. 460–462	Key Terms: 3; Practice Questions I: 4, 15; Practice Questions II: 2, 4.	Segment 1: *Personality Throughout Adulthood*
5. Explain the tendency toward gender role convergence during middle age.	pp. 463–464	Key Terms: 4; Practice Questions I: 5, 14, 19; Applying Your Knowledge: 4.	

Learning Objective	Textbook	Telecourse Student Guide	Video Lesson
6. Discuss how and why marital relationships tend to change during middle adulthood.	pp. 467–471	Key Terms: 8; Practice Questions I: 11, 22; Practice Questions II: 8; Applying Your Knowledge: 6, 7.	Introduction; Segment 2: *Family Relationships;* Segment 3: *Work and Life*
7. Discuss the impact of divorce and remarriage during middle adulthood, including reasons for the high divorce rate among the remarried.	pp. 471–473	Practice Questions I: 23, 24, 25; Applying Your Knowledge: 8.	Segment 2: *Family Relationships*
8. Describe the components of the social convoy, and explain this convoy's increasing importance during middle adulthood.	pp. 464–467	Key Terms: 5, 6, 7; Practice Questions I: 20, 21; Practice Questions II: 6, 18, 25.	
9. Describe how the balance among work, family, and self often shifts during middle adulthood.	pp. 478–485	Key Terms: 11, 12, 13, 14, 15, 16, 22; Practice Questions I: 10; Practice Questions II: 9, 10, 11, 24; Applying Your Knowledge: 9.	Segment 3: *Work and Life*
10. Define allostatic load, discuss the affects of stress in middle adulthood and explain some measures that can be employed to reduce it.	pp. 485–489	Key Terms: 17, 18, 19, 20, 21; Practice Questions I: 9; Practice Questions II: 12, 13, 14; Applying Your Knowledge: 10.	Segment 1: *Personality Throughout Adulthood*

Accepting the Challenge

Lesson 23

Late Adulthood: Biosocial Development

Preview

This lesson deals with biosocial development during the years from age 65 and beyond. It begins by discussing the myths and reality of this final stage of the life span. In modern U.S. society, which glorifies youth, there is a tendency to exaggerate the physical decline brought on by aging. In fact, the changes that occur during the later years are largely a continuation of those that began earlier in adulthood, and most elderly adults consider themselves to be in good health.

Nevertheless, the aging process is characterized by various changes in appearance, by an increased incidence of impaired vision and hearing, and by declines in the major body systems. These are all changes to which the individual must adjust. In addition, the incidence of chronic diseases increases significantly with age.

Several theories have been advanced to explain the aging process. The theories that are best supported focus on cellular malfunctions, declining immune function, and our genetic makeup. However, environment and lifestyle factors also play a role, as is apparent from studies of those who live a long life.

Prior Telecourse Knowledge that Will Be Used in this Lesson

- Biosocial development during early adulthood (Lesson 17) and middle adulthood (Lesson 20) will be referred to as we discuss normal changes in late adulthood and reasons for variations in health.
- The epigenetic theory (Lesson 2) will be referred to as we discuss the maximum life span of human beings.

Learning Objectives

Use this information to guide your reading, viewing, thinking, and studying. After successfully completing this lesson, you should be able to:

1. Define ageism, and identify two reasons for changing views about old age.
2. Describe ongoing changes in the age distribution and life expectancy of the U.S. population.
3. Distinguish among three categories of the aged, and explain the current state of the dependency ratio.
4. Differentiate between primary and secondary aging, and discuss cardiovascular disease in relationship to both types of aging.
5. Describe age-related problems in vision and hearing and discuss ageism relative to these sensory problems.
6. Discuss the adjustments older adults may have to make in various areas of life using selective optimization with compensation in order to maintain optimal functioning.
7. Identify several reasons that the incidence of chronic disease increases significantly with age, and explain the concept of compression of morbidity.
8. Explain senescence from an epigenetic theory perspective.
9. Discuss the role of genetics in aging, and explain what the Hayflick limit is and how it supports the idea of a genetic clock.
10. Identify lifestyle characteristics associated with the healthy, long-lived adult.
11. Discuss nutritional and exercise needs during late adulthood and suggest how these might best be met, and describe how drug use affects the elderly.

Read Chapter 14, "Late Adulthood: Body and Mind," pages 497–511 and 527.

View the video for Lesson 23, "Accepting the Challenge."

Segment 1: ***The Realities of Aging***
Segment 2: ***Primary and Secondary Aging***
Segment 3: ***The Genetics of Aging***
Segment 4: ***Enhancing Longevity***

Summary

Most people's perception of late adulthood is much worse than the reality. **Ageism**, or prejudice against the elderly, fosters harmful stereotypes that work to seriously limit and isolate older adults. Ageism reflects modern U.S. culture's veneration of youthfulness as well as the increasing age segregation of society, which limits contact between the oldest generation and younger ones. Ironically, many professionals who work with the elderly—including those specializing in **gerontology**, the study of old age—have inadvertently fostered ageism by focusing on the difficulties and "declines" of old age, rather than on its strengths and stability. They have also tended to base their studies of the elderly on residents of nursing homes, while largely ignoring those adults who have remained active.

Today, the fastest growing age group in the United States is persons over age 75. If present trends continue, by the year 2025, we will witness a "squaring of the pyramid": the American population will be divided into thirds, with one-third below age 30, one-third between 30 and 59, and one-third age 60 and over. This will create a somewhat unbalanced **dependency ratio** of self-sufficient productive adults to dependents.

Developmentalists distinguish between the irreversible changes that occur with time (primary aging) and changes that are caused by particular conditions or illness (secondary aging). Although many changes are apparent in the skin, hair, body shape, sensory organs, brain, and body systems of older adults, the aging process is not inevitably associated with disease. Aging does, however, make people more susceptible to chronic illness, due in part to the decreased efficiency of the immune system. In addition, the physical changes in appearance described above can have serious social and psychological implications for older adults if they accept ageist stereotypes and allow their behavior, attitudes, and self-concept to be defined and conditioned by their appearance. As the textbook describes, the examples of the **young-old**, **old-old**, and **oldest-old** indicate that aging may be optimal, usual, or impaired. Optimal aging requires active adjustment to body changes rather than passive acceptance. To have the most beneficial impact, medical interventions and lifestyle changes should take place during usual aging—typically during early or middle adulthood.

Many theories of aging have been proposed. More plausible than the usual wear-and-tear theories are cellular theories of senescence, including those proposing that increases in oxygen free radicals, declining immune function, or the eventual production of error catastrophe in cellular replication, may be instrumental in the aging process. Genetic diseases such as Down syndrome and progeria suggest the existence of a **genetic clock** that programs aging and determines the maximum life span of each species. Even when cells are cultured under ideal laboratory conditions, replication is finite—that is, constrained at a certain point, called the **Hayflick limit**.

People who live unusually long lives often share several characteristics. These include a moderate diet, daily exercise and relaxation, and life in rural, mountainous environments that promote fitness and minimize exposure to pollutants.

Review all reading assignments for this lesson.

As assigned by your instructor, complete the optional online component for this lesson.

Key Terms

Using your own words, write a brief definition or explanation of each of the following terms on a separate piece of paper.

1. ageism
2. elderspeak
3. young-old
4. old-old
5. oldest-old
6. population pyramid
7. dependency ratio
8. compression of morbidity
9. primary aging
10. secondary aging
11. cardiovascular disease (CVD)
12. maximum life span
13. average life expectancy
14. centenarian
15. calorie restriction
16. gerontology
17. healthism
18. selective optimization with compensation
19. genetic clock
20. Hayflick limit
21. epigenetic systems perspective

Practice Questions I

Multiple-Choice Questions

1. Ageism is
   a. the study of aging and the aged.
   b. prejudice or discrimination against older people.
   c. the genetic disease that causes children to age prematurely.
   d. the view of aging that the body and its parts deteriorate with use.

2. The U.S. demographic pyramid is becoming more of a square because of

   a. increasing birth rates and life spans.
   b. decreasing birth rates and life spans.
   c. decreasing birth rates and increasing life spans.
   d. rapid population growth.

3. Primary aging refers to the

   a. changes that are caused by illness.
   b. changes that can be reversed or prevented.
   c. irreversible changes that occur with time.
   d. changes that are caused by poor health habits.

4. Auditory losses with age are more serious than visual losses because

   a. they affect a far larger segment of America's elderly population.
   b. they are more difficult for doctors to diagnose than are visual losses.
   c. hearing aids, in contrast to glasses, are ineffective as a corrective measure.
   d. those who suffer from them are less likely to take the necessary corrective steps.

5. Which disease involves the hardening of the eyeball due to the buildup of fluid?

   a. cataracts
   b. glaucoma
   c. senile macular degeneration
   d. myopia

6. Factors that explain the increased incidence of chronic diseases during late adulthood include all of the following **EXCEPT**

   a. increased hypochondria.
   b. accumulated risk factors.
   c. decreased efficiency of body systems.
   d. diminished immunity.

7. A direct result of damage to cellular DNA is

   a. errors in the reproduction of cells.
   b. an increase in the formation of free radicals.
   c. decreased efficiency of the immune system.
   d. the occurrence of a disease called progeria.

8. The epigenetic theory of aging says
    a. aging is the result of cellular accidents.
    b. aging is the result of immune system deficiency.
    c. aging is caused by the interaction of genes and the environment.
    d. aging is caused by the genetic clock.

9. According to the theory of a genetic clock, aging
    a. is actually directed by the genes.
    b. occurs as a result of damage to the genes.
    c. occurs as a result of hormonal abnormalities.
    d. can be reversed through environmental changes.

10. Laboratory research on the reproduction of cells cultured from humans and animals has found that
    a. cell division cannot occur outside the organism.
    b. the number of cell divisions was the same regardless of the species of the donor.
    c. the number of cell divisions was different depending on the age of the donor.
    d. under the ideal conditions of the laboratory, cell division can continue indefinitely.

11. Which of the following is the best example of selective optimization with compensation?
    a. an older person walking more slowly to protect herself from falling
    b. a college student choosing to major in gerontology because the job prospects are good
    c. a factory worker choosing to work the night shift so that he can be home with his children during the day
    d. choosing to walk to the store instead of driving to get some exercise

12. Anti-aging remedies in the form of genetic treatments and pharmaceuticals have become popular lately. Antioxidents in the form of vitamin and food supplements are said to prevent aging by
    a. attacking free radicals.
    b. delivering more oxygen to the cells.
    c. combating the loss of bone mass.
    d. restoring collagens to the skin.

13. In triggering our first maturational changes and then the aging process, our genetic makeup is in effect acting as
    a. an immune system.
    b. a cellular accident.
    c. a demographic pyramid.
    d. a genetic clock.

14. Antibiotics impair the body's ability to absorb
    a. iron.
    b. calcium.
    c. vitamin K.
    d. all of the above.

15. Aging demands that changes be made in nutritional intake. Which of the following statements is true regarding nutrition in the elderly?
    a. The quantities of food should be increased to achieve maximum nutrition.
    b. The quantities of food should be decreased but quality of food should be increased.
    c. Older adults should drink 8 servings of fluid per day.
    d. b and c only

True or False Items

Write T (for true) or F (for false) on the line in front of each statement.

16. _____ Younger adults tend to overestimate the proportion of the elderly who suffer from infirmity just because they are old.

17. _____ Older people benefit more from lifting weights than younger people do because they are more likely to be out of shape.

18. _____ Because of demographic changes, the majority of America's elderly population is now predominantly "old-old" rather than "young-old."

19. _____ Gerontologists focus on distinguishing aging in terms of the quality of aging, that is, in terms of young-old versus old-old.

20. _____ Genetic engineering is one possibility for increasing life span, but it is considered a drastic measure by many scientists.

21. _____ The likelihood of cardiovascular disease is related less to age than to risk factors affected by health habits and genes.

22. _____ Adding or altering human genes is a trusted method for slowing the aging process.

23. _____ Although the average life expectancy is increasing, the maximum life span has remained unchanged.

24. _____ In view of changed nutritional needs during late adulthood, nutritionists generally recommend that the elderly supplement their diet with large doses of vitamins.

25. _____ The importance of lifestyle factors in contributing to longevity is underscored by studies of the long-lived.

Practice Questions II

Multiple-Choice Questions

1. People tend to view late adulthood more negatively than is actually the case because
   a. they are afraid of their own impending death.
   b. of the tendency to categorize and judge people on the basis of a single characteristic.
   c. of actual experiences with older people.
   d. they were taught to do so from an early age by their parents.

2. An important demographic change in the United States is that
   a. ageism is beginning to diminish.
   b. population growth has virtually ceased.
   c. the median age is falling.
   d. the number of older people in the population is increasing.

3. Which of the following are risks for cardiovascular disease?
   a. hypertension
   b. regular exercise
   c. smoking
   d. a and c only

4. Which of the following statements is true regarding heart disease and cancer?
   a. They are caused by aging.
   b. They are genetic diseases.
   c. They are examples of secondary aging.
   d. all of the above

5. As a result of the _______________ birth rate, the population dependency ratio in the United States is _______________ than it was at the turn of the twentieth century.

   a. increasing; higher
   b. increasing; lower
   c. decreasing; higher
   d. decreasing; lower

6. Which environmental factors can affect life expectancy?

   a. historical factors
   b. cultural factors
   c. socioeconomic factors
   d. all of the above

7. The oldest age to which a human can live is ultimately limited by

   a. cellular accidents.
   b. the maximum life span.
   c. the average life expectancy.
   d. the Hayflick limit.

8. The work of Leonard Hayflick provides support for explanations of aging that focus on

   a. wear and tear.
   b. cellular accidents.
   c. cross-linkage.
   d. a genetic clock.

9. Senile macular degeneration is

   a. the leading cause of deafness among the elderly.
   b. an eye disease in which the retina deteriorates.
   c. experienced as a ringing or rhythmic buzzing in the ears.
   d. experienced by one-third of those older than 74.

10. In studies of three regions of the world known for the longevity of their inhabitants, the long-lived showed all of the following characteristics **EXCEPT**

a. their diets were moderate.

b. they were spared from doing any kind of work.

c. they interacted frequently with family members, friends, and neighbors.

d. they engaged in some form of exercise on a daily basis.

11. Ageism affects

a. the older man who refuses a hearing aid.

b. teenagers who walk in groups through the mall.

c. the 60-year-old woman traveling down the freeway.

d. all of the above.

12. In the year 1900, the average life span in the United States was

a. 50.

b. 47.

c. 45.

d. 35.

13. The people who conduct statistical studies of populations and population trends are

a. gerontologists.

b. demographers.

c. ageists.

d. healthists.

14. The stereotype that illness and other affects of aging occur because of bad health habits is referred to as

a. healthism.

b. ageism.

c. racism.

d. none of the above.

Matching Items

Match each definition or description with its corresponding term.

Terms

15. ________	young-old	21. ________	compression of morbidity
16. ________	old-old	22. ________	oxygen free radicals
17. ________	glaucoma	23. ________	Hayflick limit
18. ________	cataracts	24. ________	primary aging
19. ________	gerontology	25. ________	secondary aging
20. ________	elderspeak	26. ________	calorie restriction

Definitions or Descriptions

a. the universal changes that occur as we grow older
b. limiting the time a person is seriously ill before death
c. the number of times a cell replicates before dying
d. unstable atoms with unpaired electrons that damage cells
e. baby talk to elders because they are old
f. the majority of the elderly
g. thickening of the lens of the eye
h. the minority of the elderly
i. the study of human aging
j. age-related changes that are caused by health habits, genes, and other conditions
k. hardening of the eyeball due to the buildup of fluid
l. reducing caloric intake to slow the aging process

Applying Your Knowledge

1. Which of the following is most likely to be a result of ageism?
   a. the participation of the elderly in community activities
   b. laws requiring workers to retire by a certain age
   c. an increase in multigenerational families
   d. greater interest in the study of gerontology

2. Loretta majored in psychology at the local university. Because she wanted to serve her community, she applied to a local agency to study the effects of aging on the elderly. Loretta is a

   a. psychoanalyst.

   b. behaviorist.

   c. gerontologist.

   d. demographer.

3. An 85-year-old man enjoys good health and actively participates in family and community activities. This person is best described as being

   a. ageist.

   b. young-old.

   c. old-old.

   d. a gerontologist.

4. The phrase "the squaring of the pyramid" refers to which of the following statements?

   a. age structure of the United States

   b. increasing birthrate, decreasing longevity

   c. decreasing birthrate, increasing longevity

   d. a and c only

5. Which developmental perspective suggests that each person is born with genetic possibilities that, along with other lifestyle factors, influence his or her life expectancy?

   a. sociocultural

   b. cognitive

   c. learning

   d. epigenetic

6. Given the changes and needs of late adulthood, an older person should probably

   a. avoid most forms of exercise.

   b. follow a regular but slower-paced program of exercise.

   c. exercise for longer periods than younger adults.

   d. focus on swimming and water exercises.

7. With regard to nutrition, most elderly should probably be advised to
   a. take large doses of vitamins and, especially, antioxidants.
   b. eat foods that are high in calories.
   c. consume a varied and healthy diet.
   d. eat large meals but eat less often.

8. Charlotte wants to make sure her elderly grandmother has every nutritional advantage to keep her mind healthy. She should suggest that her grandmother
   a. increase her intake of vitamins and minerals and decrease her caloric intake.
   b. decrease her intake of vitamins and minerals and increase her caloric intake.
   c. increase the amount of medication she takes and decrease her fluid intake.
   d. decrease the amount of medication she takes and increase her fluid intake.

9. Because age is not an accurate predictor of dependency, some gerontologists prefer to use the term ______________ to refer to the young-old, and the term ________________ to refer to the oldest-old.
   a. optimal aging; usual aging
   b. usual aging; impaired aging
   c. impaired aging; optimal aging
   d. optimal aging; impaired aging

10. In concluding her presentation on human longevity, Katrina states that
   a. current average life expectancy is about twice what it was at the turn of the twentieth century.
   b. current maximum life span is about twice what it was at the turn of the twentieth century.
   c. both average life expectancy and maximum life span have increased since the turn of the twentieth century.
   d. although maximum life span has not increased, average life expectancy has, because infants are less likely to die.

Answer Key

Key Terms

1. Ageism is prejudice against older people. (p. 497; video lesson, segment 1; objective 1)
2. Elderspeak is a babyish way of speaking to older adults, using simple sentences, higher pitch, and repetition. (p. 498; objectives 1 & 5)
3. Most elderly people in the United States can be classified as young-old, meaning that they are "healthy and vigorous, relatively well-off financially,

well integrated into the lives of their families and communities, and politically active." (p. 499; objective 3)

4. Older people who are classified as old-old are those who suffer physical, mental, or social problems in later life. (p. 499; objective 3)
5. Elderly adults who are classified as oldest-old are dependent on others for almost everything. (p. 499; objective 3)
6. Population pyramid is a graphic representation of population as a series of stacked bars in which each age cohort is represented by one bar, with the youngest cohort at the bottom. (p. 500; video lesson, segment 1; objective 2)
7. The dependency ratio is the ratio of self-sufficient, productive adults to children and elderly adults. (p. 501; objective 3)
8. Researchers who are interested in improving the health of the elderly focus on a compression of morbidity, that is, a limiting of the time any person spends ill. (video lesson, segment 2; objective 6)
9. Primary aging refers to the universal and irreversible physical changes that occur as people get older. (p. 504; video lesson, segment 2; objective 4)
10. Secondary aging refers to changes that are more common as people age but are caused by health habits, genes, diseases, and other influences that vary from person to person. (p. 504; video lesson, segment 2; objective 4)
11. Cardiovascular disease, which is disease that involved the heart and circulatory system, is categorized as secondary aging, because it is related health habits and risk factors that vary from person to person and are not necessarily age-related. (p. 504; objective 4)
12. The maximum life span is the maximum number of years that a particular species is genetically programmed to live. For humans, the maximum life span is approximately 120 years. (p. 508; objective 2)
13. Average life expectancy is the number of years the average newborn of a particular species is likely to live. (p. 508; video lesson, segment 3; objective 2)
14. A centenarian is a person who has lived 100 years or more. (p. 510; objectives 2 & 3)
15. Calorie restriction is the practice of limiting dietary energy intake, while still consuming sufficient quantities of vitamins, minerals and other important nutrients, for the purpose of improving health and slowing down the aging process. (p. 511; objective 11)
16. Gerontology is the study of old age. (video lesson, segment 1; objective 3)
17. Healthism is the idea that illness and other effects of aging are solely the result of bad health habits. (video lesson, segment 1; objective 1)
18. Selective optimization with compensation is the idea that healthy aging involves assessing abilities realistically, choosing meaningful goals, and

devising effective strategies to accomplish them, despite the limits associated with aging. (video lesson, segment 2; objective 6)

19. According to one theory of aging, our genetic makeup acts, in effect, as a genetic clock, triggering hormonal changes in the brain, regulating cellular processes, and "timing" aging and the moment of death. (video lesson, segment 3; objective 9)
20. The Hayflick limit is the maximum number of times that cells cultured from humans and animals divide before dying. (video lesson, segment 3; objective 9)
21. As applied to aging, the epigenetic systems perspective is the idea that maximum life span is not only genetically determined but also influenced by lifestyle factors. (video lesson, segment 3; objective 8)

Practice Questions I

Multiple-Choice Questions

1. b. is the correct answer. (p. 497; video lesson, segment 1; objective 1)

   a. is incorrect. This is gerontology.

   c. is incorrect. This is progeria.

   d. is incorrect. This is the wear-and-tear theory.
2. c. is the correct answer. (pp. 500–501; video lesson, segment 1; objective 2)
3. c. is the correct answer. (p. 504; video lesson, segment 2; objective 4)

   a., b., & d. are incorrect. These are examples of secondary aging.
4. d. is the correct answer. (p. 502; objective 5)

   a. is incorrect. Visual and auditory losses affect about the same number of aged persons.

   b. & c. are incorrect. Hearing losses are no more difficult to detect, or to correct, than vision losses.
5. b. is the correct answer. (p. 503; objective 5)

   a. is incorrect. Cataracts are caused by a thickening of the lens.

   c. is incorrect. This disease involves deterioration of the retina.

   d. is incorrect. Myopia, which was not discussed in this lesson, is nearsightedness.
6. a. is the correct answer. (pp. 504–505; objective 7)
7. a. is the correct answer. (pp. 504–505, 510–511; objectives 4, 7, & 9)

   b. is incorrect. In fact, free radicals damage DNA, rather than vice versa.

   c. is incorrect. The immune system compensates for, but is not directly affected by, damage to cellular DNA.

   d. is incorrect. This genetic disease occurs too infrequently to be considered a direct result of damage to cellular DNA.
8. c. is the correct answer. (video lesson, segment 3; objective 8)

9. a. is the correct answer. (video lesson, segment 3; objective 9)

   b. & c. are incorrect. According to the genetic clock theory, time, rather than genetic damage or hormonal abnormalities, regulates the aging process.

   d. is incorrect. The genetic clock theory makes no provision for environmental alteration of the genetic mechanisms of aging.

10. c. is the correct answer. (video lesson, segment 3; objective 9)

11. a. is the correct answer. (video lesson, segment 2; objective 6)

12. a. is the correct answer. (p. 511; objective 9)

13. d. is the correct answer. (video lesson, segment 3; objective 9)

    a. is incorrect. This is the body's system for defending itself against bacteria and other "invaders."

    b. is incorrect. This is the theory that aging is caused by mutations in the cell structure or in the normal course of DNA repair.

    c. is incorrect. This is a metaphor for the distribution of age groups, with the largest and youngest group at the bottom, and the smallest and oldest group at the top.

14. d. is the correct answer. B-cells create antibodies that repair rather than damage cells. (pp. 505–506; video lesson, segments 2 & 4; objective 11)

15. d. is the correct answer. (p. 506; objectives 10 & 11)

True or False Items

16. T (video lesson, segment 1; objective 1)

17. T (p. 506; objectives 10 & 11)

18. F Although our population is aging, the terms old-old and young-old refer to degree of physical and social well-being, not to age. (pp. 499–500; objective 3)

19. T (pp. 499–500; video lesson, segment 1; objective 3)

20. T (pp. 510–511; objective 9)

21. T (pp. 504–505; objective 4)

22. F (p. 511; objective 9)

23. T (p. 508; video lesson, segment 3; objective 2)

24. F Research has shown that large doses of vitamins may be harmful. (pp. 505–506; objective 11)

25. T (pp. 498–499, 505–508; video lesson, segments 2 & 4; objectives 1 & 10)

Practice Questions II

1. b. is the correct answer. (p. 497; video lesson, segment 1; objective 1)

2. d. is the correct answer. (pp. 500–501; video lesson, segment 1; objective 2)

   a. is incorrect. Ageism is prejudice, not a demographic change.

b. is incorrect. Although birth rates have fallen, population growth has not ceased.

c. is incorrect. Actually, with the "squaring of the pyramid," the median age is rising.

3. d. is the correct answer. (p. 505; objective 4)
4. c. is the correct answer. (pp. 504–505; video lesson, segment 2; objectives 4 & 7)

   a. & b. are incorrect. Over time, the interaction of accumulating risk factors with age-related weakening of the heart and relevant genetic weaknesses makes the elderly increasingly vulnerable to heart disease.
5. d. is the correct answer. (p. 501; objective 3)
6. d. is the correct answer. (video lesson, segment 4; objective 8)
7. b. is the correct answer. (p. 508; video lesson, segment 3; objectives 2 & 9)

   a. is incorrect. This is a theory of aging.

   c. is incorrect. This statistic refers to the number of years the average newborn of a particular species is likely to live.

   d. is incorrect. This is the number of times a cultured cell replicates before dying.
8. d. is the correct answer. (video lesson, segment 3; objective 9)
9. b. is the correct answer. (pp. 497–503; objective 5)

   a. is incorrect. Senile macular degeneration is an eye disease.

   c. is incorrect. This describes tinnitus.

   d. is incorrect. Senile macular degeneration affects one in six of those older than 80.
10. b. is the correct answer. In fact, just the opposite is true. (pp. 509–510; objective 10)
11. d. is the correct answer. (pp. 497–503; video lesson, segment 1; objective 5)
12. d. is the correct answer. (video lesson, segment 1; objective 2)
13. b. is the correct answer. (p. 500; video lesson, segment 1; objective 2)

    a. is incorrect. This is the study of old age.

    c. is incorrect. This is prejudice against the elderly.

    d. is incorrect. This is the weakening and decline of the body that occurs with age.
14. a. is the correct answer. (video lesson, segment 1; objective 1)

Matching Items

15. f (p. 499; objective 3)
16. h (p. 499; objective 3)
17. k (p. 503; objective 5)
18. g (p. 503; objective 5)

19. i (video lesson, segment 1; objective 3)
20. e (p. 498; objectives 1 & 5)
21. b (p. 502; video lesson, segment 2; objective 7)
22. d (p. 511; objective 9)
23. c (video lesson, segment 3; objective 9)
24. a (p. 504; video lesson, segment 2; objective 4)
25. j (p. 504; video lesson, segment 2; objective 4)
26. l (p. 511; objective 11)

Applying Your Knowledge

1. b. is the correct answer. (video lesson, segment 1; objective 1)
2. c. is the correct answer. (video lesson, segment 1; objective 2)

   a. is incorrect. A psychoanalyst does not necessarily specialize in treating the aged.

   b. is incorrect. Behaviorism describes her approach to studying, not what she is studying.

   d. is incorrect. Demographics is the study of populations.
3. b. is the correct answer. (p. 499; objective 3)

   a. is incorrect. An ageist is a person who is prejudiced against the elderly.

   c. is incorrect. People who are "old-old" have social, physical, and mental problems that hamper their successful aging.

   d. is incorrect. A gerontologist is a person who studies aging.
4. d. is the correct answer. (p. 500; video lesson, segment 1; objective 2)
5. d. is the correct answer. (video lesson, segment 3; objective 8)
6. b. is the correct answer. (pp. 506–507; objectives 6 & 11)

   c. & d. are incorrect. Older adults need not exercise longer, nor should their exercise be limited to water activities.
7. c. is the correct answer. (pp. 505–506; objective 11)

   a. is incorrect. Large doses of vitamins can be harmful.

   b. is incorrect. Older adults need fewer calories to maintain body weight.

   d. is incorrect. This is an unhealthy dietary regimen.
8. a. is the correct answer. (pp. 505–506; objective 11)
9. d. is the correct answer. (p. 500; objective 3)
10. d. is the correct answer. (p. 508; objective 2)

    a. is incorrect. Current average life expectancy is twenty-eight years more than it was at the turn of the twentieth century.

    b. & c. are incorrect. Maximum life span has not changed since the turn of the twentieth century.

Lesson Review

Lesson 23

Late Adulthood
Biosocial Development

Please Note: Use this matrix to guide your study and achieve the learning objectives of this lesson. It will also help you to view the video, which defines and demonstrates important concepts and skills as they relate to everyday life.

Learning Objective	Textbook	Telecourse Student Guide	Video Lesson
1. Define ageism, and identify two reasons for changing views about old age.	pp. 497–499	Key Terms: 1, 2, 17; Practice Questions I: 1, 16, 25; Practice Questions II: 1, 14, 20; Applying Your Knowledge: 1.	Segment 1: *The Realities of Aging;* Segment 2: *Primary and Secondary Aging;* Segment 3: *The Genetics of Aging;* Segment 4: *Enhancing Longevity*
2. Describe ongoing changes in the age distribution and life expectancy of the U.S. population.	pp. 500–501, 508–509	Key Terms: 6, 12, 13, 14; Practice Questions I: 2, 23; Practice Questions II: 2, 7, 12, 13; Applying Your Knowledge: 2, 4, 10.	Segment 1: *The Realities of Aging;* Segment 3: *The Genetics of Aging*
3. Distinguish among three categories of the aged, and explain the current state of the dependency ratio.	pp. 499–502	Key Terms: 3, 4, 5, 7, 14, 16; Practice Questions I: 18, 19; Practice Questions II: 5, 15, 16, 19; Applying Your Knowledge: 3, 9.	Segment 1: *The Realities of Aging*
4. Differentiate between primary and secondary aging, and discuss cardiovascular disease in relationship to both types of aging.	pp. 504–505	Key Terms: 9, 10, 11; Practice Questions I: 3, 7, 21; Practice Questions II: 3, 4, 24, 25.	Segment 2: *Primary and Secondary Aging*
5. Describe age-related problems in vision and hearing and discuss ageism relative to these sensory problems.	pp. 502–504	Key Terms: 2; Practice Questions I: 4, 5; Practice Questions II: 9, 11, 17, 18, 20.	Segment 1: *The Realities of Aging*

Learning Objective	**Textbook**	**Telecourse Student Guide**	**Video Lesson**
6. Discuss the adjustments older adults may have to make in various areas of life using selective optimization with compensation in order to maintain optimal functioning.	pp. 506–507	Key Terms: 8, 18; Practice Questions I: 11; Applying Your Knowledge: 6.	Segment 2: *Primary and Secondary Aging*
7. Identify several reasons that the incidence of chronic disease increases significantly with age, and explain the concept of compression of morbidity.	pp. 502, 504–505, 509–510	Practice Questions I: 6, 7; Practice Questions II: 4, 21.	Segment 2: *Primary and Secondary Aging*
8. Explain senescence from an epigenetic theory perspective.	*	Key Terms: 21; Practice Questions I: 8; Practice Questions II: 6; Applying Your Knowledge: 5.	Segment 3: *The Genetics of Aging;* Segment 4: *Enhancing Longevity*
9. Discuss the role of genetics in aging, and explain what the Hayflick limit is and how it supports the idea of a genetic clock.	pp. 509, 510–511	Key Terms: 19, 20; Practice Questions I: 7, 9, 10, 12, 13, 20, 22; Practice Questions II: 7, 8, 22, 23.	Segment 3: *The Genetics of Aging*
10. Identify lifestyle characteristics associated with the healthy, long-lived adult.	pp. 505–508	Practice Questions I: 15, 17, 25; Practice Questions II: 10.	Segment 2: *Primary and Secondary Aging;* Segment 4: *Enhancing Longevity*
11. Discuss nutritional and exercise needs during late adulthood, suggest how these might best be met, and describe how drug use affects the elderly.	pp. 505–508	Key Terms: 15; Practice Questions I: 14, 15, 17, 24; Practice Questions II: 26; Applying Your Knowledge: 6, 7, 8.	Segment 2: *Primary and Secondary Aging;* Segment 4: *Enhancing Longevity*

* The video for this lesson provides a useful exploration of these topics.

Making Memories

Lesson 24

Late Adulthood: Cognitive Development

Preview

This lesson describes the changes in cognitive functioning associated with late adulthood. The lesson first reviews the parts of the information-processing system, providing experimental evidence that suggests declines in both the information-processing and the problem-solving abilities of older adults. Next, neurological and other reasons for this decline are discussed.

Despite these cognitive declines, as the lesson next points out, real-life conditions provide older adults with ample opportunity to compensate for the pattern of decline observed in the laboratory. It appears that, for most people, cognitive functioning in daily life remains essentially unimpaired.

The main exception to the generally positive picture of cognitive functioning during late adulthood is dementia, the subject of the fourth section of the lesson. This pathological loss of intellectual ability can be caused by a variety of diseases and circumstances; risk factors, treatment, and prognosis differ accordingly.

The final section of the lesson makes it clear that cognitive changes during late adulthood are by no means restricted to declines in intellectual functioning. For many individuals, late adulthood is a time of great aesthetic, creative, philosophical, and spiritual growth.

Prior Telecourse Knowledge that Will Be Used in this Lesson

- Cognitive development during early adulthood (Lesson 18) and middle adulthood (Lesson 21) will be referred to as we discuss normal changes in information processing during late adulthood.
- The information-processing theory (Lesson 2) will be referred to as we discuss age-related changes in memory.

- Erik Erikson's psychosocial theory of development (Lesson 2) will be referred to as we discuss new cognitive development in later life.

Learning Objectives

Use this information to guide your reading, viewing, thinking, and studying. After successfully completing this lesson, you should be able to:

1. Using the information-processing approach, list the four steps of cognition as outlined in your textbook, summarize the first step of input (sensing) in late adulthood, explain the capacity of working memory, and note how long-term memory is assessed.
2. Summarize the concept of ecological validity in regard to older adults' ability to access the knowledge base and to use control processes, and explain the findings of the Seattle Longitudinal Study on cognitive output.
3. Suggest several reasons, other than the aging process itself, that might contribute to age-related declines in cognitive functioning.
4. Describe the aging brain in regard to brain slowdown and brain shrinkage, recognize the variations in brain use among older adults, and identify the benefits of using more areas of the brain in thinking processes.
5. Characterize and explain discrepancies between how the elderly perform on memory and problem-solving tasks in the laboratory, on one hand, and in daily life, on the other.
6. Identify the two most common forms of dementia and discuss the differences between them.
7. Identify and describe other dementias and their organic causes, as well as causes of reversible dementia.
8. Discuss the claims of developmentalists regarding the possibility of positive cognitive development during late adulthood, and discuss Erikson's and Maslow's ideas on integrity, self-actualization, and life review.

Read Chapter 14, "Late Adulthood: Body and Mind," pages 512–527.

View the video for Lesson 24, "Making Memories."

Segment 1: ***Changes in Information Processing***

Segment 2: ***Age-Related Changes***

Segment 3: ***Dementia***

Segment 4: ***Enhancing Cognitive Abilities***

Summary

Lesson 24 discusses the changes in information processing experienced by older adults. As measured by standardized laboratory tests (which are often biased against the older adult), some cognitive processes become slower and less efficient during late adulthood. In part, this is because laboratory techniques focus on tasks such as memorizing meaningless lists of words. This removes cultural bias but also removes the advantages of cultural knowledge, which older adults use as a memory aid to a greater extent than younger adults.

Senescence may create small decrements (gradual decreases) in the sensitivity of the sensory register. As a result, it takes longer to register sensory information and the information fades more quickly. Of all the aspects of information processing, working memory (short-term memory) is the component that shows the most substantial declines with age. In terms of both storage and processing functions, older adults seem to have smaller working-memory capacity than do younger adults. Older individuals are particularly likely to experience difficulty holding new information in mind while simultaneously analyzing it in complex ways. Research suggests that older adults may need more time to actively process items to be remembered, as well as to get information into storage. In adults, the knowledge base includes the subcomponents of short-term memory, which stores information for a minute or two, and long-term memory, which stores information for years or decades. Both short- and long-term memory take two distinct forms, each originating in a different area of the brain. **Implicit memory** is automatic, unconscious memory involving habits, emotional responses, routine procedures, and the senses. **Explicit memory** is conscious memory for words, data, concepts, and the like. Implicit memory is much less vulnerable to age-related deficits than explicit memory is. As people get older, differences in implicit and explicit memory might be reflected.

Age-related declines in cognitive functioning may result from the neurophysiological changes tied to aging, which include the progressive loss of brain cells and, more important, the slowing of brain processes as the result of reduced production of key neurotransmitters. Most older adults are not hampered in their daily life by cognitive difficulties. Through their use of compensating memory techniques, older adults are able to function acceptably. A hallmark of successful aging is selective optimization with compensation, or the ability to compensate for age-related declines in intellectual functioning. The rate at which thinking slows down with age can be reduced with regular exercise, which improves blood flow in the brain.

Lesson 24 also explores the loss of cognitive function suffered by victims of dementia. The most common forms of dementia are **Alzheimer's disease** and **multi-infarct dementia**. Several other diseases can cause dementia—among them Parkinson's disease, Huntington's disease, and multiple sclerosis. Many other problems, such as alcohol and drug abuse and psychological illness, are misdiagnosed as dementia.

As emphasized by such theorists as Abraham Maslow and Erik Erikson, many older adults show new cognitive development during later life, developing a heightened aesthetic sense, gaining in wisdom, and becoming more philosophical.

Review all reading assignments for this lesson.

As assigned by your instructor, complete the optional online component for this lesson.

Key Terms

Using your own words, write a brief definition or explanation of each of the following terms on a separate piece of paper.

1. ecological validity
2. control processes
3. dementia
4. Alzheimer's disease
5. vascular dementia (VaD)/multi-infarct dementia (MID)
6. frontal lobe dementias
7. self-actualization
8. life review
9. explicit memory
10. implicit memory

Practice Questions I

Multiple-Choice Questions

1. The information-processing component that is concerned with the temporary storage of incoming sensory information is
   a. working memory.
   b. long-term memory.
   c. the knowledge base.
   d. the sensory register/input (sensing).

2. Older adults tend to have the greatest difficulty picking up sensory stimuli that are
   a. very loud or bright.
   b. ambiguous or of low intensity.
   c. abstract or meaningless.
   d. all of the above.

3. The two basic functions of working memory are
   a. storage that enables conscious use and processing of information.
   b. temporary storage and processing of sensory stimuli.
   c. automatic memories and retrieval of learned memories.
   d. permanent storage and retrieval of information.

4. Memory for skills is called
   a. explicit memory.
   b. declarative memory.
   c. episodic memory.
   d. implicit memory.

5. Strategies to retain and retrieve information in the knowledge base are part of which basic component of information processing?
   a. sensory memory (or sensory register)
   b. working memory
   c. control processes
   d. explicit memory

6. The plaques and tangles that accompany Alzheimer's disease usually begin in the
   a. temporal lobe.
   b. frontal lobe.
   c. hippocampus.
   d. cerebral cortex.

7. Secondary aging factors that may explain some declines in cognitive functioning include
   a. fewer opportunities for learning in old age.
   b. disparaging self-perceptions of cognitive abilities.
   c. difficulty with traditional methods of measuring cognitive functioning.
   d. all of the above.

8. Which of the following is a characteristic of laboratory experiments that inhibits the older adult's memory abilities?
   a. practice
   b. priming
   c. motivation
   d. the focus on memorizing materials devoid of cultural significance

9. Dementia refers to
   a. pathological loss of intellectual functioning.
   b. the increasing forgetfulness that sometimes accompanies the aging process.
   c. abnormal behavior associated with mental illness and with advanced stages of alcoholism.
   d. a genetic disorder that doesn't become overtly manifested until late adulthood.

10. Some reversible conditions or situations among the elderly can lead to signs and symptoms of dementia. Some of these include
   a. overmedication.
   b. depression.
   c. emotional problems.
   d. all of the above.

11. Alzheimer's disease is characterized by
   a. a proliferation of plaques and tangles in the cerebral cortex.
   b. a destruction of brain tissue as a result of strokes.
   c. rigidity and tremor of the muscles.
   d. an excess of fluid pressing on the brain.

12. Multi-infarct dementia and Alzheimer's disease differ in their progression in that
   a. multi-infarct dementia never progresses beyond the first stage.
   b. multi-infarct dementia is marked by sudden drops and temporary improvements, whereas decline in Alzheimer's disease is steady.
   c. multi-infarct dementia leads to rapid deterioration and death, whereas Alzheimer's disease may progress over a period of years.
   d. the progression of Alzheimer's disease may be halted or slowed, whereas the progression of multi-infarct dementia is irreversible.

13. Medication may become associated with symptoms of dementia in the elderly for which of the following reasons?
   a. Standard drug dosages are often too strong for the elderly.
   b. The elderly tend to become psychologically dependent upon drugs.
   c. Drugs sometimes have the side effect of slowing mental processes.
   d. All of the above explanations are true.

14. The primary purpose of the life review is to
    a. enhance one's spirituality.
    b. produce an autobiography.
    c. give advice to younger generations.
    d. put one's life into perspective.

True or False Items

Write T (for true) or F (for false) on the line in front of each statement.

15. _____ As long as their vision and hearing remain unimpaired, older adults are no less efficient than younger adults at inputting information.
16. _____ Changes in the sensory register are a major contributor to declines in information processing.
17. _____ Intellectual ability is directly related to the brain's size, weight, and number of cells.
18. _____ A majority of the elderly feel frustrated and hampered by memory loss in their daily lives.
19. _____ The majority of cases of dementia are organically caused.
20. _____ Alzheimer's disease is partly genetic.
21. _____ Late adulthood is often associated with a narrowing of interests and an exclusive focus on the self.
22. _____ According to Maslow, self-actualization is actually more likely to be reached during late adulthood.

Practice Questions II

Multiple-Choice Questions

1. Research suggests that aging results in
    a. increased sensitivity of the sensory register.
    b. a significant decrease in the sensitivity of the sensory register that cannot usually be compensated for.
    c. a small decrease in the sensory register's sensitivity that can usually be compensated for.
    d. no noticeable changes in the sensory register.

2. Which of the following most accurately characterizes age-related changes in working memory?

   a. Both storage capacity and processing efficiency decline.
   b. Storage capacity declines while processing efficiency remains stable.
   c. Storage capacity remains stable while processing efficiency declines.
   d. Both storage capacity and processing efficiency remain stable.

3. Information remembered for years or decades is stored in

   a. sensory register.
   b. working memory.
   c. long-term memory.
   d. short-term memory.

4. Conscious memory for words, data, and concepts is called _______________ memory.

   a. sensory
   b. implicit
   c. explicit
   d. knowledge base

5. In general, with increasing age the control processes used to remember new information

   a. become more efficient.
   b. become more complex.
   c. become more intertwined.
   d. become simpler and less efficient.

6. Control processes include

   a. memory and retrieval strategies.
   b. selective attention.
   c. rules for problem solving.
   d. all the above.

7. Which of the following brain disorders begin with loss of motor control?

   a. Alzheimer's disease
   b. vascular dementia
   c. frontal lobe dementia
   d. Parkinson's disease

8. One study tested memory in different age groups by requiring younger and older adults to remember to make telephone calls at a certain time. It was found that
   a. older adults did worse than younger adults because their memories were not as good.
   b. older adults did better than younger adults because they were able to trust their memories.
   c. older adults did better than younger adults because they didn't trust their memories and therefore used various reminders.
   d. older adults did worse than younger adults because they were less accustomed to having to do things at a certain time.

9. Laboratory studies of memory in late adulthood fail to take into account the effects of
   a. the knowledge base of older adults.
   b. ageism and bias in measuring cognition in late adulthood.
   c. the explicit memory that is central to the functioning of older adults.
   d. the ability of older adults to rely on their long-term memories.

10. Dementia
   a. is more likely to occur among the aged.
   b. has no relationship to age.
   c. cannot occur before the age of 60.
   d. is an inevitable occurrence during late adulthood.

11. The most common form of dementia is
   a. Alzheimer's disease.
   b. multi-infarct dementia.
   c. Parkinson's disease.
   d. alcoholism and depression.

12. Organic causes of dementia include all of the following **EXCEPT**
   a. Parkinson's disease.
   b. strokes.
   c. brain tumors.
   d. leukemia.

13. Of the following psychological illnesses, which is most likely to be misdiagnosed as dementia?

   a. schizophrenia
   b. depression
   c. personality disorder
   d. phobic disorders

14. On balance, it can be concluded that positive cognitive development during late adulthood

   a. occurs only for a small minority of individuals.
   b. leads to thought processes that are more appropriate to the final stage of life.
   c. makes older adults far less pragmatic than younger adults.
   d. is impossible in view of increasing deficits in cognitive functioning.

15. A key factor underlying the older adult's cognitive developments in the realms of aesthetics, philosophy, and spirituality may be

   a. the realization that one's life is drawing to a close.
   b. the despair associated with a sense of isolation from the community.
   c. the need to leave one's mark on history.
   d. a growing indifference to the outside world.

Matching Items

Match each definition or description with its corresponding term.

Terms

16. __________	sensory register	22. __________	Alzheimer's disease
17. __________	working memory	23. __________	multi-infarct dementia (MID)
18. __________	knowledge base	24. __________	Parkinson's disease
19. __________	control processes	25. __________	integrity
20. __________	frontal lobe dementia	26. __________	life review
21. __________	dementia		

Definitions or Descriptions

a. Erikson's eighth stage of development
b. temporarily stores information for conscious processing
c. strategies for retaining and retrieving information
d. severely impaired thinking, memory, or problem-solving ability
e. stores incoming sensory information for a split second

f. caused by a temporary obstruction of the blood vessels
g. information that long term memory stores
h. caused by a degeneration of neurons that produce dopamine
i. putting one's life into perspective
j. characterized by plaques and tangles in the cerebral cortex
k. brain disorders characterized by personality changes

Applying Your Knowledge

1. Cognitive deficits emerge in late adulthood because primary aging causes
   a. sensory deficits.
   b. slower processing.
   c. a buildup of neuronal fluid.
   d. both a and b.

2. Depression among the elderly is a serious problem because
   a. rates of depression are far higher for the elderly than for younger adults.
   b. in late adulthood depression becomes extremely difficult to treat.
   c. depression in the elderly often goes untreated, contributing to a higher rate of mistaken dementia.
   d. organic forms of dementia cause depression.

3. Given the nature of cognitive development, a profession in which an individual's greatest achievements are particularly likely to occur during late adulthood is
   a. medicine.
   b. philosophy.
   c. mathematics.
   d. administration.

4. Developmentalists believe that older people's tendency to reminisce
   a. represents an unhealthy preoccupation with the self and the past.
   b. is an underlying cause of age segregation.
   c. is a necessary and healthy process.
   d. is a result of a heightened aesthetic sense.

5. Because of deficits in the sensory register, older people may tend to
   a. forget the names of people and places.
   b. be distracted by irrelevant stimuli.
   c. miss details in a dimly lit room.
   d. reminisce at length about the past.
6. Holding material in your mind for a minute or two requires which type of memory?
   a. short-term memory
   b. explicit memory
   c. long-term memory
   d. sensory register
7. Which of the following represent ways of compensating for cognitive slowing in old age?
   a. Making a grocery list.
   b. Asking for an appointment reminder from the doctor's office.
   c. Setting an alarm to signal when your favorite television program is about to begin.
   d. All of the above.
8. Which type of material would 72-year-old Jessica probably have the greatest difficulty remembering?
   a. the dates of birth of family members
   b. a short series of numbers she has just heard
   c. vocabulary
   d. technical terms from her field of expertise prior to retirement
9. Concerning the public's fear of Alzheimer's disease, which of the following is true?
   a. A serious loss of memory, such as that occurring in people with Alzheimer's disease, can be expected by most people once they reach their 60s.
   b. The risk rises steeply with age.
   c. Alzheimer's disease is much more common today than it was 50 years ago.
   d. Alzheimer's disease is less common today than it was 50 years ago.

10. Lately, Wayne's father, who is 73, harps on the fact that he forgets small things, such as where he put the house keys, and has trouble eating and sleeping. The family doctor diagnoses Wayne's father as

    a. being in the early stages of Alzheimer's disease.
    b. being in the later stages of Alzheimer's disease.
    c. suffering from senile dementia.
    d. possibly suffering from depression.

Answer Key

Key Terms

1. The idea that memory should be measured as people actually experience it, not as laboratory tests assess it, is called ecological validity. (p. 515; objective 2)
2. Memory control processes, which include strategies for retaining information in the knowledge base, retrieval strategies for reaccessing information, selective attention, and rules or strategies that aid problem solving, tend to become similar and less efficient with age. (p. 516; objective 2)
3. Dementia is severely impaired judgment, memory, or problem-solving ability. (p. 517; video lesson, segment 3; objectives 6 & 7)
4. Alzheimer's disease, a progressive disorder that is the most common form of dementia, is characterized by plaques and tangles in the cerebral cortex that destroy normal brain functioning. (p. 518; video lesson, segment 3; objective 6)
5. Vascular dementia (VaD), or *multi-infarct dementia* (MID), which accounts for about 15 percent of all dementia, occurs because an infarct, or temporary obstruction of the blood vessels (often called a stroke), prevents a sufficient supply of blood from reaching an area of the brain. (p. 519; video lesson, segment 3; objective 6)
6. A form of dementia characterized by personality changes caused by deterioration of the frontal lobes and the amygdala is called frontal lobe dementia. It can also be called *frontotemporal lobar degeneration*. (p. 519; objective 7)
7. The final stage in Maslow's hierarchy of needs, characterized by aesthetic, creative, philosophical, and spiritual understanding, is called self-actualization. (p. 523; objective 8)
8. In the life review, an older person attempts to put his or her life into perspective by recalling and recounting various aspects of life to members of the younger generations. (p. 524; objective 8)

9. Explicit memory is memory of consciously learned words, data, and concepts. This type of memory is more vulnerable to age-related decline than implicit memory. (video lesson, segment 1; objectives 1 & 2)
10. Implicit memory is unconscious or automatic memory involving habits, emotional responses, routine procedures, and the senses. (video lesson, segment 1; objectives 1 & 2)

Practice Questions I

Multiple-Choice Questions

1. d. is the correct answer. (p. 514; video lesson, segment 1; objective 1)

   a. is incorrect. Working memory deals with mental, rather than sensory, activity.

   b. & c. are incorrect. Long-term memory, which is a subcomponent of the knowledge base, includes information that is stored for several minutes to several years.
2. b. is the correct answer. (p. 514; video lesson, segment 1; objective 1)
3. a. is the correct answer. (p. 514; objective 1)

   b. is incorrect. These are the functions of the sensory register.

   c. is incorrect. This refers to long-term memory's processing of implicit and explicit memories, respectively.

   d. is incorrect. This is the function of long-term memory.
4. d. is the correct answer. (video lesson, segment 1; objectives 1 & 2)

   a. & b. are incorrect. Explicit memory is memory of facts and experiences, which is why it is often called declarative memory.

   c. is incorrect. This type of memory, which is a type of explicit memory, was not discussed.
5. c. is the correct answer. (pp. 515–516; objective 2)
6. d. is the correct answer. (p. 518; video lesson, segment 3; objective 6)
7. d. is the correct answer. (video lesson, segment 2; objective 3)
8. d. is the correct answer. (video lesson, segment 2; objectives 3)
9. a. is the correct answer. (p. 517; video lesson, segment 3; objectives 6 & 7)
10. d. is the correct answer. Each of the other answers is an example of subcortical dementia. (pp. 521–522; objective 7)
11. a. is the correct answer. (pp. 518–519; video lesson, segment 3; objective 6)

    b. is incorrect. This describes multi-infarct dementia.

    c. is incorrect. This describes Parkinson's disease.

    d. is incorrect. This was not given in the textbook as a cause of dementia.
12. b. is the correct answer. (pp. 518–519; video lesson, segment 3; objectives 6 & 7)

a. is incorrect. Because multiple infarcts typically occur, the disease is progressive in nature.

c. is incorrect. The textbook does not suggest that MID necessarily leads to quick death.

d. is incorrect. At present, Alzheimer's disease is untreatable.

13. d. is the correct answer. (pp. 521–522; video lesson, segment 3; objective 7)
14. d. is the correct answer. (p. 524; objective 8)

True or False Items

15. F The slowing of perceptual processes and decreases in attention associated with aging are also likely to affect efficiency of input. (pp. 514–516; video lesson, segment 1; objectives 1 & 4)
16. F Small reductions in power and sensitivity of sensory register do occur, but they generally can be compensated for. (pp. 514–515; video lesson, segment 1; objective 1)
17. F These affect intellectual activity only in cases of extreme malformation, damage, or disease. (pp. 512–513; video lesson, segment 2; objectives 3 & 4)
18. F Most older adults perceive some memory loss but do not feel that it affects their daily functioning. (pp. 515–516; video lesson, segment 2; objective 5)
19. T (pp. 517–522; video lesson, segment 3; objectives 6 & 7)
20. T (p. 518; video lesson, segment 3; objective 6)
21. F Interests often broaden during late adulthood, and there is by no means exclusive focus on the self. (pp. 522–525; video lesson, segment 4; objectives 8)
22. T (p. 523; objective 8)

Practice Questions II

1. c. is the correct answer. (p. 514; video lesson, segment 1; objectives 1)
2. a. is the correct answer. (pp. 514–515; video lesson, segment 1; objective 1)
3. c. is the correct answer. (p. 515; video lesson; segment 1; objective 1)

   a. is incorrect. The sensory register stores information for a split second.

   b. is incorrect. Working memory stores information briefly.

   d. is incorrect. Short-term memory is another name for working memory.
4. c. is the correct answer. (video lesson, segment 1; objectives 1 & 2)

   a. is incorrect. Sensory memory, or the sensory register, stores incoming sensory information for only a split second.

   b. is incorrect. This is unconscious, automatic memory for skills.

   d. is incorrect. Explicit memory is only one part of the knowledge base. Another part—implicit memory—is unconscious memory for skills.
5. d. is the correct answer. (p. 516; objective 2)

6. d. is the correct answer. (p. 516; objectives 1, 2, 3, & 5)

   a. & b. are incorrect. Age-related deficits in these types of memory are minimal.

   d. is incorrect. Although explicit memory is part of the knowledge base, another part—implicit memory—shows minimal age-related deficits.

7. d. is the correct answer. More than half of all people inherit neither the protective nor the destructive gene. (p. 519; video lesson, segment 3; objective 7)

8. c. is the correct answer. (p. 513–517; video lesson, segment 1; objectives 1, 3, & 5)

9. b. is the correct answer. (p. 515; objective 5)

10. a. is the correct answer. Although age is not the key factor, it is true that dementia is more likely to occur in older adults. (p. 517; video lesson, segment 3; objective 6)

11. a. is the correct answer. (p. 518; video lesson, segment 3; objective 6)

    b. is incorrect. MID is responsible for about 15 percent of all dementia.

    c. & d. are incorrect. Compared to Alzheimer's disease, which accounts for about 70 percent of all dementia, these account for a much lower percentage.

12. d. is the correct answer. (pp. 519–522; objective 7)

13. b. is the correct answer. (p. 521; objective 7)

    a. & c. are incorrect. These psychological illnesses are less common in the elderly than in younger adults, and less common than depression among the elderly.

    d. is incorrect. This disorder was not discussed in association with dementia.

14. b. is the correct answer. (pp. 522–525; objective 8)

    a. & d. are incorrect. Positive cognitive development is typical of older adults.

    c. is incorrect. Pragmatism is one characteristic of wisdom, an attribute commonly associated with older people.

15. a. is the correct answer. (pp. 523–525; objective 8)

    b. & c. are incorrect. Although these may be true of some older adults, they are not necessarily a key factor in cognitive development during late adulthood.

    d. is incorrect. In fact, older adults are typically more concerned with the whole of human experience.

Matching Items

16. e (p. 514; video lesson, segment 1; objective 1)
17. b (p. 514; video lesson, segment 1; objective 1)
18. g (p. 515; video lesson, segment 1; objective 2)
19. c (pp. 515–516; video lesson, segment 1; objective 2)
20. k (p. 519; objective 7)
21. d (p. 517; video lesson, segment 3; objectives 6 & 7)
22. j (p. 518; video lesson, segment 3; objective 6)
23. f (p. 519; video lesson, segment 3; objective 7)
24. h (p. 519; objective 7)
25. a (p. 523; objective 8)
26. i (p. 524; objective 8)

Applying Your Knowledge

1. d. is the correct answer. (pp. 512–513; objective 4)
2. c. is the correct answer. (p. 521; objective 7)

   a. is incorrect. In general, psychological illnesses are less common in the elderly than in younger adults.

   b. is incorrect. Depression is quite treatable at any age.

   d. is incorrect. Symptoms of depression are often mistaken as signs of dementia.
3. b. is the correct answer. (pp. 522–525; objective 8)
4. c. is the correct answer. (pp. 522–525; objective 8)

   d. is incorrect. This would lead to a greater appreciation of nature and art, but not necessarily to a tendency to reminisce.
5. c. is the correct answer. (p. 514; video lesson, segment 1; objective 1)

   a. & d. are incorrect. The sensory register is concerned with noticing sensory events rather than with memory.

   b. is incorrect. Age-related deficits in the sensory register are most likely for ambiguous or weak stimuli.
6. a. is the correct answer. (video lesson, segment 1; objectives 1 & 2)

   b. is incorrect. Explicit memory involves words, data, concepts, and the like. It is a part of long-term memory.

   c. is incorrect. Long-term memory includes information remembered for years or decades.

   d. is incorrect. The sensory register stores information for a split second.
7. d. is the correct answer. (pp. 515–516; objectives 2 & 5)

8. b. is the correct answer. Older individuals are particularly likely to experience difficulty holding new information in mind, particularly when it is essentially meaningless. (pp. 515–516; objective 5)

   a., c., & d. are incorrect. These are examples of long-term memory, which declines very little with age.

9. b. is the correct answer. (pp. 518–519; video lesson, segment 3; objective 6)

   c. & d. are incorrect. The textbook does not indicate the existence of cohort effects in the incidence of Alzheimer's disease.

10. d. is the correct answer. (pp. 521–522; objective 7)

   a., b., & c. are incorrect. The symptoms Wayne's father is experiencing are those of depression, which is often misdiagnosed as dementia in the elderly.

Lesson Review

Lesson 24

Late Adulthood
Cognitive Development

Please Note: Use this matrix to guide your study and achieve the learning objectives of this lesson. It will also help you to view the video, which defines and demonstrates important concepts and skills as they relate to everyday life.

Learning Objective	Textbook	Telecourse Student Guide	Video Lesson
1. Using the information-processing approach, list the four steps of cognition as outlined in your textbook, summarize the first step of input (sensing) in late adulthood, explain the capacity of working memory, and note how long-term memory is assessed.	pp. 513–517	Key Terms: 9, 10; Practice Questions I: 1, 2, 3, 4, 15, 16; Practice Questions II: 1, 2, 3, 4, 6, 8, 16, 17; Applying Your Knowledge: 5, 6.	Segment 1: *Changes in Information Processing*
2. Summarize the concept of ecological validity in regard to older adults' ability to access the knowledge base and to use control processes, and explain the findings of the Seattle Longitudinal Study on cognitive output.	pp. 515–517	Key Terms: 1, 2, 9, 10; Practice Questions I: 4, 5; Practice Questions II: 4, 5, 6, 18, 19; Applying Your Knowledge: 6, 7.	Segment 1: *Changes in Information Processing*
3. Suggest several reasons, other than the aging process itself, that might contribute to age-related declines in cognitive functioning.	*	Practice Questions I: 7, 8, 17; Practice Questions II: 6, 8.	Segment 2: *Age-Related Changes*
4. Describe the aging brain in regard to brain slowdown and brain shrinkage, recognize the variations in brain use among older adults, and identify the benefits of using more areas of the brain in thinking processes.	pp. 512–513	Practice Questions I: 15, 17; Applying Your Knowledge: 1.	Segment 1: *Changes in Information Processing;* Segment 2: *Age-Related Changes*
5. Characterize and explain discrepancies between how the elderly perform on memory and problem-solving tasks in the laboratory, on one hand, and in daily life, on the other.	pp. 515–516	Practice Questions I: 18; Practice Questions II: 6, 8, 9; Applying Your Knowledge: 7, 8.	Segment 2: *Age-Related Changes*

* The video for this lesson provides a useful exploration of these topics.

Learning Objective	Textbook	Telecourse Student Guide	Video Lesson
6. Identify the two most common forms of dementia and discuss the differences between them.	pp. 517–519	Key Terms: 3, 4, 5; Practice Questions I: 6, 9, 11, 12, 19, 20; Practice Questions II: 10, 11, 21, 22; Applying Your Knowledge: 9.	Segment 3: *Dementia*
7. Identify and describe other dementias and their organic causes, as well as the causes of reversible dementia.	pp. 519–522	Key Terms: 3, 6; Practice Questions I: 9, 10, 12, 13, 19; Practice Questions II: 7, 12, 13, 20, 21, 23, 24; Applying Your Knowledge: 2, 10.	Segment 3: *Dementia*
8. Discuss the claims of developmentalists regarding the possibility of positive cognitive development during late adulthood, and discuss Erikson's and Maslow's ideas on integrity, self-actualization, and life review.	pp. 522–525	Key Terms: 7, 8; Practice Questions I: 14, 21, 22; Practice Questions II: 14, 15, 25, 26; Applying Your Knowledge: 3, 4.	Segment 4: *Enhancing Cognitive Abilities*

Staying in the Game

Lesson 25

Late Adulthood: Psychosocial Development

Preview

"The older you are, the more important your choices are." So begins Lesson 25, which focuses on psychosocial development during late adulthood. Because the choices we make are so different, adults in their later years are more diverse in terms of their development than at any other time. Even so, negative stereotypes about the elderly too often distort people's perceptions of the later years. Certain changes are common during this stage of the life span—retirement, the death of a spouse, and declining health—yet people respond to these experiences in vastly different ways.

Individual experiences may help to explain the fact that theories of psychosocial aging, discussed in the first part of the lesson, are often contradictory. The second section of the lesson focuses on the challenges to feeling fulfilled during late adulthood, such as finding new sources of achievement once derived from work. In the third section, the importance of marriage, friends, neighbors, and family in providing social support is discussed, as are the different experiences of married and single older adults. The lesson concludes with a discussion of the frail elderly—the minority of older adults, often poor and/or ill, who require extensive care.

Prior Telecourse Knowledge that Will Be Used in this Lesson

- Psychosocial development during early adulthood (Lesson 19) and middle adulthood (Lesson 22) will be referred to as we discuss psychosocial development during late adulthood.
- The major theories of development (Lesson 2) will be referred to as we discuss psychosocial development in later life.

Learning Objectives

Use this information to guide your reading, viewing, thinking, and studying. After successfully completing this lesson, you should be able to:

1. Explain the central premises of self theories of psychosocial development during late adulthood.
2. Discuss Erikson's stage of integrity versus despair and the process of achieving integrity in old age.
3. Identify and describe the stratification theories of psychosocial development during late adulthood.
4. Discuss dynamic theories of late adulthood.
5. List and discuss several activities and alternative sources of achievement during late adulthood.
6. Explain the social convoy's increasing importance during late adulthood.
7. Describe how, and why, marriage relationships tend to change as people grow old, and discuss the impact of retirement.
8. Discuss the impact of being old and single (never-married, divorced, or widowed) on both women and men.
9. Discuss friendships among older people.
10. Discuss the relationship between the generations as it exists today, and identify several reasons for conflict between generations.
11. Describe the frail elderly, define ADL and IADL, and discuss their importance.
12. Identify the measures that can protect the elderly from becoming frail, discuss caring for the elderly (including long-term care), and demonstrate an understanding of elder abuse.

Read Chapter 15, "Late Adulthood: Psychosocial Development," pages 529–561.

View the video for Lesson 25, "Staying in the Game."

Segment 1: ***Theories of Late Adulthood***
Segment 2: ***Keeping Socially Active***
Segment 3: ***Importance of the Social Convoy***
Segment 4: ***Quality of Life***

Summary

The major theories of adulthood include self theories, stratification theories, and dynamic theories. **Self theories** emphasize the active part played by each person in fulfilling his or her potential. A central concept for self theory is that older adults set goals, assess abilities, and find a way to accomplish what they want to achieve despite age-related declines. One of the ways they may do this is through **selective optimization with compensation**, a process by which they optimize remaining abilities in order to compensate for declines in other abilities.

According to Erikson, the final challenge of development is that of integrity versus despair, in which older adults attempt to come to terms with the personal choices and events that have shaped their lives and integrate them into a meaningful whole. Partly as a result of changes in appearance, health, and employment, maintaining a coherent and consistent sense of identity during late adulthood may be particularly challenging.

Stratification theories maintain that social forces are particularly powerful during late adulthood, when a person's ability to function depends largely on the person's position in society. **Disengagement theory** maintains that during late adulthood the individual and society mutually withdraw in order to prepare for the individual's impending death. Critics of disengagement theory point out that older people choose to keep their social networks small because they are interested in maximizing the quality of their social relationships. Furthermore, **activity theory** holds that the more active the elderly are, the greater their life satisfaction and the longer their lives.

Contemporary theories of adult development also focus on the impact of stratification by gender and race. **Feminist theory** points out that most social structures and economic policies have been established by men, and consequently, women's needs are often devalued. **Critical race theory** maintains that racial separation shapes the experiences and attitudes of both racial minorities and racial majorities.

Dynamic theory emphasizes the diversity of development, as each person shapes his or her life within specific social contexts that are constantly changing. According to **continuity theory**, people cope in late adulthood in much the same way that they did earlier in life. Thus, even though the social environments of adults may change as they age, those who coped well earlier in life continue to do so.

Compared to younger adults, older adults are more likely to feel a strong obligation to serve their community and become involved in volunteer work. Many older adults stay busy by maintaining their homes and yards, reflecting their desire to age in their own home. One result of this is that many of the elderly live by themselves.

The continuity of older adults' **social convoy** is an important affirmation of who they have been and what they will continue to be. Older people's satisfaction with life bears relatively little relationship to their contact with younger members of their own family but correlates significantly with the quantity and quality of their contact with their social convoy. Long-standing friendships are particularly cherished by older adults and correlate with feelings of well-being and self-esteem. Thus, older adults are likely to have smaller social convoys, but these are the friends with whom they greatly enjoy spending time.

The **frail elderly**—the physically infirm, the very ill, or the cognitively impaired—are differentiated by their inability to perform adequately the **activities of daily life (ADLs)**, including eating, bathing, toileting, walking, and dressing. Equally important to independent living are the **instrumental activities of daily life (IADLs)** that require some intellectual competence, such as paying bills, shopping, and so forth.

In every nation, the number of frail elderly is increasing. However, many elderly persons never become frail because of four protective factors: their attitude, their social network, their physical setting, and their financial resources. Although being female, a minority member, or poor puts a person at increased risk of frailty, this is not inevitable. Some people enter late adulthood with many buffers in place: family members and friends, education, a pension, a lifetime of good health habits, and so on.

Review all reading assignments for this lesson.

As assigned by your instructor, complete the optional online component for this lesson.

Key Terms

Using your own words, write a brief definition or explanation of each of the following terms on a separate piece of paper.

1. self theories
2. integrity vs. despair
3. continuity theory
4. positivity effect
5. stratification theories
6. disengagement theory
7. activity theory
8. age in place
9. naturally occurring retirement community (NORC)
10. AARP
11. filial responsibility
12. frail elderly
13. activities of daily life (ADLs)
14. instrumental activities of daily life (IADLs)
15. assisted living
16. identity theory
17. selective optimization with compensation
18. feminist theory
19. critical race theory
20. social convoy
21. socioemotional selectivity theory
22 dynamic theories

Practice Questions I

Multiple-Choice Questions

1. According to disengagement theory, during late adulthood people tend to
   a. become less role-centered and more passive.
   b. have regrets about how they have lived their lives.
   c. become involved in a range of new activities.
   d. exaggerate lifelong personality traits.

2. Elderhostel is
   a. a special type of nursing home in which the patients are given control over their activities.
   b. a theory of psychosocial development advocating that the elderly can help each other.
   c. an agency that allows older people of the opposite sex to live together unencumbered by marriage vows.
   d. a program in which older people live on college campuses and take special classes.

3. Integrity has been reach when the elder individual
   a. feels anxious and unsure in regard to life achievement.
   b. feels comfortable with oneself in regard to life achievement.
   c. feels jealous of young people because of their youth and opportunity.
   d. feels none of the above.

4. Elderly people typically realize
   a. their life can remain the same if they take very good care of themselves.
   b. close family members are more important than they thought.
   c. its important how people remember them.
   d. b & c only.

5. In general, older people are
   a. more likely to retire at a later age.
   b. likely to retire for health-related reasons.
   c. likely to retire simply because they want to.
   d. more likely to retire at their employers' request.

6. The idea that individuals set their own goals, assess their abilities, and figure out how to accomplish what they want to achieve during late adulthood is referred to as
   a. disengagement.
   b. selective optimization with compensation.
   c. dynamic life-course development.
   d. age stratification.

7. After retirement, the elderly are likely to
   a. get a part-time job.
   b. become politically involved.
   c. do volunteer work because they feel a particular commitment to their community.
   d. do any of the above.

8. Which of the following theories does **NOT** belong with the others?
   a. disengagement theory
   b. feminist theory
   c. critical race theory
   d. continuity theory

9. Which of the following is most true of the relationship between the generations today?
   a. Because parents and children often live at a distance from each other, they are not close.
   b. Older adults prefer not to interfere in their children's lives.
   c. Younger adults are eager to live their own lives and do not want to care for their parents.
   d. The generations tend to see and help each other frequently.

10. The importance of long-standing friendships is reflected in which of the following?
    a. the intensification of friendly bonds between in-laws
    b. the mother–daughter relationship becoming more like one between two friends
    c. the intensification of friendly bonds between members of the extended family and/or the social convoy
    d. a change in the husband–wife relationship to one of friendship

11. In general, during late adulthood the fewest problems are experienced by individuals who

    a. are married.
    b. have always been single.
    c. have long been divorced.
    d. are widowed.

12. Which of the following is true of adjustment to the death of a spouse?

    a. It is easier for men in all respects.
    b. It is initially easier for men, but over the long term it is easier for women.
    c. It is generally easier for women.
    d. It is determined primarily by individual personality traits, and therefore shows very few sex differences.

13. According to dynamic theories,

    a. self-integrity is maintained throughout life.
    b. adults make choices and interpret reality in such a way as to express themselves as fully as possible.
    c. people organize themselves according to their particular characteristics and circumstances.
    d. each person's life is largely a self-propelled process, occurring within ever-changing social contexts.

14. Which of the following most accurately expresses the most recent view of developmentalists regarding stratification by age?

    a. Aging makes a person's social sphere expand.
    b. Disengagement is always the result of ageism.
    c. Many elderly disengage, but most studies show the elderly as quite happy, filling various roles.
    d. Older adults need much less social activity to be happy than they did earlier in life.

True or False Items

Write T (for true) or F (for false) on the line in front of each statement.

15. _____ As one of the most disruptive experiences in the life span, widowhood tends to have similar effects on men and women.

16. _____ Remote grandparents are active in the day-to-day lives of their grandchildren.

17. _____ Continuity theory assumes that the primary goal of adult development is adapting to change.

18. _____ Most developmentalists support the central premise of disengagement theory.

19. _____ Most older people suffer significantly from a lack of close friendships.

20. _____ Nearly one in two older adults makes a long-distance move after retirement.

21. _____ Loneliness during late adulthood is greater for individuals who were never married than for any other group.

Practice Questions II

Multiple-Choice Questions

1. Critics of disengagement theory point out that
   a. older people want to substitute new involvements for the roles they lose with retirement.
   b. disengagement usually is not voluntary on the part of the individual.
   c. disengagement often leads to greater life satisfaction for older adults.
   d. disengagement is more common at earlier stages in the life cycle.

2. A beanpole family is one that consists of
   a. fewer generations with fewer members than in the past.
   b. fewer generations with more members than in the past.
   c. more generations than in the past but with only a few members in each generation.
   d. more generations with more members than in the past.

3. According to continuity theory, during late adulthood people
   a. become less role-centered.
   b. become more passive.
   c. become involved in a range of new activities.
   d. cope with challenges in much the same way they did earlier in life.

4. Developmentalists who believe that stratification theory provides an unfairly negative picture of women and minority groups point out that
   a. European Americans are more likely than African Americans to be placed in nursing homes.
   b. elderly women are less likely than men to be lonely and depressed.
   c. multigenerational families and churches often nurture Hispanic Americans.
   d. all of the above are true.

5. Which of the following reduces the amount of time the average elderly person needs help with ADLs and IADLs?
   a. financial resources and personality
   b. attitude and social setting
   c. compression of morbidity and good medical care
   d. social network

6. The major U.S. organization affecting the elderly is
   a. Elderhostel.
   b. the American Association of Retired Persons.
   c. Foster Grandparents.
   d. Service Corps of Retired Executives.

7. Which of the following would **NOT** be included as an instrumental activity of daily life?
   a. grocery shopping
   b. paying bills
   c. making phone calls
   d. taking a walk

8. One of the most important factors contributing to life satisfaction for older adults appears to be
   a. at least one close friend.
   b. contact with younger family members.
   c. the number of new experiences to which they are exposed.
   d. the ability to travel.

9. In general, the longer a couple has been married, the more likely they are to
   a. be happier with each other.
   b. have frequent, minor disagreements.
   c. feel the relationship is not equitable.
   d. do all of the above.

10. Adjustment to losing a spouse in late adulthood tends to be
    a. equally easy for men and women.
    b. more difficult for women.
    c. easier for men.
    d. none of the above.

11. The average nursing home cost in the United States is
   a. $75,000 per year.
   b. $150,000 per year.
   d. $200,000 as a one time only fee.
   c. none of the above.

12. According to Erikson, achieving integrity during late adulthood above all involves
   a. the ability to perceive one's own life as worthwhile.
   b. being open to new influences and experiences.
   c. treating other people with respect.
   d. developing a consistent and yet varied daily routine.

Matching Items

Match each definition or description with its corresponding term.

Terms

13. __________ disengagement theory
14. __________ self theories
15. __________ continuity theory
16. __________ activity theory
17. __________ stratification theories
18. __________ activities of daily life (ADLs)
19. __________ instrumental activities of daily life (IADLs)
20. __________ dynamic theories
21. __________ Elderhostel
22. __________ social convoy

Definitions or Descriptions

a. theories such as Erik Erikson's that emphasize self-actualization
b. an educational program for the elderly
c. eating, bathing, toileting, walking, and dressing
d. theory that a person's life is an active, largely self-propelled process that occurs within ever-changing social contexts.
e. theory that people become less role-centered as they age
f. actions that require intellectual competence and forethought
g. the family members, friends, acquaintances, and even strangers who move through life with an individual
h. theories such as feminist theory and critical race theory that focus on the limitations on life choices created by social forces
i. theory that elderly people become socially withdrawn only involuntarily
j. theory that each person copes in late adulthood in the same way he or she did earlier in life

Applying Your Knowledge

1. Which of the following statements most accurately describes psychosocial development in late adulthood?
   a. Many leading gerontologists believe that people become more alike as they get older.
   b. Older adults generally fit into one of two distinct personality types.
   c. Many gerontologists believe that the diversity of personalities and patterns is especially pronounced among the elderly.
   d. Few changes in psychosocial development occur after middle adulthood.

2. An advocate of which of the following theories would be most likely to agree with the statement, "Because of their more passive style of interaction, older people are less likely to be chosen for new roles"?
   a. disengagement
   b. continuity
   c. self
   d. dynamic

3. An advocate for feminist theory would point out that
   a. since most social structures and economic policies have been established by men, women's needs are devalued.
   b. women in the United States make up the majority of the elderly and the elderly poor.
   c. many elderly women are expected to care for frail relatives even if it strains their own health.
   d. all of the above are true.

4. Professor Martin states that "membership in certain groups can place the elderly at risk for a number of dangers." Professor Martin evidently is an advocate of which theory of psychosocial development?
   a. self theories
   b. social stratification
   c. dynamic
   d. continuity

5. An elderly man with dementia is most likely to be cared for by his spouse in ________________ and by his children in ________________.
   a. Korea; the United States
   b. the United States; Korea
   c. Japan; Sweden
   d. Sweden; Japan
6. Research indicates that the primary perpetrators of elder abuse are
   a. professional caregivers.
   b. mean-spirited strangers.
   c. other relatives.
   d. middle-aged children.
7. Which of the following best describes the relationship between the elderly and younger generations?
   a. If children move, the elderly will also move in order to continue to be near them.
   b. The elderly enjoy social contact with the younger generation and particularly enjoy having long visits from their grandchildren.
   c. Family members throughout life typically support one another.
   d. The relationship between mothers and daughters improves with age, with conflict decreasing substantially.
8. Of the following older adults, who is most likely to be involved in a network of intimate friendships?
   a. William, a 65-year-old man who never married
   b. Darrel, a 60-year-old widower
   c. Florence, a 63-year-old widow
   d. Kay, a 66-year-old married woman
9. Following a heated disagreement over family responsibilities, Sidney's grandson stormed away shouting "Why should I listen to you?" Later, Sidney is filled with despair and feels that all his years of work to build a strong family were wasted. An identity theorist would probably say that Sidney is trying to
   a. dominate his grandson.
   b. teach his traditions to his grandson.
   c. pass the customs of the past to the younger generations of his family.
   d. do b & c only.

10. Claudine is the primary caregiver for her elderly parents. The amount of stress she feels in this role depends above all on

a. how frail her parents are.

b. her subjective interpretation of the support she receives from others.

c. her relationship to her parents prior to their becoming frail.

d. her overall financial situation.

11. Wilma's elderly mother needs help in taking care of the instrumental activities of daily life. Such activities would include which of the following?

a. bathing

b. eating

c. paying bills

d. all of the above

12. Jack, who is 73, looks back on his life with a sense of pride and contentment; Eleanor feels unhappy with her life and that it is "too late to start over." In Erikson's terminology, Jack is experiencing ______________, while Eleanor is experiencing ________________.

a. generativity; stagnation

b. identity; emptiness

c. integrity; despair

d. completion; termination

Answer Key

Key Terms

1. Self theories such as Erik Erikson's theory focus on how adults make choices, confront problems, and interpret reality in such a way as to express themselves as fully as possible. (p. 530; video lesson, segment 1; objective 1)
2. In Erikson's theory, the final crisis of development is that of integrity versus despair, in which older adults attempt to integrate their personal experiences with their vision of the future of their community. (p. 530; video lesson, segment 1; objective 2)
3. According to the continuity theory of aging, each person copes with late adulthood in much the same way that he or she coped with earlier periods of life. (p. 532; video lesson, segment 1; objectives 1 & 4)
4. Positivity effect is the tendency for elderly people to perceive, prefer, and remember positive images and experiences more than negative ones. (p. 532; objective 1)

5. Stratification theories emphasize that social forces limit individual choices and affect the ability to function. (p. 533; video lesson, segment 1; objective 3)
6. According to disengagement theory, aging results in social withdrawal and passivity. (p. 534; video lesson, segment 1; objective 3)
7. Activity theory is the view that older people remain active in a variety of social spheres and become withdrawn only unwillingly. (p. 534; video lesson, segment 1; objective 3)
8. Age in place refers to a preference of elderly people to remain in the same home and community, adjusting but not leaving when health fades. (p. 540; objectives 5 & 11)
9. A neighborhood or apartment complex whose population is mostly retired people who moved to the location as younger adults and never left is referred to as a naturally occurring retirement community, or NORC. (p. 541; objective 5)
10. AARP is a U.S. organization of people aged 50 and older, which advocates for the elderly. It was originally called the American Association of Retired Persons, but now only the initials AARP is used, to reflect the fact that the organization's members do not have to be retired. (p. 543; objective 5)
11. Filial responsibility is the idea that adult children are obligated to care for their aging parents. (p. 548; objective 10)
12. The frail elderly are the minority of older adults who are physically infirm, very ill, or cognitively impaired. (p. 553; video lesson, segment 4; objective 11)
13. In determining frailty, gerontologists often refer to the activities of daily life (ADLs), which comprise five tasks: eating, bathing, toileting, dressing, and transferring from a bed to a chair. (p. 554; video lesson, segment 4; objective 11)
14. The instrumental activities of daily life (IADLs) are actions that require some intellectual competence and forethought, such as shopping for food, paying bills, and taking medication. (p. 554; video lesson, segment 4; objective 11)
15. Assisted living is a living arrangement for elderly people that combines privacy and independence with medical supervision. (p. 559; objective 12)
16. An example of a self theory, identity theory emphasizes the impact of the choices adults make on their self-concepts. (video lesson, segment 1; objective 1)
17. Selective optimization with compensation is the idea that healthy aging involves assessing abilities realistically, choosing meaningful goals, and devising strategies to accomplish them, despite age-related losses and limitations. (video lesson, segment 1; objective 1)
18. A stratification theory, feminist theory points out that since most social structures and economic policies have been established by men, women's

needs are devalued by society. (pp. 534–535; video lesson, segment 1; objective 3)

19. Another stratification theory, critical race theory maintains that racial stratification shapes the experiences and attitudes of both racial minorities and racial majorities. (pp. 535–536; video lesson, segment 1; objective 3)
20. The social convoy is the network of people with whom we establish meaningful relationships as we travel through life. (video lesson, segment 3; objective 6)
21. According to socioemotional selectivity theory, as people get older they tend to have fewer, but more important, friendships and relationships. (video lesson, segment 3; objectives 6 & 9)
22. According to dynamic theories, each person's life is an active, largely self-propelled process that occurs within ever-changing social contexts. (video lesson, segment 1; objective 4)

Practice Questions I

Multiple-Choice Questions

1. a. is the correct answer. (p. 534; video lesson, segment 1; objective 3)

   b. is incorrect. This answer depicts a person struggling with Erikson's crisis of integrity versus despair.

   c. is incorrect. This answer describes activity theory.

   d. is incorrect. Disengagement theory does not address this issue.
2. d. is the correct answer. (p. 541; objective 5)
3. b. is the correct answer. (p. 530; objective 1)
4. d. is the correct answer. (p. 530; objective 1)
5. c. is the correct answer. (p. 538; video lesson, segment 2; objective 5)

   a. & b. are incorrect. Workers are retiring earlier than in the past, and not always for health-related reasons.

   d. is incorrect. Mandatory retirement is illegal in many nations.
6. b. is the correct answer. (p. 532; video lesson, segment 1; objective 1)

   a. is incorrect. This is the idea that the elderly withdraw from society as they get older.

   c. is incorrect. This is the theory that each person's life is a self-propelled process occurring within ever-changing social contexts.

   d. is incorrect. According to this theory, the oldest generation is segregated from the rest of society.
7. d. is the correct answer. Contrary to earlier views that retirement was not a happy time, researchers now know that the elderly are generally happy and productive, spending their time in various activities. (pp. 537–544; video lesson, segment 2; objective 5)

8. d. is the correct answer. The others can be categorized as stratification theories. (pp. 532–536; video lesson, segment 1; objectives 3 & 4)
9. d. is the correct answer. (pp. 547–548; objective 10)
10. c. is the correct answer. (p. 552; objective 6)

    a., b., & d. are incorrect. These may occur in some cases, but they are not discussed in the textbook.
11. a. is the correct answer. (pp. 544–545; objective 7)
12. c. is the correct answer. (pp. 546–547; objective 8)
13. d. is the correct answer. (video lesson, segment 1; objective 4)

    a. is incorrect.

    b. is incorrect. This expresses self theory.

    c. is incorrect. This expresses stratification theory.
14. c. is the correct answer. (p. 534; objective 3)

    a. is incorrect. This is the central idea behind disengagement theory.

    b. & d. are incorrect. These ideas are expressions of activity theory.

True or False Items

15. F Men fare less well than women (p. 547; objectives 7 & 8)
16. F Involved grandparents are active in the day-to-day lives of their grandchildren. (p. 550; objective 6)
17. T (p. 532; video lesson, segment 1; objectives 1 & 4)
18. F In fact, disengagement theory has few serious defenders. (p. 534; video lesson, segment 1; objective 3)
19. F Most older adults have at least one close friend and, as compared with younger adults, are less likely to feel a need for more friendships. (p. 552; video lesson, segment 3; objective 9)
20. F A minority of older adults move to another state. (pp. 540–541; objective 5)
21. F If anything, loneliness tends to be less in never-married older adults. (p. 552; objective 9)

Practice Questions II

Multiple-Choice Questions

1. a. is the correct answer. (p. 534; video lesson, segment 1; objective 3)

    b. is incorrect. If disengagement were not voluntary, this would not be a choice of the elderly.

    c. & d. are incorrect. Neither of these answers is true, nor a criticism of disengagement theory.
2. c. is the correct answer. (p. 547; objective 10)
3. d. is the correct answer. (p. 532; video lesson, segment 1; objectives 1 & 4)

a. & b. are incorrect. These answers describe disengagement theory.

c. is incorrect. This answer pertains to activity theory.

4. d. is the correct answer. (pp. 533–536; video lesson, segment 1; objective 3)
5. c. is the correct answer. (p. 554; objectives 11 & 12)
6. b. is the correct answer. (p. 543; objective 5)

   a. is incorrect. Elderhostel is an educational program for older adults.

   c. & d. are incorrect. These service organizations affect a much smaller percentage of the elderly.
7. d. is the correct answer. (pp. 554–555; video lesson, segment 4; objective 11)
8. a. is the correct answer. (p. 552; objective 9)

   b., c., & d. are incorrect. The importance of these factors varies from one older adult to another.
9. a. is the correct answer. (pp. 544–545; objective 7)

   b. & c. are incorrect. The longer a couple has been married, the less likely they are to have frequent disagreements or feel that the relationship is not equitable.
10. d. is the correct answer. (pp. 546–547; objectives 7 & 8)
11. c. is the correct answer. Many nations spend substantial money on services for the elderly. (p. 558; objective 12)
12. a. is the correct answer. (pp. 530–531; video lesson, segment 1; objective 2)

Matching Items

13. e (p. 534; video lesson, segment 1; objective 3)
14. a (p. 530; video lesson, segment 1; objective 1)
15. j (p. 532; video lesson, segment 1; objectives 1 & 4)
16. i (p. 534; video lesson, segment 1; objective 3)
17. h (p. 533; video lesson, segment 1; objective 3)
18. c (p. 554; video lesson, segment 4; objective 11)
19. f (p. 554; video lesson, segment 4; objective 11)
20. d (video lesson, segment 1; objective 4)
21. b (p. 541; objective 5)
22. g (video lesson, segment 3; objective 6)

Applying Your Knowledge

1. c. is the correct answer. (pp. 530–533; objective 1)
2. a. is the correct answer. (p. 534; video lesson, segment 1; objective 3)

   b. is incorrect. Continuity theory, a type of dynamic theory, maintains that older adults cope with aging in much the same ways as when they were younger.

c. is incorrect. Self theories emphasize the quest for self-actualization.

d. is incorrect. Dynamic theories emphasize that life is a self-propelled, ever-changing process within an ever-changing social context.

3. d. is the correct answer. (video lesson, segment 1; objective 3)
4. b. is the correct answer. "Groups" are the social "strata" that this theory focuses on. (p. 533; video lesson, segment 1; objective 3)

   a. & c. are incorrect. These theories emphasize the efforts of the individual to reach his or her full potential (self theories) by interpreting experiences in the face of ever-changing social contexts (dynamic theories, of which continuity theory is one [d.]).
5. b. is the correct answer. (pp. 534–535, 556; objectives 3, 11, & 12)

   c. & d. are incorrect. The textbook does not compare care for the frail elderly in these countries.
6. d. is the correct answer. (p. 557; objective 11)
7. c. is the correct answer. (p. 547; objective 10)

   a. is incorrect. Even if children move, their parents prefer to stay in their homes.

   b. is incorrect. Although the elderly enjoy social contact with the younger generations, they prefer shorter visits.

   d. is incorrect. Tension and conflict continues throughout life in mother–daughter relationships.
8. c. is the correct answer. (pp. 546–547; objective 8)

   a. & b. are incorrect. At every age, women have larger social circles and more intimate relationships with their friends than men.

   d. is incorrect. Widows tend to be more involved in friendship networks than married women.
9. b. is the correct answer. (p. 531; objective 1)
10. b. is the correct answer. (pp. 556–557; objective 12)
11. c. is the correct answer. (p. 554; video lesson, segment 4; objective 11)

    a. & b. are incorrect. These are examples of "activities of daily life."
12. c. is the correct answer. (pp. 530–531; video lesson, segment 1; objective 2)

    a. is incorrect. This is not the crisis of late adulthood in Erikson's theory.

    b. & d. are incorrect. These are not crises in Erikson's theory.

Lesson Review

Lesson 25

Late Adulthood
Psychosocial Development

Please Note: Use this matrix to guide your study and achieve the learning objectives of this lesson. It will also help you to view the video, which defines and demonstrates important concepts and skills as they relate to everyday life.

Learning Objective	Textbook	Telecourse Student Guide	Video Lesson
1. Explain the central premises of self theories of psychosocial development during late adulthood.	pp. 530–533	Key Terms: 1, 3, 4, 16, 17; Practice Questions I: 3, 4, 6, 17; Practice Questions II: 3, 14, 15; Applying Your Knowledge: 1, 9.	Segment 1: *Theories of Late Adulthood*
2. Discuss Erikson's stage of integrity versus despair and the process of achieving integrity in old age.	pp. 530–531	Key Terms: 2; Practice Questions II: 12; Applying Your Knowledge: 12.	Segment 1: *Theories of Late Adulthood*
3. Identify and describe the stratification theories of psychosocial development during late adulthood.	pp. 533–536	Key Terms: 5, 6, 7, 18, 19; Practice Questions I: 1, 8, 14, 18; Practice Questions II: 1, 4, 13, 16, 17; Applying Your Knowledge: 2, 3, 4, 5.	Segment 1: *Theories of Late Adulthood*
4. Discuss dynamic theories of late adulthood.	*	Key Terms: 3, 22; Practice Questions I: 8, 13, 17; Practice Questions II: 3, 15, 20.	Segment 1: *Theories of Late Adulthood*
5. List and discuss several activities and alternative sources of achievement during late adulthood.	pp. 534–544	Key Terms: 8, 9, 10; Practice Questions I: 2, 5, 7, 20; Practice Questions II: 6, 21.	Segment 2: *Keeping Socially Active*
6. Explain the social convoy's increasing importance during late adulthood.	pp. 544–553	Key Terms: 20, 21; Practice Questions I: 10, 16; Practice Questions II: 22.	Segment 3: *Importance of the Social Convoy*

* The video for this lesson offers a useful exploration of this concept.

Learning Objective	**Textbook**	**Telecourse Student Guide**	**Video Lesson**
7. Describe how, and why, marriage relationships tend to change as people grow old, and discuss the impact of retirement.	pp. 544–547	Practice Questions I: 11, 15; Practice Questions II: 9, 10.	Segment 3: *Importance of the Social Convoy*
8. Discuss the impact of being old and single (never-married, divorced, or widowed) on both women and men.	pp. 546–547, 552–553,	Practice Questions I: 12, 15; Practice Questions II: 10; Applying Your Knowledge: 8.	
9. Discuss friendships among older people.	pp. 552–553	Key Terms: 21; Practice Questions I: 19, 21; Practice Questions II: 8.	Segment 3: *Importance of the Social Convoy*
10. Discuss the relationship between the generations as it exists today, and identify several reasons for conflict between generations.	pp. 547–552	Key Terms: 11; Practice Questions I: 9; Practice Questions II: 2; Applying Your Knowledge: 7.	
11. Describe the frail elderly, define ADL and IADL, and discuss their importance.	pp. 553–555	Key Terms: 8, 12, 13, 14; Practice Questions II: 5, 7, 18, 19; Applying Your Knowledge: 5, 6, 11.	Segment 4: *Quality of Life*
12. Identify the measures that can protect the elderly from becoming frail, discuss caring for the elderly (including long-term care), and demonstrate an understanding of elder abuse.	pp. 540, 554–560	Key Terms: 15; Practice Questions II: 5, 11; Applying Your Knowledge: 5, 10.	

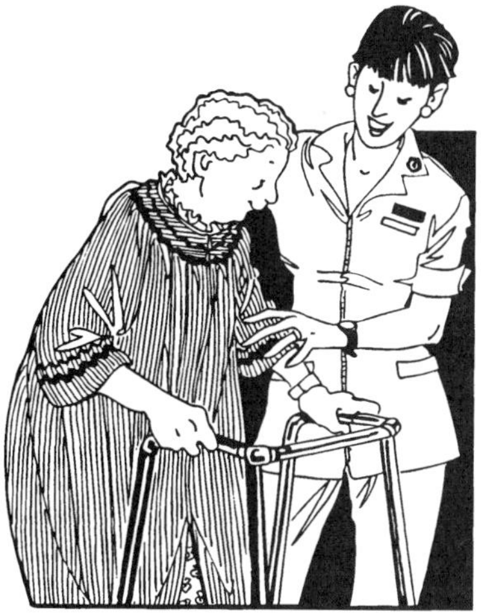

Lesson 26

Epilogue:
Death and Dying

Preview

Depending upon an individual's age, experience, beliefs, and historical and cultural context, death can have many meanings. Death marks the close of the life span, and is another area that reflects the vast complexity of human development in the way people grieve, accept, or deny death due to their social, religious, and cultural differences.

The lesson begins by exploring the dying person's emotions, noting that the reactions that death prompts vary from individual to individual. Although contemporary psychologists consider the experience of dying to be variable and not subject to an unvarying sequence of stages, the pioneering work of Elisabeth Kübler-Ross was nevertheless instrumental in revealing the emotional gamut of terminally ill patients and the importance of honest communication.

Next, the lesson deals with how dying patients and their families plan for death and the controversial issue of whether and when the death of a loved one should be hastened. This section also discusses hospice and other forms of care designed to help the terminally ill patient to die "a good death."

The final section explores the social context of dying, noting that perceptions of death vary markedly according to their historical and cultural context. This section also deals with changing expressions of bereavement and how people can be aided in the process of recovery.

Learning Objectives

Use this information to guide your reading, viewing, thinking, and studying. After successfully completing this lesson, you should be able to:

1. Describe a good death, and identify Kübler-Ross's stages of dying, and discuss these stages in light of more recent research.
2. Discuss age-related differences in the conceptualization of emotional reactions to death.
3. Discuss the steps that patients, family members, and medical personnel can take to plan for a swift, pain-free, and dignified death.
4. Explain the concept of palliative care, focusing on the advantages and disadvantages of hospices, and describe the conditions under which individuals choose to avoid medical intervention.
5. Discuss issues surrounding assisted suicide and active euthanasia, noting the Dutch experience with legislation regarding assisted dying.
6. Describe some cultural and religious variations in how death is viewed and treated.
7. Describe recent changes in the mourning process, and suggest steps that can be taken in helping someone to recover from bereavement.

Read Epilogue, "Death and Dying," pages 565–589.

View the video for Lesson 26, "Living and Dying."

Segment 1: *Emotional Reactions to Death*

Segment 2: *Deciding How to Die*

Segment 3: *Social Context of Bereavement*

Segment 4: *Cycle of Life*

Summary

Elisabeth Kübler-Ross proposed that the dying go through five emotional stages, beginning with *denial*, during which the patient refuses to believe that he or she will die. Denial is followed by *anger*; *bargaining*, in which the patient tries to negotiate an alternative with God or fate; *depression*; and finally *acceptance* of death as the last stage of this life and possibly the beginning of the next. Although the theory brought needed attention to the experience of dying, recent research shows that Kübler-Ross's stages, when and if they occur, do not always occur in the sequence she proposed.

Most people agree that a "good death" is one that occurs swiftly, with little pain, and allows the individual to die with dignity, surrounded by loved ones. There is a growing consensus that the patient should be the ultimate authority regarding what life-sustaining measures should be used in terminal cases. Some people make a **living will** to indicate what medical intervention they want if they become incapable of expressing those wishes.

Individual reactions to dying vary across the life span. Young children are usually upset by the thought of dying because it suggests the idea of being separated from loved ones. Adolescents may be focused on the ways their condition may affect their appearance and social relationships. Middle-aged adults may be primarily concerned about meeting important obligations and responsibilities. An older adult's feelings about dying depend more on the situation. If one's spouse has already died, and if the illness brings pain and infirmity, death may be more readily accepted.

When medical interventions appear not to be working and terminally ill individuals are near the end of life, **palliative care** is designed to ease suffering through such methods as pain-killing medication or **DNR (do not resuscitate)** orders. Few doctors and nurses are trained to handle the psychological demands of palliative care. **Passive euthanasia** occurs when life-saving care methods are available, but are not used to allow death to occur.

The **hospice** is an alternative to hospital care that seeks to minimize suffering and to make the last days of life filled with love and meaning. Hospices provide the dying with skilled medical care but shun the use of artificial life-support systems. Both palliative care and passive euthanasia may be used in hospice. The hospice concept has its critics, however, and raises many legal and ethical questions that center around the wisdom of a patient's accepting a death sentence, perhaps prematurely, and simply waiting to die. In addition, because candidates for the hospice program must be diagnosed as terminally ill, participation is restricted to a minority of the dying. Especially controversial are issues concerning **physician-assisted suicide**, in which someone provides the means for a person to end his or her life, and **active euthanasia**, in which someone intentionally acts to terminate the life of a suffering person.

The specific meanings attached to death vary from individual to individual, and according to their cultural and historical context. In most African traditions, elders take on an important new status through death, while in many Muslim nations, death affirms faith in Allah and caring for the dying is a holy reminder of mortality. Among Hindus and Sikhs, helping the dying to relinquish their ties to this world and prepare for the next is considered an obligation for the immediate family. Preparations for death are not emphasized in the Jewish tradition because hope for life can never be extinguished. Many Christians believe that death is the beginning of eternity in heaven or hell, and thus welcome or fear it.

The larger cultural context often has more influence on variations in death practices than religion does. Customs of **mourning** also vary tremendously. Two themes that emerge in cultural variations of death practices are that religious and spiritual concerns often reemerge and that returning to one's roots is a common urge.

In recent times, mourning has become more private, less emotional, and less religious. As a result of these trends, there is an increasing tendency toward social isolation for those who have lost a loved one and increased likelihood of physical illness. Mourning may be affected by the conditions under which the loved one died; deaths that are expected and occur after a long period of illness may be easier to cope with because they permit anticipatory **grief**. However, even those who have had time to prepare for the loss of the loved one may be surprised at how much additional grief they may experience afterwards.

Bereaved persons are comforted by social support: a friend who listens, sympathizes, and does not ignore the real pain and complicated emotions involved in the recovery process. Those who would comfort the bereaved should be aware that **bereavement** is likely to be a lengthy and demanding process that may last for months or even years. The experience of grief may vary markedly from one individual to the next, and there is no one "correct" way to deal with the loss.

Review all reading assignments for this lesson.

As assigned by your instructor, complete the optional online component for this lesson.

Key Terms

Using your own words, write a brief definition or explanation of each of the following terms on a separate piece of paper.

1. thanatology
2. terror management theory
3. near-death experience
4. good death
5. hospice
6. palliative care
7. double effect
8. passive euthanasia
9. DNR (do not resuscitate)
10. active euthanasia
11. physician-assisted suicide
12. slippery slope
13. advance directive
14. living will
15. health care proxy
16. bereavement
17. grief
18. mourning
19. absent grief
20. disenfranchised grief
21. incomplete grief
22. anticipatory grief
23. voluntary euthanasia

Practice Questions I

Multiple-Choice Questions

1. Kübler-Ross found that doctors often chose not to inform terminally ill patients of their condition and sometimes concealed the information from families as well. Such an approach would tend to
   a. minimize possibilities for grief.
   b. increase feelings of isolation and sorrow.
   c. discourage the family from retaining memories of the deceased.
   d. maximize possibilities for passive euthanasia.

2. Medical advances have meant that death today can be
   a. far less painful for the dying individual.
   b. emotionally far less painful for the bereaved.
   c. a solitary, lengthy, and painful experience.
   d. predictable, and therefore a less traumatic experience.

3. Kübler-Ross's stages of dying are, in order
   a. anger, denial, bargaining, depression, acceptance.
   b. depression, anger, denial, bargaining, acceptance.
   c. denial, anger, bargaining, depression, acceptance.
   d. bargaining, denial, anger, acceptance, depression.

4. Recent research regarding the emotions of terminally ill patients has found that
   a. all patients reach the stage of acceptance.
   b. emotional stages generally follow one another in an orderly sequence.
   c. most dying people want to spend time with loved ones and to talk honestly about their condition.
   d. most experience depression.

5. Most adults hope that they will die
   a. with little pain.
   b. with dignity.
   c. swiftly.
   d. in all of the above ways.

6. A pain-free death is least likely to be experienced by
   a. the oldest-old patients in hospitals.
   b. hospice patients.
   c. children dying of cancer.
   d. patients who fail to make a living will.

7. Hospice is best defined as
   a. a document that indicates what kind of medical intervention a terminally ill person wants.
   b. mercifully allowing a person to die by not doing something that might extend life.
   c. an alternative to hospital care for the terminally ill.
   d. providing a person with the means to end his or her life.

8. Palliative care refers to
   a. heroic measures to save a life.
   b. conservative medical care to treat an illness.
   c. efforts to relieve pain and suffering.
   d. allowing a terminally ill patient to die naturally.

9. Which of the following describes a situation in which, at a patient's request, caregivers are ordered not to take extreme measures to intervene in life-threatening health events?
   a. involuntary euthanasia
   b. active euthanasia
   c. physician-assisted suicide
   d. DNR

10. Which of the following is a normal response in the bereavement process?
    a. experiencing powerful emotions
    b. culturally diverse emotions
    c. a lengthy period of grief
    d. All of the above are normal responses.

11. A "double effect" in medicine refers to a situation in which
    a. the effects of one drug on a patient interact with those of another drug.
    b. medication relieves pain and has a secondary effect of hastening death.
    c. family members disagree with a terminally ill patient's proxy.
    d. medical personnel ignore the wishes of a terminally ill patient and his or her proxy.

12. Criticisms made against hospices include all of the following **EXCEPT**
    a. the number of patients served is limited.
    b. in some cases a life is being ended that might have been prolonged.
    c. burnout and the rapid growth of hospices might limit the number of competent hospice workers.
    d. the patient is needlessly isolated from family and friends.

True or False Items

Write T (for true) or F (for false) on the line in front of each statement.

13. _____ The terminally ill generally want to know about and discuss their condition.

14. _____ Subsequent research has confirmed the accuracy of Kübler-Ross's findings regarding the five stages of dying.

15. _____ Modern life-prolonging medical technologies have tended to make dying a pain-free, dignified death more difficult and less likely to occur.

16. _____ Following the death of a loved one, the bereaved can best ensure their psychological health and well-being by increasing their social contacts and the number of activities in which they are involved.

17. _____ To help a bereaved person, one should ignore the person's depression.

18. _____ Many dying people never receive hospice care because it is expensive, especially if curative therapy is continued.

19. _____ Physician-assisted suicide and active euthanasia are legal almost everywhere in the world.

20. _____ Hospices administer pain-killing medication but do not make use of artificial life-support systems.

21. _____ Joan Didion wrote *The Year of Magical Thinking*, a book on her own grief after the sudden death of her husband.

22. _____ Murders and suicides trigger police action that can enhance the grief process.

Practice Questions II

Multiple-Choice Questions

1. Kübler-Ross's primary contribution was to
   a. open the first hospice, thus initiating the hospice movement.
   b. show how the emotions of the dying occur in a series of clear-cut stages.
   c. demonstrate that varied and contradictory emotions are normal among the terminally ill.
   d. show the correlation between people's conceptualization of death and their developmental stage.

2. Mourning customs are designed to
   a. make the grief stricken feel whole again.
   b. move the grief toward reaffirmation of life.
   c. allow a public expression of grief.
   d. all of the above.

3. The kind of grief in which the bereaved person does not seem to mourn at all is called
   a. interrupted grief.
   b. disenfranchised grief.
   c. absent grief.
   d. none of the above.

4. Legal experts and medical personnel increasingly agree that the ultimate authority in deciding how a terminal patient is treated should be
   a. the patient's physician.
   b. the legal system.
   c. the patient's family members.
   d. the patient.

5. Recent research reveals that Kübler-Ross's stages of dying
   a. occur in sequence in virtually all terminally ill patients.
   b. do not occur in hospice residents.
   c. are typical only in Western cultures.
   d. make feelings about death seem much more predictable and universal than they actually are.

6. Today, it may be more difficult for the terminally ill to die a swift, dignified, and pain-free death because
   a. modern medicine can sustain life beyond its time.
   b. many doctors view death as an enemy to be fended off at all costs.
   c. the dying often are in discomfort or outright pain because analgesic medications are underprescribed.
   d. of all of the above reasons.

7. Living wills are an attempt to
   a. make sure that passive euthanasia will not be used in individual cases.
   b. specify the extent of medical treatment desired in the event of terminal illness.
   c. specify conditions for the use of active euthanasia.
   d. ensure that death will occur at home rather than in a hospital.

8. In explaining the death of a family member to a child, one should
   a. tell the child Grandma is sleeping.
   b. tell the child that God wanted his sister.
   c. tell the child that Grandpa went on a trip.
   d. none of the above.

9. The hospice made acceptable three basic principles regarding death and dying, including all of the following except that
   a. an interdisciplinary team can provide the best care for any sick person.
   b. death is a family affair.
   c. the dying person should be left alone to reconcile his or her feelings about life.
   d. palliative care is a worthy medical goal.

10. To develop the greatest understanding of variations in mourning practices, a person would do best to focus on
   a. the age and gender of terminally ill patients.
   b. religious differences among the bereaved.
   c. cultural differences among the bereaved.
   d. whether the death permitted anticipatory grief reactions among the bereaved.

11. Healing after the death of a loved one is most difficult when
    a. the death is a long, protracted one.
    b. the bereaved is not allowed to mourn in the way he or she wishes.
    c. a period of grief has already elapsed.
    d. there are no other mourners.

Matching Items

Match each definition or description with its corresponding term.

Terms

12. ________	DNR	16. ________	physician-assisted suicide
13. ________	hospice	17. ________	palliative care
14. ________	living will	18. ________	health care proxy
15. ________	double effect	19. ________	anticipatory grief

Definitions or Descriptions

a. hospice treatment that relieves suffering and safeguards dignity
b. an alternative to hospital care for the terminally ill
c. hospital chart order to allow a terminally ill patient to die naturally
d. a document expressing a person's wishes for treatment should he or she become terminally ill and incapable of making such decisions
e. providing the means for a terminally ill patient to end his or her life
f. an individual chosen to make medical decisions for someone if that person is unable to do so
g. reduces shock and eases the acceptance of a loved one's death
h. situation in which a pain-relieving drug also hastens the death of a terminally ill patient

Applying Your Knowledge

1. People who know they will die soon are more likely to
    a. believe in life after death.
    b. begin acting out in bizarre ways.
    c. isolate themselves.
    d. do none of the above.

2. The terminally ill patient who promises to live a better life if spared from dying is probably in which of Kübler-Ross's stages?

   a. denial

   b. anger

   c. depression

   d. bargaining

3. The terminally ill patient who is convinced his laboratory tests must be wrong is probably in which of Kübler-Ross's stages?

   a. denial

   b. anger

   c. depression

   d. bargaining

4. Dr. Welby writes the orders DNR (do not resuscitate) on her patient's chart. Evidently the patient has requested

   a. a double effect.

   b. passive euthanasia.

   c. active euthanasia.

   d. an assisted suicide.

5. The doctor who injects a terminally ill patient with a lethal drug is practicing

   a. passive euthanasia.

   b. active euthanasia.

   c. an assisted suicide.

   d. an act that became legal in most countries in 1993.

6. Summarizing her presentation on the process of mourning, Rita states that most developmentalists view mourning as

   a. an unnecessary and emotionally crippling process.

   b. a disruptive force in development.

   c. a necessary and healthy process.

   d. important for some, but not all, individuals.

7. Which of the following statements would probably be the most helpful to a grieving person?
   a. "Why don't you get out more and get back into the swing of things?"
   b. "You're tough; bear up!"
   c. "If you need someone to talk to, call me any time."
   d. "It must have been his or her time to die."

8. Dr. Robinson is about to counsel her first terminally ill patient and his family. Research suggests that her most helpful strategy would be to
   a. keep most of the facts from both the patient and his family in order not to upset them.
   b. be truthful to the patient but not his family.
   c. be truthful to the family only, and swear them to secrecy.
   d. honestly inform both the patient and his family.

Answer Key

Key Terms

1. Thanatology is the study of death. (p. 565; objective 1)
2. The idea that people adopt cultural values and moral principles in order to cope with their fear of death is referred to as terror management theory (TMT). This system of beliefs protects individuals from anxiety about their mortality and bolsters their self-esteem so they react harshly when other people go against any of the moral principles involved. (p. 570; objective 6)
3. A near-death experience is an episode in which a person comes close to dying but survives and reports having left his or her body and having moved toward a bright, white light while feeling peacefulness and joy. (p. 573; objective 6)
4. Good death is a death that is peaceful, quick, and painless and that occurs at the end of a long life, in the company of family and friends, and in familiar surroundings. (p. 574; objectives 1 & 3)
5. A hospice is an institution in which terminally ill patients receive palliative care. (p. 575; video lesson, segment 2; objective 4)
6. Palliative care, such as that provided in a hospice, is care that relieves suffering while safeguarding the person's dignity. (p. 576; video lesson, segment 2; objective 4)
7. A double effect is a situation in which medication has the intended effect of relieving a dying person's pain and the secondary effect of hastening death. (p. 576; objectives 3 & 4)

8. Passive euthanasia is a situation in which a seriously ill person is allowed to die naturally, through the cessation of medical intervention. (p. 578; objective 3)
9. DNR is an acronym for "Do Not Resuscitate," which is a medical order to not use extreme measures to resuscitate a patient in the face of a life-threatening event. (p. 578; video lesson, segment 2; objective 4)
10. Active euthanasia is a situation in which someone takes action to bring about another person's death, with the intention of ending that person's suffering. (p. 578; objective 3)
11. A physician-assisted suicide is one in which a doctor provides the means for a person to end his or her life. (p. 578; video lesson, segment 2; objective 5)
12. Slippery slope is the argument that a given action will start a chain of events that will culminate in an undesirable outcome. (p. 580; objective 5)
13. A document that contains an individual's instructions for end-of-life medical care, written before such care is needed, is called an advance directive. (p. 580; objective 3)
14. A living will is a document that specifies what medical intervention a person wants if he or she becomes incapable of expressing those wishes. (p. 580; video lesson, segment 2; objective 3)
15. A health care proxy is an individual chosen by another person to make medical decisions if the second person becomes unable to do so. (p. 580; objective 3)
16. Bereavement is the sense of loss following a death. (p. 582; objective 7)
17. Grief is an individual's emotional response to bereavement. (p. 582; objective 7)
18. Mourning is the ceremonies and behaviors that a religion or culture prescribes for bereaved people. (p. 582; objective 7)
19. Absent grief is a situation in which overly private people cut themselves off from the community and customers of expected grief; can lead to social isolation. (p. 585; objective 7)
20. Disenfranchised grief is a situation in which certain people, although they are bereaved, are not allowed to mourn publicly. (p. 585; objective 7)
21. Incomplete grief is a situation in which circumstances, such as a police investigation or an autopsy, interfere with the process of grieving. (p. 585; objective 7)
22. Anticipatory grief occurs before the death of a loved one and it is said to reduce the shock of death. (video lesson, segment 1; objective 7)
23. When someone, at the dying person's request, helps that person end his/her life it is called voluntary euthanasia. (video lesson, segment 2; objective 5)

Practice Questions I

Multiple-Choice Questions

1. b. is the correct answer. (p. 575; video lesson, segment 1; objective 1)
2. c. is the correct answer. (pp. 574, 576–577; video lesson, segment 2; objectives 1 & 3)
3. c. is the correct answer. (p. 575; video lesson, segment 1; objective 1)
4. c. is the correct answer. (p. 575; video lesson, segment 1; objectives 1 & 2)
5. d. is the correct answer. (p. 574; video lesson, segment 2; objective 1)
6. a. is the correct answer. (p. 574; objective 1)
7. c. is the correct answer. (pp. 575–576; video lesson, segment 2; objective 4)

   a. is incorrect. This is a living will.

   b. & d. are incorrect. These are forms of euthanasia.
8. c. is the correct answer. (p. 576; video lesson, segment 2; objective 4)
9. d. is the correct answer. (p. 578; video lesson, segment 2; objective 4)

   a. is incorrect. There is no such thing as involuntary euthanasia.

   c. is incorrect. In this situation, a doctor provides the means for a patient to end his or her own life.
10. d. is the correct answer. (pp. 582–587; video lesson, segments 3 & 4; objective 7)
11. b. is the correct answer. (p. 576; objectives 3 & 4)
12. d. is the correct answer. A central feature of hospices is that the dying are not isolated from loved ones, as they might be in a hospital. (pp. 575–577; video lesson, segment 2; objective 4)

True or False Items

13. T (pp. 574–575; objectives 1 & 2)
14. F Later research has not confirmed Kübler-Ross's findings that the emotions of an individual faced with death occur in orderly stages. (p. 575; video lesson, segment 1; objective 1)
15. T (pp. 574, 576–577; objectives 1 & 3)
16. F The psychological well-being of the bereaved depends above all on their being able to openly express their grief. (pp. 582–583; objective 7)
17. F A friend should listen, sympathize, and not ignore the mourner's pain. (p. 587; objective 7)
18. T (p. 577; objective 4)
19. F These practices are illegal throughout most of the world. (p. 578; video lesson, segment 2; objective 5)
20. T (pp. 575–576; video lesson, segment 2; objective 4)

21. T (p. 582; objectives 6 & 7)
22. F (p. 585; objective 7)

Practice Questions II

Multiple-Choice Questions

1. c. is the correct answer. (p. 575; video lesson, segment 1; objective 1)
2. d. is the correct answer. In recent times, mourning has become less religious than formerly. (p. 583; objective 7)
3. c. is the correct answer. (p. 585; objective 7)
4. d. is the correct answer. (pp. 574, 576–580; objectives 1 & 3)
5. d. is the correct answer. (p. 575; video lesson, segment 1; objective 1)

   b. & c. are incorrect. There is no evidence that hospice residents experience different emotional stages than others who are dying, or that these stages are a product of Western culture.
6. d. is the correct answer. (pp. 574–577; objectives 1 & 3)
7. b. is the correct answer. (p. 580; video lesson, segment 2; objective 3)
8. d. is the correct answer. (p. 567; video lesson, segment 4; objective 2)
9. c. is the correct answer. (pp. 574–577; objectives 1, 3, & 4)
10. c. is the correct answer. (pp. 571–573; objective 6)

    a. is incorrect. Age is an important factor in both mourning and the dying person's emotions; gender, however was not discussed as a source of variation in dying practices.

    b. is incorrect. Culture often has more influence on variations in death practices than religion does.

    d. is incorrect. Anticipatory grief primarily influences the ease with which the bereaved are able to accept the loss of their loved one.
11. b. is the correct answer. (pp. 582–588; objective 7)

    a. & c. are incorrect.

    d. is incorrect. This issue was not discussed.

Matching Items

12. c (p. 578; video lesson, segment 2; objective 4)
13. b (p. 575; video lesson, segment 2; objective 4)
14. d (p. 580; video lesson, segment 2; objective 3)
15. h (p. 576; objectives 3 & 4)
16. e (p. 578; video lesson, segment 2; objective 5)
17. a (p. 576; video lesson, segment 2; objective 4)
18. f (p. 580; objective 3)
19. g (video lesson, segment 1; objective 7)

Applying Your Knowledge

1. a. is the correct answer. (p. 570; objective 6)
2. d. is the correct answer. (p. 575; video lesson, segment 1; objective 1)

   a. is incorrect. People in this stage refuse to believe that their condition is terminal.

   b. is incorrect. In this stage, the dying person directs anger at others for his or her condition.

   c. is incorrect. In this stage, the dying person mourns his or her own impending death.
3. a. is the correct answer. (p. 575; video lesson, segment 1; objective 1)
4. b. is the correct answer. (p. 578; video lesson, segment 2; objectives 4 & 5)
5. b. is the correct answer. (p. 578; video lesson, segment 2; objective 5)
6. c. is the correct answer. (pp. 571–588; objectives 6 & 7)
7. c. is the correct answer. (pp. 582–588; video lesson, segment 3; objective 7)

   a., b., & d. are incorrect. These statements discourage the bereaved person from mourning.
8. d. is the correct answer. (pp. 576–580; objective 3)

Lesson Review

Lesson 26

Epilogue
Death and Dying

Please Note: Use this matrix to guide your study and achieve the learning objectives of this lesson. It will also help you to view the video, which defines and demonstrates important concepts and skills as they relate to everyday life.

Learning Objective	Textbook	Telecourse Student Guide	Video Lesson
1. Describe a good death and identify Kübler-Ross's stages of dying, and discuss these stages in light of more recent research.	pp. 565, 574–575	Key Terms: 1, 4; Practice Questions I: 1, 2, 3, 4, 5, 6, 13, 14, 15; Practice Questions II: 1, 4, 5, 6, 9; Applying Your Knowledge: 2, 3.	Segment 1: *Emotional Reactions to Death;* Segment 2: *Deciding How to Die*
2. Discuss age-related differences in the conceptualization of emotional reactions to death.	pp. 566–571	Practice Questions I: 4, 13; Practice Questions II: 8.	Segment 1: *Emotional Reactions to Death;* Segment 4: *Cycle of Life*
3. Discuss the steps that patients, family members, and medical personnel can take to plan for a swift, pain-free, and dignified death.	pp. 576–580	Key Terms: 4, 7, 8, 10, 13, 14, 15; Practice Questions I: 2, 11, 15; Practice Questions II: 4, 6, 7, 9, 14, 15, 18; Applying Your Knowledge: 8.	Segment 2: *Deciding How to Die*
4. Explain the concept of palliative care, focusing on the advantages and disadvantages of hospices, and describe the conditions under which individuals choose to avoid medical intervention.	pp. 575–578	Key Terms: 5, 6, 7, 9; Practice Questions I: 7, 8, 9, 11, 12, 18, 20; Practice Questions II: 9, 12, 13, 15, 17; Applying Your Knowledge: 4.	Segment 2: *Deciding How to Die*
5. Discuss issues surrounding assisted suicide and active euthanasia, noting the Dutch experience with legislation regarding assisted dying.	pp. 578–580	Key Terms: 11, 12, 23; Practice Questions I: 19; Practice Questions II: 16; Applying Your Knowledge: 4, 5.	Segment 2: *Deciding How to Die*

Learning Objective	Textbook	Telecourse Student Guide	Video Lesson
6. Describe some cultural and religious variations in how death is viewed and treated.	pp. 570–573	Key Terms: 2, 3; Practice Questions I: 21; Practice Questions II: 10; Applying Your Knowledge: 1, 6.	Segment 1: *Emotional Reactions to Death*; Segment 4: *Cycle of Life*
7. Describe recent changes in the mourning process, and suggest steps that can be taken in helping someone to recover from bereavement.	pp. 582–588	Key Terms: 16, 17, 18, 19, 20, 21, 22; Practice Questions I: 10, 16, 17, 21, 22; Practice Questions II: 2, 3, 11, 19; Applying Your Knowledge: 6, 7.	Segment 1: *Emotional Reactions to Death;* Segment 3: *Social Context of Bereavement;* Segment 4: *Cycle of Life*